Experiments in Contradiction

Part One   **The Different Forms of Contradiction**

with C. L. Bonnet, J. P. Bronckart,
A. Bullinger, A. Cattin, J. J. Ducret,
A. Henriques-Christophides, C. Kamii,
A. Munari, I. Papandropoulou, S. Parrat-Dayan,
M. Robert, and T. Vergopoulo

Part Two   **The Relations between Affirmations and Negations**

with A. Blanchet, G. Cellerier, C. Dami,
M. Gainotti-Amann, C. Gilliéron,
A. Henriques-Christophides, M. Labarthe,
J. de Lannoy, R. Maier, D. Maurice,
J. Montanegro, O. Moisimann, C. Othenin-Girard,
S. Uzan, and T. Vergopoulo

Experiments in Contradiction

JEAN PIAGET

Translated by Derek Coltman

The University of Chicago Press
Chicago and London

JEAN PIAGET is director of the International Bureau of
Education in Geneva, Switzerland. His many publications
include *Language and Thought in the Child, Judgment and
Reasoning in the Child,* and *The Early Growth of Logic
in the Child,* as well as *Biology and Knowledge* and
Adaptation and Intelligence, both published by the
University of Chicago Press.

Originally published in two volumes as *Recherches sur la
contradiction,* ©1974 by Presses Universitaires de France, Paris.

The University of Chicago Press, Chicago 60637
The University of Chicago Press, Ltd., London

84 83 82 81 80   5 4 3 2 1

Library of Congress Cataloging in Publication Data

Piaget, Jean 1896–
    Experiments in contradiction.

    Translation of Recherches sur la contradiction.
    Includes bibliographical references and index.
    1. Cognition. 2. Cognition in children.
3. Contradition. I. Title.
BF311.P51813   155.4'13   80–14248
ISBN   0–226–66779–0

Contents

Foreword

Experiments in Contradiction marks a major shift in the focus of the investigations carried out by Jean Piaget's *Centre International d'Epistémologie Génétique*. For a number of years, the work of the *Centre* and, consequently, the successive volumes of *Etudes d'épistémologie génétique* have centered on the problem of causality. Out of that effort have come detailed analyses of the way in which explanations of concrete physical systems are constructed. With the present volume, Piaget shifts his attention to the process by which all knowledge is created. He is no longer concerned only with causal explanations or with wome particular physical problem to be solved. He is interested in the general procedures used by people when they think, whatever they may choose to think about.

From the time of the Greeks until the beginning of this century, the principles of contradiction, identity, and excluded middle were held to be the fundamental "laws of thought." Two developments forced this view to change, however. The first of these was the dawning realization that no logical system could be constructed on the basis of these laws alone. The second development, or rather series of developments, consisted of demonstrations that logical systems could be invented which did not obey one or another of these laws. One example would be the polyvalent logics which allow propositions to be something other than simply true or false. These undermine the idea that there is something fundamental about the principle of excluded middle. Other examples would be Brouwer's "irreversible" mathematical operations and Griss's "logic without negation," both of which seemed to speak against the principle of contradiction. If noncontradiction, identity, and excluded middle are not, therefore, the basis of reason, why has Piaget taken up the topic of contradiction?

The answer really is quite simple. Certainly Piaget does not wish to reinstitute the principle of contradiction as a "law of thought" in the old-fashioned meaning of that phrase. Much thought is contradictory, and for that reason the principle of contradiction cannot rule all thinking. But people do at times think logically, and when they do, contradiction becomes important. In *Essai de logique opératoire* Piaget has demonstrated that both Brouwer's "irreversible" mathematical operations and Griss's "logic without negations" are constructed using fully reversible systems of mental operations. Contradiction, or rather its absence, noncontradiction, is a property of such systems, and, in fact, Piaget contends that reason in all its forms, i.e., praxeological, concrete, formal, and mathematical, rests on systems of this sort. There is no reason, therefore, to interpret the work of Brouwer and of Griss as a refutation of the principle of contradiction, and its existence does not obviate the interest of this principle.

The importance Piaget places on reversibility is clearly illustrated by the following excerpt from his *Introduction à l'épistémologie génétique.*

> The great problem of every epistemology, but principally of every genetic epistemology, is to understand how the mind succeeds in constructing necessary relationships which appear to be "independent of time" when the instruments of thought are psychological operations ... constructed over time ... The fundamental law which appears to rule the progressive mentalization of action is the law of passage from irreversibility to reversibility.

Despite its great importance, reversibility is not easy to understand. It is a concept related to what is now referred to as teleonomy. This science makes use of a form of explanation related to Aristotle's explanations in terms of final cause. It attempts to explain the behavior of self-regulating systems in terms of function or purpose. It differs from Aristotelian teleology because it restricts the domain to which finalist explanations apply. It does not attribute functions or purposes to all phenomena, only to those which arise from biological or psychological systems or from the artificial self-regulating systems devised by man, and it limits consciousness to intentional behavior.

In biology, teleonomic science is concerned with the nature and mechanisms of organic adaptation. It tries to ascertain how living systems have been formed and how the various functions of their constituent parts conserve and reproduce the species. In psychology, teleonomy becomes the study of mental adaptation. Since most adaptation of this sort, excepting instincts and habits, involves intelligence, psychological teleonomy focuses largely on intelligent behavior. According to Piaget, intelligence is synonymous with intention or the ability to adapt thought or action to a goal by recombining the means one has at his disposal. The relationships brought out by these definitions are helpful because by comparing intentional to causal phenomena, Piaget's reasons for attaching so much importance to mental reversibility become apparent.

Causal phenomena are understood in terms of "causes" which come before and produce "effects." Intentional phenomena, on the other hand, require that causal phenomena be arranged in such a way that some desired effect may be achieved. For this to happen, the effect, or, in teleonomic terms, the "goal," must come before the cause or "means." Thus, intentional organization of thought or action requires *reversal* of the causal order. To be able to accomplish this, the subject must be able to carry out his thoughts or actions in both causal and teleonomic sequence. He must be able to do or think things in both directions. For this reason, reversibility is crucial to intelligence and to Piaget's theory.

That noncontradiction must also be a property of reversible systems can be seen by comparing the definition of contradiction and the factors that make reversibility possible. Contradiction is usually defined in terms of formal structures. For example, in propositional logic contradiction is the simultaneous assertion of a proposition and its inverse. It is saying that p and $\bar{p}$ are both true. In these studies, however, Piaget broadens the concept of contradiction. Instead of defining it in terms of structures, he defines it in terms of functional disequilibrium. From that perspective, contradiction on the sensorimotor level becomes incomplete compensation between the positive effects of action directed toward some goal and the negative effects produced by the same action or by environmental factors. An example of a negative effect of the first variety would be, say, the failure of an infant with sticky fingers to disembarrass himself of a feather. If he picks it off one hand, it sticks to the other. An example of the second sort of negative effect would be the difficulty babies encounter in trying to draw a long object horizontally through the vertical bars of a crib. In this instance, the bars provide a negative effect which must be compensated. Under Piaget's new conception, the most general form of contradiction on the logical level becomes "incomplete compensation between affirmations . . . and negations." Here, affirmations take the form of the attribution of some quality, say "blue," to all members of a class. By negations, he means the attribution of the negative of that quality, i.e., "not blue," to members of the complementary class. The p and $\bar{p}$ of the first definition become, therefore, instances of affirmation and negation respectively. The quality attributed to p is that it is "true." To avoid contradiction, the quality attributed to $\bar{p}$ must be that it is "not true." This change in definition is advantageous because it extends the notion of contradiction to every logical level and even to the prelogical level of sensorimotor action.

Turning to reversibility, one finds that it, too, is defined in terms of compensating effects. It occurs only when a system is composed in such a way that every possible transformation of the system is coupled to an equal and opposite transformation. It differs from contradiction in that it is a concept which applies to material as well as to psychological systems. The notion of reversibility is, therefore, broader than the notion of contradiction, but it is easy to see that contradiction and reversibility are related. The attribution of a quality to the members of a class is an act or transformation of a mental system. The corresponding negation is another transformation. Hence, contradiction may be interpreted in terms of irreversible mental systems and is, in fact, synonymous with them.

As Piaget states in the quotation given earlier, the great question of epistemology is how the passage from irreversibility to reversibility occurs. From what has been said, it is clear that if one could understand the reason for contradictions and the exact procedures by which contradictions are overcome, one would comprehend the mechanism of this passage. In other texts, Piaget has called this mechanism equilibration. In this book, he discusses the close relationship between contradictions and equilibration. In effect, then, contradiction becomes a way of understanding how the irreversible is made reversible and, thus, comes to bear directly on the central epistemologic question.

This indicates why Piaget took up the topic of contradiction. His conclusions are too exciting to reveal ahead of time. Suffice it to say that they constitute a major step forward in the construction of his epistemologic theory. At the same time, they lead to new and challenging questions.

One of the difficulties in interpreting *Experiments in Contradiction* is that it brings to the fore an ambiguity in what is meant by the passage from irreversibility to reversibility. On the one hand, Piaget has defined a series of mental "periods" that children pass through as they grow up. He has called these the sensorimotor, concrete operational, and formal operational periods. They are defined in terms of the child's general powers of organization. The first period is characterized by the organization of motor action, the last two by the organization of thought on different levels of complexity. Certainly, if one observes the subject as he traverses these periods, his action and thought become much more reversible and noncontradictory. On the other hand, Piaget indicates that the passage from irreversibility to reversibility occurs within each developmental period. Sensorimotor actions are at first irreversible and contradictory in the broad sense of the term. Through the process of disequilibration and reequilibration, they become reversible and noncontradictory within the sensorimotor period. It is the same with the two periods of thinking. The "preoperational" part of the concrete period is a time when thought is not reversible. It gives way within the same period to concrete operations which are. From the point of view of the formal operations, however, thought remains irreversible and contradictory. It will be another four or five years before reversibility is achieved in this higher system. Since ontogentic and equilibrational forms of passage or development are not kept separate in *Experiments in Contradiction,* the reader is not clear whether overcoming contradictions is a psychogentic or an equilibrational affair.

This ambiguity is apparent in the way the experiments are designed and in the results obtained. The experiments are carried out with children of different ages and, therefore, of different developmental periods. The youngest children, of course, exhibit more contradictions than the others, the older children fewer. This makes the passage from irreversibility to reversibility appear to be a matter of the ontogenetic passage from one period to another. At the same time, every experiment demonstrates that some subjects begin with contradictions and, in the short time interval during which the experiment is conducted, go on to correct their initial contradictory answers. With these subjects, the passage from irreversibility to reversibility appears to be a matter of equilibration.

The upshot of all this is that the reader is left to decide for himself what the relationship between psychogenesis and equilibration is. The studies suggest but do not make clear that Piaget has used ontogentic immaturity as a tool to expose the stages of equilibration. How this is possible may be grasped by recalling the factors responsible for mental development. Piaget believes there are four of these, i.e., biological factors, physical experience, social experience, and equilibration. All together they produce movement from one developmental period to another. The biological factors provide, apparently, certain possibilities for organization. Given these, experience is equalibrated within a single level. Transition to higher stages, as far as anyone can be certain, requires both structures equilibrated at the lower level and biological changes which make more complex organization possible. The first are necessary because the general forms of lower level structures become the elements organized into higher level structures. The second provide a qualitative jump in the subject's organizing power.

In trying to solve any problem, a person begins with the knowledge that he has. He makes a primary assimilation and then evaluates it in terms of the goal he is seeking. If the goal has been achieved, he lets the solution stand. If there is disequilibrium or contradiction, however, he attempts to correct it by constructing compensations. If the difficulty is only a matter of equilibration within his mental powers or of easily attainable experience, he may be able to do so on the spot. If, however, greater organizing powers than he has are needed, he will have to await ontogenetic progress. From this it is obvious that one way to halt equilibration in midstream would be to use problems about which the subject has some knowledge but which cannot be solved on his mental level. He will be able, therefore, to begin the equilibration process but not to complete it. In other words, the primary assimilation will be effected but contradictions either will not be detected or, if they are, the subject will not be able to correct them. This does not mean, however, that equilibration is an ontogenetic affair. It only means that ontogenetic immaturity can be used to halt equilibration for a certain class of problems.

In closing, it should be pointed out that foreknowledge of this ambiguity should not discourage readers. That could hardly be the aim of any foreword, and it would be doubly undesirable in the case of a book that offers as much as this one does. The ambiguity is not, strictly speaking, a defect in these researches. Rather, it is an object lesson in how knowledge is constructed. It should be viewed in light of something Piaget has constantly repeated. In *L'équilibration des structures cognitives,* the volume of the *Etudes* coming after *Experiments in Contradiction,* he writes:

> Cognitive equilibration never indicates a stopping point except provisionally, and this is not a situation to be deplored. . . . On the contrary, the fact that states of equilibrium are always transcended is due to something very positive. All knowledge consists in bringing up new problems at the same time that it resolves preceding ones.

Experiments in Contradiction illustrates this very well.

T. A. Brown

Introduction

The aim of this work is to seek out the relations between contradiction and disequilibriums of action or thought. Is a cognitive disequilibrium simply the result of contradiction, a contradiction of which the subject may or may not be aware, but on which it is possible from the outset to confer a logical form, as if all the definitions and inferences involved had already been given and made explicit, so that the contradiction then consists in a formal error of calculation which is the sole cause of any perturbations or disequilibriums? Or, on the contrary, does disequilibrium, in this cognitive domain as in others, constitute an elementary fact occurring in the form of adaptation failures, conflicts, oppositions, and so on, all of which are difficult to formulate for lack of sufficient structuring of the notions involved, and of regular deductive procedures, but all of which will sooner or later be manifested in the subject's consciousness as contradictions? These contradictions could in that case take multiple forms, either conscious or unconscious, and pass through a variety of stages before becoming logically formulatable. Such a problem is more meaningful than it may seem at first glance, for the following reasons.

First, it runs parallel to another problem, that of the relations between operatory reversibility and equilibration. A few years ago, in a critique of our research, J. Bruner wrote that the notion of equilibration was unnecessary, and that the notion of progressive reversibility was sufficient in itself. But in that case, where does this progress come from, since if the interplay of reversals and reciprocities is not given in the first place, it still remains to establish how it comes about. Examination of the facts has since enabled us to recognize operatory reversibility as the end product of an uninterrupted and progressive sequence of regulations, or, in other words, of a process of equilibration. If that is the case, then one is in a position to expect, even if only by way of counterproof, a filiation of contradictions to disequilibriums, and not the reverse.

In the case of contradiction, however, the problem is at once more difficult and more serious. More serious because, when analyzing disequilibriums of action and thought one always, in practice, finds contradictions; and if one were to take the view that the contradictions are the source of the disequilibriums, then one would be limiting oneself to providing a merely logicist explanation of development, as if all progress must consist purely in correcting errors of reasoning, and as if those errors were really no more than unfortunate accidents that it would have been possible to avoid from the very beginning. It is true that all the dialectical schools, so fashionable today, posit contradiction as a primary and necessary fact, and one that constitutes the motive force for all noetic as well as praxeological progress. But the point here is precisely that what dialectics calls contradiction is not a logical or formal contradiction, otherwise it could never be "transcended" but only corrected and eliminated. And this remarkable nonformal character of what dialecticians term "contradiction"—or sometimes, more prudently, "opposition" and "conflict"—thus leads us inevitably back to the problem of the relations between contradictions and disequilibriums.

It is, however, a more difficult problem than that of the relations between reversibility and equilibrations. For one thing, regulations and reversibility are positive facts, relatively easy to observe in the subject's behavior and reasoning, even independently, of that subject's awareness of them, whereas contradictions are much less easy to track down, since when the subject is wholly unaware of some particular contradiction, however glaringly obvious to the observer, the latter must always ask himself if he is not perhaps projecting his own logic onto the reactions (though admittedly this can be remedied by referring to the later stages that the subject himself will very soon reach), and also, above all, if he is really succeeding in reconstituting with sufficient acumen exactly what is happening in the child's thought or action at the level under consideration.

If the legitimacy of our problem appears, nevertheless, to be beyond dispute—and the reference to dialectics shows that the question involved is in fact a very general one—what then are the guiding hypotheses that will enable us to achieve its solution? In the first place, of course, it will be a matter of establishing quite clearly, in any particular piece of research, not only whether the manifestations of disequilibrium arise before or after a detailed awareness of contradiction—that is obvious—but also whether they arise before or after the signs which indicate that there is a problem for the subject. However, this still only displaces the problem, since one still has to find out what any such initial disequilibrium consists of, which is to say, a disequilibrium capable of later becoming a contradiction without the latter being presupposed.

The two most general characteristics of a state of equilibrium (physical and biological as well as cognitive) are stability and that which makes stability possible, which is to say compensation of perturbations. For example, a series of elements of increasing magnitude will be said to be in equilibrium if it maintains itself (and gives rise, among other things, to constant inferences of transitivity), and if the introduction of fresh elements does not perturb relations previously established. We shall say therefore that the first manifestation of a disequilibrium capable of leading to contradictions related to lack of stability will be that one and the same action (including actions interiorized int the form of assertions or judgments) does not always lead to the same result. In this case, the subject will sooner or later experience a difficulty which is the functional—but not yet structural—aspect of contradiction: the contradiction will begin to become structural when there is comparison of the differing results and questioning as to whether the identity of the actions is real or only apparent.

If instability in the results of an action is a primary form of the disequilibrium that produces contradiction, then a second form must necessarily arise from it: insofar as the same action does not always lead to the same result, the contrary action (that is, the action that formally compensates the first) will not always cancel out the first. The end results of this situation are thus incomplete compensations, and it is on this point that the disequilibrium of systems of actions comes closest to logical contradiction, which is reducible to a nonzero product (and thus to incomplete compensation) of a statement and its negation.

Third, if there is disequilibrium in the double sense of instability of the action's results and also of incomplete compensation, then, from the cognitive point of view, a third characteristic must follow: that inferential compositions (coordination of actions or statements) cannot lead to necessary products, but allow indecisions and thus partial incoherences to subsist, thereby providing a third source of possible contradictions.

Might it not be said, however, that these three aspects of praxeological and cognitive disequilibriums already imply contradictions proper from the very outset, rather than being the constituting factors that will explain the formation of those contradictions, as we shall seek to show? We think not,

since it seems to us that, on the contrary, two fundamental differences exist
between the psychogenetic roots of logical contradiction and the characteristics of this type of contradiction. The first is that we are as yet dealing
with function only, whereas contradiction proper presupposes structures—either functions or identities, then operations. Functioning precedes
and prepares structures, hence the anteriority of disequilibrium in relation to
contradictions relative to structures. More importantly, there is a second
difference, not far removed from the one just mentioned, yet not the same. It
is that the oppositions arising from disequilibriums are exclusively dependent upon the contents of action or thought. Logical contradiction presupposes a minimum of formalization, in the sense of a construction of
forms comprising at the very least an interplay of definitions, since two
statements are logically contradictory or not according to the definitions of
the notions employed, whereas oppositions between contents, or the
rudimentary functional kind of contradiction, fall into the domain of immediate intuitions, which is to say that of subjective feelings of disequilibriums, or else of not yet conceptualized, or insufficiently conceptualized, actions.[1]

For all the reasons given above, it seems to us that the problem we intend
to study here can be posed in legitimate terms. To seek for the sources of
contradiction in situations where the same action appears not to give the
same results, in which two contrary actions do not completely compensate
each other, and in which the inferential coordinations lack necessity, does
mean in one sense, it is true, that we are referring forward to logical contradictions caused by errors in identity, of reversibility (for example, when
an involution does not return to its starting point), or of deductive composition. Yet such a course is unavoidable insofar as the problems of conservations, reversibility, and inferential production appear in prelogical
forms at very early, elementary levels, a fact that obliges us to look very
closely indeed into the relations between contradictions and disequilibriums
as a complement to the relations between reversibility of thought and
equilibration.

Part 1 of this work will consist in an analysis of a certain number of facts
relating to the considerations just mentioned: disequilibriums or "contradictions" deriving from false identities, incomplete compensations, or
incorrectly regulated inferences. These facts will be grouped into two
categories according to whether they belong to the logico-mathematical domain (chapters 1 to 3) or the physical domain (chapters 4 to 6). Since the
result of these analyses is to show that such disequilibriums always result
from insufficient compensation between affirmations and negations (which
goes without saying, but it still remained to be shown in what a great variety

of forms this general characteristic occurs), we were then faced with the principal problem to be solved: why do these initial disequilibriums and failures in compensation occur?

Part 2 of this work is therefore devoted to the solution of that problem, again dealing separately with the same two domains, chapters 7 to 11 concerning logico-mathematical questions, and chapters 12 to 15 physical questions. In fact, this solution, which would have been easy to imagine at the outset, or to derive from previously known facts, did not actually impose itself until all the results of the experiments described here had been collated, and thus without our having used it as our working hypothesis, probably because it was just too simple. It is that if a lack of compensation exists between affirmations and negations at elementary levels, this is not by virtue of some kind of primitive state of disorder or chaos (or, worse still, as a result of that cognitive original sin existing in the imaginations of certain dialecticians who would like to make contradictions, conflicts, and oppositions the source of all developing knowledge), but for a very much more natural reason: that the spontaneous tendency of every action, perception, or cognition in general is to direct itself toward affirmation and the positive characteristics of reality, while negation, in its necessary forms, is the product of secondary developments only, and, in its contingent forms, of perturbations. Action consists in modifying reality, and thus in tending toward a positive goal, whereas it requires an additional effort of retroactive reflection to perceive that any approach to that goal implies a moving away from one's starting point and a negation of the initial state. To perceive consists in grasping given positive properties, and it requires a disappointed expectation or anticipation to observe that a presence counted upon has failed to materialize (though this goes beyond the field of pure perception). To represent or to judge entails the affirmation or attribution of positive predicates, and it is only by means of a nonimmediate process that a subject can discover that each predicate a is not merely different from other equally positive predicates b, c, and so on, but by the very fact of its affirmation renders them negative (non-a) in accordance with a series of relative and variously interlocking complementaries. In a word, if a lack of compensation between affirmations and negations lasts for any appreciable time, it is not, except in the case of local and specific perturbations, because there is any conflict between them, but, much more simply, because the impress of affirmations possesses a greater immediacy and thus systematically outweighs negations for want of symmetries understood as necessary at the outset. This is why the contradictions arising from these dissymmetries generally remain unconscious for so long, since achieving awareness of them presupposes construction of the negations not given at the start. And when this construction does take place, it then leads simultaneously to both conscious apperception and transcendence of any such contradictions. It is only in cases where an anticipation is invalidated by an external fact that the contradiction between the two is more or less rapidly made conscious, but only because the negation there has been imposed from outside and did not require endogenous contruction.

Such are the general themes developed in part 2 of this work. I have one further observation to make about the composition of the chapters into a whole. Some of them deal with fresh facts not described in our previous collective works. In those cases, the experiment is given in detail, level by level according to our usual method. Others, however, are reexaminations of facts already known, although viewed here solely from the point of view of contradiction and the relations between affirmations and negations. In these cases, the account of the experimental data (even though they have all been freshly gathered and in as much detail as for the other chapters) will be much more summary, since the reader can refer back to previous publications; the discussion of them will be limited to the central questions being considered in this book.

Finally, it would probably be as well to repeat that, though the writer of this introduction is in fact the author of the work as a whole, his coworkers did not simpy ask the questions, but took a decisive part in devising those questions and refining the techniques employed.

EDITOR'S NOTE: Throughout the book, the subjects are identified by three-letter code names. The numbers in parentheses that follow each name indicate the subject's age in years and months.

Part One

The Different Forms of Contradiction

One

Transitivity and Additivity of Subliminal Differences

with A. Bullinger

The contradiction we shall be dealing with here is that pointed out by Poincaré in his famous differentiation between mathematical and physical continuity: the latter alone remains contradictory because of the fact that perceptually (and sometimes even metrically) one has $A = B$, $B = C$ but $A < C$, and overcoming this contradiction necessitates the intervention of logico-mathematical operations that enable one to construct infinitely small differences and then to subject them to the laws of transitivity and additivity. Keeping within the psychophysical domain, W. Köhler has invoked the same contradiction, when the differences $A < B$ and $B < C$ remain subliminal and the difference $A < C$ is alone perceived, to show that the whole ABC is not perceptually equal to the sum of its parts, and therefore does not entail any additive composition, since perception in this case gives $A = B$, $B = C$ and $A < C$. But what Köhler omitted to say is that the distinguishing characteristic of intelligence is precisely to introduce such compositions, even in this case, a fact that renders it irreducible to the *Gestalts* perceptual model.

In what follows, however, we shall not be examining our material from the point of view of perception theory, but rather trying to establish how forty-five subjects aged from five to twelve years old have gradually achieved awareness of, then attempted to remove, the contradiction between their perceptual observations of seven apparently nondifferent elements in the order $A = B = C = D = E = F = G$ and a perceptible inequality between the two end elements $A < G$. The interest of this problem is twofold. First, it involves a contradiction that is not directly given between the two statements p (G is greater than A), and $\bar{p}$ (G is equal to A), but between a statement p with an observable content ($G > A$) and statement p which must be deduced from $A = B$, $B = C$, and so on, up to $F = G$. It is thus evident that, without the particular inference based on transitivity ($A = G$ if $A = B$, $B = C$, up to $F = G$) the subject cannot be aware of the initial contradiction, or of those he encounters later when attempting to construct the subclasses of equivalence ($=A$ and $=G$). On the other hand, in order to overcome this contradiction between the deduced $\bar{p} = A = G$ and the observed $p = A < G$, it is insufficient to make the hypothesis of imperceptible differences (something already very difficult for young subjects): it is also necessary to construct a new operation on the level of intelligence, and to understand the possible additivity of these apparently nonexistent differences, so that the imperceptible differences $\Delta 1 + \Delta 2 + \Delta 3$, and so on, shall be equal in sum to the observable difference ΔAG, or $(\Sigma \Delta 1 \rightarrow 6) = (\Delta AG > 0)$. Now, since this is an operation that can in itself seem like a contradiction to seven- to eleven-year-olds at the concrete level, it will be interesting to establish experimentally how this pseudocontradiction is removed.

§1. Technique

The equipment consists of a rectangular board with seven sockets into each of which a disk is fitted. These disks are all of the same thickness, but their diameters increase progressively by imperceptible steps of 0.2 mm, so that disk A is 58.8 mm across, and disk G 60.0 mm. The disks are arranged in two staggered rows $^a\diagdown{}_b\diagup{}^c\diagdown{}_d$ and so on, and disks A through F are all held in place by a fine chain that permits each to be compared physically only with its immediate neighbors in the line, up to and including F with G. The last disk, G, on the other hand, is unattached, so that it can be directly compared with A (the difference in size between these two being clearly perceptible) as well as with each of the others.

Questioning begins with an exploration of the equipment. The child's attention is concentrated first on the size of the disks (their diameters). At first sight, the subject often claims to be certain that all the disks are equal in size from simple visual observation. Then the questioner suggests more precise measurements, and it is interesting to note the subjects' own spontaneous suggestions (measurement by superimposition or congruence cannot be taken for granted before seven to eight years in this case). This phase lasts until the child produces a judgment about the disks as a whole, and during it one examines the possible role of transitivity by testing for it if necessary (it is of particular interest to note if measurements are made in the order AB, BC, and so on, or simply AB, CD, EF, without any cross-linking of the pairs).

When the child concedes that all the disks are equal in size, he is questioned about the relation of G to A, which he is first asked to predict, then to verify, after which he is asked for an opinion on the result. If the subject's previous measurements have been carried out in a manner influenced by transitivity, then he usually becomes aware that there is a contradiction. If the measurements followed no order at all, then one persuades the subject to make fresh ones in an order that will suggest transitive connections, so that the subject begins to see a problem in the distribution of the equalities and inequalities.

It is here that the most important part of the questioning begins. This consists in finding out how the subject attempts to remove the contradiction, or how he envisages the totality of the elements A to G and their relationships to one another. If, as is almost always the case, the subject decides that there are two classes of equivalence involved, for example $E F G$ being equal to G and $A B C D$ equal to A, one then asks what the relationship is between E and D, and then asks the subject to check it physically. If the subject then rearranges his classes into $D E F G$ and $A B C$, one asks the same question about D and C, and so on.

It is generally during this investigation of how the subject conceives of the structure as a whole that one encounters the most interesting contradictions, which must then be inventoried and examined to see if and how the subject has achieved a conscious awareness of them, and, finally, how he is experiencing them or succeeding in eliminating them.

§2. Stage 1, Five to Seven Years

The subjects at this stage have not yet acquired transitivity, and so remain unable to perceive the contradiction involved in the relations of the other disks to *G*. Here are two examples from level 1A.

Jos (5–0) says all the counters (disks) "*are as big as each other.*" He is then shown how to check *A* against *B*, and then goes on to place *B* on *C*, *D* on *E*, and so on, without paying any attention to the relation of *C* to *D*. "So what can you tell me now? — *Those [E and F; C and D; A and B] are all the same size.*" But when he has compared *A* with *G* he concludes quite simply that *A B C D E* and *F* "*are the same size, littler than G* — What about *G* and *F?*— *F will be littler.* — Try and see. — *Yes, that one sticks out* (in other words he is denying their apparent equality)."

Pas (6–1) affirms the equality of all the disks, first by just looking, then after having put both hands around them. He accepts equality after superimposition of *A* on *B*, then *B* on *C*, as also the equality of *A* and *C*, but "*by looking*" and not as a result of inferential transitivity. He goes on measuring, then: "*They're all the same — G* and *A* too? — *They're the same too.* — Look carefully. — *No, they're not.* — So are they all the same? — *All except G and A.* — So *G* is the same as what? — *As B C D E F.* — And *A?* — *That's the same as B C D E F.* And *A* and *G?* — *They're not the same.* — Is that a good explanation? — *Don't know.* — Explain it to this gentleman (observing student) — [Pas repeats that *G* = *B C D E* and *F*, that *A* = *B C D E* and *F*, but that *G* is bigger than, *A*] — What about *G* and *C? — I think G is a bit bigger.* — And *G* and *B?* — *G is bigger.* — And *G* and *F? — The same.* — And *G* and *D? — The same.* — And *G* and *E? — The same.* — So? — *So G is bigger than A B C and it's the same as D E F.* — And what about *C* and *D? — I don't know.* — What do you think? — *D is bigger than C.* — See if it is. — *D is a little bit bigger. . . . No, they're the same.* — And *G* and *D? — They're the same.* — Is that right? — *Yes.* — So all of them together, what are they like? — *G is bigger than C B A and it's the same as D E F.* — And *C* and *D? — The same.* — So what would you call these three (*A B C*)? —

They're little. — And *D E F* and *G? — They're big. —* And there's a difference between the big ones and the little ones? — *G and D are the same, and so are C and D . . . Ah! I understand it all now: G is the same as F E and D and A B C D are all the same, but G is bigger than C B A!''*

At level 1B, on the other hand, we do find hints of transitivity, but these are still insufficient to force the subject into consciousness of the contradiction.

Ala (6–6) measures *A* and *B: "They're equal because it doesn't stick out. —* Now *B* and *C. — The same. —* And *A* and *C? —* (He attempts to measure them together, but of course can't) — What do you think? — *They're the same because all of them are the same. — D* and *E? — Same thing. — F* and *G? — Them too. —* And when you put *G* on *A? — They'll be the same because they're all the same size. —* Try. — *They're the same. —* It doesn't stick out? — *Well, just a bit, so G is bigger than A. —* Is that how it should be? — *I don't know. —* Just now you said they were all the same. — *It's only G that isn't. —* So what about *F* and *G? — They're the same. No, no, G sticks out. —* So what about them all together? — *A B C D E F are the same, G is bigger, and G is the same as F. —* Now put *G* and *A* together. — *G sticks out; it's bigger. —* Now *G* and *B? — G sticks out. — G* and *C? — It still sticks out. — G* and *D? — It still does. — G* and *E? — They're the same. — G* and *F? — The same too. —* So what do you think of them all now? — *They're all the same except G. —* Think carefully. — *Well, AB, CD are the same and they are littler than G. —* And *E F* and *G? — Those are all the same* (as each other). — And *D* and *E? — They are the same size but G is bigger than A.''*

Cri (6–5) begins with visual estimates, then would like to put the two disks to be compared *"side by side* (so that he can envisage lines across the tops and bottoms).[11] — What if they were cookies? — *I'd put them on top* (of each other). — Good. Do that then. — *[F and G] They're the same size. [D E] So are they. [BC] And those. [A B] And those. —* Is *A* the same size as *B? — Yes. —* And *B* the same as *C? — Yes. —* And *A* and *C? — They're the same size because they both fit on B. —* Good. Try *CD, The same size. —* And *AB? — They are too. — BC? — The same. — AC? — The same. — CD? — The same. — AD? — We haven't done those two. —* But what do you think? — *It's hard. —* Can't we tell? — (He tries to place *A* on *D*). — *Ah yes, we can tell because D is the same as C and C is the same as A so that means D and A are the same.''* He then continues measuring, *E* and *F, F* and *G,* and concludes that *"they're all the same size. —* Is it worth trying *G* and *A? — I'm not very sure about that* (Cri's growing transitivity is not yet accompanied by necessity). — What would you expect usually? — *They're all the same. —* Try then. — *It [G] sticks out a bit!* Is that what ought to happen? —

No, it's F that isn't the same as G." He then compares *G* and *F:* *"They're the same."* Then *G* with *C: "G is bigger than C,"* then *"It's bigger than B,"* and also than *D,* yet *G* and *E,* then *F "are the same."* — Good. So what do you say about them all together? — *There are some big ones [E F G] and some little ones [A B C D].* — And *D* and *E? — D is littler than E.* — Try it. — *They're the same.* — So how do you think that happens? — *I don't know. Perhaps G gets bigger when you touch it."* Cri is given the true explanation. "Do you think that's possible? — *Yes.* — You've understood what I explained? — *Yes.* — So can you tell it back to me? — *Well, A is little, B is bigger, C is littler, D is bigger, E is littler, F is bigger, and G . . . gets bigger!"*

Sia (7–1). The same reactions: *G* is sometimes equal to *D* and sometimes bigger. "How does that happen? Does it change? — *Yes, its size does.* — How do you know? — *Because of seeing it."*

Ick (7–3). Having at first thought, from his observations, that $D = E$, he then decides that *D* is smaller than *E.* "What's happened then? — *It changes.* — It's size? — *Yes.* — Is that possible? — *Yes."*

Oli (7–0). After comparing *G* with *A,* then with *B: "The G is not the same with all of them.* — So at one time *A* is the same as *B* and at another time it's smaller than *B,* is that it? — *Yes, it's A. Sometimes it's little, other times it's big.* — It changes in size, in how big it is? — *Yes."*

Level 1A subjects display two sorts of contradiction. The more elementary of them seems rather lacking in interest from the logical point of view, but it involves a factor that must occur before awareness of any contradiction is achieved: the memory of previous data (observations or inferences). When Jos affirms the equality of all the counters from *A* through *G,* then discovers that *G* is larger than *A,* he concludes immediately that *G* is therefore superior to all the others as well, including *F,* without perceiving any contradiction, since he immediately forgets that he has already physically established that $F = G$. In the immediate present, therefore, there is no contradiction, especially since when he repeats the *F* to *G* comparison he denies the perceptually observable fact confronting him, namely their apparent equality. Yet there is a contradiction in relation to a previously accepted fact, which is not reexamined but merely forgotten, and this is the simplest form of contradiction. Despite this, however, it is not entirely without a logical meaning too: when a previous affirmation is erased so easily from the memory it is because there is nothing necessary in its character, and that is quite natural with subjects like Jos, who display neither transitivity (see his measurements of *EF, CD,* and so on, without attempting to compare *D* and *E*), nor any spontaneous tendency to verify facts by congruence, remaining quite content with purely visual estimates.

Pas, on the other hand, does recall previously accepted facts, and subsequently attempts to remove the contradiction between "all the same" and "G is bigger than A" by subdividing "all" into two distinct classes, each containing equal elements. The fundamental fact here, however, is that he then falls into another systematic contradiction which he seems at first to be totally unaware of. For Pas's two classes are defined, in practice, either by equality with G, giving the "big ones" (that is $X = B\,C\,D\,E\,F$), or by equality with A, comprising the little or non-X disks. The trouble is, however, that the class non-X is made up of the selfsame elements $B\,C\,D\,E\,F$, with the results that the two classes, which ought to be disjunct (since one is defined by equality with G and the other by nonequality with G) are conceived of as identical. If noncontradiction can be defined by complete reversibility or compensation ($X \cap$ non-$X = 0$), we are thus faced here with the very maximum possible contradiction: $X =$ non-X. However, after further physical comparison of G with the other counters, Pas finds a better solution: X (equality with G) $= D\,E\,F$, and non-$X = A\,B\,C$. These classes are thus disjunct, so that the contradiction has apparently been overcome, thus leading quite logically to Pas's conclusion that D must be bigger than C. Unfortunately, however, physical comparison once again shows that $C = D$, which plunges him into further difficulty. He then overcomes this ("Ah! I've understood it all now") by once again accepting a contradiction, but this time a less obvious one: $X = D\,E\,F$, and non-$X = A\,B\,C\,D$. Thus compensation remains incomplete, since $X \cap$ non-$X = D$, or, in other words, D is seen as equal to both G and A despite the fact that G is bigger than A. The subject's imperviousness to this contradiction is certainly due in some degree to a lack of transitivity, but probably also to the attribution of insufficient meaning to negation.

As for the level 1B subjects, in whom one can observe the beginnings of transitivity, the case of Ala remains analogous to that of Pas (except that he does not begin with $X =$ non-X): he accepts, for example, that G "is bigger and the same as F", then constructs two nondisjunct classes $A\,B\,C\,D$ and $E\,F\,G$, while accepting D and E as equal, which is equivalent to the partial compensation accepted by Pas in relation to C and D. Cri reaches the same blind alley: D is simultaneously equal to $E\,F\,G$ and to $A\,B\,C$, even though G is bigger than A. His solution then is quite simply that G changes size according to which of the other disks it is compared to, and that otherwise they all remain equal in size. When Cri is given the correct explanation, based on imperceptible differences, he fails to understand it and reduces it to a simple alternation of sizes with G still "getting bigger." Finally, Sia, Ick, and Oli remove the contradictions between $G>D$ and $G = D$, and so forth, by accepting, like Cri, that G (or even D or A) "changes size."

In short, the characteristic of stage 1 subjects is to establish classes of equivalence whose distinguishing characteristics are exclusive (x is equal to G and y is unequal to G, therefore $y = \overline{x}$), except that this exclusiveness is conveniently ignored, or not experienced as such, in the case of the two sections of these classes that overlap, when in fact they ought to be either complementary or disjunct. Either the subject accepts this situation, which to us is contradictory, or else he tries to explain it by invoking nonconservation of size on the part of G. But he does not try to remedy the contradiction, as we shall find 2A level subjects doing, by modifying his classes of equals in the hope of hitting on a true dichotomy.

§3. Stage 2, Level 2

This stage is characterized by the acquisition of transitivity and an awareness of the contradiction present, even though the subject does not succeed in transcending it. On level 2A he puts his faith in a movement of the boundary between the "little ones" and "the big ones," as if successive manipulations along these lines will eventually provide a solution. Here are some examples, beginning with an intermediate case:

Sté (7–6) thinks all the disks are equal *"because I can look at them and see. —* And if you want to find out if they really are? *— You put them on top of one another* (Sté is thus the first of our subjects to employ congruence spontaneously.)" — Try with A and B — *Yes, they're the same size, because there isn't one sticking out.* — And B and C? *— The same size. — A* and C? *— No, C is bigger than A, I think.* — You said that $A = B$ and $B = C$, so what about A and C? *— Oh! But C is the same size as A because A = B and B = C!* — What about all the counters together? *— You have to try them all to see* (he proceeds to measure them in pairs, with cross-references between pairs, AC, BC, and so on, but omitting CD)." — What about all of them now? *— The same size.* — And G and A? — (After tracing the zigzag line of disks with his finger) *The same, because A = B, B = C, C = D [and so on, up to F =g].* — Try them then. *— It's bigger than A.* — Is that what we ought to expect? *— Don't know. No, because they're all the same size so you wouldn't* [expect it]. — What do you think of them all now? *— They're different sizes.* — All of them? *— No, G is the biggest of all.* [He makes further physical comparisons then divides them into "little" (A and B) and "big" (C to G inclusive]." — And B and C? *— C is bigger than B. Oh no!* (having compared), *all those [A B C] are little and those [D through G] are big."* Then he tests C and D. "Why are you doing that? *— Because I've made a mistake."* In other words, he was doubting the coherence of his dichotomy: "*Ah, no, C is bigger.* — But you're tilting it. *— All the same,* *it's bigger.* — Sure? — *Yes* (he once more makes the division into *A B C* and *D E F G*, then corrects this without prompting into *A B C D* and *E F G*). — And *D* and *E*? — [without testing] *They're different."* Then after a further comparison he reverts to *A B C* "little" and *D E F G* "big". "So what's happening? — *That one [C] is changing its size! I don't know, I can't see it properly.* — So sometimes it's big and sometimes it's little? — *Because before I made a mistake; I couldn't see it properly. I must see if I made a mistake."* Again he checks *D* against *E*, and laughs: *"I did make a mistake. G and F are big and the rest are little."* He then places *G* on various other disks and laughs every time: *"It's a trick, because it changes. Bigger and smaller. It's funny how it does it.* — Does it change its shape? — *No, but perhaps it's because of the holes* (meaning according to whether a particular disk is in its socket or out of it)." Finally he is given the correct explanation, and he concludes: *"You need a microscope then. Or a magnifying glass. It's funny because it does* (seem to) *change size."*

Lau (7–3) observes that *A* = *B* and *B* = *C*. *A* and *C* are *"the same size.* — But we haven't put them together. — *It's because A = B and B isn't bigger than C."* — Likewise *D* = *C*, therefore *D* = *A*, and so on. After acknowledging that *G* > *A*, Lau concludes that *G "will be bigger than F."* After testing, he deduces that *F* and *G* are big while *A B C D E* are little. "And *E* and *F*? — (test) *Same size.* — So? — *A B C D are little and E F G are bigger."* Then after a comparison of *D* and *E*, it is *A B* and *E* alone that are little. "And *C* and *D?* — *C will be smaller than D."* After observing their equality, Lau then concludes that *"they're all big."* We then return to *G* > *A*: *"A is littler than all the others."* — Littler than *B?* — *Yes.* — Try. — *B is bigger* (distortion of apparent observable fact.)"

Nad (8–1) says that to be sure of the apparent equality *"we'll have to put them on top of one another."* This done, she concludes that *C* = *A "because A is the same as B, B the same as C, so C and A come to the same,"* and likewise with *E* and *B*, and so on, until she reaches *G* and *A:* "Is it worth testing *G* and *A?* — *No.* — Well I think we'd better, all the same. — *Yes. No, G is bigger than A.* — Is that what we ought to expect? — *No, no. Perhaps I didn't look properly at G and F.* — Well look again then! — *They're the same, so F is bigger than A.* — Now *F* and *E*. — *They're the same too.* — So that means *E* is bigger than *A* too, does it? — *No.* — What about *F* and *A?* — *They're the same. It's G that's bigger than A.* — So *F* and *A* are the same size, so are *G* and *F*, and *G* is bigger than *A?* — *Yes, that's right. No, it's not.* — What then? — *These four [A B C D] are the same, these four [C D E F] as well, E and F too, and F and G too, and G isn't the same as A.* — If you had to call them all something, what would it be? — *Middle-sized.* — Are some big and some little? — *No, all the same.* — What about *G* and *A?* — *No, G is bigger than A.* — Tell me how that happens. — *These two are the same. I didn't look properly before.* [She does a second comparison.] — What is happening? — *Don't know. G is bigger than all the others except F.* — What about *E* and *F?* — *The same. Yes, F is the same as G, E is the same as F, but perhaps G isn't the same as E.* — How does that happen?" After further comparisons, Nad then begins dividing the disks up: *E F G* are equal, all the others smaller, and *A* the smallest of all. Then, after comparing *A* and *B*, "*A B C are little and D E F G are big.* — And if you try *C* and *D?* — *They're the same.* — So *C* is little, *D* is big, and they're both the same? — *Oh no, that's not right.* — Try *G* against all of them. — (She does so, and concludes that *G* = *F E D* and *C,* while *G* is bigger than *B* and *A.*) Then: "*A and B are littler than C D E F G.*" — And *B* and *C? — C is bigger than B.* — Try. — *They're the same.* — How is that? — *Don't know.*" The correct explanation is given. She accepts the idea of small invisible differences well enough, but instead of conceiving of them as equal and additive she imagines them as increasing in size: "*the difference between B and C is bigger than the difference between A and B.*"

Tio (8–10) thinks all the disks are equal, then after comparing *G* and *A* places *G* on each of the others and concludes: "*G is bigger than A B but C D E and F are the same size as G.*" But he then wants to check the relation between *B* and *C,* without any prompting, "*to see if it is what it should be.* (He compares.) *They're the same size!* — *G* and *B? — B is smaller.* — So? — *So A and B are smaller than G. C D E and F are the same as G, and those four there* [*C D E and F*] *they're the same as A and B.* — Is that possible? — *Either they're all the same or they're littler than G.*" He then ends up with the hypothesis: "*A B and C are smaller than D E F and G.* — And if we put *D* on *C? — C will be smaller than D.* — Do you want to try? — *No, they're the same after all!* — Does it change size? — *No, it's stayed the same, it's me that's made a mistake.* — So how are they all together, the counters? — *They look as though they're all the same.* — And if *G* sticks out over *B? — That means they're not the same.*" When given the correct explanation, Tio is not really convinced by it.

Once the contradiction between $G > A$ and the general equality suggested by a two-by-two comparison has been observed, the solution offered by these subjects is naturally, as in stage 1, to divide the disks into two distinct classes of equivalence. But the big step forward they have taken due to the acquisition of transitivity and reversibility (taking into account reverse operations and thus negations) then prevents them from remaining content with an approximate compensation $X \cap$ non-$X \neq 0$, or, in other words, accepting the existence of an overlapping section displaying both X and non-X

characteristics at the same time. For example, having divided the disks into *A* and *B* (smaller than *G*) and *C D E* and *F* (equal to *G*), Tio then spontaneously compares *B* with *C* "to see if it's what it should be," that is, to see if *C* really is bigger than *B* rather than equal to it. Among the other subjects, who all had to be prompted to make this comparison, the existence of a term that could be equal and different simultaneously was experienced immediately as a contradiction, and they all looked for something to replace it. The usual solution consisted in changing the make up of the classes of equivalence by moving the boundary between < *G* and = *G*. Two problems thus present themselves. First, if these subjects believe in transitivity, do they not know in advance that moving the boundary will simply lead to a recurrence of the same problem in relation to the two new disks on either side of their new boundary? Second, and most important, given their constant sense of contradiction from this point on, why don't they try to remove it by moving toward the idea of a serial structure rather than simply sticking to dichotomies between classes?

The answer to the first question is, clearly, that once a sequence of transitive equalities from *A* to *G* has been observed, followed by the unexpected inequality *A* < *G*, it is natural for them to have doubts about the accuracy of their measurements ("I made a mistake," Sté says, for example), and so they can continue to hope for a more satisfactory boundary between their two classes *X* and non-*X*. But that presupposes a dichotomy, and that in turn produces the second problem.

In this respect, the interest of the reactions observed here is to present us with a development comparable to that of simple seriation, but with a timelag that is easily explicable by the fact that the differences between the adjoining elements are imperceptible. Even in the case of perceptible differences, younger subjects begin, in fact, by reacting as if to a dichotomy: a little one and a big one, and so on, in a sequence of juxtaposed pairs, or little ones and big ones divided into two classes. Only later do we find trios (little ones, middle-sized ones, big ones), and, eventually, attempts to establish continuity (*A* < *B* <*C* <*D* . . .). The reason for this is that the characteristics "little" and "big" are absolute predicates and thus easier to handle than relations such as "littler" = "less big". Similarly, in the present case, the conflict between the observation *A* < *G* and the sequence of apparent equalities suggests a simple duality, and so it is natural for our subjects to begin by trying to establish dichotomies between classes of equivalents.

That said, the contradiction due to the artificial boundaries thus established cannot, of course, be overcome. So the subjects get out of this difficulty either, as in Lau's case, by distorting observable fact (over *B* and *A* at the end), or, as with Sté, by once more accepting that *G* varies in size, albeit subjectively (according to the perceptual comparisons made and changes in position), or by giving up all hope of understanding, like Nad and Tio.

§4. Level 2B

The criterion for this level, from nine to ten years old, is that the subject, though not yet successful in overcoming the contradiction by means of an additivity of invisible differences, nevertheless does catch momentary glimpses of two ideas that lead in the right direction, and that combine in support of a relation that requires clarification. The first of these ideas is that of multiple, if not serial, differences, as opposed to simple dichotomies of big and little. The second is the possibility of nonperceptible differences. Here are some examples, beginning with an intermediate case.

Pie (9–4): *"They're the same size. No, there are two little ones, two middle-sized. It's like a family of dolls: there are little ones, then bigger ones, till you get to papa. —* But how can you be sure? *— You have to arrange them in sizes, you can put them on top of one another. —* Right. Have a try then. *— C and D, they're the same size. A and B, well I think B is fatter* [bigger] *than A. E and F, they're almost the same but it's F that wins, it's fatter than E. —* How can you tell that? *— Because there's a tiny little edge sticking out. —* Look again. *— No, they're the same."* He then changes his position, and after saying they are all equal goes on to subdivide them into $AF < G$ then into $AE < FG$, and so on, even going so far as to accept $F = G$, $G > A$, and $F = A$, all three simultaneously.

Mar (9–9) begins from a position of general equality, then after observing G bigger than A thinks he *"measured it wrong before."* He tries again and assumes $AE < FG$. *"And if you do E and F? — Then F will be bigger than E. —* Try. *— No, they're the same size. Perhaps it's because EG are the same and those [AD] are smaller. —* And D and E? *— Ah, but we've seen they're the same. It's funny . . . perhaps they're all becoming smaller all the time, but you can't manage to see it. —* How do you know? *— Because we've tried them all. —* But we saw that they're all the same size. *— Yes, but you can't manage to see when they're getting smaller all along all the time. —* Between A and B for examples? *— The B gets bigger but you can't manage to see it."*

Tim (10–6) performs comparisons A through F, and after observing $F = G$ concludes, with transitivity, that there is general equality. Once she has observed $G > A$ she says first that (G) is simply *"bigger than the others. —* But wouldn't you have noticed that before? What's happening then? Is it changing size? *— No, I think they were all a little bit bigger* (than one another). — I don't understand. — *I think that A and B are almost the same size, so you don't see the difference. Then it's like that all along, and then when we put G on A it did make a difference."* So Tin appears to have reached the correct solution, including the additivity of imperceptible differences. But it only takes one leading question to make her change her mind: "A difference so small you can't see it? Do you think such a thing exists? — *No, I don't think they're all a little bit bigger.* — She then retreats to the equivalent classes hypothesis *A B C* smaller than *D E F G*, but later returns to her previous idea for *C* and *D*: "D will be bigger than C, there'll be a little difference. — Try. — Yes. . . . No."* She tries *G* again on *B* then *C* then *D*, and concludes: "C is bigger than B, and B is bigger than A. G and D, they're the same size, there's only a little difference: D is bigger than C, just a tiny bit.* — And *G* and *E*? — *The same size.* — And *E* and *D*? — *E is a little bit bigger after all, but it's difficult to say.* — Perhaps there's a little difference we can't see? — *No, I don't think so. I think A B C D E F are the same size and they're smaller than G.* — Why do you think your explanation about the tiny differences is wrong? — *Because I measured and I couldn't see them.* But what if they were very, very tiny? — *If they were very very tiny, then perhaps you couldn't see them.* — And all those very very tiny differences all together, perhaps that would make a big difference? — *Oh no, that couldn't happen."*

Roc (10–8) wavers in a similar way. After accepting general equality, then observing *G > A*, he claims that *"there is the same difference"* (1 mm) between *F* and *G*. *"They're not all equal. Yes, they are all different. — There's a difference between G and E? — A half a millimeter more. — And between G and C? — Whew! Either they're equal or there's a quarter of a millimeter. — G and B? — Well there you can see the difference! — And between D and B? — They're different. I can't say exactly. You can feel it with your fingers though."* But later he is sure that *D = F = G: "Yes, these three are equal. The others are in another family. No, they're all equal, unless you have to split them up.* — What about *E* and *C*? — *Wait. No, I can't work it out any more."* "But could it be that there is a difference between each counter in the row and the next? — *Yes, I've told you I couldn't tell exactly."*

The case of Pie shows first that at the stage of equilibrated concrete operations, reached at about nine years, when a certain number of notions become relational, our seven disks with their imperceptible size relations are just as likely to suggest a serial model as a dichotomy into classes of equals: in fact Pie refers at the very ouset to the possibility of there being "little ones" "middle-sized ones" and "big ones". Thus there is nothing untoward about the other subjects on this level, when faced with the contradictions their dichotomies cause, thinking of multiple and serial differences rather than remaining with the idea of discontinuous categories. But this idea leads to two opposing consequences. The first is that by imagining differences between each element and the next the subject is led toward a recognition of them as nonperceptible. As Mar so strikingly puts it: "Perhaps they're all becoming smaller all the time, but you can't manage to see it. — How do you know? — Because we've tried them all!" In other words, in order to overcome the difficulties, they are forced to resort to imperceptible magnitudes. But this leads in turn to a second consequence, and one that tends to dampen the hopes the first may have raised, given the limits imposed on the subject's thought by the modes of reasoning inherent in concrete operations: if such magnitudes can be neither perceived nor measured, they cannot in that case be subjected to composition, and hence cannot be additive. Just as, on the physical level, one has to wait for the stage of formal operations that will enable bodies to be accepted as being composed of microscopic smaller bodies (with the exception of sugar, in which the crystals can be seen to grow progressively smaller), with the result that concrete compositions remain semimacroscopic, so, in these questions of differences conceived of as imperceptible, subjects at this level, that is the nine- to ten-year-olds, are undoubtedly led to make such a hypothesis in order to overcome the contradiction between the apparent equalities and the final AG inequality. But they are not yet in a position to deduce that the latter is made up by the sum of the imperceptible differences, because what is imperceptible appears to them to be different in nature to magnitudes accessible to the laws of rational composition, so that even its very existence cannot be guaranteed with any certainty: "I told you," Roc concludes, "that I didn't know exactly." And Tin, who at the beginning of her interrogation seemed to have understood, and thus to have reached stage 3, put up no resistance when doubt was sown in her mind as to whether invisible differences "exist". In the end, she says "perhaps we can't see them," meaning that they do exist after all, but even then "it couldn't happen" that they might add up to make a big difference. So that ultimately the waverings displayed by all these various subjects can be said to be due, when taken all together, to their failure to decide between the two models: seriation with imperceptible differences or classes of equivalence with the contradictions they inevitably entail.

§5. Stage 3 and Conclusions

Our last group of subjects, those between eleven and twelve, having first believed in a general equality of all the elements, then observed the inequality $G > A$, overcomes the contradiction by accepting the existence of nonperceptible differences of magnitude capable of being progressively added to produce a visible inequality. Here are some examples, beginning with a case transitional between levels 2B and 3.

Nad (10–10) perceives only equalities until $G > A$: "Well? — *A is the smallest of all. — And A and B are the same? — No. — Test it. — They're the same! There's something wrong. — Explain. — They are . . . G is bigger than the others. — And yet F = G? — No. Yes, they're the same. — So G is bigger? — No.*" Further comparisons, then Nad gives up the attempt to understand. "Is it that G gets bigger? — *No.* — Does A get smaller? — *No.* — Is there a very small difference between A and B and B and C, and so on? — *Yes!* — Is that possible? — *Yes. — Explain. — A is just a little bit smaller than B, B than C, and so on. So then that makes it a big difference between G and A. — And between F and G? — The same thing. — Can one see it? — No. — And between G and C? — There you can see it. — Between G and E? — There you can't. — Are they the same? — No. Every time there's a little difference, so in the end there's a big difference . . . because G and A are further apart and they've been put in order.*" So one simple question suggesting the possibility of small differences immediately triggered off understanding, whereas at previous levels even a complete explanation by the questioner had no effect.

Pat (11–4) first assumes general equality, then, after observing that $G > A$, says that "*it wasn't quite exactly what I did before.*" His first reaction is to think there are two classes ($A = B = C = D$) and ($E = F = G$). "And D with E? — *They're not quite equal. — Can you see they're not? — I can feel it. — A big difference? — Very small. — Then F and E? — They're unequal too. — Could it be a small difference you can't see? — I'll see. You might say there isn't any at all. If you looked with a magnifying glass it's possible they aren't the same size. — So are they equal? — They're all equal but there's such a small difference that several small differences makes one big difference. — Were you surprised when you put G on A? — Yes, but because there were a lot by then it made it into one big one.*"

Jer (11–9), after checking the equalities, observes that $G > A$ and concludes that "*F must be smaller than G — Test it then. — It's the same. It's one of the others that's smaller. Perhaps E. — Test that. — Same size.*" Then he goes on, E and D, D and C, and so on, right up to A. "Is it what we ought to expect? — *No, they get smaller and smaller, with very tiny differences between them. — Can you have differences so small you can't see them? — Yes.*"

Arc (12–0). "*They're equal. And G and A? — They're equal. — Sure? — Yes.* [Physical comparison]. *Oh! No, there is a difference. — Does that surprise you? — Oh yes! — It doesn't fit in then? — Yes, because some*

are just a little bit smaller, so you can't see it with the naked eye. — So?
— *There's a little difference between each counter.* — And did you see
them, these little differences? — *Because if you add all the little differences up and put them on G, then G is bigger.* — How did you come
to think of little differences all adding up? — *Because when you put them
together you can't put the big difference all at once because we'd see it*
(in other words because there is a continuous series)."

Asc (12–7): "*They're all equal.*" After G on A: "*It's bigger than A!* —
How can that happen? — *I didn't measure properly.*" He compares
again: *AB, BC,* right up to *FG,* saying each time: "*Just a little bit bigger.
Not much. You can't see it. You can feel it . . . with your fingers.* — Can
you feel it easily? — *No. Hardly anything. A tiny bit.* — So the difference
between *A* and *B* is the same as that between *B* and *C,* and so on? —
(further superimpositions beginning at the *A* end) *It's always the one
underneath that's bigger. They get bigger and bigger all the way along,
and the last one is bigger than the first* [meaning visibly bigger]."

The additivity of imperceptible differences has thus been acquired, making it possible to remove the contradictions. As to where this new operation
comes from, one might regard it as simply a generalization from the addition
of visible differences, which does produce a coherent structure at the concrete operations level. It is probable, however, that what is really involved is
a process of reflective abstraction, with its two characteristics of projection
from one plane to another (from the actually perceptible to the possibly
imperceptible, deduced in a necessary way) and of reorganization, since this
additivity of possibles does undoubtedly go hand in hand with distributivity.

Taken as a whole, these results are quite instructive about the nature of contradiction, about how consciousness of it is achieved, and about the logical
processes enabling it to be transcended. As to its nature, we have already
observed that it can be traced back to incomplete reversibility or compensations: when the intersection of two classes of equivalence (X and non-X) is
not seen as zero (complete compensation), so that the subject instead endows both classes with an overlapping segment whose characteristics must
consequently be x and $\bar{x}$ simultaneously, then there is a contradiction. We
have also seen that this contradiction possesses degrees according to the
extent of the overlap between the classes (which in the case of Pas in section
2 at first comprises *B C D E* and *F,* in other words all the elements except *A*
and *G,* these five elements being simultaneously equal to *A* and equal to *G,*
even though *G* is acknowledged to be larger than *A*).

It goes without saying, however, that to define noncontradiction by the
fact that the negation (non-X) exactly compensates the affirmation (X) is to
subordinate the notion of contradiction to that of negation: to say that class

X is made up of elements smaller than G is first of all to accept that "smaller" constitutes a negation of "equal", at least within the whole made up of seven elements, none of which is larger than G. But is that in fact the belief of the five- to six-year-old subjects, since they perceive no difficulty in accepting that one, two, three, or even five elements are simultaneously equal to and also smaller than G. In fact, one of two things is happening: either the child conceives the characteristic "littler," as we do, as being equivalent to "unequal" and therefore as a negation of "equal," while being unable as yet to compound this negation with its corresponding affirmation and achieving complete compensation, or else the child is introducing an extra, middle term between our negation and affirmation, in which case this middle term remains uncompoundable in terms of compensation.

Against this, what is clear is that the child is not saying (in its language) that such and such an element is at the same time "the same" and "not the same" as G. So, intervening between "littler" and not equal or "not the same" there is an inferential process that for us is immediate in a serial form, but which could very well find no place in the mind of a five- to six-year-old in any form at all. So we say that the child remains impervious to the notion of contradiction. But have we that right, and would it not be better to maintain that in the absence of that inference there is in fact no contradiction? In that case, $E = G$, $E = A$, and $E > A$ would be three distinct statements that one should not attempt to link together, each one being true in its own limited context (and, the 1B subjects add, the elements G and A may very well be changing their size from one situation to another). Surely, however, no one supposes that in moving from stage 1 to stage 2, the child turns overnight into a nuclear physicist capable of delighting in such complex occurrences. and seeing them as elementary cases of complementarity. The fact is that stage two subjects do find those three statements contradictory, which enables us to say that at five to six years old an awareness of that contradiction was already latent, but that the subject was not yet able to make it conscious for want of the necessary inferences. From this there follows our second conclusion: conscious awareness of contradiction presupposes an inferential structuring of what is observed, and we have seen this actually at work in the form of a transitivity conceived of as necessary, and of the composition of affirmations and negations.

Finally, where transcending the contradiction is concerned (levels 2B and 3), we find the two usual complementary aspects: in extension, a broadening of referential awareness (hypothesis of imperceptible differences) and, in comprehension, a relativization of the notions involved, the absolute predicates "little" and "big" being transformed into relations of serial differences. It is also noteworthy that in this progress toward supraliminal seriation we find a development occurring between the seven- to eight-year-old group and the eleven- to twelve-year-old group very similar to that which occurred between the three- to four-year-olds and the seven- to eight-year-olds: transition from dichotomies (seven to eight) to trichotomies (Pie at 9–4) and on to continuous differences. In both cases absolute predicates (little or big) are replaced by ordered relations; in one case, however, the latter are manipulatable, and in the other they must be constructed by inference alone.

As for the type of contradictions examined in this chapter, we might see them in terms of a conflict between one observed fact $(A < G)$ and a schema of anticipation $(A = B = C = \ldots G)$; but it goes without saying that the later conflicts are much more concerned with relations between quite separate schemes (classes of equivalence or seriation) applicable to the objects' observable characteristics as well as their unobservable ones. Finally, as to the general meaning of the development observed, we shall return to that in section 5 of chapter 2, which deals with a parallel problem.

Two

Contradictions in Partitive Compositions

with J. J. Ducret (part 1) and A. Henriques-Christophides (part 2)

In the introduction to this book, we put forward the hypothesis that functional situations giving rise to contradictions in the cognitive behavior of a subject can be divided into three categories. The first involves defective identity, when the same action does not lead to the same results, and hence, by derivation, when the same object used in the action is no longer characterized by the same properties. The second category is that of incomplete compensations between an affirmation and a negation, which is the same thing as accepting the existence of a nonzero overlap between a class X and its complementary class non-X. As for the third category, we have already mentioned nonnecessary inferences, in other words noncoherent compositions, and supposed that they result from a combination of the identity errors and incomplete compensations that constitute the first two categories.

One of the aims of this chapter is to examine the validity of this last hypothesis by taking one of the simplest possible examples of inferential coordination, the case of additive composition involved in the notion that the whole is equal to the sum of its parts. The subjects are presented with a number of small squares and small triangles, all having the same surface area, but such that the child will perceive the triangles as being larger than the squares. What will the subject's reactions be when the four triangles and the four small squares are both arranged to form two larger squares whose surface areas are visibly equal? If, as the psychologist naturally hopes, the younger subjects entangle themselves in a contradiction by saying that the two totalities are equal while at the same time denying equality of area to the two kinds of constituent element, the problem will then be to find out how this contradiction comes about (since perception alone will certainly not account for it), how it is made conscious, and finally how it is transcended, which takes much longer than one might have supposed in subjects who, in simpler tests, have already displayed an awareness of area conservation.

§1. Technique

One begins by showing the child two cardboard squares A and B with equal areas (16 cm by 16 cm) and asks, without allowing juxtaposition or superimposition, if they take up the same amount of "room" (for playing on, say) or whether there's more room on one than the other. These squares were accepted as equal by all subjects. After that, the child is shown four small, right-angled isosceles triangles (which we shall call $t1$ and whose total surface area when combined is 16 cm^2) and asked to check by congruence (superimposition) that they are equal. The same procedure is then followed with four small squares each 8 cm^2 (which we shall call s). Next, a $t1$ is placed several centimeters above an *s* (with its hypotenuse or the angle opposite the hypotenuse nearest the square), and one asks if there is the same room or not on the two figures. The answer is almost always that *t1* > *s*, under the double influence of the triangle's larger perimeter and the fact that its hypotenuse will project at both ends beyond any side of the square.

Next, child and experimenter simultaneously construct two large squares, one with the four *t1*, which we shall call *T1*, and one with the four *s*, which we shall call *S*. During this, the experimenter's hands are screened from the child's view. The child is then asked to predict what the relation of the two surfaces will be. (Objectively it is, of course, that *T1* = *S*) When the child has made his prediction, the screen is removed and he is asked to judge visually whether they are equal or not. If equality is contested, one can then conduct a transitivity test using the two squares *A* and *B* that were shown first. The subject is led to observe that *T1* = *A* and *S* = *B*, so that T1 = S because *A* = *B*. When equality has been acknowledged, the child is reminded of his judgment on *t1* and *s*, and one observes his reactions when confronted with the relations *T1* = *C* and *t1* > *s*.

Next, one goes through the same procedure with eight small triangles (called *t2* and each with a surface of one-half *t1*) and eight small rectangles (called *r* and each with an area of four by eight cm), eventually building up a big square *T2* with the eight *t2* and a big square *R* with the eight *r*. Once again *T2* = *R* (and both are equal to the previous sets of large squares *T1* and *C*, and *A* and *B*), although the subject will usually have said that *t2* > *r*.

In addition, as a means of reinforcing comprehension of the additive composition, one can also make two squares with the four *t1* and four of the *t2*, termed respectively *T1* and *T2*[1], whose inequality is made even more glaring by the fact that their constituent elements are unequal as well.

Finally, one goes on quickly to test for conservation of number and area in order to evaluate the child's operatory level.

§2. Stage 1

Here are some examples from level 1A:

Gab (5–8): "If you look at that (a *t1*) and that (an *s*), is one bigger than the other or not? — *The triangle is bigger.* — And if we take four of one sort and four of the other and make squares (subject arranges squares, the experimenter triangles) we have two big squares (*T1* and *C*). Now, is one bigger than the other? — *They're the same.* — And the *t1* and the *s*, do they take up the same room? — *That one [t1] takes up more room.* — And my big square and your big square? — *The same room for both of them.*"

Béa (6–0): "Do you think one of these big squares takes up more room than the other (*A* and *B*) or the same? — *They're both the same.* — And these little squares (four *s*) as well? — *Yes.* — And are these triangles (*t1*) all the same as one another? — *Yes.* — And if we take this (*s*) and this (a *t1*), does *s* take up more room than *t1* or the same room? — *That one* [*t1*] *is bigger.* — Now together we're going to make a big square with all these little triangles and a big square with all these little squares. Is one of these big squares bigger than the other? — *They'll be the same* (prediction). — How do you know? — [Silence.] — Are you sure? Have you seen that they are? — *No, but they're the same.* — And these, (*t1* and *s*), does one of them take up more room? — *Yes, the triangle.* — And we made two big squares with these triangles and these little squares, and you think the big squares are the same? — *Yes.* — What did we make with the little squares? — *A big square.* — You took them and put them together yourself? — *Yes.* — Are there more little squares or more little triangles in the big squares? — *Both the same.* — And *t1* is bigger than *s* yet now there's the same room in both big squares? — *Yes.* — So *t1* is bigger than *s*, and I put four *t1* and you put four *s* and the big squares are the same? — *Yes.*"

Bos (6–6) begins by anticipating then observing that the big squares *T1* and *C* are equal. Similarly with the elements *t1* and *s*: "*they're the same.*" Then, reflecting on *t1* and *s*, he adds: "*because they both belong to the house,*" which appears to be a judgment based on qualitative kinship rather than surface area. He is then given four *t2* and four *t1* to compare and arrange into two big squares, of which *T1* is much the larger. He anticipates: "*Mine is bigger because it has bigger triangles.*" So Bos seems quite ready for additive composition, but faced with *T2* and *R*, although he says the two big squares are equal he also thinks that "*the triangle* [*t2*] *is bigger*" than the rectangle *r*. "And the big squares are the same? — *Yes.* — How many triangles do you have? — *Eight.* — And how many rectangles in mine? — *Eight.* — How do you know? — *They* (the big squares) *are the same size.* — And these (*t2* and *r*)? — *No, the triangle is bigger.* — And when I use *t1* and *t2*, the square *T1* (with four elements for each big square so that *T1* is much larger) is bigger? — *Yes, because the t2 are smaller than the t1.* — And with *t2* and *r* you say that the little triangle *t2* is bigger than *r*, and there's the same room in both the big squares, is that right? — *Yes.* — And if another boy said that if *t2 > r*, then the big square (*T2*) will be bigger than the other (*R*), that would be wrong? — *Yes.*"

At level 1B, the beginnings of additive composition appear. They are still episodic, however, and not without contradictions between reactions to different questions.

Tan (6–8): *t1* is bigger than *s*, but with the big squares *T1* and *C* (made up of four elements each) she anticipates that "*they are both the same because they have the same number in them.* — But you haven't counted, have you? — *Yes, with my eyes.* — Can each *t1* be put with an *s? — Yes* — But one takes up more room? — *Yes, the triangle [t1].* — And both big squares take up the same room. But there's one thing I don't understand. You say t1 takes up more room than *s* (Each *t1* is compared with each *s.*) So what about the two big squares? — *They take up the same room.''* She is shown *t1* and *t2,* then two squares are made with four *t1* and eight *t2: "There's more room on my square [T1=4] because the t2 are little and the t1 are big.* Does that fit in with what you said before? — *No.* — Now then (the *t1* and *s* triangles and squares are shown), look again. Is one bigger? — *The triangle [t1].* — And if we make our squares? — *They're the same.* — And these (*t1* and *s*)? — *The triangle is bigger* — And the big squares? — *They both take up the same room.''*

Ful (6–3): *t1* and *s: "The triangle takes up more room.* — Now we're going to make two big squares together. — [Prediction.] *This one [T1] takes up more room because there are four big t1, and that makes a square a bit bigger than the other because it's made with four squares a little bit littler.* — Do you remember how we made them? — *There are four squares.* — Is one of the big squares bigger than the other? — (Perception.) *Both the same. I thought it was littler because the little squares didn't take up as much room.* — (Each *t1* and *s* compared again. Constant reaction: *t1 > s.*) And when they're put together? — *T1 is the same size as C.''* With the eight *t2* and eight rectangles there is the same reaction: equality of the big squares and inequality between the two sets of eight elements: "How can that be? — *Because they are* [all] *little, because there were little triangle and little rectangles.* — But *t2* and *r? — The triangle is bigger.''* Next, a comparison of two big but unequal squares made up of four *t2* and four *t1: "That one [T1] is bigger because there's more room here [t1 > t2].''* We go back to *t1* and *s: "The triangle [t1] isn't the same as the little square [s] but they both make a square the same size.* — I don't understand — *Because it is big [t1] and this one is smaller [t2] that makes it* [when totaled] *smaller. This one [t1] is almost the same size as s, but not quite, but it makes the same size all together all the same.* — Is that possible? — *Yes.''*

Dom (7–1). Prediction: "*Yours [T1] is bigger because you have triangles [t1 > s].* — And what does that mean? — *It won't be the same size, but a little bigger . . . no, the same size, the same room.''* Shown the *t2* and rectangles (*r*): "*The triangles take up more room.* — And the big squares? — *They're the same.* — Why? — *If* [= although] *the rectangles are smaller they take up the same room* [when totaled]. — Why? — *There's the same number. To make things the same you need the same number of them.* — And these (*t2* and *r*)? — *The triangle is bigger.''* But the big squares are still seen as equal.

Mey (7–9). The triangle *t1* are bigger than the squares *s,* but the big squares $T1$ and C are equal (both prediction and perception): "Can you have $t1 > s$ and $T1 = C$? — *Yes, it all depends how you put them together. You can have $T1 = C$, that's quite all right.*"

Thus subjects at level 1A see no contradiction in square or triangular elements being unequal in surface area even though equal numbers (Béa and Bos have both acquired conservation of number) of those same elements produce wholes with equal surface areas. It is true that these subject have not yet acquired conservation of area, but this is not an explanation, since what they are lacking, in the present experiment as in tests for conservation, is additive composition of spatial magnitudes, and it is this lack we in fact need to explain. First, we must remember that at this level (1A) there do already exist certain quantitative relations between parts and wholes, albeit of a particular type, deriving as they do from insufficient differentiation and coordination between extension and understanding of classes. For example, it can happen that subjects consider ten elements drawn from a collection of fifty as being "more" than ten drawn from a collection of twenty, as if the "more numerous" characteristic of the fifty were transferred to the ten in the same way as a qualitative characteristic. When Bos accepts that $t1 = S$ because $T1 = C$, which would be a 2B level response if it were based on an additive composition, he is in fact reasoning like such young subjects in accordance with simple qualitative kinship, since he says that the $t1$'s and the s's "both belong to the house" (the house being the big square). On the other hand, in the case of the four $t1$ and four $t2$ there is no problem of composition, since the differences $t2 < t1$ and four $t2$ (as a square) $<$ four $t1$ are perceptually obvious because so extreme, simply because the $t1$ triangles are twice the size of the $t2$'s.

The problem, then, is why such additive noncomposition (as in $t1 < s$ but four $t1$ [or $T1$] = four s [or S]) occurs, given that this flagrant contradiction — and above all the fact that subjects at this level are totally unaware of it—clearly derives from the absence of such an inferential mechanism. To understand the nature of this lack, and therefore of this contradiction, we need to go on an examine how the first indications of this mechanism begin to appear at level 1B, even though 1B subjects still remain on the whole unable to generalize from it, and are therefore still powerless to recognize the contradictions already encountered.

Tan, for example, anticipates that $T1 > T2$ (even though these squares are perceptually equal), because the elements composing them are unequal, and Ful reacts in exactly the same way with respect to $T1$ and $T2$, yet in the case of the triangles $t1$ and squares s he says that the difference is much less, hence the possibility that $T1 = S$. And Mey is quite definite that one can make two equal totalities out of unequal elements because "that all depends on the way you put them together. That's quite all right." So it seems that two conditions are necessary before additive composition can occur. The first, naturally, is that any particular element, whether $t1$, s, or whatever, shall retain its identity when entering into the composition of the big square so that one can no longer say, as Ful does, that "almost the same size...that makes the same size anyway," or in other words, that little differences can disappear during the course of composition. But the second condition is less obvious. It is, as Mey says, "how you put them together," implying that skillful arrangement enables one to compensate for inequalities in the separate elements of the whole. Moreover, it should be noted that Mey, like Ful and Dom, is successful in the simple conservation of area tests, as, for example, when one changes a square into a rectangle or cuts it up into smaller squares that can be put together again to reconstruct the original whole. In these cases, a lengthening of one side is compensated for by a shrinking of the other, and so on, while the operation is made easier by the fact that one is dealing with closely related shapes (all quadrilaterals). On the other hand, we should remember[1] the great difficulty experienced by subjects until the age of nine or ten in imagining how it is possible to construct a square with four triangles by combining them in precisely the same positions as we use here to make the square $T1$. So that in comparing $T1$ to square S, made up of smaller squares s, the subject is being presented with a new conservation problem, one involving heterogeneous rather than homogeneous forms, hence the impossibility of perceiving immediately the dimensional compensations involved. It is thus "quite all right," as Mey says, that without lacking a precise representation of this composition of triangles into a square, the subject should suppose that the differences of size accepted between the $t1$ and the s can be cancelled out by compensations when the two big and equal squares $T1$ and S are formed. The idea here is that if $t1 > s$, these differences, albeit always in the same direction (for the subject has compared them in pairs and always found the triangle bigger), can be compensated for and prevented from adding up by means of the new positions that one gives to the small triangles $t1$. In practice, the greater length of one side, which plays an obvious role in teh judgment $t1 > s$ (ordinal evaluation), no longer comes into play when the triangles are arranged in a circular way inside the big squares $T1$ or $T2$, and even when a momentary intuition of additive composition has made the subject anticipate that $T1$ will be greater than S (Ful and Dom), the perception of equality does not shock him.

§3. Level 2A

Unlike the previous subjects, those of level 2A achieve awareness of the contradiction from the outset, even though they are not always able to overcome it.

Dan (6–8): *s* is smaller than *t1*, and the square *T1* "*is bigger because s is smaller to make a big square.* — Can you explain it a bit more? — *Those [t1] were bigger than those [s].* — And I've put the same number of *s* as you have of *t1*? — *Oh! Yes, because there is four and four, the two squares [T1 and S] are the same.* — But out of *t1* and *s* there's one that takes up more room? — *Yes, the triangle.* — And is there more room on *T1* or *S*? — *No.* — Does that fit in? — *No.* — What's wrong then? — *The two little ones [t1 and s] are the same.* — How do you know? — *[Silence.]*"Hesitation over *T2* and *R*, then the same solution (*t2* = *r*). "How can you tell? — (Silence.) — Can you explain? — *No.*"

Sta (7–4): *t1* is bigger than *s*. "What about the big squares we've made? — *They take up the same room because all the bits of cardboard take up the same room* [but there may be no relative differentiation here between the *t1* and the *s* and between the *t1*'s and *s* among themselves]. — You said that t1 = *s*? — *Yes, no, t1 is bigger.* — And the big squares? — *T1 is bigger because the s's are smaller than the t1's.* — And did I use more *t1*'s than you did *s*'s? — *No, we both took one* [at a time]. — And what do you see when you look? — *T1 is bigger.*" *T1*, then *S* is now compared with large, undivided squares (*X*). Sta accepts that *T1* = *X*, as also *S* = *X*, yet continues to believe that *T1* > *S* (even though he has already acquired the notion of transitivity in general, as well as conservations of number and area). We then go on to *T2* and *R*: *t2* is bigger than *r* but of *T2* and *R* he says: "*there is the same room in those because those [t2] are bigger than those [r], but two r's make the same as two t2's.*" And of course 2*r* = 2*t2* = ¼ of the big square. "And if I make the big square by putting together two *r*'s and two *t2*'s we'll have? — *The same room, because the t2's are bigger, but they make a big square* [= ¼ of the square] *just like the r's do.*" On the other hand, when we introduce smaller rectangles, Sta observes a perceptible inequality between the total squares, and when we return to *T2* and *R* he now says: "*They're both the same size, because the rectangle [r] is the same size as the little triangle [t2].*" But after further visual examinations his doubts return.

Guy (7–9) finds that *t1* > *s* and concludes from this that the square *T1* "is bigger. — Explain. — *Because the t1 is bigger than s, that's why T1 is bigger than S.*" But when he thinks about the numbers (four in both), he concludes that *T1* = S and deduces from this that "*there's the same room in t1 as in s.* — But you did say it (*t1*) is bigger? — *If you cut up t1 you'd make it the same as s.*" So everything is now logically explained; but a further visual examination causes Guy to revert to *t1* > *s*. "But then *T1* is the same as *S*? — *Yes.* — Sure? — [Further visual check.] *I think so.* — And now *t1* and *s*? — *t1 is bigger and s is smaller.* — Doesn't it make a difference, one being bigger than the other? — *Yes, it means they're not the same! And they should be the same* ... [but] *the triangle [t1] is bigger than the square [s].* — And that doesn't make a difference? — *No.''* *T2* and *R* produce the same waverings, with *T2* > *R* at first because t2 > r, followed by equality in both cases and finally, after careful visual checks: "*They* [*T2 and R*] *are the same size.* — And t2 and r? — *There's more room in t2.''*

Lam (8–0) finds that r < t2 and *T2* = *R*. "Is that peculiar? — *Oh ! Yes it is, because there's the same number, and the t2 is bigger, so I wonder why those* [the big squares] *are as big as one another. I suppose r must be the same as t2.* — And is it? — *Oh! No, the t2 is bigger.''* Back to *T1* and *S*: "*The same room in both* (even though t1 > s). — Is that what you'd expect? — *No! Now I understand. This is a triangle and this is a square, they're different shapes and they've been put in* [to the big square] *differently, so they make the same size.''*

When the elements are compared once again in detail, he continues to accept the small triangles as being larger than the small squares or rectangles when compared one by one, whereas two triangles put together are equal to two rectangles put together, and so on, because the shapes arrived at then become comparable.

Cos (8–6): t1 > s, but when made up into large square (*T1*) "*they take up the same room.* — Why is that? — *I don't know.''* With *T2* and *R*, on the other hand, the result is *R* < *T2* because r < t2. But when presented with unequal rectangles giving clearly different wholes, Cos concludes that both *T2* and *R* as well as their elements are equal. Later, however, she returns to her original solution.

It will be seen that all these subjects are aware of the requirements of additive composition, and therefore sense a contradiction between t1 > s and T1 = S. But they are unable to overcome it entirely (except Dan, the youngest, but without being able to find an explanation, as will be the case at level 2B) for two reasons. The first is naturally perceptual in nature[2], arising from the fact that t1 appears bigger than s while the big square *T1* is visibly equal to *S*. Perception alone, however, is far from being the whole explanation, since that remains the same at level 2B, where it is held in check by adequate inferences: "You can see that t1 > s, but it isn't true," Rol will say (§4), and there is nothing to prevent subjects on level 2A, since they have already mastered the first concrete operations, from reasoning in the same way if they could manage to apply the laws (already acquired) of additive composition not only in cases involving homogeneous shapes but also in those involving heterogeneous ones. The main reason for their relative failure is therefore the persistence of the reasoning process already pointed out at the end of section 2: in order for correct additive composition to occur between heterogeneous shapes (triangles and quadrilaterals), it is not only necessary that every element shall conserve its identity, but also that when two different kinds of elements are put together, their inequalities of shape shall be compensated for quantitatively. But, in fact, these subjects continue to believe in false compensations, clinging to qualitative factors (position), and so cannot break through to the notion of quantitative compensations, even though they do so quite easily in tests of area conservation in which the elements are all the same shape and only the total areas formed change in configuration.

Lam is remarkable in this respect: he accepts that two triangles when placed side by side to form a square cover the same area as two rectangles placed side by side to form an equal square, and that is a decisive step. But at the same time he goes on thinking that one of those two triangles is larger than one of those rectangles. His way of reconciling this discrepancy has a very clear meaning: "they're different shapes and they've been put in differently, so they make the same size." So we have a deliberately incomplete compensation from the quantitative point of view, but one that appears adequate for qualitative reasons of position. It is clear that Sta is reasoning in the same way when he says that "the triangles are bigger, but they make a big square just like the rectangles do." Guy reaches level 2B momentarily when he says that "if you cut up the triangle you'd make it the same as the square," which is a complete compensation because it is quantitative. However, it proves no more than a fleeting gleam, and he then returns to his previous qualitative compensation and the contradiction it entails, saying in the end that it doesn't matter.

§4. Level 2B and Stage 3

2B subjects do succeed, though not without hesitations, in removing the contradictions and offering good reasons. They are for the most part aged from nine to ten, though there were three precocious cases just under or over eight.

Jul (7–11) doesn't know whether *tl* is bigger or smaller than *s*, depending on their positions. As for *Tl* and *S*, the latter will be "*bigger: there there are squares, here there are triangles, and that makes a difference. — Is S* bigger? — *I don't know.* [Visual check.] *I think they're the same . . . I think tl and s are the same size anyway.* — Then why does *S* = *Tl*? — *I don't know how to explain. Ah! because the tl and s are the same for bigness. Each of the s is the same size as each of the tl.*"

Rol (7–11): "*It's Tl that's bigger, because the tl are bigger than the s.* — Look. — *The big squares are the same size.* — I don't think I quite understand. — *Now I think that tl = s became Tl = S.*" But can one see how? — *All you can see is that tl and s, are not the same size.*

You can see that t1 > s, but it isn't true. — Why isn't it true? *— Because the big squares are the same size."* Long hesitations over the relation of *t2* to *r*, but as soon as the big squares have been made: *"So t2 = r because T2 = R."*

Bar (8–4) thinks that *t1 > s* and *T1 > S*. "Why? *— It isn't true. If the four s together take up the same room as the four t1, then t1 = s. —* But when you look at them? *— Then t1 seems bigger, but they're the same: if you cut up this triangle to make a square [t1 to make s], then they come to the same."* Then *T2* and *R:* "*T2 is maybe bigger, but perhaps not. —* What does it depend on? *— "It depends on r and t2. If you cut up t2 it would have to make an r* [in order for *T2* to equal *R*]."

San (9–5): *"I said that s > t1, I don't know. —* And the two big squares can take up the same room if it is? *— Yes . . . t1 and s must be the same size then."*

Cri (9–8) says of *T2* and *R:* "*If t2 is bigger, the big square is bigger."*

Lau (9–11): *"If R = T2 then t2 = r,"* after hesitations over this last point.

Dia (10–6) thinks that *t2 > r*, then: *"no, when you put them together [two t2] that makes like a square, [two r] that makes the same together as two t2, it makes the same thing,"* and *"when you make the two big squares they make the same thing."*

Sem (10–6): same reasoning for the *t2*'s: they equal *r*. *"Looking, you'd say t2 is bigger, but it's the same size."*

The two new and linked factors that characterize the reactions of these subjects are thus that they succeed in removing the contradiction (between $t > s$ and $T = S$, and so on) definitively, not just momentarily, and that they justify their final position with an explanation that makes explicit reference to additive composition (as opposed to Dan at level 2A, who applies it but doesn't isolate it). Note, for example, the speed with which Rol, Bar, and San deduce the equality of the elements $t1 = s$ or $t2 = r$ on the basis of the observed equality of the large squares $T1 = S$ or $T2 = R$, because for these subjects the equality of the parts (an equal number of triangles and quadrilaterals) is a necessary consequence of the equality of the wholes they form, and vice versa. Jul offers his proof in the direction parts → whole, but his discovery stems no less from the equality of the large squares. When Dia and Sem proceed from the part to the whole, they do so on the basis of a logical analysis of those parts: if one "cuts up the triangle *t1*," Bar says, "to make a square, then it's the same thing." And Dia, like Sem, discovers spontaneously that two *t2* triangles put together are equal to two rectangles *r* put together, hence $t2 = r$ and $T2 = R$.

As for the reactions of Stage 3 subjects, they differ from the ones just noted only in the immediacy of their comprehension:

Cor (11–7): "If you look at one of these triangles and one of these rectangles, does one have a larger area than the other? — *No, because two of those triangles make a square, and so do two rectangles.* — What about *T2* and *R*? — *They're both the same because one t2 = one r and there are eight of one there and eight of the other there.*"

Rib (12–0): "*t2* and *r*? — *The same area. If you put one t2 on one r there's a bit sticking out and a bit not covered, so they're the same.* — And *T2* and *R*? — *If one t2 = one r the two big squares must be equal because there's the same number in each.* — But if one looks at one *t2* and one *r*? — *If you didn't think about it then it t2 might look bigger, but it isn't true.* — Why is that? — *Because our eyes deceive us.*"

§5. Conclusions

The first conclusion to be drawn from this development from level 1A to level 2B or 3 is, naturally, that in such an experiment (as in that described in chapter 1), unawareness of the contradiction, then growing consciousness and finally transcendence of it, are due to the lack, then to the acquisition of an inferential mechanism for dealing with conflicts between perception and deduction. In chapter 1 we were dealing with nonvisible differences, and therefore with apparent perceptual equalities (other than the obvious differences between the extreme ends of the series). But in order to reconstruct that series, it was essential to base one's reasoning on an inferential mechanism of transitivity that was absent at the outset (hence the unawareness of any contradiction), and was then constituted despite difficulties caused by the conflicts it entailed with perception. In the present investigation, the situation is exactly parallel, but moves in the opposite direction: perception imposes apparent inequalities, except in the final configuration (the totalities represented by the big squares), and in order to establish the real equalities subjects must employ an inferential mechanism of additive composition which, at the outset, is not there, and which is only constituted with difficulty in the specific case when the elements to be joined and compared are heterogeneous.

In these two parallel developments (for in chapter 1 there is a necessary additivity of the unperceived differences, and the transitivity required is itself an additive composition of relations, since $ARC = ARB + BRC$), the initial lack of the inferential mechanism derives in reality from a combination of two components: the lack of identity between the terms involved, and the incomplete character of the necessary compensations. There is a lack of identity because one term (the size of the disks in chapter 1 and of the triangles or quadrilaterals in this experiment) is conceived of as being sometimes equal and sometimes not equal to a second. As for the incomplete compensations, we have seen in chapter 1 that the complementary classes of equivalence constructed by the subject possess an overlapping group of characteristics that is at once x and non-x. Similarly, in the results of this present experiment, the subjects believe, up to and including level 2A, that the differences between the elements they judge to be unequal can be compensated for because their positional relationships are seen as acting as quantitative relations, as is conceivable from an ordinal viewpoint.

But incomplete compensations constitute, in all domains, the fundamental characteristic of states of disequilibrium, since it is the property of equilibrium to be a total compensation (algebraic sum equaling zero) of the virtual tasks concerned. Some such consideration is probably the only way of explaining why the subject becomes troubled by the contradiction long before being able to express it logically. An adequate formulation would require, in effect, that one regard the equality of the whole and the sum of its parts as a necessary norm: in this case, and only in this case, it is inadmissible to affirm simulatneously that $t1 > s$ and that $T1 = S$. In other words, rendering the contradiction explicit brings about its suppression. Yet it is not until level 2B that such a way of thinking imposes itself on the subject. Before that, he merely experiences uneasiness, with momentary but local solutions, as though he were achieving an intuition of additive composition for fleeting moments now and then, but mingled with others, and without perceiving its necessity or, above all, its generality. But what are these fragmentary intuitions if not the expression of schemas of action, each valid in its own area of application and limited only by an inability to adjust it sufficiently when those areas are extended? Hence the interferences observed between applications (affirmations) and nonapplications (negations). Thus again we encounter incomplete compensations; but now we see them occurring not just between classes of objects but at an even earlier state—between the schemas of action themselves.

For example, the subject judges the triangle $t1$ to be larger than the square s because its baseline sticks out beyond any one side of the square, a criterion that is correct when it is two lines that are to be compared (and especially when the starting point is the same), but which, in the case of $t1$, obscures the other dimensions. The result is, that in the big square $T1$, in which the triangles $t1$ are placed differently and form an area equal to the square S made up of four s's, these differences in the length of sides no longer play any role, so that the equality $T1 = S$ does not appear surprising. Similarly, the subject may judge that $t1 > s$ because he perceives the perimeter of $t1$ as larger than that of the square, forgetting that perimeters and areas are not proportional; but in the large squares *T1* and *S* the perimeters of the smaller elements are contained inside those of the total squares, which once more leads to a false compensation. Or else the subject bases his judgment on the equality of the numbers involved, but forgetting the possible nonequivalence of the units. On the other hand, he will accept additive composition when the elements involved are homogeneous in shape, but without generalizing it to apply to the hetrogeneous shapes, for the reasons just given. In short, the subject has at his disposal a series of partially valid schemas not yet sufficiently regulated to extend their areas of application, and this leads both to his inadequate compensation between affirmations and negations and also to the disequilbrium that is expressed in the subject's feeling of uneasiness, which persists until he succeeds in formulating the contradictions clearly and consciously. This formulation, in fact, presupposes precisely such a previous regulation of extensions, that is, of "all" and "some," while the subject's unease stems from the absence of such delimitations, and persists until he has found a principle of integration in the generalization of additive compositive, which in fact goes hand in hand with the regulation of extensions.

However, the problem has not been solved, but only displaced, since we still have to explain this lack of coordination between affirmations and negations. One might well wonder if it wouldn't be simpler, in this chapter as in chapter 1, to attribute the initial disequilbriums to nothing more than the conflicts experienced between perception and inferences, and equilibration to the final success of those inferences. That is, of course, partly the case, on the condition that we insert this initial primacy of perception, and this ultimate victory of inferential composition, within a broader development whose meaning will become clear in later chapters (7–9).

In fact, the subject in our preoperatory stage begins by being centered on the object with its positive characerics provided by perception, whereas negations and limitations (regulation of "all" or "some" as "not-all", and so on) are derived only later on by means of secondary relational adjustments or inferences. The result of this initial primacy of the positive over the negative is that in cases where the object changes shape (conservation tests), the subject regards the transforming action (rolling out a ball into a sausage) as additive and augmentatory, without perceiving that what is added in one dimension is necessarily removed in another. The notion of conservation is constituted, on the contrary, when such an action is conceived of as a displacement of some parts of the object in relation to others, with these additions and subtractions being necessarily linked and compensated, so that the conservation of the total quantity is based on a simple "commutability" or commutativity in a broad sense (see chapter 10).

In the situations examined in chapter 1, and in the present investigation, we are observing a partly analogous development, even though the individual objects involved are not transformed by the actions, but simply compared. The subject begins, as is only natural, by concerning himself solely with the perceptible and positive characteristics of the object in the form of equalities or differences, without paying attention to their possible limitations or negations. Then, when presented with conflicts (simultaneous equalities and differences, or the one leading to the other), one frequent reaction, sometimes made explicit but more often only implicit, is to accept that the disks in chapter 1 can change size when handled ("perhaps it gets bigger when you touch it"—Cri at 6–5; "sometimes it's little, sometimes it's big"—Oli at 7–0), and that the triangles $t1$ cease being larger than the squares s when suitably arranged. Here we have an equivalent, in attenuated form, of the actions that in conservation tests are thought to bring about a material modification in the individual objects and change their quantitative characteristics.

It is only after this stage has been gone through that the solution is sought, and found, in the direction of additivity, and in opposition to the initial perceptual data. Now on this point (due allowance being made for the delaying role played by non-perceptible facts or appearances in conflict with observed equalities), a progressive victory of this kind for the addition of the parts into a stable whole constitutes the equivalent, in the field of logical comparisons, to that of displacement over transformations in the quantitative tests. It is a long while now since E. Meyerson, in the field of concrete actions, compared addition to a displacement, whether practical or mental. And indeed, in such elementary cases of addition, the displacement is necessarily accompanied by a subtraction, since what is added to one collection is necessarily removed from another. In the case of parts being joined to form a whole, the result is that whatever is introduced into the sum is necessarily drawn from the parts and therefore can no longer be produced, as so many stage 1 subjects imagine, during the course of the process. Inversely, whatever is missing from the sum (as the big square $T1$ may lead subjects to suspect after they have predicted that it will be bigger than S) did not exist in the parts, and has not been disposed of during the construction process by arranging the final whole spatially in such a way as to eliminate inequalities in the parts.

To sum up, then: even though we have not been dealing in these experiments with actions that materially modify the shapes of the objects involved, but only with logical comparisons (at the heart of which the transformations involved bear solely upon the structures of the totalities or of the process by which they are brought into relation), the transition from initial disequilibriums to final equilibrium presents general features that can be found in other areas: a lack of compensations, leading to contradictions and persisting as long as the subject remains centered upon the positive characteristics of the object, followed by operational or inferential compositions, whose additivity is regulated by the interplay of implicit subtractions or negative operations and thus attains reversible necessity.

Part 2. Complementary Experiments into Logical Contradictions and the Composition of Heterogeneous Shapes

Another experiment, made independently of the previous one, was undertaken with the aim of investigating the reactions of subjects to instructions that are either contradictory (for example: "draw me a square with three sides") or not in themselves contradictory but possibly appearing so to the children (for example: "fold a rectangle into four little triangles" or "make me a triangle with the same space in it as this square"). Since sections 2 to 5 of this chapter have led us to suppose a late development of logical contradictions, based upon structural compositions as opposed to conflicts of contents, as wellas a difficulty in arriving at spatial compositions involving heterogeneous shapes (triangles and squares or rectangles), it would be as well to give a brief account at this point of the results obtained in this second experiment, which complements the first.

The two instructions "draw me a square with three sides" and "draw me a rectangle with four sides all the same length" ("all as long as one another") are logically contradictory if we follow their definitions: "a square is a closed figure possessing four equal sides (and four angles, and so on)" and "a rectangle possesses two pairs of parallel sides unequal in length." However, if the subject does not abide by these definitions, but takes the words "square" and "rectangle" to refer to variable contents between which he assumes it is possible to establish certain equivalences (for example, conserving the overall shape of a square but only drawing three sides of it so as to leave the figure open, or drawing three sides of it so as to leave the figure open, or drawing two of its sides linked by a diagonal), then it will be possible to view such responses as possessing a greater or lesser degree of coherence, albeit outside the domain of formal contradiction.

In practice, out of about fifty subjects ranging from five to twelve years of age, it was not until one reached the seven to eight-year-olds that one received answers (five out of twelve at the age of seven) plainly denying the possibility of a three-sided square from the outset. And it was only among the nine- to ten-year-olds that such reactions became unanimous. At five to six years, all the subjects involved began by attempting some kind of graphic construction, and although half of them finally came to announce the impossibility of the task, the remainder, while accepting that they couldn't achieve it themselves, still thought that an adult, being cleverer, would undoubtedly do so.

Xan (5–3) draws three of the sides of a square, but after the original request has been repeated says: "*It's not quite a square with three lines.*" He closes the figure, then observes that it now has four sides. He tries again, but this time draws the fourth side with a gap in the middle, so that the two sections he has drawn can be seen as extensions of the adjacent sides. "*No, you can't do it.*" But he only means that he can't. He still believes that an adult could: "Are you sure I can? — *Yes.*" For the rectangle with four equal sides, at first Xan simply draws a rectangle smaller than the one displayed: "Does it have all four sides as long as one another? — *Yes.* — Explain how. — *You can do it like this* [he draws the two medians, thus joining the sides into pairs, which to him seems to be an assurance of general equality, by showing that they are all little and that there are no more big ones]. — And now draw me a triangle with four sides. — [He draws two adjacent sides, then gives the third a hump so that is counts for two.] — How many sides? — *Four* [pointing them out]." Then he draws another, but making dots halfway along two adjacent sides, thereby indicating that they can be joined by a straight line cutting the triangle in two (which he studiously avoids actually doing) and fulfilling the role of fourth side.

Nic (5–6) for the four-sided triangle draws a triangle with its bisector and maintains that he now has "*four sides.*" for the rectangles with four equal sides he draws a very little oblong beside the large one offered as a reference. He then claims they are "*all little.* — Isn't that one there littler than that one? — *No.* — It's the same littleness? — *Yes.* — Exactly the same littleness? — *Yes.*"

Vic (5–10) for the three-sided square draws a square without a fourth side, or in other words open: "And that's a square? — *Yes.*"

Isa (6–7) draws three of the sides of a square: "*Yes.* — Is that a real square? — *No, it has three lines.* — Can it be done? — [Silence.] — Is it impossible, or just difficult? — *Difficult.* — Could this gentleman do it? — *Yes.* — And the teacher? — *Yes.* — So it's possible? — *No.* — Why not? — *It doesn't exist.* — But the gentleman could do it? — *Yes.*"

Noc (6–9): "*A square isn't hard, but with just three lines, I can't do that.* — And could this gentleman do it? — *Yes.* — Why is that? — [Silence.]"

As a reference, here are two examples of answers given by older children.

Mon (12–6): a square with three sides "*that's not possible. —* Why not?

— Because squares have four sides. — Is it impossible to do or just hard? *— It's impossible. —* And a rectangle with four equal sides? *— That won't work because if it's not like that it isn't a rectangle. A rectangle has sides that aren't the same, and squares have equal sides."*

Phi (12–2): *"It's impossible because a square is a quadrilateral."*

These results show very clearly the difference between logical contradiction—which is necessarily relative to a previously established system of classes well-defined in comprehension as well as clearly outlined (and therefore clearly quantified) in extension—and prelogical contradiction involving only nonformalized contents. In the latter case, the contradiction consists solely in a disequilibrium between actions, and is relative solely to a more or less realizable coherence between the schemas governing those actions, the sole criterion of which remains the degree of difficulty the conciliatory or equilibrating action presents, the ultimate limit being presented, of course, by impossibility, though it is a limit that is never reached and, above all, not susceptible of justification. Thus the five- to six-year-old subjects end up in some cases by giving up their attempts, but because the solution is too "difficult," not because it is impossible (Isa). And if what they are asked for "doesn't exist," that only means they haven't found it yet, since they believe an adult could. As for the solutions offered, they consist in retaining the square's overall shape but eliminating one side, in giving the third side of a triangle a hump which is seen as an extra, fourth side, in calling an internal or bisecting line a "side," in drawing a smaller rectangle so that its four sides shall "all be little" (Nic) and consequently equal (cf. Xan also). The solution arrived at for reconciling the contradictory schemas thus consists in accommodating them to the extent of possible reciprocal assimilation, the sole question then being to ascertain, by means of a kind of introspective or internal logical (or prelogical) experiment, whether that accommodation does in fact provide stable satisfaction, or whether it remains in a state of disequilibrium. If the latter is the case, then there is uneasiness or a sense of contradiction. But even then it is clear enough that the contradiction remains wholly relative to the complete or incomplete compensations of a process of equilibration between the schemas of action, and is not yet related to a deductive and formalizing construction, this being a characteristic of the forms of equilibrium achieved by the final stage alone.

The second part of this experiment, after the impossible requests, consists in asking the subject to draw "the longest possible line" between two points. This request is preceded, however, by an introductory question bearing on the shortest possible line. The results show a complete contrast between the reactions of eleven- to twelve-year-olds and five- to six-year-olds. The former all answer: "*It goes to infinity.*— Is it possible to draw it? — *there isn't any end to it* (Phi 12–2)." The young ones, on the contrary, all draw a line that sticks out beyond the two points, or various curves, or later, beginning at about seven years old, lines running around the edge of the paper, and so on.

When we come to compositions of heterogeneous shapes (folding a rectangle into four triangles either before or after having folded it into four small rectangles, or transforming a square into a triangle with the same surface area), the difference between these questions and the previous ones is that the younger subjects still view the tasks as impossible but sometimes more rapidly and with greater conviction: it is not until nine to ten years old that the questions are resolved by seventy-five and fifty percent of the subjects, and this always after hesitations.

Nar (6–6) attempts to fold a rectangle into four triangles, but only succeeds in producing small quadrilaterals "*because there are squares on both sides.*" Transformation of a large square into a triangle is not possible "*because there isn't any triangle* [contained or implied in the square]. — Do you think someone else could do it? — *No.* — But could they make a rectangle? — *Yes.*"

Mic (6–6) fails to make four triangles from the rectangle. He too produces four smaller rectangles: "*It's not possible. No one can do it because it's too hard.* — No one? — *No, because if you fold it into four it makes a square.* — Do you want to try again, with this square piece? — [He fold it into squares] *It makes a square, four squares.* — Is it just hard or is it impossible to make four triangles? —*Impossible.* — Can't anyone do it? — *Yes* [= no]. — Sure? — *Yes.* — Try to draw them. — [He draws a little triangle in each of the square's four corners, though without folding them down, then puts them all along the square's top side.] — But why not take up the whole sheet, the way you did with the four squares? — *That's impossible. No one can do that.*" When asked to make a square into a triangle his reaction is the same: "*That's impossible.* — Could someone else doe it? — *It's too hard.* — But when you're grown up, you'll be able to do it then? — *No.*"

Art (7–3) (who had successfully resolved the first set of questions) finally draws an oblique line across one corner of the rectangle to produce a small triangle. "But what if you draw over the whole rectangle? — [She then draws a second triangle, its top angle touching the oblique line already drawn but its base occupying only a sector of the rectangle's base line: hence two triangles plus one irregular quadrilateral and one irregular pentagon.] — Try again —*Impossible.* — Could I do it? — *No.*"

The next set of reactions (one subject aged 5–10, several aged 6–0 or even 7–8) consists in folding down the four corners of the rectangle, giving four triangles that do not take up the rectangle's entire area.

Flo (6–7) then proceeds as follows: "But there is some of it left over. — *That's the only way you can do it.*" But given a square she does laboriously (after first folding it several times into quadrilaterals) succeed in producing one diagonal fold, then two. On the other hand she fails to make a triangle out of the square.

Son (7–2) does not get beyond the stage of folding down the four corners, and in the case of the square draws a big triangle inside it that is, of course, not the same in area.

It is not until level 2B, however, that these problems are completely mastered. This makes it clear why, in the case of the questions investigated in sections 1 to 5 of this chapter, the solutions are not reached until nine to ten years old: at the outset of this development there exists for young subjects a sort of systematic contradiction (in fact a pseudocontradiction) in attempting to transform quadrilaterals into triangles because, to them, these heterogeneous shapes appear irreducible.

Three

Reactions to the Irrational and Double Reversals

with M. Robert

One very general tendency of the scientific mind consists in viewing the universe as intelligible, and consequently as noncontradictory. No doubt some aleatory element exists, and in consequence irreversible processes of intermixture, but such things are matters of disorder only, not of contradiction, and rational deductive methods like the theory of probabilities can render even these intelligible. It is also true that "the dialectics of nature" has attempted to reveal contradiction in the multiple oppositions to be found within phenomena; but all these are in fact contravections—in other words "vections" moving in opposite directions—and not true contradictions. By this I mean that they are not oppositions between the "statements" of a subject, even though contravections may in fact exist within that subject's actions, so that the problem then arises—but only then—of what the relations are between inadequately compensated contravections, which will in fact be contradictory to varying degrees, and those contravections that are completely compensated and, for that reason, the source of rational compositions.

If we examine the development of such contradictions when they are apparently linked to real objects, there are two particular questions that merit examination. The first is whether a belief in the intelligibility of the real world is found at all levels where questioning of the subject is possible, or whether it is something that develops. In order to investigate this question, the best method is to present the child, not with aleatory phenomena (we are already relatively well informed on that point), but with a series of conjuring tricks that will provide an image of continual contradictions. In this particular experiment we shall use large, flat matches, the nonhead ends of which are marked with a clearly visible line drawn by the child on one of the flat sides, leaving the other blank. If the experimenter then turns the matches over twice, by turning his hand and the matches held in it at the same time, he can give the impression that the lines are still visible whenever the matches are rotated, or, if he so chooses, never visible. What will the subjects' reactions be to this type of contradiction, apparently inherent in the object itself? Secondly, when the subject attempts to explain the contradiction, he will invoke a variety of possible actions on the part of the experimenter, and our second problem will be that of the relations between those actions and the effective or imaginary transformations of the object.

Technique

The technique used in the experiment is extremely simple, provided the experimenter possesses a certain manual dexterity. The child is first shown two long, flat matches (two is the optimum number because of the final question) and asked to drawn lines in blue pencil on one side of both at the nonhead end. The subject is then asked to observe that there are no marks of any kind on the other (blank) side. The matches are laid on the table with the marked sides uppermost, and the child is asked what he will see when the matches are turned over. "No lines," is the usual answer. The experimenter then holds the matches up vertically, with the lines showing, and asks what the subject will see when they are turned round. But then he executes two simultaneous movements (here termed "rotations"): (1) he twists his hand so that the other side of the match should become visible; (2) at the same time he rotates the two matches with his fingers, thereby cancelling the effect of (1), so that the lines are still visible. These gestures are repeated several times (and rapidly of course), in order to elicit amazement from the subject. The matches are then laid on the table again, with the lines showing, and the child is again asked what he will see if they are turned over: "the lines still" or "no lines this time," the subject replies. The matches are turned, still on the table, and the subject observes the lack of lines on the other side. Then the process is repeated and the subject is asked for explanations.

When the subject realizes that there is a trick involved, the experimenter tries to get him to perform it himself, or to analyse it verbally. If he fails, the "rotations" in the air are repeated in slow motion until final success or failure is established. The questions asked should bear upon the details of the movements executed (the two rotations: one longitudinal as the hand twists, the other transversal as the fingers turn the matches over). To subjects beyond a certain level one can then put a final question, while showing them the matches with one blank side and one marked side showing: how would one set about making the line seem to move from one match to the other? In this case, of course, simply rotating the matches once with the fingers, without the longitudinal rotation, is sufficient.

§1. Stage 1

First a few examples:

Pol (4–10): "Now, what if we turn the matches over? — *We won't see the lines.* — Let's see. — *No lines.* — [Double rotation.] — *Little lines!* — Is that what you'd expect? — *Yes, because you turned them the other side, the lines.* — [Matches on table again.] — What if I show you the other side? — *No little lines* [observation]. — [Double rotation again]. — *The lines.* — Is that peculiar? — *Yes.* — [Matches on table, lines showing.] — What's on the other side, do you think? — *Lines.* — Why? — *Because they'll be there.* — What makes you think that? — [Double rotation.] — *Why don't you show the other side?"* [Blank sides then shown in the hand.] — "Now what if I turn them? — *There'll be lines.* — [Two sets of double rotations.] — What can you see? — *Blank.* — And the other side? — *No lines.* — And the other again? — *No.* — Have they vanished? — *Yes.* — Let's look. Do you think they've vanished, or are they there? — *They're there.* — Make up your mind. — *They're not there.* — Look. — *They haven't disappeared!* — [Both sides shown again, then double rotations so that blank sides always show, but with subject saying each time that the lines are still there on the other side.] — What if I show the other side? — *No.* — What do you mean, no? — *No.* [= you won't see them if they're up in the air.] *We have to put them on the table* [then you can see the lines on the other side]. — [More double rotations from blank to blank.] — Where are they? — *On the other side, they've disappeared.* — Is that possible? — *Yes.* — How? — *Because they've disappeared.* — Can that happen? — *Yes and they come back afterwards.* — [Matches on table. Pol turns them over and sees lines: surprise.] — Why didn't we see them and now we do? — *Because before* [in the air] *they'd vanished.*"

Vin (5–4): "What if we turn them over? — *There won't be anything, there aren't any lines.* — Every, every time I turn the matches over? — *No lines, because there aren't any.* — [Double rotation.] — *There are marks!* — Why? — *Because on the other side there aren't any. Look behind!* — And what if I show you the other side? — *Perhaps we'll see them?* — Why? — *Because I'd drawn on that side* [i.e. the invisible side, which means he rejects the lines on the visible side as not being the ones he made.] — And if I turn again? — *We'll see lines.* — Why? — *Because before we saw them.* — And if I show you the other side? — *There'll be lines.* — And if I showed you the other side again? — *Lines.* — Will they be on the other side? — *Yes.* — Why? — *Because before we saw them.* — [Matches on table.] — [Vin turns them himself.] — *Oh! No!* — Why aren't there any there? — *Because we put them* [the matches] *on the table.* — And before (in the air)? — *It's like flames from matches, you can see them from the other side.* — But how is it that we can see the line on both sides? — *There's a bit of the line that comes through from the other side* [= that is visible through the match like a flame.] — [On table.] — [Vin does the turning.] *No, there aren't any.* — And before (in the air)? — *There's a bit that comes out* [= through from the other side]."

Cla (5–1). Double rotation: "Why can we see them? — *Because.* — What if I show you the other side again? — *Nothing, I don't know.* — [Process repeated.] Why? — *Because that's how it is.* — And the other side? — *There'll be lines there. No. I don't know.* — [Double rotation.] — *There'll be lines because you've got them on the other side.* — Sure? — *Yes* [he looks]. *No, I can't see them. Just now there were some there. Now there aren't.* — Why not? — *You're doing magics.* — I'm doing a little trick. Have a go. — *I don't know how.* — [Another double rotation.] — *Why are they on my side again?* — Ah. And what about the other side? — *The lines were on the other side. Now they've come here.* — Do the lines move then? — *No they stay on the same side.* — So what happens? — *I don't know.*"

Dal (6–2). Double rotations and amazement. Matches on table, lines showing. "If I turn them over, what shall we see? — *Blue* [color of lines], *because it was blue before* [in the air]. — Go on then. Turn them over. — *Blank!* — How does that happen? — *Don't know.*" Another double rotation. Dal predicts the blank side correctly this time; but when the lines continue to appear he once more begins to believe that they will be there on the other side even with the matches on the table. He confesses he can't understand, because "*they can't move round if they're drawn on.*"

Two things seem clear in the reactions at this level. First, the subjects sense very strongly that there is a contradiction between the presence of the lines after double rotations and the fact that both matches have a blank side. And indeed, there is more involved than a simple failure on the part of the facts to confirm the subject's anticipation, since in this particular case the prediction made is not due to previous observations that have been more or less well encoded, and therefore leave a certain margin for interpretations. The constraint here is in fact much stronger, since it results directly from an action that the subject has just performed, and about the meaning of which no doubt is possible. So, having himself drawn the lines on one side of a flat match and nothing on the other, the subject cannot help but be perturbed when he sees them still there after the match appears to have been turned over (if Pol is not at first, that is only because he failed to grasp immediately what it was he had seen).

The second clear point that emerges is that the subjects, although aware of a contradiction situated, as it were, within the object, do not accept it in the slightest, and are in no way satisfied at finding themselves in the presence of the unintelligible, whereas one might have expected them to be delighted and amused when confronted at last with a fantastical object daring to defy the most elementary laws. This dissatisfaction leads to attempts to resolve the conflict; but with the exception of Vin (the only one to think up a causal explanation, based on a sort of transparency or permeability attributed to the match, a hypothesis that will be found again in one or two level 2A subjects), their attempts at overcoming it go no further than a search for laws that merely displace the problem while themselves remaining in part contradictory. One of these laws is that, if one sees lines while the matches are in the air on the side where they haven't been drawn, then one will find them similarly on the blank side when they are turned over on the tables, as if the lines were from then on present on both sides (Pol at times, Dal, and so on), even though such a law contradicts the child's own initial action. Another frequently recurring law is that the lines appear on the wrong side up in the air, but that they won't be there when the matches are turned over on the table (Pol at first, Vin before his transparency interpretation, and Dal); but the contradiction in this case is only being displaced. Pol, when shown double rotations always producing a blank side, ends up by accepting that the lines can vanish but "come back afterwards," which is simply a tautological displacement of the problem. Taken as a whole, these subjects admit their noncomprehension.

What is interesting, however, in these stage 1 reactions, is that although the presence of the lines on one side of the matches only is due directly to the action of the child himself, it never occurs to him for a moment to seek the solution of the conflict in the direction of other possible actions, in other words, in the manipulations of the experimenter; he rather concentrates all his efforts on the object itself, as though an analysis of its properties will enable him to liberate those properties from their unintelligibility.

The reason for this exclusive concentration on the object is, presumably, that the double rotations, and above all the reversals of reversals they produce, are part of the subject's own geometry, whereas the two sides of a flat match are spatial properties of the object. And it is undoubtedly easier to begin with notions derived from the latter by empirical abstraction than to construct new ones by means of reflective abstraction, since the first involve only static characteristics, whereas the second express transformations.

§2. Level 2

First some examples:

Reg (7–1). Double rotation: "*The lines* [astonishment]. — And again? — *The lines.* — Why is that? — *Because if it's like the first time, now it's the same.*" And so on. Matches on table, lines showing: "What if we turn them over? — *They'll be there. No, I don't know.* — But will there be lines or not? — *No. Before you had them in your hand, and it's possible there could be lines in your hand, but then not when they're put down.* — Is it possible they could be there all the same? — *Yes, because there were before and it's possible there may be again.* — Can they move round to the other side on their own? — *No.* — Look. — *There, I only drew the lines on one side!* — So it's magic then? — *I don't think so. If it was magic, when you put them down, then there'd still be lines, because you didn't touch them* [= didn't modify them before putting

them down]. — So the lines move round to the other side? — *No.* —
Then perhaps it's something I'm doing? — *Yes it might be.* [She picks up
the matches and turns them over.] *No lines!* — So? — *You twisted them
like that to show me* [rotation, but not double]." Reg attempts the trick
but fails.

Jea (7–3) thinks at first that a second set of matches has been substituted.
The double rotation is repeated with the experimenter standing to prove
the impossibility of this, then the matches are placed lines up on the
table: "Will we see lines if we turn them over? — *Yes, there were lines
on both sides.* — Look. —*No, there weren't.* — Why's that? — *Because
we didn't put them* [= draw them on both sides]. — So? — *I don't
know.*" Jea takes the matches and rotates them in the air (single rotation
only): "*They aren't there on both sides.* — [Experimenter shows double
rotation again.] — Is it the matches doing it, or me on purpose? —
*You're doing it on purpose because they can't come round on their own,
the lines.* — [Double rotation in slow motion.] — *You turned them
around!* [He tries himself.] *I can't do it.* — What happens when I turn
them like that? — *There are lines on both sides.* — And when you do it?
— *Nothing.* — So? — *Don't know.*"

Syl (6–8) after being shown double rotation, is "*not very sure,*" when the
matches are laid on the table, whether she will find a blank side underneath because "*before* [= in the air] *they were on both sides.*" When the
idea of a trick has been suggested to her, Syl tries to perform it, then
supposes that "*you can make as if you're turning them then not turn
them.*" Then she succeeds in copying the slow motion double rotation.

Phi (8–0). Same reaction when matches replaced on table: "*I don't know.
I don't think there'll be any lines. Yes there are. I don't know.* — Why is
that? — *Because I only drew them on one side and not on both.* — And
why (in the air) did you see them on both? — *I don't know. Perhaps I
pressed too hard and the lines came through on the other* side [cf. Vin in
§1 and his transparency theory]. — Look— [He checks that there are no
lines visible on the blank side] *I understand: you pretend as if you're
turning them over, but you don't.*" Eventually, and with help, he succeeds in grasping the principle after further demonstrations.

Cia (8–1) repeats both Phi's hypotheses. "*I drew very hard and it's come
out the other side,*" then the turning of the matches said to be only apparent. Also grasps principle with help in the end.

Pau (8–1) doesn't understand "*how you can make them go away then
come back.* — You can look (matches laid on table). — *They aren't
there! I don't understand it at all. . . . Because they're on the table and
there's only one side with them not the other; and why when they're in*

your hand were they on both sides? — Well, which would you expect ordinarily, lines on one side only or on both? — *Perhaps on the table there's just the one side with them and in your hand both sides.* — Try yourself (he can only manage a single rotation). — *You have to turn you hand like this. When it moves quickly no one can see."* After further demonstrations he finally achieves a double rotation.

It should be noted that at the beginning of each of these interrogations the question was asked: "Every time we turn the matches over what will we see?" This was to make sure that all the subjects possessed an immediate intuition of the law of double reversal: "One time we'll see the lines and one time there won't be any," Jea answered for example. The same question when put to stage 1 subjects, on the other hand, did not elicit—or not at first—this intuition of necessary alternation (see Vin's first answer in §1). This make it all the more curious that out of a dozen seven- or eight-year-old subjects there were only three (quoted in the next section) who attributed the reappearance of the lines right away to the experimenter's manipulations, a reaction that ought to be typical of level 2B. At level 2A, on the other hand, the subjects (unless they begin by making an accusation of cheating, like Jea) start by reasoning about the object, as in stage 1, either imagining that by pressing too hard when drawing the lines they have made them visible on the other side (Phi and Cia), or else accepting, without understanding it, that two new lines have come into being and will therefore be visible on what was the blank side whether the matches are on the table or in the air. Once they have been made to check, on the table, that there really are lines on one side only, they return to the stage 1 hypothesis: "it's possible that in your hand there are lines (on both sides) but when they're put down (on the table) they aren't there any more" (Reg and others). It is at this point, but only at this point, that in his efforts to remove this so far merely displaced contradiction, the idea comes to the subject (and even then only after a leading question in some cases) that, if the lines on the "wrong" side appear only "in the hand," then that hand may well have something to do with it: the matches were turned "very quickly" (Pau), or the experimenter only pretended to turn them (Syl), or, finally, they were turned twice. Although the principle of the solution has thus been reached, it sitll remains to define the necessary physical movements more precisely, and at this level failure on this score is the usual result, and even subjects who succeed do so only with considerable help.

§3. Level 2, Stage 2, and Conclusion

Level 2B is reached by almost all the nine- to ten-year-olds and by three advanced subjects of seven and a half to eight: it is characterized by a rapid comprehension of the double rotation present in the experimenter's manipulations.

Max (7–5) is ahead of his age group in reaching the correct factual solution, undoubtedly because, even during the early double rotations, he successfully tries to peer round and see the other side of the matches during the manipulations. He concludes that if the lines always appear on the side presented *"it is because you turn so quickly."* He tries right away to copy what he has seen: "[A single rotation.] *No.* [He does two twists with his hand alone.] *Yes, that's all it is: you turn them quickly . . . you turned them round twice."* Although he has grasped the principle, however, he still can't reproduce the double rotation using fingers as well as hand. He puts in an extra rotation and ends up with the blank side showing.

Mar (8–2): *"You turned them around. Perhaps I can't see because you do it so quick. —* How many times do I turn them? *— Two."* Unlike Max he succeeds in doing the trick himself after several attempts.

Mic (8–10). The same reactions, but he has difficulty combining the two movements of hand and fingers.

Ifu (9–5) thinks at first that the experimenter is merely pretending to turn the matches without actually doing so. Then he accepts that this is not the case and attempts the manipulations himself: *"If you could make your hand go all the way round* [thus making a double rotation with the hand alone],"* then he turns the matches over once, then twice, but each time using the hand movement only. "But what if you made the matches turn over in your hand too? *— You need to make two turns . . . a turn all the way around and back."* He eventually succeeds: *"If your hand changes its position* (logitudinal rotation), *then the matches will too. So you only need to make a turn half way round."*

Cib (9–2) talks from the very outset about there being two turns involved, but in an attempt to combine the two movements observed in the experimenter's manipulation, she begins by turning the matches with her fingers, lowering her hand and turning it front to back at the same time, thus producing a total of three rotations.

Ter (10–7): *"If you have very quick hands then you can turn them very fast." —* What do you mean? *—* [She demonstrates a double rotation] *That's the only answer. —* Can you do the same thing so that one doesn't see the lines? *— The same system for with the lines, and you turn. —* And to make it look as though a line is going from one match to the other? *— You just show one match with its line and the other without* [the matches side by side], *then you do the turning and on the other side* *you see the lefthand one with the line if the line was on the righthand one before.* She tries, but turns them as well as rolling them, which cancels the effect. Then she turns her hand back to front, etc., but finally rotates the matches without turning her hand, even though she can't explain exactly what she did.

Rho (10–7): *"It's a trick. The lines can't move* [tries himself: he moves his hand alone.] *I can't do it, you do something with your fingers."* Then he turns either his hand or the matches. *"So? — You have to turn your hand and the matches as well, otherwise the lines come one time and the blank side the next."* When he tries to make the line seem to move from match to match, at first he turns one match only, then: *"Oh! Yes, that's it. You turn them both. —* And before? *— You had to turn the hand and the matches. —* And now? *— Only the matches. Before the lines were on the same side, but now one's on one side and the other on the other."*

The progress achieved in stage 3 consists in the fact that the subject understands not just the necessity for a double reversal, something already acquired at level 2B, but also grasps immediately that the two reversals are effected by the experimenter in different ways: one along the longitudinal axis by raising or lowering the hand, the other along the transverse axis by rotation of the matches.

Joh (12–11): *"The lines! As you pulled your hand up you moved your fingers. —* You saw them move? *— No, I guessed. You turned the matches over at the same time as you showed me* [= as you raised your hand]. *—* Do you want to try? *—* [He immediately tries to turn the matches at the same time as raising or lowering his hand.] *—* How many movements are you making? *— Two: turning my wrist and rolling with my fingers. —* Why the two? *— If you don't turn your wrist they see the other side. So you have to turn your wrist so that they see the same place each time."* When asked how to switch the lines: *"No, you can't, because if you turn the matches* [while also reversing the hand], *you always see the same thing. Oh! Yes you can* [rotation of matches alone]."

Tof (12–3) begins by making the hand movement alone: *"Ah! A twist! You have to pull your hand up and turn it over too. —* Why? *— Otherwise you don't see the line. You have to do it quickly, and both at once, otherwise they'd see* [the trick]. *—* It's just one movement then? *— Pulling up your hand and turning it, that's two movements. —* Why not three? *— I pull up, I turn, I turn again, and that gives the wrong side.* [Switching the line from match to match.] *I'll just turn them once . . . you only make one movement."* He also achieves the same thing by simply turning his hand around.

At level 2B the apparent contradiction between the constant reappearance of the lines and the fact that they have been drawn only on one side of each match is overcome immediately by hypothesizing a double rotation. In other words, the subject is no longer seeking to extract from the object, by empirical abstraction, some property or other that will explain its mysterious behavior. Instead, he reasons from the outset in terms of transformations derived from coordinations of actions by reflective abstractions, which leads immediately to an understanding of the double reversal. The interest of these reactions thus lies in the fact that this understanding occurs first in an abstract form. In other words, the subject correctly deduces that it requires two rotations to make the lines reappear on the visible side of the match before being able to say exactly how those rotations are being achieved by the experimenter in practice. She is in fact executing two distinct movements, one longitudinal (a raising or lowering of the hand), the other transversal (rotation of the matches), each of which changes the side of the match that is visible, and thus equivalent to two rotations, but achieved in different ways. The tendency of the subject at this point is to turn either the hand or the matches twice. Hence their initial failures (three rotations, and so on) which are then gradually understood, so that they finally achieve a correctly analyzed success. The characteristic of stage 3, then, is to reach this successful stage right away.

So what do these facts teach us? Between stage 1 and stage 3 we are presented first of all with a particular subclass of those contradictions that occur between fact and anticipation, since the prediction here is based not upon some kind of observation but upon the results of one or more actions on the part of the subject. This subclass possesses a certain interest, since it presents us in its simplest form with one of the situations described in the introduction to this book, that in which the contradiction stems from the fact that one and the same action can seem to produce different results: the child himself has drawn lines on one side of the matches only, yet the act of rotating those matches appears to lead to his sometimes seeing no lines on the other side and sometimes to his seeing them. Hence the conflict in the subjects: they no longer know what to predict, and often attempt to take refuge in a second contradiction, according to which the same action gives different results on the table or in the air (which is a less violent contradiction incidentally, the progress consisting in differentiating the same action into two distinct forms). Moreover, the fact contradicting the previous action is not contradictory except when it is interpreted as emanating from the object, and ceases to be so once it is understood as being dependent upon a coordination between schemas of actions. Here again, then, we come up against one of the usual characteristics of contradiction, which is that it results from an incomplete compensation (insofar as the permanence of the lines appears to the subject to be achieved by a single rotation), while it is removed by the complete compensation represented here by the law of double reversal.

However, to reach this very simple solution a complex development has been shown to be necessary, and the interest of that development lies in the relations between the actions carried out on the object and that object's supposed or real properties. The subjects' initial reactions are all based, in fact, on the deep-rooted idea that the object itself has been modified, and the subject's attitudes have to be totally reversed in order for him to succeed in grasping that the experimenter's actions consist in nothing more than rotating the matches twice, not the once that perception at first seems to indicate, so that he is quite simply seeing the same side of them again and again.

In this respect, the development encountered here, despite clear differences, does present an analogy to what one observes in the domain of conservations. There, the subject's action is conceived of at first as materially modifying the object itself: by making it longer one increases its quantity, and so on, without the subtractive effects of that action (diminishing the object's width, and so on) being taken into consideration. Only after this stage is the action understood as a simple displacement, which by adding part of the object in one direction must by that very fact remove it elsewhere, thus leading to the principle of conservation of the totality (see chapter 10). Similarly, in the present experiment, the subjects on our pre-operatory level imagine that the actions imposed on the object when it is turned over (in the air, if not on the table) actually transform it in a material way, thus leading to an elimination of the blank side without lines. It is not until the operatory stage that the action begins to be reduced to a mere displacement that, in this particular case, modifies the object's positions alone, thus leading to an immediate solution on level 2B, which is to say the concept of a double rotation. At this level, then, the subtractive or negative aspect of the transformations (blank side) is given as much attention as their positive aspect (side with lines on.)

The great difference between these two situations, however, is that in the area explored by our usual conservation test, the subtractive aspect of the action is at first ignored, whereas in the case of the matches it is precisely with maintaining the subtractive aspect that the subjects are most concerned, since the existence of a blank side is a result of their own previous and intentional actions. In this case, therefore, we have merely an initial lack of coordination between the positive and negative characteristics of the actions. But this makes it all the more instructive to observe that, in both cases, the coordination of the two aspects is blocked as long as the action is conceived of as materially modifying the object, whereas, again in both situations, once the action has been reduced to displacements, this composition of the two aspects, now seen as inseparable from changes of position, is assured.

Four

Contradictions Experienced with Springs

with A. Munari and I. Papandropoulou

The problem set for the subject in this case involves the relations between the variable length of a spring and the invariable length of the wire of which it is composed. There may well be an apparent contradiction here for the subject, and in that case it will be interesting to see how it is resolved. More particularly, when a method of measuring the two lengths is introduced, as, for example, by means of a column of beads introduced inside a plastic tube spirally cut to form a spring, or by counting the number of windings or "rings" with the spring in different stages of extension, one may find further contradictons arising, according to whether the subject attributes one or other of the observable properties to the variable length S of the spring as a whole or to the constant length W of the wire or plastic strip of which the spring is made.

In fact, then, the problem we are addressing here is that of the coherence or incoherence of the causal model that a subject constructs for himself in order to explain a phenomenon, and thus of the contradictory or noncontradictory character of the properties attributed to objects. But since it is clear that these properties are interpreted, and thus always consist (except on the plane of action alone) of conceptualized observable facts, and since it is equally clear that the relations between these properties entail some degree of inference or significant implication (pulling the spring implies lengthening it, and so on), the problem of the contradictions or noncontradictions within a causal model is analogous to that of the coherence of a logical system (cf. the additivity disscussed in chapter 2). The difference is that the observable facts, although always interpreted, correspond in the causal system to properties belonging to the object itself, whereas in the logical system they are introduced by the subject (as order, classes, correspondences, and so on), who does of course take into account the properties of the objects, but also adds frameworks that do not exist in those objects themselves. It follows that, in the case of causal attributions, what the subject attributes to the object is no more than an approximation relative to the not entirely known characteristics of the object, whereas in the case of logico-mathematical structuration, what is added to the object (even though the subject himself cannot necessarily distinguish between attribution and adjunction) is transparent for the subject, since those adjunctions come from him and include their own intrinsically necessary characteristics. Only (since in causality the operations or actions attributed to the objects derive from those of the subject, with the addition of those indispensable accommodations aimed at reaching the object in itself), it is still the case, in a causal model, that the coherence and the contradictions must be comparable to what is encountered in the construction of a logico-mathematical system (such as those in chapters 1 and 2), and it is this comparison that we shall attempt to draw in this chapter.

§1. Technique

One begins by showing the subject a steel spring six centimeters long (when unstretched) and asking whether stretching it will increase the length of the steel wire itself. In other words, the child is led to make a distinction between the overall length of the spring (S) and the length (W) of the wire as such: "Does the wire become longer? Is there more steel wire?" and so on. It may help to make comparisons with a longer (twelve centimeter) spring that stretches proportionately less than the small one.

A second spring is made up of an orange plastic tube (fifteen centimeters in length) spirally cut into five windings and twenty millimeters in diameter. The same question is asked regarding the length and quantity of the tube. One also asks whether the number of winding (rings) will increase or not when the tube is stretched. One also adds that the tube can be filled with fifty contiguous beads, and the question then is whether lengthening the spring will enable one to put more beads inside it (or fewer).

Similarly, one shows the subject a steel wire spring mounted vertically on a plinth with beads strung on the wire of the spring: will one be able to put on more beads if one stretches the spring? For comparison, a similar spring without beads is fixed beside the first but (like its companion) situated around a vertical rod. Beads can then be slipped onto this rod, inside the second spring, and since in this case their number will vary with the length of the spring, this will help the subject to distinguish between the two lengths S and W in the case of the springs themselves. Finally one has a spring, thirty centimeters in diameter, made of a length of green hosepipe inside which there is a wire of the same length that keeps the hosepipe coiled. The questions are: "If I pull the spring, will we have to put more wire inside, or is there enough already?" and "Will the pipe and the wire be the same length if we pull?"

§2. Stage 1

For four- to five-year-old subjects on level 1A there is no opposition between the overall length of the spring S and the length of the wire W (or hosepipe, or plastic strip, and so on), because both are generally assumed to lengthen correlatively. The arguments they use, on the other hand, present a number of contradictions of which they themselves are unaware, lacking as they do inferential coordinations between analogous or neighboring elements, or else because they have forgotten their previous statements Here are some examples:

Vui (–7). Comparison of two wire springs: "Which has most wire in it?
— *That one*. — Why? — *It's bigger* [when not stretched]. — And now?

— (The other one is stretched.) — *That one* [the second]. — Why? — *Because it's littler.''* The orange tube gets longer if it's pulled (*''there's more tube now''*) and it has to have more beads put in it, whereas another spring already strung with beads won't take any more when it's stretched *''because it's too little, the wire. —* And why did we have to put more in the orange one and not here? — *Because there are too many beads* [already strung] *and you can't put any* [more] *on.''*

Luc (4–10), when shown the orange spring expects the number of windings (rings) to increase when it is stretched: "Look? — *No.* — And if I stretch it more? — *There'll be lots.* — Look. — *Five, the same as before.* — Why's that? — *Don't know.''* But he says you'll be able to put a lot more beads in *''because it's bigger now.''*

Mar (5–3): *''There'll be more* [length of wire W] *because it gets longer. —* And more rings? — *No, because it's always the same rings that come away from each other. —* And the wire? — *More wire.* — Where does it come from then? — *The rings are pulled apart, and then it goes* [stretches]. — (Orange plastic spring) Count the rings — *Five.* — And if you pull? — *There'll be more.* — [He pulls.] — Now count. — *Five.* — Is there a way of making more than five? — *No.* — What if I fill the tube with these fifty beads, is there a way of making room for some more? — *Yes, if you pull ever so hard.* — How is that? — *Because it gets flat* [= rectilinear.] — And will there be more rings? — *Yes ... I don't know.* — (Spring with wire inside) What if we pull? — *It gets straight but there isn't any more wire ... there isn't any more because the rings come apart.''*

At level 1B, from six to seven years, however, the subjects are more consistent in their statements and accept the constancy of length W; but, being unable to differentiate sufficiently between the overall length S and that of the wire W, they tend to draw contradictory inferences.

Bue (5–8): "Will there always be the same amount of wire, or less or more? — *Always the same amount.* — How is that? — *When it's closed* [unstretched] *then there's not much, but when it's open there's more.* — (Orange tube) How many rings are there? — *Five.* — And if I pull? — *More will come if you pull. And when you don't touch it there's five.* — [Tube is stretched.] — *Five again, because there aren't very many. When you pull there's still five.* — I'm putting fifty beads inside. If I pull can I put in more? Or no more? — *No more.* — Why not? — *Yes, more. Because it'll be bigger.''*

Cri (6–0): "What happens when we pull? — *It makes the rings of the spring come apart.* — Does that mean there's more wire? — *Oh no! But when you pull, it comes apart from itself.* — I can put fifty beads in this orange spring when it's like this. If I stretch it can I put in more? Or not? — *Yes lots more, you can put in one hundred beads if the rings come very apart.* — And does the number of rings stay the same or not? — *Yes, even when you stretch it. If you pulled very hard, then it would be all straight.* — When can you put in the smallest number of beads? — *When it's tightest together.*"

Bar (6–1). Orange tube: "How many rings? — *Five.* — And if I pull it? — *There'll be five, because you stretch it, so ... yes there'll be more because you stretch it* [tube is stretched]. *Five, but there are spaces.* — It isn't odd that there are still five? — *No, it isn't odd.* — Is there still the same amount of tube? — *Yes, still the same amount, and there are still five* [rings] *too* [in other words, there is a coordination between the number of windings and the length of the plastic strip]. — We can put in fifty beads. Now what if we pull? — *Fifty.* — And if we pull very hard? — *More.*" On the other hand, faced with the small metal spring with thirty windings, Bar thinks the number of rings will increase with stretching, while still maintaining that the five rings of the orange tube will remain the same.

Sté (6–5) also thinks that "*there's the same amount of wire,*" but "*it will be open* [there will be spaces visible]. — Will there be more rings? — *No.* But it will get longer? — *Yes.* — So why won't there be more rings? — *Because it will be pulled.*" — Orange tube — "*When it's tight to-gether the beads will spill out because there's not so much room. If you can put in fifty beads like that* [unstretched] *then you can put in sixty or seventy like that* [stretched]. — And when can you put in most? — *When it's like this* [almost straight]."

Pao (6–5) thinks first of all that the wire doesn't get longer when the spring is stretched, but then accepts that the number of rings increases, and concludes that the wire must therefore get longer. With the orange tube, on the other hand, he sees both as remaining constant. "And if you stretch the orange one, will we have to put in more beads to fill it or not? — *The same.* — Not more? — [He counts the windings with the tube stretched.] — *No. You could put some more in, but only when the tube is pulled out straight.* — Because there's more tube then? — *No.* — Even if it's quite straight? — *No.* — So why can you put in more beads? — [Silence.]"

Col (6–9). Orange tube: he says we'll have to put in more beads when it's stretched "*because it gets bigger,*" but in the case of the beads threaded onto the wire spring: "*No, you wouldn't need any more.* — Why more in the big tube and not here? — [Silence.]"

The contradictions displayed by level 1A are of limited interest because they derive from a defect in the psychological functioning of the subjects' thought processes (continual disequilibriums) rather than from the in-temporal structure of their momentary states of equilbrium. In practice, the subjects in this substage appear to forget or ignore what they have just said, both when dealing with one and the same object and also when moving from one kind of spring or one situation to another. Vui, for example, when comparing a large diameter spring to a smaller diameter one, says that the first contains more wire because it is "bigger," but that the second has more wire when it is stretched "because it's littler." Luc thinks that the number of windings increases with stretching, then, having observed that this is not the case, he nevertheless predicts that one will be able to put in more beads "because it's bigger." Mar uses the notion of the rings "coming apart" at one point as justification for the absence of an increase in wire length (at the end), at another to explain the fact that the wire does become longer.

Among subjects from level 1B, on the other· hand, the contradictions become more systematic or structural: the wire doesn't change, despite the stretching of the spring, but you can but more beads on it, as though it were in fact longer. For example, Bue thinks that the wire doesn't get longer but that the number of windings, as well as the number of beads you can put in, increases. Cri is categorical: there isn't any increase in wire length, "Oh no! But when you pull it it comes apart from itself," which is moreover a good justification for the supposed invariance, and the number of windings also remains the same, yet one can put in one hundred beads instead of fifty if you stretch the spring. Pao alone begins by resiting the notion that one will be able to put in more beads; but then he adds, unprompted, that "you could put some more in, but only when the tube is pulled out straight." It is true that such increases are no longer predicted when it is a question of the beads threaded onto the spring (as opposed to those dropped into the tube), be-cause from the perceptual point of view the threaded beads, being visible, suggest the idea of an already completed whole, but the contradiction re-mains glaring in the case of the beads in the tube, and without there being any intervening misunderstanding as to the increased length of the column they form when the spring is stretched.

It is nonetheless clear that such contradictions do not consist in explicitly formulating the simultaneous truth of a statement p and its negation non-p, as if the subject were saying at the same time "the wire (W) is getting longer" and "it is not getting longer." On the contrary, the contradiction is mediate only, and consists, for example, in maintaining that the wire or the tube does not get longer while also accepting some other statement (increase in the number of beads inserted) that in fact implies an increase in the length of that tube without the subject being aware of that implication. Similarly, in chapter 1, a child at this level did not say that an element (disk)—say D—is at the same time equal to G and not equal to G: he said that D is simultaneously equal to G and to A, even though $A < G$, without feeling obliged by the rules of transitivity—which he has not yet acquired—to conclude that D must in that case be displaying two incompatible characteristics. In a word, the contradictions in this present chapter derive from the interplay of the subject's inferences, and what the child is saying in practice, is that if the wire (or plastic strip) W does not increase in length, the reason is that the windings of the spring are moving apart, but that this space that appears between the "rings" produces more room (the compensating decrease in the spring's circumference with increasing length not having been grasped) so that a longer column of beads can be inserted. In other terms, the source of these contradictions is to be sought in a relative inability, still persisting, to differentiate between the overal length S of the spring and the local or elementary length W of the wire or plastic spiral. The result is that the apparent conservation of the length W is not yet an authentic conservation—something that goes without saying at this preoperatory level—and that it still remains in the state of a qualitative identity. What the child understands is that he has to distinguish between two actions; stretching the spring S as a whole, or acting upon the wire or plastic strip when unwound and separated from this overall stretching effect. What the subject affirms, therefore, is that by pulling the spring one is not acting upon the wire; but in practice his reactions show that these two actions, though distinguished in principle in the subject's intention, remain relatively undifferentiated when one probes more deeply into his evaluations of the two lengths involved, in other words when one moves from the qualitative (the wire doesn't change) to the quantitative (implicit reference to the interstices: more "room").

§3. Substage 2A

At the 2A level the subjects present analogous contradictions but are already becoming conscious of them and succeed to some extent in overcoming them.

Gil (7–6): "How many rings are there? — *Five.* — And what if I pull? — *There'll be a lot more* — [Tube is stretched]. — What's happened? — *We haven't pulled out any more.* — Can we pull so that there'll be less? — *Yes, you have to pull more* [= total extension would eliminate windings altogether]. — And if there are fifty beads in the tube, when I pull can we put in more? — *A lot more.* — Why — [Silence.] — And will there be more rings? — [Silence.]'' Wire spring: "If I pull, will there be more wire? — *No.* — Why not? — *You'd need a lot* [= more than there actually is]. — And if I squash it up? — *There's less.* — So? — *Perhaps it's always the same.* — Why would that be? — *I don't know. Because there are the little holes* [interstices between windings] *that move apart.* — And if I fill the tube with beads and pull, will we need more or less? — *Less.* — Why? — [Silence.] — Explain. — *Don't know.*''

Pil (7–6). Orange tube: "How many rings? — *Five.* — And if I pull? — *Let's try and see.* — Guess — *Less, no the same.* — Why less? — *When you pull it'll become extra long and there almost won't be any rings at all.* — Shall we try? — *Five.* — Pull harder. — *Still five, but if I pulled even harder there'd be less.* — Now, fifty beads, that fills it up. What if we pull? — *It'll be longer, so we'll have to put in more.*'' Spring with threaded beads: "If we pull, will there be room for more? — *No, I don't think so, perhaps, but I don't know.* — With the beads in the tube you said we could put in more, didn't you? — *I think it would still take the same . . . you'd need to try to your hands* [on the tube] *and if its gets longer you'd need more.* [She stretches the tube and looks.] *Yes, it doesn't get bigger.* — So you don't need more beads? — *No.*''

Gra (7–6). Orange tube: "When I pull is there more of the tube? — *No, still the same amount.*'' But when asked about the beads: "*it will need a lot more in it when it's pulled.*'' With the beads threaded on the wire spring, however, you can't add any more "*because they'll still be all squeezed together.* — But the wire gets longer? — *Yes, because it's stretchy* [the spring as a whole poorly differentiated from the length W].''

Rob (8–0): Same reactions, but made more explicit. The wire remains the same length when one pulls the spring: "*You'd think there was more, but there's the same, it's just pulled apart.* — How would you explain it to a little boy who thinks it gets longer? — *I'd tell him it only look longer because it's pulled apart.*'' Orange tube, same response: the number of windings will remain constant. "*There are five, you can't make any more by pulling it.*'' With the fifty beads, on the other hand, "*there'll be more room. You pull and that pulls apart the room inside the tube. When you pull the tube that makes room inside because it's pulled apart.* — But is there more tube? — *No, the same, because there are five rings and if you pull there are still five.* — And can you put in more beads with the same length of tube? — *Yes. Because you've pulled like that you can put in more beads because you widen it* [make the interstices wider] *and that makes a bit more room.*'' With the beads threaded on the wire spring, however, you won't be able to put on more: "*No, there's no room, because here it's already full* [or to be more precise, the contradiction is evident from the outset]. *So that means with the tube too, you can't, because that's full, so you can't put in any more.''* In other words, the tube isn't "getting wider" any more.

Mor (8–5) thinks that pulling the spring lengthens the wire. *"Of course, because the wire gets bigger. — And if we weighed it? — It would still weigh the same.''* Orange tube: "Count the rings. — *Five.* — And if we pull? *The same. Because if you pull it won't change.''* Tube filled with beads: *"You'll have to put in more because if you pull there'll be more room. It gets bigger.* — And will there be more rings then or not? — *Yes, because it gets bigger.* [Pulls.] *that's funny!''* He then abandons the idea that the tube gets bigger and that it will take more beads.

Rey (8–6) thinks that the wire gets longer and that the number of rings will increase. After demonstration: *"There's five rings, so there'll always be five.* — Why's that? — *Because* [to achieve a greater number] *you'd have to have more stuff* [more W].'' Orange tube with beads in: *"You'd need another ten.* — Why? — *Because of pulling it.* — And how many rings? — *Well, I think what I said wasn't right and it stays the same.''*

Sel (8–7): there's *"not more''* wire when you pull the spring *"because it's harder''* which is to say nonelastic, and the windings remain the same in number *"because you can't make any more than there are.''* But you can add ten beads to the fifty in the unextended tube. "What if we measured? — *Sometimes it's longer when you pull it, because pulling on it makes it stretch.''* Hesitation over the beads threaded on the spring: *"It will be bigger''* so you can add more; but when he tries: *"No, there's not enough room, it's the same as before.* — And with the tube, could you put in more beads? — *That's the same.''*

Bri (8–8): when you pull the spring there will be more wire *"because it will be longer.* — And with this one (green pipe)? — *There's more when you pull, it's like the other spring.''* Orange tube: the number of rings remains the same but *"it will need more beads* [to fill it], *because when the tube stretches it makes some room.''* On the other hand, when he is helped to make a spring of his own with wire wrapped around a pencil, he concludes that the length of wire *"is always the same.* — And all the other springs? — *There's the same in those too all the time.* — And the big tube? — *It stretches, yes, no, no I don't think so.* — And the beads on the wire? — *I don't think you can put more beads on, because there isn't any more wire when you pull.''*

Pod (9–0): the wire increases in length. "Where does the extra wire come from? — *From the spring.''* The number of windings, however, remains constant. You will be able to put more beads in the orange tube, and if an ant crawled round and round it after it was stretched *"it would have to crawl farther because it's longer.''* After seeing the beads threaded on the wire spring, however, he says one can't put on any more, either on the wire or inside the orange tube.

The striking characteristic of these answers is their apparent regression relative to those given at level 1B: whereas 1B subjects asserted the constancy of the lengths W of the wire, while in fact denying it over the question of the beads inside the tube, these 2A subjects are much less categorical and much more hesitant. In general, by the end of the questions they arrive at correct answers and overcome the contradictions, but at the outset they are very much torn between two contradictory tendencies. On the one hand there is the solidarity they cannot bring themselves to reject between the lengthening S of the spring and the length W of the wire, and so on. This relative nondifferentiation is not new, since it is the explanation behind the contradictions characteristic of level 1B (increase in column of beads while asserting the constanty of W). But the 1B subjects were not conscious of the contradiction and were prepared to make a verbal distinction between the conservation of the wire W, which was before all else a qualitative identity to them, and the lengthening of the spring. With the quest for quantification, which is the main characteristic of stage 2 generally, it at first becomes more difficult to distinguish the lengthening of the spring S and the length of the wire W itself, because, as Sel says, "pulling on it makes it stretch," or Bri, "when the tube stretches it makes some room," or Pod, when he claims that the extra wire comes "from the spring." The second tendency, however, due to a gradual sharpening of this quantifying analysis, consists, when talking about the length W of the wire, in trying to view it henceforward as an authentic, which is to say a quantitative, conservation, one that can no longer be reduced to the verbal affirmation "the same amount of wire," but also includes the decisive check that one can't thread any more beads on it because "there's no more room." And it is indeed just such a clear differentiation that the majority of subjects have achieved by the end of the questioning: "I think what I said wasn't right and it stays the same" (Rey) or "I don't think you can put more beads on, because there isn't any more wire when you pull" (Bri).

So these subjects waver between two contradictory tendencies during the questioning, but they also make notable progress, and in two ways: they become gradually conscious of the contradictions, and they develop greater inferential power, enabling them to link a statement or an observation with its consequences: an increased length W must entail a greater number of beads, but a constant length will make it impossible to add any; a variable number of windings implies a lengthening of the wire, and a constant number the invariance of that length W (there won't be any more tube, Rob says, "because there are five rings and if you pull there are still five,"). Moreover, these two advances are intersupportive: it is clear that consciousness of the contradiction depends upon the operatory capacity to coordinate statements with one another, just as that capacity consists in a composition of statements and negations entailing an interplay of compensations that is the basis of noncontradiction.

§4. Level 2B and Conclusions

Subjects at level 2B find the solution right away and experience no contradictions.

Loz (7–11): "When we pull the spring will it get longer? — *Yes.* Is there more wire then? — *No, because it gets longer but it's still the same.*" Orange tube: "How many rings? — *Five.* — And if we pull? — *Still five.* — But the tube is longer when we pull? — *No, it doesn't get bigger.* — So how does it get longer? — [A zigzag gestrue.] *It does that.* — We can put fifty beads inside. If we pull, can we put in more? — *No, because the tube doesn't get bigger.*"

Pau (8–4): "*When it gets longer there isn't any more wire in it.* — (Orange tube.) How many rings? — *Five.* — And if we pull? — *Still five, because if you stretch it and there are more rings, that's a miracle.* — Isn't there any way of having more? — *Yes, if you keep turning it* [if the coil is twisted tighter] *there'll be more rings but littler ones.*" Beads inside tube: he says you can't put in more beads by pulling harder. "And if we used water? — *No.*"

Gua (9–4). Length W remains the same "*because when you pull it's still the same, you can't make any more of it.*" Beads inside: "*Still the same number.*"

Kam (10–2): "Is there more wire? — *No, because the wire, if it's twisted, you can't make it longer without having more of it.*" Beads inside tube: "*It will be the same thing, because you don't put on any more tube, so it's like the* [wire] *spring.*"

The great majority of level 2B subjects are between nine and ten years old. As for the older, stage 3 subjects, their answers are much the same, with the one difference—that they sometimes introduce, without prompting, the notion of a compensation between the vertical spacing of the windings and their reduction in diameter.

Cer (11–2): "*If you pull there's still the same length of wire.* — And the rings, if I pull? — *Still five.* [the tube is pulled] *Now the rings are smaller. You automatically diminish them.* — Could we put in more beads? — *Oh no. The same number.*"

Cho (11–11): *"The rings aren't so wide now. Yes, when one pulls the spring out one makes rings that are wider."* "Wide" means greater in diameter the first time but "further apart" and therefore actually narrower when used the second time.

This doesn't mean that the 2B subjects didn't take these compensations into account, since they no longer believed that the greater spaces between the windings increase the length W, but it is not until stage 3 that we find them being commented on explicitly.

So what conclusions are we to draw? The contradictions observed in this chapter obey the usual schema of an uncompleted reversibility; in other words, that of an incomplete compensation between affirmation and negation. If we start with the conservation of the length W of the wire or spiral tube during the stretching of the spring, this conservation is characterized by a class of observable facts X, which are those given priority by these 2B subjects: same number of windings, same space occupied along the wire or tube by beads, water, and rigid inner wire, lack of elasticity in the material itself, and so on. The complementary class non-X (change in the length W of the wire or material forming the spring) will be characterized, on the contrary, by the inverse of the first set of characteristics: increase or decrease in number of windings, of the space occupied by the beads, and so on. As for the lengthening of the spring S, that is characterized by a class of observable facts Y: increase in the distance between the ends of the spring, increasing interstices between the windings, and so on, plus all the properties of X, whereas the nonstretching of the spring, non-Y, entails the negation of that first set of characteristics, but the maintenance of the attributes of X. That being so, it is clear that the observed contradictions consist in the first place in not dividing the observable facts into complementary and disjunct classes X and non-X, but in viewing these two classes, illegitimately, as overlapping to some extent: the length W is thus said to be constant because nothing has been added to it, yet it can provide more room for the beads, and so on.

The main interest does not lie in that fact, however, although it provides a useful confirmation of the general characteristics of contradiction. The psychological problem here is to isolate the reasons for these particular incoherences, and it is easily seen that they derive from inferential difficulties, for, even if the predicates of the classes X and non-X all correspond to observable facts, the links between them are not the product of immediate classifications or definitions, but rather of mediate relations or inferential coordinations, and it is by no means just chance that these relations and coordinations are not mastered until levels 2B and 3. Until then, the subjects are constantly tripped up by a false inference: when the spring is stretched, the windings, though remaining constant in number, move further apart, thereby giving the impression of "more room" and leading them to think that it will be possible to insert more beads. Because he fails to grasp that this extra vertical space is compensated for by a decrease in each winding's diameter, the subject then postulates a lengthening, without seeing that it is contradictory to the invariability of the wire length W. Later, interreference between class Y and class non-X enables the subject to attribute these wider interstices to the stretching of the spring S and not to any modification in the length W of the wire or plastic strip.

In a word, the contradictions observed derive from false inferences and the lack of necessary inferences resulting from a relative lack of differentiation between the increases in length of the spring S and the wire W, and thus between classes Y and non-X. The process by which the contradiction is transcended thus becomes quite clear: it consists, through the possibility of new inferences brought about by advances in quantification, in a double interplay of differentiation and integration. On the one hand, the subject succeeds in differentiating—to some extent at level 2A and completely at level 2B—between what is due to the stretching of the spring and what to the invariable length of the wire, thus enabling him to construct the classes of observable facts X and non-X, as well as Y, in a valid way. On the other hand, this very advance enables him—for the two processes are intersupportive—to achieve a new integration in the form of conservations based upon compensations (length of the wire) and manifesting themselves in transformations (stretching of the spring producing modification in the form of the windings).

It is now possible to appreciate the kinship between this development and that described with respect to logico-mathematical contradictions in chapters 1 and 2. In both cases, the contradiction consists in incomplete compensations, and thus in an insufficient composition of affirmations and negations. In both situations, this initial inadequacy derives from the lack of inferences at the outset, while the transcendence of the contradictions is due to new signifying implications. Finally, in both cases the transcendence entails differentiations leading to a widening of the referential scope, and to an integration that makes itself known by the relativization of the subject's notions. These, then, are the general features of any process leading to a contradiction and then to the transcendence of it, but there remain notable differences, nevertheless, between the two situations, the logico-mathematical and the physical. In the former case, the subject begins with partly erroneous relations $D = A$, $D = G$, and $A < G$ that he then succeeds in correcting once he has succeeded in imagining another structure such as $A \leqslant$

$D \leq G$ or $A < D < G$ in order to resolve the problem. In the present (physical) case, on the other hand, the subject is presented with two observable lengths S and W that are at first improperly differentiated, and when he affirms that W is invariable while also accepting that stretching the spring makes it possible to put on more beads, the contradiction arises from the fact that he is attributing to W not only its rightful properties of conservation but also others borrowed from S. So even supposing a logico-mathematical (but here spatial) structuring comparable to that in chapters 1 and 2, transcending the contradiction here will require in addition an improved level of empirical abstraction from objects and their observable characteristics, which is to say an implicit or explicit use of the physical experience itself. The ensuing differentiation between notions thus possesses a more complex significance than in the purely logico-mathematical case, where the additivity of the imperceptible differences can be constructed by means of pure reflective abstraction.Put another way, the composition of affirmations and negations is no longer a matter of form only, but also of content. Moreover, this recourse to content also entails in its turn—particularly when it comes to differentiating them—a compensation between affirmations and negations since, as we saw just now, it involves both of them equally.

As for the reasons for the rather persistent lack of differentiation between S and W, they obviously revolve around the fact that the claimed invariability of W is not at first a true conservation. The latter presupposes, in effect, that any increase in one dimension entails a corresponding decrease somewhere else, while nonconservations depend on the absence of any such reference to the negative (see chapters 10 and 11). And in fact, the subjects who do not get beyond saying that W stays the same length but that one can put more beads on it are still not making any reference of this kind; it is not until stage 3 that the child will declare explicitly—despite its implicit acceptance as early as level 2B—that the rings are always smaller in diameter when stretched. With these results, then, we are already encountering the conflict between positive and negative characteristics, and the initial primacy of the former, which we shall meet so often in later experiments.

Five

Differing Attitudes toward
Nonconfirmation of a Prediction

with T. Vergopoulo (part 1) and C. Bonnet (part 2)

Part 1. Contradiction in the Paradoxical Behavior of a Wheel

When the subject anticipates an event in terms of a law that he considers to be general (for example that a wheel standing on its rim will always roll down an inclined plane), and is confronted with a rebuttal of his former experience (if the rim of the wheel has a concealed weight in it on the side facing the upward slope so that the wheel rolls upward slightly), can we speak of contradiciton in such a case, and will such a contradiction obey the same laws as in more usual cases? Certainly, if we remain on the plane of strict legality, this is in fact no more than a counter-proof, and the consequence to be drawn from it is that the supposed law is not in fact general, thus leading to a revised statement of it in order to make it adequate to the observed facts. In that case, it would be improper to term it a contradiction. On the other hand, it is clear that as soon as a search for causes is involved—and such a search always arises—the affirmations and negations inherent in the schemas and the explanatory model constructed by the subject will raise problems of contradiction.

The technique employed in this experiment, which was suggested by R. Carreras, is very simple. The apparatus consists of a sloping board and two apparently identical wheels, the first of which, *A*, rolls normally down the slope while the second, *B*, has a weight concealed at a certain point in its rim. If the wheel is positioned with the weight on the "down" side, then the wheel will roll downhill. If the weight is right at the bottom then the wheel will remain motionless. And if it is on the "up" side, then the wheel will roll a few centimeters uphill. The experimenter asks the subject to predict the behavior of the wheels, then explains the anomaly inherent in *B*. One can also use a third wheel, *C*, with a concave rim into which the child can press modeling clay in order to make it the same weight as *B* (which proves useful when the subject uses the weight of *B* as his sole explanation).

§Stage 1

We shall begin with some examples from level 1A.

Dec (4–8). Wheel *A:* "*It will roll. —* Why will it? *— Because you've got that board there. —* And if it's like this (board flat?) *— No, because when you take that away* [gesturing indicating slope] *it won't roll. —* Wheel *B* on board: "*It stays there. —* Why ? *— Because it's too far from there* [top of slope]. *—* Is it natural? *—* [Silence.], *—* What should it have done? *— Rolled. —* Why? *— Because it's a wheel. —* But instead? *— It's staying in the same place. —* Why's that ? *— Because. —* Is there a reason? *—* [Silence.] *—* And now? *— It's rolled the other way* [upwards]. *—* Why? *— Because it was put the other way round.* [Dec has noticed that the experimenter turned the wheel]. *—* (Both wheels displayed.)

What are they going to do? — *A will roll, B won't roll.* — Why's that? — *Because.* — Are they both exactly the same? — [After shaking them and banging them on the table.] *One makes the same noise, the other not the same noise.*" A difference in weight is suggested, and Dec accepts that it is the heavy one that won't roll. She is then given *C* with some clay, which she puts "anywhere" and makes no discovery, dropping the weight question apart from saying she wants the wheel to be "*light.*"

Lis (5–5). Wheel *A: "It will roll down.* If we let it go here (middle of slope)? — *It won't roll because it has to have that up there* [upper section of slope] *and then it rolls* [i.e., it must be put at the top of the slope]." We try, and *A* rolls down. Wheel *B: "It won't roll because the board isn't up high to here* [= because *B* isn't at the very top]." *B* is tried: "*It doesn't roll.* — Is that normal or peculiar? — *Peculiar.* — What's wrong then? — *When you turn it* [with weight downhill] *it rolls, and when you don't turn it it doesn't* — (More demonstrations.) Can we make it roll upwards? — *Yes.* — Is it peculiar that it does so many things? — *No, it's all right. When the ball's at the bottom it goes up and when it's at the top it goes down.*" Explanation: "*Because it doesn't roll very well . . . you need to turn it till it goes up again.*" Weight is suggested as a factor, but there is no reaction. With *C* she puts the clay all the way round it.

Far (5–9) supposes that the anomalies presented by *B* are due to the fact that it isn't round enough: "*It's oval and the other's round.* — Draw a circle round *B.* — *It's round.* — So it is round then? — *No, a bit oval.*" Weight is suggested: "*It is heavy.* — And does that make a difference? — *A bit: it rolls and it doesn't roll.*"

Now here are some examples from level 1B in which the subjects invoke weight as a factor without prompting:

Pig (5–6): "*That one doesn't roll! It hasn't gone down it's gone up!* — Are they the same? — *No, one's rounder than the other.* — [*B* not moving] *It's because it's very heavy.* — What else can it do? — *Go up, stay there, or roll* [down] *. . . because you always turn it the other way.*" He is given *C*, to which he adds clay randomly while comparing its weight to that of *B*, then: "*It can't go upwards because it isn't turned round.*" However, he succeeds quite by chance in making it remain motionless, then roll downward. He immediately turns it round and it rolls upward: "Have you understood now? — *There are wheels that go up, some that go down, and some that stay there.*" Tries again and fails: "Why won't it go up? — *Don't know.*" Asked to recapitulate: "*It's because B is more heavy, so it doesn't roll* [down]."

Mon (5–10) doesn't understand what's happening, except when *B* remains stationary: "*It stays like that on the spot, but I know. I know it's because it's heavy.* — And what do heavy wheels do? — *They roll down.*

— And why doesn't *B?* — *Because it's all heavy."* With *C* he tries to achieve the same weight, but observes that *"they're not the same, this doesn't go up."* The weight is shifted to one side and Mon makes it roll upward: "Why? — *Don't know.* — Is it because it's heavy? — *No."*

Mur (6–0). *B* rolls up or stays still: "Is that what you'd expect? — *Yes, because wheels when they're heavier don't go round.* — And if I put it here (center of board)? — *It will go up because it's in the middle.* — And here (at the top)? — *It will go down.* — Why? — *It will roll down because it's heavy.* — Can we tell which it will do? — *Yes, sometimes that way* [down] *sometimes that* [up]. — But why *B* and not *A?* — *Because it's too heavy, so it does what it wants.* — And *A?* — *It rolls because it's light.* — And *C?* — *When you put on the plasticine it's heavy so then it rolls down."*

Gal (6–2): *"It's because of what's inside.* — What? — *I don't know, but there's something. It weighs a lot.* — What does this thing do? *It makes it not roll.* — And when it does roll? — *The thing makes it roll."*

The following subjects were helped with the suggestion that they put the modeling clay on one side of *C* only.

Oli (6–7) thinks that *B "is hard"* and *"goes backward and stays on the spot,"* whereas *A "rolls because it isn't hard."* *"Inside B there's some iron. It makes it stay where it is."* After he has hesitated over *C* it is suggested he put the clay on one side only. After several failures he succeeds in making it roll uphill or remain stationary: "Where do you put the weight for it to stay where it is? — *At the bottom.* — And to go backwards? — *Near the top uphill* [correct]. — So why does it go uphill? — [Silence.] — And to make it go down? — *You can't because it's heavy."*

Isa (6–7): *"Before it rolled down, but now it won't* [when placed on board by experimenter]. *It's because I put it on right up at the top* [of board]. — Is that what you'd expect? — *It ought to roll down, but it doesn't move."* Then Isa discovers the difference in weight. "Is that important? — *Yes, that one* [b], *if it wanted to be light it could be light* [= roll down], *and that one* [A], *if it wanted to be heavy it could be heavy* [and roll uphill]. — And why does *A* do only one thing? — *Ah! B is hard inside.* — And does that do something? — *Yes, if you push it then it rolls down, but if you don't it won't."* With *C,* Isa observes that the weight makes no difference. The clay is put on one side and *C* made to remain stationary. Isa succeeds in reproducing this effect, but can't see that the weight is at the bottom: *"Yes, it's because I put it across* [on the side]." Similarly with the downward and upward motions: *"Yes, because there* [on the side] *it's much more full."*

Cri (6–6): "*It's heavier. There's something inside!* — What? — *Ball bearings!* — But does it roll? — *No.* — But don't ball bearings make things roll more easily? — *Then it's because it's heavier it doesn't roll* [down]." He makes no discovery with C. Putting the clay on one side is suggested and he does so: "*It's stays where it is because now it's a trick.* — What is the trick? — *There's more here, so it doesn't roll.* — What does it do? — *It goes down, it stays there, but it doesn't go up.* — Try." He succeeds in making it do all three, but can't explain. "What did you do? — [Silence]." and so on. "If you had to explain B to someone little who doesn't understand, what would you say? — *That it has a trick in it like* C. — And what have you understood? — *It's thicker here* [the clay]. *That's the trick.*"

Vin (6–5) has almost reached level 2A: "*It goes frontward and backward.* — Is that usual? — *Yes, because sometimes there are balls that bounce and others that don't . . . but there's something that makes one of them stay and the other roll.* [He experiments.] *It's too heavy.*" Given C, he manages to make it remain stationary: "*It's staying still, I think there's plasticine all around B.*" Clay on one side only is suggested, and C rolls uphill. "Why does it go uphill? — *You try it there where it's heavier. It rolls because you hold it where it's heavier.* — What should you do to make it roll downhill? — *Put the plasticine at the bottom.* — [He discovers his error.] — And to make it stay where you put it? — *The plasticine at the bottom* [*success*]. — And to make it go upwards? — [Demonstrates successfully.] *I held it where there isn't any plasticine* [meaning he'd put the weighted side on the uphill side] *so it went backwards.* — Is there a reason? — *You hold it where it's heaviest, you put it down and it goes downwards.* — So what have you understood about them both? — *B is heavier than A, it's B that has something inside. The lightest one hasn't got anything inside.*"

It is clear from these reactions that the fact of B remaining stationary or rollling uphill is not viewed by 1A subjects as in any way shocking: "No, it's all right," Lis says at five and a half, "when the ball's at the bottom it goes up and when it's at the top it goes down." Similarly, Dec thinks it stays motionless because it wasn't put at the top of the slope, and believes, like Lis, that one only need turn it around to make it go upwards, since one is thereby indicating to it the way it should go. Far alone assumes that there is something abnormal going on, and thinks it is because B isn't quite round, then is apparently satisfied by the suggestion that it is something to do with weight, since weight can make things "roll" and "not roll." None of the subjects brings up the question of weight unprompted, and although they sometimes seem to accept the idea when it is put to them, it is without conferring any stable meaning on it: Dec wants to make C "light", Bal to make it heavy like B, but only momentarily, while both Lis and Far ignore the whole idea of weight.

With the 1B subjects, on the othere hand, ther is clear disagreement between their anticipation and the unexpected facts constituted by B's immobility or ability to move uphill, and they are aware of this disagreement. This leads to two problems. The first, which is to establish what exactly the contradiction between a prediction and an observation consists of, will be dealt with after we have analyzed the reactions at later levels; the second, which is best examined here, at the 1B level, is to establish how the subject tries to overcome this contradiction by finding a model that will explain both the usual facts (those upon which his prediction is based) and the new data threatening the generality of the law derived from those facts. It is clear, in fact, that even at this elementary level the child is indeed seeking to fulfill this double condition, and it is on this point that the question becomes most interesting: will the subject manage, without encountering further contradictions, to reconcile the unexpected new data with the data he has already acquired and, above all, already interpreted?

The tendency common to all these subjects is that of seeking such a reconciliation in the direction of weight (with some quickly surmounted exceptions where the subject begins by invoking the positioning of the wheel on the board or a difference in circularity between A and B). In effect, from the age of five and a half, almost all the children turn to the notion of weight as a means of explaining why a ball or any circular object rolls downhill: they roll because they are heavy (Mon, Mur, and others), or else, more rarely, because they are light (Mur and Isa), presumably because they conceive of lightness as facilitating movement in objects. It is thus normal for the child, when trying to explain the immobility or uphill motion of B, to make use of the difference in weight between A and B when he discovers it. Isa goes no further than supposing that descent implies lightness and the other possibilities implied by heaviness, yet at the same time accepting that both A and B have the power to become heavy or light at will, which is of course tautological, if not contradictory. The others, unlike Isa, invoke B's heaviness as an explanation of its immobility, then generalize that explanation when it moves uphill, as though the greater weight preventing its descent (immobility) also, and for the same reason, causes the contrary (upward) motion. Now it is clear to us that this represents a series of contradictions; but the subject senses them in part only. Faced with the immobility of B, Mon exclaims with satisfaction: "but I know. I know it's because it's heavy," but immediately afterwards he adds that heavy things "roll downwards." then, suspecting a contradiction, he attempts to circumvent it by characterizing B as "all heavy." The other subjects likewise distinguish between "very heavy" (causing immobility) and "heavy" (causing descent). But it would be going much too far to interpret this as a principle of *extremum* or *optimum:* it is no more than a prerelational form of thought proceeding by discontinuous categories, similar to that observed in the early stages of seriation ("little" "middle" and "big"), whereas when he begins reasoning by relation, as will be the case at level 2A, the subject understands that, although the weight makes the wheel descend, an increase in weight will reinforce or accelerate that descent. It is certainly true that great weight can prevent motion, but only on condition that it is localized at the bottom of the wheel, and that is what these subjects fail to see when they link B's immobility with the total wheel-weight, whereas in reality that weight ought to help it descend. Moreover, when supposing that its weight explains B's immobility, the subject ignores the fact that it has also moved upwards, except to reason that, if a normal weight brings about descent, then too great a weight will bring about everything that is not descent, including upward motion.

The reactions to wheel C are very significant in this respect. The experimenter's suggestions in fact make the child understand that the weight, in order to have an effect, must be unequally distributed, whereupon, his confidence boosted by this hint, the subject usually succeeds, after trial and error, in obtaining the desired effects. But that doesn't mean he has understood what is happening, and he is still a long way from grasping that this localized weight does in fact always move downwards, even on those occasions when it makes the wheel itself move upwards. What the child discovers, in the most advanced cases, is the power possessed by the weight to direct the wheel in one or other direction; but he still thinks of it as a motive force, capable of moving in any direction, that one can make use of at will to make the wheel go down or up or remain stationary (just as, at this stage, a pebble at the bottom of a glass of water is conceived of as pushing the water upwards and thereby raising its level). Oli and Vin, in fact, eventually reach conclusions based entirely on the total weight of the wheel.

Taken as a whole, the contradictions inherent in the uses that 1B subjects make of the notion of weight derive in practice from its nonrelational character, but also, and equally, from the fact that the categories or subclasses the subject constructs as he encounters a need for them ("heavy," "very heavy," "all heavy," light," and so on) are arrived at *ad hoc,* without any systematic ordering of "all" and "some" relations. And in order for a system of classes to be noncontradictory, it is essential that the characteristics x and non-x of the complementary classes shall compensate each other exactly: $x \cup$ non-$x = 0$. It is this reversible composition of affirmations and negations that is still lacking at this level.

§2. Level 2A

Here are some examples, beginning with an intermediate case:

Lau (6–5). Wheel *B*: "*It's heavy* [manipulation]. *It has one side made specially so it rolls and one specially made so it doesn't.* — [Further manipulation.] — What is it doing? — *It rolled backward, it stays in the same place, it rolls forward.* — Why does it do all that? — *Because it's heavy.* — And heavy things do all that? — *Yes* [a sigh] *because . . . it has sides made to do two things.*" With *C* Lau first puts clay on one side then "*everywhere there are holes* [where it's concave]." Experiments: "*It still goes forward, it doesn't want to stay still: it's too light* [comparison]. *No, it's too heavy.* [Lau removes some clay, making weight asymetrical, then experiments some more.] *It has sides to roll and sides not to roll.* — Which one to roll down? — *The lightest one . . . when the heavier side is at the bottom it can't roll.*" Lau then succeeds in making it roll uphill: "*The heaviest side has to be at the top for it to go backwards.*" — And to stay still? — *A little bit to the left or right, there* [near the *bottom*]. — Do you understand it? — *When it's heavy it can stay still, or go backwards or forwards.*"

Kam (7–9): "*You push it and it doesn't go down.* — Why not? — *Because it's heavy.* — Because it's heavy? — *No. Usually a heavy wheel rolls down.*" Handed *C*, he puts clay on one side, but by chance only: "*It won't roll.* — Look (it rolls down). — *It was turned the other way round.* — Can you make it go up? (He does.) And down? (He turns the wheel round.) What changes when you turn it? — *It has more weight* [on one side]. *When you turn again it has less weight.* — Where should we put the heavier side? — *At the top.* [He succeeds in making it roll down]. — And to make it stay still? — *At the bottom.* — And to make it go up? — *On the heaviest side at the bottom* [it remains stationary]. — *On the lightest side* [it rolls down]. *Now I see.* — Make it go up then. (He does so.) — *You put the plasticine near the top uphill. And downhill it's empty.* — And to make it go down? — *You put the heavy side downhill.* — Is that peculiar or normal? — *Peculiar.* — Do you know why it happens like that? — *No.*"

Cas (8–7) thinks initially that *B* is not perfectly circular, then notices the difference in weight but without seeing this as an explanation of *B*'s behavior. He is given *C* with clay three-quarters of the way around it. Cas manages to make it stay still or roll down but not to roll up, and has not at first really paid attention to the positioning of the clay. "To make it stay still? — *You have to put the hollow bit at the front.*" To make *C* roll uphill he adds more clay, then takes some off, and discovers: "*you have to put the hollow bit toward the slope* [on the downhill side] *and the heavy bit there* [the uphill side]. — So? — *It's the plasticine that makes it go.* — Is it because of the weight? One little boy said that. — [Silence.]''

Luc (8–7): Same reactions. Eventually: *"So I put the heavy there and the light there and then it rolls down"* or up, or remains stationary (after he has succeeded in making it do so). No explanation.

Gal (8–9) notes that *B* is heavier and will therefore roll more readily or fall over, then, after observing that it doesn't, hesitates to attribute its immobility to its weight. With *C* he only succeeds at first in making it roll down, and *"like that* [weight at bottom] *it stays still."* Several attempts before achieving uphill motion, then *"when the plasticine is on the right it rolls to the right and when it's on the left it rolls to the left.* — Why does it stay still when it's there? — *Because it's heavier at the bottom.* — So how do you explain it all? — [Silence.]''

The advances made at this level are of two kinds. The first is important, despite its negative character: the subjects have achieved awareness of the contradictions entailed in using the total weight of the wheel as an explanation. Kam, for example, begins with an explanation characteristic of level 1B: *B* remains stationary "because it is heavy." But he immediately sees the contradiction: "Usually a heavy wheel rolls down." Lau, after invoking weight as an explanation, sighs as he realizes the inadequacy of this and switches to the idea of the "two sides" with different functions. Cas and Gal both give up the idea of total weight as an explanation very quickly.

The second advance is the idea, which will be more clearly formulated at level 2B, of an inequality between specific actions: Lau imagines "one side made specially so it will roll" and another "so it won't roll," though without perceiving that he is dealing with asymmetrical weights, even though he grasps this later with wheel *C*. Generally speaking, *C* puts all the subjects on the right track, first of all by means of successful practical experiments, then by enabling them to become aware of the positions and distribution of the wheel's weight as a result of their actions. Yet they are still unable to derive any general explanation from their observations: the intermediate subject, Lau, simply returns to the theory of total weight, while the others all prudently confess that they just don't understand. In other words, the localized weight on one or other side of the wheel remains for them a motive force imposing a particular direction on the wheel, but without the general hypothesis that weight must always move down. Thus they succeed in avoiding the the contradictions of level 1B, but not in transcending them by means of an overall interpretation. However, it should be remembered that this lacuna is to be expected, since it is not until level 2B, that the verticality of the weight's descent is truly understood, as much by reason of the ability to construct systems of coordinates as because of advances in the grasp of dynamics (the horizontality of water explained by its weight being directed downward, and so on).

§3. Level 2B, Stage 3, and Conclusions

The two correlated advances characterizing level 2B are, first that the experiments with *B* suggest to the subject an asymmetry of weight, and second, after his experiments with *C*, that he isolates more or less clearly the underlying explanatory principle of the weight's constant tendency to move downward.

Zur (7–11) observes *A* descend in the normal way and says that if it were heavier it would go at the same speed but make more noise, then "*the heavier one goes quicker because there is the push.*" But seeing *B* remain stationary he immediately supposes: "*It doesn't go down because it's somehow heavier at the bottom. — Why? — There's something down there that makes it heavier.*" *B* moves upward. "*It has more weight high up than down at the bottom. — Can we make C do the same as B? — That depends how you've filled it in: perhaps you've left sides empty.*" He puts clay three-quarters of the way round: "*That will make it go down on one side and stop afterwards.*" And if it's filled only half way round: "*That will make it go to and fro.* [Experiments.] *It doesn't make it do what I said. — What if we want to make it (C) go uphill? — You must put the plasticine on this side* [correct]. *— And for it to stay still? — The plasticine at the bottom. —* Why does the weight make it go round? *— Because it's heavier than the light one. I can't explain it properly: the weight doesn't like being up high.*"

Pic (8–8): "*It's heavier. It will roll down quicker because it's heavy.* [Experiment.] *It doesn't work. Ah! there's a ball bearing inside: something that makes it stop, so it doesn't want to roll down. —* And to make it roll uphill? *— You have to make sure the thing that makes it heavy is a little bit down from the top on this side. To make it go down it has to be a bit down from the top on the other side.*" Wheel *C*: Pic begins by putting the clay "*on one side, quite squashed up. —* What are you trying to do? *— Make it go down like that. So I have to put the plasticine on this side.* [It goes down.] *—* And now? *— To make it stay still you have to put the heavy part at the bottom. —* And to make it go up? *— On this side at the top.* [It goes up.] *—* Why is that? *—Because the heaviness presses down on where it isn't heavy. —* (uphill motion)? *— Yes, because the plasticine is heavy, so it tries to go down if it's here and up if it's there.*"

Laz (9–3): "*Because it's heavier, the weight pulls it along quicker. —* [*B* stationary] *— It doesn't go! —* [*B* uphill.] *— My word, there must be a* *weight in there. You've put a piece of lead there* [pointing to correct spot on rim]. — What makes you say that? — *There must be a place where there's more lead, so then the lead pulls it, and then you can put it one way or another and the wheel goes towards where the lead is."* Wheel *C:* he puts a large piece of clay on one side and a small piece on the other, to unbalance it. But he fails at first to place the wheel correctly in order to make it go up, though he succeeds immediately in making it go down: *"Ah, if I put it the other way round that will be it. Because where the biggest weight is that's the way it turns."*

Bra (9–8). *B* stationary: *"It's heavier! — So? — It should have rolled quicker. Ah! It's just where it's sitting that the weight is."* Wheel *C:* experiments successfully, then: *"If you put the weight uphill it goes uphill, and downhill that's the way it goes."*

Rin (8–4): "Can you make *C* go uphill? — *Yes,* [put] *the heavier bit at the top on this side, then it can't help turning that way.* — Do you think that's peculiar? — *No, that's what should happen. It must go backwards according to how you put the plasticine.* — What is the weight doing then? — *Where the weight is it weighs down and so it goes lower."*

Bru (10–4): *"Because before it began to move it held back a bit, so I thought there was a weight in the wheel.* — So can you make it go uphill? — *Yes.* [He places it correctly.] *The weight goes down and the wheel goes up.* — And why does it stay still? — *Because the weight is heavy and it weighs down at the bottom and then the wheel doesn't move."*

The stage 3 reactions add nothing new except fuller explanations:

Dam (12–5). *B: "Ah! it has more weight on one side than the other, that's why it goes up. Yes, the weight wants to be at the bottom because the earth attracts heavy things more than light ones.* — You don't find it peculiar? — *Of course not. It's what you'd expect, because there's more weight in one place than another."*

Since the general opinion typifying level 2B is that weight causes descent, and accelerating descent with increasing weight (Zur, Pic, Laz, and others), the immediate reaction of these subjects when confronted with the behavior of *B* is that the wheel contains asymmetrically distributed weights. It should be noted that this deduction is very different from the superficially similar one sometimes encountered at level 1B: when Gal, for example (§1), says that the wheel there "is something there (inside)," and adds that this thing causes the wheel either to roll or not to roll, he conceives of this thing, just like Cri with his imaginary "ball bearings," as some kind of all-purpose machine with inexplicable powers. At level 2B, on the contrary, Zur's "something that makes it heavier," is acting in a very rational way by weighing down toward the bottom because "weight doesn't like being up high," and thus makes the wheel move forward on the side where the "something heavier" moves downward. Similarly, with Pic, the wheel goes uphill provided that "what is heavy is a little bit down from the top on this side," the internal asymmetry of the wheel's weight thereby enabling "the heaviness to press down on where it isn't heavy." Compare also the correct formulations given by Rin, "where the weight is it weighs down and so it goes lower," and above all by Bru: "the weight goes down and the wheel goes up."

In other words, by level 2B the contradictions of the explanatory model have been transcended by means of a differentiation between the total wheel weight and the weight added to one side of the rim, and by the integrating relation according to which the weight must always move down. In this case, even if the other parts of the wheel have a weight such that the wheel tends to roll down, the greater weight placed high up on the rim can make that spot on the rim move downward in the uphill direction (Laz alone goes so far as to employ two unequal weights to achieve this imbalance). As usual, then, the problem of contradiction is resolved here by an extension of the powers of reference and the arrangement in relational form of notions that were at first limited and distorted by their absolute predicates, or, more briefly, by the interplay of differentiations and integrations.

As for our question as to the nature of the contradictions between a factual datum and a subject's anticipation, the overall development here from level 1A to stage 3 shows that there is no fundamental difference between this situation and that of the conflicts between two schemas being applied to the same objects, because the new fact causing the problem is always inter-dependent upon successive schemas of interpretation, just as it is upon the previous facts upon which the interpretation was based. Once again, then, we are dealing with a coordination between schemas that are at first in-compatible but are later combined into a higher unity. What is specific to situations such as this, however, is that the new object or event that is to be explained in a way that conforms with previous facts, is of a physical nature, so that the new constructions devised by the subject must in consequence be based upon data that he must discover by progressive analysis rather than just inventing them himself. Hence the possibility of multiple compromises such as those listed by B. Inhelder, H. Sinclair, and M. Bovet in *Learning and the Development of Cognition* (Cambridge, Harvard University Press, 1974). However, these compromises once more consist in incomplete compensations, and the power of logic, by imposing the obligation to achieve authentic noncontradictions, then plays a formative role just as indispensable as experimental analysis. This is why the subjects at our level 2A, even though they are still unable to find the explanations being sought, do take a decisive step forward in freeing themselves from the contradictions relating to the polyvalent notions of weight characteristic of level 1B, and by ordering the relations of "all" and "some" in an adequate fashion.

In the latter respect, it would be as well to end with an observation that will assume growing importance as our experiments continue. In logico-mathematical areas, as in physical ones, the subject starts off with positive statements and the development of positive characteristics; it is only secondarily, under pressure from the data involved, that he comes to wrestle with negations or limitations. But there is a fairly notable difference between the negations that present themselves in the physical domain and those that occur in logico-mathematical territory. In the first, the contradiction between factual datum and the subject's prediction impinges more or less rapidly upon the child's consciousness, because the negation is, in a sense, being imposed on him from outside. The difficulty, then, is to overcome that contradiction without incurring new ones, in other words to achieve a logical regulation of any new negations that prove necessary. In practice, however, it is still possible simply to increase the number of positive statements in an effort to link the facts with other positive characteristics: thus we find 1B subjects attributing multiple significations to "heavy" and "light" in order to legitimize what they have perceived, without feeling the slightest need for counter-examples. Indeed, even those counter-examples provided by simple observation are interpreted in a positive sense by further positive statements differing only slightly from the original ones. Hence the multiple compromises to which we referred a little earlier.

In the case of logico-mathematical systems, on the other hand, the negation is not imposed from outside, but is constructed by the subject himself. The result is that the child does not achieve consciousness of the contradiction until the level at which he has become capable of transcending it—along with others related to it—by a regulation of the negations involved. In such situations, therefore, we do not find the compromises so frequently encountered in the physical domain, and, since the solutions are of the all-or-nothing kind, success depends entirely upon operatory reversibility.

We shall return to these various problems in our general conclusions, particularly in section four.

§4. Contradiction in Unexpected Phenomena Relating to Balance

It may be of interest here to examine the results of a complementary experiment whose schema is the same as that of the preceding one: the transcendence of an apparent contradiction between an opposing fact and a prediction based upon weights, though with the difference, in this second case, that the addition or positioning of the parasitic weights appears less paradoxical than with their concealment in the rim of a wheel. The tests employed consist first of all in presenting the subject with various pieces of chipboard and asking him to predict their position of equilibrium when suspended asymmetrically, but without telling him that some of them contain an invisible screw (weight). Then one presents him with two ordinary boxes (one square, one round) containing a marble—sometimes with the child's knowledge, sometimes without—and finally a circular box inside which is a square box followed by a square box containing a circular box, both inner boxes containing a marble. The subject knows that the marble is present but not that there is a differently shaped box inside the outer one.

Even subjects at stage 1 predict how the pieces of chipboard will hang, by taking into account the weight or size of the sections on either side of the point of suspension, but they are unable to guess the causes of the irregularities observed.

Kat (5–6): "*The big side goes lower.* — Why? — *I don't know.* — And this piece? — *The same.* [Experiment.] *No.* — Can you explain that? — *No.*" But after handling the boxes: "*That piece* [of chipboard] *going up* [above the point of suspension, although it is the larger] *is light.* — And the other side? — *They're both light.* — So why does the little side go down? — *Because the hole's in the middle.*" [Wrong.]"

Mas (5–6): "*The big side goes down.* — Why? — *The big side is heavier.* — And with this piece? — *The same.* [Experiment.] *No.* — Can you explain? — *The hole* [to which the string suspending it is attached] *is too little.* — What if I make it bigger? — *The big side will go down.* [Experiment.] *No.* — Can you explain? — *No.*"

With stage 2 subjects, the hypotheses move in the direction of concealed additions.

Fer (7–9): The smaller portion "*is heavier.*" There are "*pebbles hidden inside,*" and so on.

Cro (7–10): "*You've put something inside. It's possible there's something heavier in that little side.*"

Clearly then, despite identical predictions based upon the correct principle, at stage 1 the contradictions imposed by the facts engender only explanations that strive to limit themselves solely to the facts being observed at the actual moment, even to the extent of distorting them in any way that presents itself, including negation of what has previously been stated. At stage 2 one naturally still finds residues of such behavior. But since the

contradiciton is merely displaced by such explanations, the budding operatory logic of the seven- to eight-year-old obliges him to seek further, and
leads him to venture beyond the immediate perceptual data.

The boxes containing the marbles present three (or two) successive problems: imagining the presence of a heavy body when the balance of the box
does not obey the rules (and the presence of the marble hasn't been di-
vulged); predicting the differing positions of balance for the single square or
circular box with marbles in; and finally, in the case of the double boxes,
deducing from the observed facts that the outer box contains another one
different in shape.

It is hardly worth spending time on the first of these problems, since it is so
closely analogous to that of the pieces of chipboard. As for the second, it is
remarkable that the solutions offered at stage 1, although not complete,
already go a long way toward the correct solution.

> Kat (5–6): the weight will go *"right to the bottom."* With the square box
> she localizes the marble in the lowest corner, but without any precise
> relation to the axis. After observation: *"In the low down corner. —
> Why? — It's heavy, and it can go into all the corners.* But why into this
> one? *— the marble goes down. —* Why not into another corner? *— Be-
> cause it can't bounce up."*

> Cor (6–7): *"It will go down . . . into the low corner."*

> Nad (6–7) *(without having been told about the marble): "There's some-
> thing that goes down every time you turn it. Every time you turn it's
> heaviest down at the bottom. —* What do you think is there? *— A cube:
> it's stuck inside."*

Nad, like other 1B subjects, thus goes as far as deducing from the positions the box takes up that there is a heavy body, "a cube," inside it, just as
the 2A subjects did with the blocks of chipboard; but we must remember that
this supposition is undoubtedly easier to make in the case of the boxes, since
it is a specific characteristic of boxes, generally speaking, to have contents.
The interesting problem now is to establish when and how the subject will
conclude that there is another box concealed inside the one he is manipulat-
ing. In practice, one finds suspicions of this fact as early as level 2A and
direct statement of it at level 2B.

> Cro (7–10). Single square box: the marble *"goes into the corner. —* And
> if I let go of the box? *— There. —* And if I turn it? *— There,"* and so on,
> in each case the lowest point. "And with this (round) box? *— Always at
> the bottom. —* Like with the square one? *— No, the marble goes round.*
> — Why did the marble stay in the corners with the square box? *— It*

slopes. — And here? *— It can always go to the bottom, so it's always there.''* When confronted with the trick boxes, Cro is surprised to see a square box come to rest in an unexpected position: "Where is the marble? *— There. —* Is this doing the same as the other box? *— no. —* Can you explain it? *— [It is spun again.] — It does the same as a round box* — Do you see why? *— No ... it's doing what a round box does.''* When the trick round box is spun he is once more surprised to see that it can come to rest in four positions: *"It's like the square box!''*

Odi (7–9). Trick round box: he predicts the same position as for a normal round box—the marble *"will stop anywhere. [Experiment.] It doesn't do the same thing! It does the same as a square box!''* Odi then supposes that the marble has been made immoveable inside, but that doesn't explain the four positions. He then imagines that *"some cardboard''* has been inserted, and finally: *"you've put a square box inside it.''*

Gen (7–5). Round trick box: "What does it do? *— What the square box does. You'd have to make the round box into a square box* [inside].''

Gil (8–10). With the trick round box, right away: *"There's something in a corner that's heavy* [the presence of the marble had been divulged] *and glued. —* And the marble? *— It's stuck there. —* So there's nothing peculiar about it? *— No.* [he turns it slightly]. *The marble isn't glued. Now it's stuck here. There's something holding it back, a little square piece of cardboard. —* Everywhere? *— No* [Experiments.] *—* How many times does it get stuck? *— Four, it's a* [big] *piece of square cardboard. There's a square box inside. The marble is going into the corners.* Faced with the trick square box he concludes right away: *"There's something inside, a round box, and the marble's in the round box.''*

Clearly, then, the overall development involved is the same as in the case of the weighted wheel: complete solution of the problem at level 2B and partial solutions at level 2A sufficient to remove the apparent contradictions. But since it is easier to suppose the presence of additional objects inside a box than on the rim of a wheel, the subjects at substage 2A succeed in progressing more rapidly from the observation "it's doing the same as a round box" or "as the square box" (Cro) to the conclusion that something (a piece of "cardboard" say Odi and Gil) has been inserted so as to affect the positions in which the box comes to rest, and then that this "something" is round or square in shape. These solutions do not require the hypothetical-deductive thought of stage 3, since there is no need as yet to take the plunge into the system of all the possibilities inherent in the observed transformations. Provided the subject is clearly aware of the contradictions, as is the case here from the earliest concrete operations, and consequently does not distort what he observed, he is then able to conclude that his observations so far are not providing an acceptable explanation, and that he must therefore add further objects, hidden ones, it is true, but still operating in the same way as the observable factors in simple situations.

Part 2. Mechanical Curves

To link contradiction with incomplete compensations, as we have consistently done so far, undoubtedly implies a disequilibrium between negations and affirmations, as later analyses will show more clearly. As a preparation for those analyses, it may be useful at this point to give a brief account of some further reactions, in addition to those already described, in cases where contradictions arise between an observable fact and a subject's anticipation of it. Once more we shall be dealing with revolving wheels, but this time with a pencil fixed through it at some point to provide a graphic record of the wheel's movement by drawing various mechanical curves. The interest of this situation is that it entails three variables: the movement of the wheel or wheels; the movement of the pencil propelled by the subject and fixed to one of the wheels; and the line drawn by the pencil as it moves (for from the subject's point of view, this line is viewed as more or less correct without being determined univocally by the movement of the pencil in straight or curved lines). When observations of the result do not conform to the subject's predictions there will therefore be four of five possibilities for negations: (1) that the line is not in conformity with the actions of the subject or of the pencil, both of which are seen as correctly executed and predicted; (2) that the movement of the pencil has been adversely affected by the apparatus despite the subject's action, which again he conceives of as correctly executed and predicted; (3) that the subject's action in pushing the pencil has been badly executed; and finally, that his prediction was incorrect, either (4) because of some local disturbance opposing the generality of the predicted law (which will remain valid in other cases), or (5) because the subject has failed to differentiate the movement of the wheel from the pencil itself, or, in other words, failed to predict the law in its complete and correct form. If this order of negations corresponds to the development we are about to examine, this would thus represent an interesting evolution of the negations involved, advancing from the periphery (resistance of objects) to the center (limitations of the subject's own affirmations), and achieving equilibration only at the late stage of positive operations.

The technique adopted concentrates not on the causal or geometric explanation of how the mechanical curves are produced, but on the subjects' reactions to the failure of their predictions. For example, one pushes a pencil through the middle of a little disc so that its point just emerges on the underside, then rolls the disc round the outside of a big ring: the prediction, an easy one, is that the pencil will draw a big "ring". The same is true if the disk is rolled around the inside of the big ring. On the other hand, when one rolls the disk along a straight ruler, with the pencil still through the disk's center, the line is straight, despite the circularity of the disk. If the pencil is fixed on the circumference of the disk, then rolling it along the ruler produces a cycloid. And more difficult still is the case where one has a disk exactly half the diameter of a big ring, fixes the pencil at a point on the disk's circumference, and rolls the disk round the inside of the ring: what happens is that the pencil draws a straight line across the diameter of the ring.

In each of these situations the experimenter asks for a prediction (both spoken and drawn) without paying too much attention to the reasons that the subject gives, often unasked, then lets the subject perform the action in question, thus producing a line on the paper. The subject is then asked whether the line he has made corresponds with "what he thought," then what he thinks now "of this line," whether "it's gone right," and also whether it would be the same if he tried again. If need be, other analogous situations can be devised and used, and one can end by making use of a "spirograph," a child's toy working on the same principles already used but considerably more complicated, so that by inserting the pencil in a variety of places one can obtain from an apparently circular trajectory a whole variety of curves, stylized flowers, and even squares and triangles with rounded corners. There is naturally no question of requiring an explanation for these results but, as before, simply of seeing what the subject's reactions are to the nonconfirmation of his predictions.

§5. Level 1A.

The youngest subjects (level 1A) attribute the failure of their predictions to the drawing itself:

Dia (4–0), for the disk with the pencil in the middle circling a large circle, predicts "*a round.* [Draws.] *Yes.*" But when the disk draws a straight line across the diameter of the big circle when rolled around inside, he says that " *that* [disk] *went all around,*" but of the line, "*that didn't go around,*" as if the line had not in fact followed the movement of the pencil. He then insists on trying again somewhere else on the paper; then "*we must have another piece of paper*"; then he draws a circle himself, by hand, around the circumference of the big circle. Later, having produced more straight lines with the disk, he says "*we must use a different pencil*", discards the disk, and draws another circle by hand with the edge of the big circle as guide. Finally, he discards the big circle as well and draws the rings he had incorrectly predicted by hand alone.

Rob (4–3) similarly predicts nothing but circles, and when the pencil makes almost straight lines complains that *"it's not quite round. — So? — It's not very nice. —* How can you make it look nice then? *— Go all around. —* And what do you think of this line? *— It's cockeyed* [= the drawing is wrong]."

Isa (4–5) inserts the pencil in one corner of a square, then of a big cross, then of a rectangle, all of which are pivoted round their centers, and anticipates drawings of a square, a cross, and a rectangle, rather than the circles that of course result. She predicts circles when the pencil is inserted in the center of a disk which is rolled around a larger disk (correctly), but also when the disk is rolled along a straight ruler. Whereupon she condemns the resulting lines as failures: *"it looks a bit funny."* Again, in order to confirm her predictions, she discards the small disk and draws the circles she had anticipated freehand.

Wil (4–8) expects circles in every case because the pencil is in the center of the little disk. When the latter is rolled around a large circle, his prediction is, of course, correct, but when the disk draws a straight line along the ruler, despite his prediction (*"like the other; it will make a round"*), he corrects the drawing by dragging the pencil forcibly into a circular path. When the test is repeated he at first predicts a sinusoidal curve (a compromise between circle and straight line), then: *"It will make a proper line —* How do you mean? *— It will be a round."* When both predictions prove incorrect, he says of the pencil: *"It does things it shouldn't, things that aren't nice."*

The reactions on this earliest level are thus of three kinds. First, failure to comprehend the pencil's movements because they have not been differentiated from the shape of the object guiding or framing it, or from the shape of the disk in which it is fixed. This is the same as saying that (unless, like Isa, one inserts the pencil in one corner of a quadrilateral or cross) these subjects predict circular lines only, even if the small disk is rolled along a straight ruler, which ought to facilitate the anticipation of the correct, rectilinear result (Isa and Will). Next, the fact that, if the drawing does not confirm the prediction, then it is the drawing as such that is viewed as the seat of the error, as negating what is "right" and not the prediction of the subject; indeed, this "wrong" drawing is not conceived of as a failure on the subject's part: it is the pencil in its role as graphic tool that is thought of as failing to obey the pencil in its role as moveable object subject to the form of the partner object. Inside the big circle, Dia says, the pencil "went all round" (which is an exaggeration), but the drawing "didn't go round"; the drawing "isn't nice," it is "cockeyed" (Rob), it is "a bit funny" (Isa) and "does things it shouldn't," things "that aren't nice" (Wil). Third, there is then only one remedy: the drawing must be corrected, as though it were not in fact the necessary result of the pencil's movement; hence Dia's changes of paper or pencil, the forcible imposition of a circular trajectory upon the pencil (Dia and Wil), and even the rejection of all ancillary apparatus in order to make freehand drawings that ensure the pencil verifies the subjects' predictions.

§6. Levels 1B and 1C

At the second level, 1B, the line drawn is no longer an independent variable but depends entirely on the movements of the pencil; but those movements are in their turn linked to the frame-objects imposing particular directions upon the pencil-holding disk. It follows from this that when the observations do not conform with the prediction, this negative result is attributed essentially to the equipment. There may also be a suggestion that the fault lies in the action itself, in that it has failed to follow the lines of the equipment properly, but this displacement of the negative element onto the subject's own action sems to belong to a slightly later level, intermediate between 1B and 2A, and which we may term 1C. Here are some 1B examples:

Jan (5–6) predicts circles when the disk follows the circumference of the big circle, whether inside or outside. When the disk rolls along the ruler, with the pencil in the center, he no longer predicts a circle like the 1A subjects, but says that it will draw *"straight along"* and draws a straight line to show what he means. "And like this (pencil at circumference of disk)? — *It will make a lot of rounds* [a series of separate and noncontiguous circles] *and then a line* [a straight line corresponding to the ruler, as though the pencil could trace that in addition to the perimeters of his circles]. — Let's see. (Cycloid lines begins to appear.) Is that what you thought? — *Yes . . . no, like that* [his own drawing]. — Is it going the way it should? — [Silence.] — And what about like this (disk with pencil on circumference revolving around inside of circle twice the diameter and producing a straight line across the diameter of the big circle)? — *This* [he predicts a circle]. — Watch. — *A line! What a rascal!* — Who? — *That* [the big circle]. *That's being a rascal."* With the spirograph he predicts a circle and is astonished when it draws a triangle: *"It's more normal if a round makes another round.* — Well what can we do?" He draws his "round" without the equipment and continues to deprecate the behavior of these rascals. "What if it wasn't a rascal? — *It would behave and always do the same thing."*

Phi (5–6) predicts a straight line when the disk follows the ruler with the pencil in the center, but then makes the same prediction with the pencil on the circumference, which in fact produces a cycloid curve. Seeing the cycloid appearing, he calls it a square, but doesn't think it ought to happen "*because rounds don't make squares* — But they make lines (since he had predicted a line instead of the cycloid)? — *Yes. No. They don't make lines. Rulers make lines.*" Subsequently attempts are made to help him predict the pencil's various paths, but he fails to differentiate them from the shapes of the moving disk or the guide shapes.

Cla (5–7), having made wrong predictions: "*it's the pencil that's wrong* [in its role as guide for the disk, not in that of producer of the actual line], *it went the wrong way, and it should have gone the right way* [= should have followed the outline of the framing object]."

Cha (6–0) similarly predicts a straight line for the cycloid as well as for the actual straight line. He then tries to correct the result by forcing the disk to draw lines in conformity with his prediction.

Clearly, then, although the negative element is not yet being attributed to prediction error, or even to some deficiency in the subject's own action when holding or guiding the pencil, the responsibility for failure is no longer seen as lying with the drawings because they haven't reproduced the movements of the pencil correctly, but with the pencil itself (Cla), because it hasn't followed the big object properly, or with the frame-objects themselves because they prevent the pencil from making the predicted circles, or even because they are actively playing the "rascal" by refusing to "always do the same thing" (Jan).

The following are some examples from level 1C (mostly about six years of age) in which the negative is beginning to move in the direction of the subject himself, but, interestingly enough, only in that he suspects himself of "drawing badly," or, in other words, of failing to produce a correct copy of the objects or displacements he still believes he has correctly predicted, and not yet in that he suspects himself of a wrong interpretation; he is still unable to distinguish between the positive cases, where his predictions are confirmed, and the negative cases where other factors have intervened.

Col (5–2) correctly predicts a straight line with the pencil in the center of the disk rolling along the ruler, but when it comes to drawing it he insists on rotating the pencil itself. When the pencil is inserted at the top of the disk's circumference he predicts "a line along the top," meaning a straight line across the peaks. When he sees the cycloid beginning to appear: "*It's making a bridge, we've gone wrong: down and then up.* — What should it be like then? — *Like this* [straight line], *we must get it to do that.* — [Tries again. Cycloid starts again.] — *I need to hold the pencil a bit lower down, but if it starts drawing the same thing again, then we'll just have to try again.* — [Further attempt.] — *It still looks like a bridge. We must get it right. It keeps on and on going wrong.*" He alters the position of the pencil, twists it, and so on, but won't give in: "*It's because I didn't turn it properly.*"

Ret (6–1) is faced with a straight line instead of the predicted circle: "*It's because I didn't put it on right* [= didn't keep the disk against the inside of the big circle tightly enough, hence the diameter line instead of the predicted circle]." The cycloid is predicted as a straight line, then, after seeing the cycloid appear: "*It's because I did that* [shaking hand]. *I moved it.*" With the Spirograph he gets no further than 1B reactions: "*It's rounds making squares!*"

Pel (6–3) refuses to accept the cycloid he has obtained: "*I don't think that's any good. — What would it be like if it were good? — It would be straight. It's no good because it's a hump. I ought to have stayed on the line and I curved up. — What if you were to try again? — It would go wrong again, no, perhaps once or twice it would, but not every time!*" He then manages to drag the disk along the ruler without revolving it, producing a straight line: "Did it turn properly like that? *— Yes.*"

Cor (7–0), seeing the cycloid: "*It's come out wrong. I didn't turn it properly.*"

These cases are very instructive. The correctness of the predictions is still not being questioned, which means that the child still doesn't entertain the notion that the negation can be attributed to his own reasoning (error as to the generality of a law and need to distinguish subclasses in which it can be modified by local factors), but attributes the negative result to the purely physical aspects of the action performed, because it has failed to conform to the factual data. In other words, there is very little difference between the 1B and 1C reactions apart from a slight advance on one point: that the negative result, instead of being seen as simply the result of faulty equipment distorting the lines, is here viewed as residing in the defective copy produced by deficiencies in the subject's own action. On the other hand, we must take care to distinguish these 1C reactions from those at level 1A, first because the average ages are four years old for 1A and six years old for 1C (with 1B at five years old in between), but above all because at the 1A level the child is viewing the drawing as something quite independent of himself, even though his hand is holding the pencil. The pencil, in other words, is seen as being entirely controlled by the shape, whether circular or otherwise, of the apparatus, so that it must necessarily reproduce that shape. If this fails to occur, then the fault lies in the drawing or the pencil, as though what has occurred is a mechanical accident, of which the subject is a victim, rather than being a mistake on his part. The 1C subjects, on the other hand, have begun to entertain the notion of their own lack of skill being to blame. And that is a step forward in the subjectivization of the negation, if one may so express it, even though the subject's activity is still viewed as being entirely determined from outside, by the circular or linear objects he believes he simply has to copy. In practice, therefore, beneath this persistent realism a remarkable change of direction has taken place: in passing over to the subject, even if it is on the plane of action alone, the negation becomes instrumental, and from now on will play a role increasingly complementary to that of affirmation.

§7. Levels 2A and 3

This is in fact what is beginning to happen on level 2A (seven to nine years old).

Ast (7–6) predicts a straight line when the disk with center pencil is rolled along the ruler. Then seeing the cycloid beginning to emerge: "*I was wrong. It makes a shape like funny squashed spectacles.*" He rejects the hypothesis of juxtaposed circles as a continuation of this figure "*because you can't squash them together,*" then he makes a distinction between those cases when the pencil draws straight lines and those when it draws curves by saying of the disk: "*You make it turn a different way.*"

Ort (7–6), seeing an unpredicted cycloid: "*It was wrong when I drew a round there,*" then, "*if I was to do it on the spot* [= if the disk was turned without moving forward, i.e., simply pivoted round its center] *it would make a round then.*"

Rib (7–6), with the pencil in the center rolling along the ruler predicts a circle, then, observing the resulting straight line: "*It's not the same, the round has been turned the wrong way* [in relation to its overall motion in a straight line].*"

Gug (8–11) predicts for the cycloid a series of very definitely separated circles, then proceeds to roll the disk: "*It's not the same at all. — Why not? — Because here I drew with the little round, and there I imagined it* [anticipation].*"

Cap (8–7) says it's impossible to obtain a straight line with one circle rolling inside another, and informs the experimenter that he is asking him "*a pointless question. I won't try any more.*" Then, observing the result: "*There it is. It's because I began there* [with the pencil fixed to the circumference of the disk.]*" But "*you could make a circle, too*" by inserting the pencil elsewhere.

With the beginning of concrete operations (2A), negation is thus acquiring a different status. To begin with, the subject recognizes from the outset that his predictions can be right or wrong: "I made a mistake" (Ast, Ort, and others), "Here I drew with the little round, and there I imagined it" (Gug).

But above all, the subject then immediately assigns the negation a status of stable operatory usability, and not just a heuristic role of recognition and elimination of errors: given a rejected prediction (say a circle), it can still remain true in certain cases A, and is invalidated only in other cases A', hence the possibility of putting A and A' together to form a class B in which the A' are non-A B's and the A are non-A' B's. For example, Ort, having predicted one or more circles instead of the cycloid, recognizes that this is not in fact the case when the pencil is positioned on the rim of the rolling disk (hence the sub-class A' substituted for A) but he maintains the continued existence of a subclass A in which the drawing of a circle is in fact possible "if I was to do it on the spot." It now remains for the subject to discover the general law proper to class B $(= A + A')$, but that can only be achieved (in the present experiment) by successfully coordinating the overall translations of the wheel/disk (movement of the pencil drawing it forward) with its local rotations, and the subjects at level 2A are still only partly successful in this respect. The furthest they go—although this already represents a consider-able advance—is to show why their prediction, which remains valid in other cases, does not work in such and such a specific case by pointing out the various modifying factors as they go along.

By the time we reach level 2B (nine to ten years old), however, we do begin to find coordination of this kind between the translations and the local rotations, in other words, between the movements of the pencil and those of the circle, which are at last being clearly differentiated.

Abu (9–8), with the pencil at the center: "*Turning it all the time* [the disk], *it rolls along, but this* [path of pencil] *will be straight all the same.* — And with the pencil here [on circumference]? — *Not quite straight.* [He draws a semicircle, then tries with disk.] *Like this, when it turns, it keeps getting further away, but it can't make the whole circle, it can't go back again* [hence the observed cycloid]."

Pil (9–10). Pencil at center. "*The round turns round and around on itself, and the pencil isn't going lower or higher.* — So? — *A straight line.* — Is that possible? — *The pencil stays in the middle so it makes a straight line.* — And like this (pencil at circumference)? — *When the pencil turns it does this as it goes along* [drawing an epicycloid with overlapping loops.] — Watch. — *It didn't work because the pencil couldn't keep on going lower* [= move backward] *and it couldn't make a circle* [= a loop, hence a cycloid not an epicycloid]." On the other hand, with the disk drawing a straight diameter across the inside of the large circle with twice the diameter, he wonders if he has "*slipped turning it around and made a straight line.*"

At stage 3, after questioning only a few subjects, we encountered no correct predictions for this last question, but some good explanations after the event:

> Jan (12–0), who was expecting segments of cycloids, explains the line across the diameter of the larger circle by the fact that the disk inside it is *"a bit too big. It depends on the diameter of the circle* [that of the disk in relation to that of the outer one], *and where you made the hole* [for the pencil]: *right at the edge, inside, or in the middle."*

This onset of the ability to coordinate the translations and rotations already clearly differentiated at level 2B recalls the reactions at the same level to the weighted wheel in section 1 of this chapter: just as the 2B subjects realize that the weight always moves downward (class B), but that when positioned at the center of the wheel or toward the front it pulls the wheel downhill (subclass A), while when positioned on the upslope side of the wheel near the top it causes the wheel to move uphill slightly (subclass A' = those B that are non-A), so here the 2B subjects understand, in the cases of mechanical curves, that there is always rotation of the circles upon themselves coordinated with the movements of the pencil (generally translations) that cause the disk to move along, but that, according to the positioning of the pencil, the frame-objects, and the sizes of the disks used in relation to those objects, one can obtain apparently contradictory results (hence the non-A B's), such as circles, straight lines, cycloids and even (at stage 3) straight lines produced by the rotation of a circle within a circle, when a point on the circumference of the inner one traces the diameter of the outer one.

§8. Conclusion

As a whole, then, when summarized in retrospect, the development of the negations here (or of the unfulfilled predictions) from level 1A through levels 2B and 3 seems to entail a very general meaning. The initial negative characteristics (when were are dealing with subjects who insist on maintaining the validity of their failed predictions at all costs) are at first attributed solely to external objects, which are viewed as simple perturbation factors: inadequacy of the resulting drawing interpreted not as due to the subject's own actions, but to the lack of a necessary dependence of the graphic result upon the movements of the pencil; then due to the resistance of the objects involved (moving disk, frame-objects, or the pencil itself), which are seen as failing to execute the tasks they ought to perform in order to verify the predictions, which are still viewed as correct. Then the negation is attributed to the actions of the subject, but still in a realist mode, which is to say that those actions are seen as not attaining their goal, which is a copy of reality verifying predictions that are again still viewed as correct. It is only later, at level 2A, that the subject's prediction is seen as false, with the onset of understanding as to the why of his failures or successes, but still without sufficient structuring or classifications of the successful outcomes (confirmation of affirmations) and the unsuccessful ones, whereas by level 2B this understanding has made further advances and already foreshadows a stable equilibrium between affirmations and negations.

What this development means, therefore, is that there is, so to speak, a progressive subjectivization or interiorization of negation, insofar as it evolves from an external, contingent perturbation into a necessary operation of thought. In the beginning, affirmation exercises a systematic primacy, because the object's properties take immediate, absolute, and quasi-infallible possession of the subject's mind, so that his prediction errors are conceived of as due solely to material perturbations that are preventing a triumphant affirmation (in theory) from attaining its objective (in fact), thus creating the necessity of compensating for those perturbations by cancellations or corrections. A step forward is taken at level 1C when the failure of the prediction is attributed to deficiencies in the subject's own action, but that still does nothing to shake the realism of his affirmation, since the necessary compensation now consists simply in correcting the perturbations falsifying the action directed at fulfilling the prediction. With level 2A, on the other hand (in these experiments), comes subjectivization: the predictions are conceived of as being susceptible to error (a development that can, of course, occur earlier in simpler experiments), and this means that affirmation has ceased to be an immediate conquest, but must proceed in stages. This in turn means, however, that negation gains what affirmation loses: it becomes both a limitation on the subject's affirmations and a complement to those affirmations, which, though correct for one subclass of objects, can be false for another, and vice versa. In this case, the external pertubations, which exist, but were hitherto wrongly viewed as the very substance of the errors made (that is, as obstacles to the success of the subject's affirmations), now begin to be integrated into the system, and, losing the status of perturbations to be cancelled or compensated for materially, acquire that of variations to be considered as positive elements, albeit distinct from (or the reverse of) others of which they thus become the negative. By level 2B in the present experiment—and generally whenever the observable facts are clearly recognized and understood—affirmations and negations are being equilibrated to a greater extent, and at stage 2 achieve exact compensation: what is true but particular to a class A is not so in the case of its complementary class A', though both are included in the properties of B (but not of B'; any subclass or class A is then necessarily characterized by as many negations (being non-A' but being B) as affirmations. Thus the subjectivization of the negations is achieved simultaneously with the relativization of the affirmations, these two conjunct and interdependent processes thereby finally achieving the delayed but obligatory equilibration of the positive and negative aspects of any operatory system.

Six

Contradictions in the Coordinations of
Observable Facts (Scales)

with C. Kamii and S. Parrat-Dayan

The problem presented by scales has been studied many times, and the psychological information to be derived from it may seem to have been exhausted. We have chosen it, nevertheless, in order to study a particular question that presents itself with regard to the elementary forms of contradiction: can one view as contradictory, and in what sense, predictions observed at a certain level of development that will appear manifestly absurd to subjects at later levels; for example, the prediction that if one puts the same weight into both pans of a scale then both pans will move downward? Clearly the first answer that comes to mind is that there is nothing contradictory in such an event for a subject ignorant of the fact that such weights are exerting equal and opposite forces on the two pans, or a subject who thinks that the beam of the scales is flexible. But if one adopts the point of view, as we do, not of logical contradiction (i.e., contradiction between statements inferred from defined notions), but of the equilibrium between the subject's actions or operations, it is clear that the problem presents itself differently: on the one hand it is a matter of knowing how far the subject is making progress with the consequences of his suppositions, or whether those suppositions remain unstable by their very nature; and on the other hand it is a matter of establishing how far he is capable of sensing further possibilities along the line of his "virtual efforts" in both a physical sense (which may modify the state of the scales) and a cognitive one (the different hypotheses that the situation suggests).

Technique

The scale employed consists of two pans, A and B, hanging by chains at either end of a beam. Just above the points on the beam where the chains are attached, there are two small vertical rods sticking up, A' and B'. The weights, all equal in size and weight, consist of thick disks pierced in the center, so that they can either be placed in the pans or impaled on the vertical rods.

One begins by asking what will happen if one places a weight in A or B, then what the other (empty) pan will do. If it is predicted that A will move down and B will rise, then one asks by how much, to see if the subject is predicting equality or not between the differences, or whether one is expected to move down more than the other moves up, and so on. One also asks if these movements are simultaneous or successive. After he has observed what actually does happen, and has been asked analogous questions about A' and B', he is asked to predict the effects of a weight being placed in both pans (with accompanying gesture to indicate simultaneity of the two operations). After he has seen the actual result, the next question deals with the addition of one more weight in each pan (making two in both). Then one asks for a prediction of what will happen with eight weights in A and none in B, after which one asks the child to do whatever he thinks necessary to bring the pans level again. When he has succeeded in reaching eight against eight, one asks what will happen when one removes two from one side (then four, and so on) or when, with the scales at eight = eight, one adds five to both sides at once (there may be prediction of equal levels but accompanied by a general lowering). And if we have one in A and none in B, how far will B move down and A rise if we put one in B too?

A last question concerning the AB system, and just as essential as the others, consists in placing four in A and four in B then asking the subject to make A go up. The point of interest here is to find out whether the sole method that occurs to him is adding to B, or if he also thinks of the other possibility: subtracting from A.

Finally, one goes on to the $A'B'$ system. With eight in A and eight in B, what will happen if one moves two weights (then four and so on) from B to B'? Then, with four in A and four on A', one asks the subject to make the two pans level by putting whatever he chooses into B or on B', but with the single proviso that he must not exactly match the four + four of AA'. For example, he might put six in B and two on B' or vice versa.

§1. Level 1A

Here are our results:

Gab (4–10): "If I put one in B? — *I'd like to try to put two* [one in A, one in B, which she does]. — [The weights are removed again.] — And with one in B? — *It will go down.* — How far? — [Points to the ground] — And the other pan (pointing to unweighted A)? — *That will go down the same* [she demonstrates descent, but by 5 cm only]. — *Will they both go down if I put just one here* [in B]? — *Yes, that one will go right down to here* [B to ground]. — But the other? What will happen to that? — [This time indicates 2 cm above A's present position]. — It will go up? — *Yes,* — Why? — *Because that one* [B] *will go down.* — So why does it go down? — [Silence.] — Do you know why? — [Silence.] — Where will it go? — [This time demonstrates a 3 cm descent for A.] — Watch. (Weight placed.) Is that right? — *Yes.* — Is it what you said? — *A little bit higher.*" For one in A she first predicts that B will go down and A rise (which she has just witnessed for the opposite placing), but then "*They'll go down together,*" then once more one rising and one falling. One placed on B': "*It will go down* [but by 3 cm only, much less than if in B]. — And there (A)? — [Rise of 5.5 cm] — So it will go up more than the other will go down? — *Yes.* — Why? — [Silence.]" After observation of one on B' we move on to one on A': "*That one* [B] *will go up more* [i.e., same error repeated]." A weight hooked on underneath pan *B:* "Will it move? — *No, it won't go down because it* [weight] *isn't in there or up there* [*B* or *B*]." One in *A* and one in *B:* "*I don't know. They'll go down to there* [2.5 cm each]. — Watch. Now, is that what you said would happen? — *Yes* [they have both stayed in the same position but with a slight seesawing as the weights were put in]. — If I add one in here and there (*A* and *B*)? — *It'll go down.* — Both or just one? — *Both* [indicates 2 cm]. — Shall we put a finger underneath to check? Now in they go. Is it like you said? — *Yes.* — Has it come down to the lady's finger? — *Not quite.* — But it did go down? — *Yes.* — Now I'll put another one in both again (making three each in *A* and *B*). — [Gab indicates a descent of about 1 cm.] — Put your finger underneath to see. (Weights in.) Is it right? — *Where* [she moves her finger upwards!]. Did you cheat just a little? — *No* [she means it]." Eight in *A* and none in *B:* "What do we do to make *A* go up? — *Put eight in there* [*B*]," but she is expecting a very slight rise of *A* and a slight descent of *B*, so is very surprised to see them level. "Now what if we add five to both? — "*That one* [*B*] *will go down* [by 3 cm]. — And the other? — *The same* [but indicating descent of 5 cm]. — Why? — *Because they are heavier on both the sides.* — [five added to both] — *It hasn't gone down!* — Why not? — *Don't know.* — [eight in each again]: "Now what if we take out two from here *(B)*? — *It will go down lower.* — And the other? — *Down as well.* — And if I take out all of the eight here (*B*)? — *It will be all empty and the other one* [*A*] *will go down.*" — And *B*? — *It will stay the same where it is.* — Will it? — *Or go down a little.* — And with none in *A* and eight in *B*? — *That* [*A*] *will stay still and that* [*B*] *will go down.*" — All weights removed. Then: "What if we put eight in *A* and eight in *B* like before? — *They'll both go down* [1 cm each]. — When? — *Both together.* [Weights placed. She cheats again.] *They've gone down.* — But didn't you cheat a little? — *No.*" Asked to make *A* rise (for example seven in *A* and eight in *B*), she is canny enough to add weight to *B*, but does not conclude from this that removing weight from *B* will make *A* go down. If there are four each in *A* and *B* and also on *A'* and *B'*, asked to predict what will happen if the four in *B* are moved to *B'*: "*B will go up because it will be more light.*" If a weight is hung from a string, *B* will go down 1 cm and *A* will rise 5 cm.

Jua (4-11) sees the analogy with a seesaw and predicts that one in *B* will make it swing in a horizontal plane. "*And then that one* [*A*] *will go up.* — And if I put one in *A*? — *It will touch the ground and that one* [*B*] *will go up.* — And with one in both? — *They'll both go down* [by 1 cm then 5 cm each]. *Can I try?* [He puts one in both simultaneously, and is amazed.] *Ah! It hasn't gone down! They've stayed the same both sides. But if I take away one from B, that* [*A*] *will go down.*" To keep both at the same height, he suggests "*one here* [*A*] *and some here* [*B*]," then by visual symmetry "*and some here* [*A*]." He succeeds without counting: "And if

I take one away from *B? — It [A] will swing to and fro* [left to right] *like that. —* Won't *B* go up? *— No. That one [B] will go up if we take the two rings off* [= everything from both pans]. How far? *— To there* [5 cm each side]. — If I empty *A* and leave some in *B*, will it go up? *— Yes, I think so. —* And *B? — It will stay like that* [same height]."

Pai (4–11): "*I've got a seesaw like that at home.*" He nevertheless predicts that with one in *B* and none in *A*: "*they will both swing like this* [horizontally]," then both will go down, but not at the same time. After he has watched what does happen, he predicts that with one in *A* and none in *B*, *A* will go down and *B* will go up. "And what if there is one in *A* and one in *B? — The'll both go down. —* Let's see *— Yes* [no] *they'll both go up. —* How do you know? *— Because I have a seesaw and I've already seen it happen.* [Weights in.] *No, they've stayed like that. —* And if I add one to each? *— They'll both go like that* [up or down]*...stay like that. —* Why? *— Because a lot of seesaws are like that.*" Later, having seen eight and eight produce equilibrium also, he thinks that if you add five and five "*That one [B] will go down. —* And the other? *— Up. —* Why? *— Because of putting five here and five there . . .* [no]*. . . it will go the same as it is. —* Which do you think? *Don't know.* [Weights on.] *Yes, because there's a lot there and a lot there* [symmetry]."

Del (5–0) thinks that with one in *B* and none in *A* "*It will swing* [both will go up and down vertically]. — And if I leave the one in *B? — It goes on swinging. —* Doesn't it stop at all? *— When you hold it it doesn't,*" otherwise "*it doesn't stop.*"

Cla (5–4). One in B: "*That will make it heavy. —* Will the pan move? *— No. —* And the other pan? *— No. —* Watch *— Well! It's tilted down [B].* — And *A? — It's gone up.*" One in *A*: "*It will go down and the other will stay up high,*" then *B* will go up, "*because the round thing is heavy,*" but *B* will not go up very much "*because that* [the pan] *isn't so big.*" Moreover one will go down "*before, and then that one will go up.* [Weight on.] *They went together.*" One in *A* and one in *B*: "*Both* [will] *go down together.*" With the weights on she is amazed to see the pans level, and again with eight and eight. "And what if I put on five and five now? *— Well, they'll both go down. —* Where to? *— Right down. At the same time. —* And with four and four? *— They'll stay* [in equilibrium]. *—* And with five more? *— They'll go down.* [Weights on.] *I wasn't right.*" A week later, one in *B*: "*It will go down. —* And *A? — That one too. —* How far? *— There* [10 cm] *—* Sure? *— It will stay up high. —* It won't move? *— No.* [Weight on.] *No. —* And one in *A? — I think the two will go down then come up again high the same as now. —* At the same time? *— Yes.* How does that happen? *— Because it's heavy.*" With two and two: "*They'll go down.* [Weights on.] *They don't go down. Because* *it's heavy they stay still.''* Eight in B: *"I'll put a lot in there [A] then they will come the same height. —* What if we take everything out of *A? — It will go down to the bottom* [down 50 cm]. — Why's that? — *Because there's nothing left. –* And *B?* — It will go up because it has some in. — And if we put five more in each one? — *Then they will both go down to the bottom.''* Then changes mind: predicts equilibrium but for four and four: *"It will go down.''*

Wic (5–10). Same predictions of simultaneous descents, and so on, then after demonstrations: *"I don't know any more, I don't think anything at all.''* Every question then gets the answer: *"You have to try and see,''* even with equal weights. And for eight and eight: *"It's stayed there again. If we said it would go up* [B, because A alone had the eight weights on at first], *that wasn't right.''*

Bis (5–11), on the other hand, makes a brilliant start: for one in B, and none in B, he predicts A down and B up, then the reverse for one in B and none in A. But for one in both: *"That one [B] will go up and that one [A] will go down to the bottom —* And if we put one more in each (now two and two)? *They'll both go down.* [Weights on.] *Hm! They stay the same. —* Why? — *Because we put in two and two, so it still stays up in the air. —* And with another one in each? — *That one [A] will go down and that one [B] will go down too. —* Both? — Yes. [Weights on.] *Ah! Always* [strong stress on always] *the same. —* Is that what we should expect? — *There's something wrong somewhere.''* Later, Bis perceives one method only to achieve equipoise: *"Take away everything out of there and there [A and B]. —* And like this (four in A, none in B)? — *It went down because they aren't the same. —* So what shall we do to make them level? — [Silence.], — Try. — *Put in ten [in B].''*

Can (6–6) displays analogous reactions despite his age. Moreover he thinks at the beginning that if there is one in A and none in B, then A *"will swing* [up and down] *and the other [B] won't.''* After the demonstration, when asked to predict the results of one in B and none in A, he thinks that B will swing while A *"will swing a bit but it will stop very quickly and the other one will go on.''*

Two previously acquired pieces of knowledge seem to be having a marked effect on these reactions, which taken as a whole seem to be beating all known records as far as number of contradictions is concerned. And not only do these two pieces of knowledge differ from each other, in that one is realtively stable whereas the other is quite the opposite, they also have the power to contradict one another. The first is that weights generally tend to move downwards, even though there are exceptions to this: Pai says that one in A and none in B will make "both go up" (having changed from "both go down"), but this may be a wrongly interpreted memory of his seesaw;

Cla, on the other hand, without referring to seesaws, thinks that if there are none in A and eight in B, then the former will go down because it no longer has to hold anything up, and the latter will go up, presumably because the weight is a strong force. The second piece of previously acquired knowledge, probably due to experience of seesaws (but in this case correctly assimilated), is that a weight moving downward at the end of a bar can cause the rise of another weight at the other end of that bar; and this is what Gab, Jua, Pia, Cla, and Bis all maintain at times. However, there are two fundamental circumstances limiting the application of this link at level 1A. One is that it is to some extent in contradiction with the tendency of weights to descend: hence the remarkable frequency among these 1A subjects of the idea that the two pans A and B at the two extremities of the beam will both move down when weighted (and then, but in fewer cases, both move up again if you take everything out, as Jua says). The second circumstance, which overlaps to some extent with the first, is that the behaviors of pan A and B (or of the weights in them) are seen as independent of each other, so that the beam is not viewed as providing any necessary link between them, as though in fact it were flexible and could accommodate any combination of movements.

It is clearly this lack of coordination between the two sides A and B of the scales that is the source of the innumerable incoherences evident in the subjects' replies: when one pan rises or descends, the other can do the same, the opposite, or stay where it is; when one goes up when the other goes down there is no equality in the changes of level, and the movements do not necessarily take place at the same time, since the rise can begin after the descent (and is never explained causally); when one of the pans swings (either horizontally or vertically) the other can do the same or remain stationary, and so on. The only really wise one is Wic, who concludes "I don't know any more, I don't think anything at all," and who, after having said that B would go up (with no weights in when A had eight already), announces that "that wasn't right" because with even weights (eight and eight) it remained stationary. The two problems that face us, then, are to establish whether this lack of coordination between A and B already constitutes a contradictory situation on its own, and, and second, to ascertain the nature of the contradiction it entails. Although, from the logical point of view, the hypothesis of an elastic beam permitting both pans to rise or fall together contains nothing contradictory, it must be pointed out, from the psychological point of view, that the subject does not in fact say or even clearly conceive anything of the kind. What he is trying to do is predict what one side of the scales will do with such and such a number of weights in it, and also, because it is requested of him, to anticipate the relation of that movement to the movement of the other side. Yet even after the subject has seen what actually happens in a number of cases, both kinds of prediction still present this amazing characteristic of almost total randomness, as if the effects of the weight on one side, and above all its repercussions on the other, present no element of necessity. In other words, the subject makes a minimum of inferences while seeming anxious to exploit the maximum of possibilities he can think up. Thus he will say in general that weight makes things go down, but never thinks that the addition of a weight must exclude the possibility of it making the pan go up (Pai even goes so far as to suppose at first that adding five to both pans when they are level will make one go up and the other down). A subject will sometimes say that if a weight makes one side go down the other will go up, but there is no inevitability involved (since they are usually both expected to go down), so that it is in no way excluded that the opposite may also happen.

From the point of view of contradiction, then, the situation is quite clear. There are no logical contradictions to be found, in the sense of a disagreement between inferred statements and definitions or premises, since there are no stable definitions or premises involved, and very little in the way of inferences. However, there is continual disequilibrium and incoherence of the thought process, since affirmations constantly triumph at the expense of exclusions or negations, whereas any coherent process of deduction must entail an exact compensation between the two. The lack of a functional link between the two sides of the scales is therefore the expression of a general absence of coordination, which cannot take place without necessary inferences, in other words, reversibility of operations. This emerges with particular clarity in the questions relating to equal weights, which one would have thought the simplest of all. In certain cases, the subject does predict equilibrium for reasons of symmetry (it will stay still with thirteen and thirteen, Pai says, "Because there's a lot there and a lot there," but only after having predicted that one side will go up and the other down), but there is still no question here of two contrary actions compensating one another, and Bis in particular, despite her outstanding start (B will go up and A will go down, and so on), thinks that there will likewise be a rise and a fall with one in A and one in B, then that both will go down if one adds two and two, and so on, and she ends by concluding: "There's something wrong somewhere." That is the only exclusion observed among all these subjects, and even then, as is only too apparent, what it excludes is the most rational relation of all.

§2. Level 1B

Onset of coordinations, but in one direction only.

Mar (5–9), for one in *B* and none in *A: "That one [B] a little lower and the other a little higher [A]. And if you put it there* [weight in *A*], *it's that one [B] that will go up. —* How far? — [Rise of 25cm fall of 7 cm.] — So it will go up more than the other goes down? — *Yes, because the little weight* [in *A* or *B*] *will make this weight* [the empty pan] *go up. —* And with one in *A* and one in *B? — Oh! You can't tell if that one [A] will go lower or if that one [B] will. —* How do you mean? — *There's no tell-ing . . . perhaps that one will go down, perhaps that one. —* Not both? — *No, not both, because if there's one that's heavy enough then the other will go up. And if that one goes down it will make that one go up. —* Do both these rings weigh the same? — *Yes. –* So? — *So they'll both go level with each other. —* Where? — *Here or here* [all possible heights down to the ground]." With eight in *A* he can think of no way to make *B* level with it. "How many are there in the pan? — *Eight. Ah! You have to put in eight."* But then, if you take one out of *B "it will go lower. —* Why? — *Because there'll be . . . no, it will go up, that one [A], because there'll be more rings in it,"* whereas the other will go down *"because there won't be so many rings."* Then, if all weights are removed from *A "that one [B] will go down because it's heavy. —* But didn't you tell me just now that it goes up when it's heavy? — *Ah! Yes, that's true, that's true. —* What do you think now? — *No, it will go down."* With five and five he still thinks you can't tell which will fall or rise, then concludes that *"it will stay the same size."*

Wou (5–3). One in *B: "It will go down* [indicates 10 cm fall]. — And the other? — *It will go up. —* How far? — [14 cm rise.] — With one in *A* and none in *B? — A will go down and B will go up. —* And with one in both? — *It will stay in the same place because they both weigh the same. —* And with five and five? — *It will stay the same height."* So far Wou would seem to have reached level 2A, but after the pans have been equalized with eight and eight: "If I take away one from *B? — It will go lower —* And if I add one to *A — It will be lower. —* And if I take one away from *A? — It [A] will go down and B will go up. —* And if I take one away from *B? — It will go up and A will go down. —* And if I take away all eight from *A? — It will go down —* Watch (eight removed from *A*) — [As soon as first weights removed] *It will go up, it will go up! —* (eight in *B* and none in *A*.) If I take one out of *B? — It will go up just a little,"* but for eight in *A* and none in *B*: "If I put eight in *B? — B will go down and A won't go up. —* Sure? — *No.* [She then demonstrates a small rise for *A* and a large fall for *B*.]" With weights on *B'* she thinks that it will go down further than with the same weight in *B "because there [B'] it's high up."* With eight and eight in *A* and *B*: "If I take one from *B* and add it to *B'? — That [B] will be lower. —* And two from *B* to *B'? — Lower still."* With two in *A* and two in *B*: "I'd like you to make *A* go up. — *If*

we put some more there [*B*], *the other will go up.* — But can you do it without putting any more on at all? — (Wou can't see the solution to that.)
What if I take one from *B*? — *It will go up, and the other down.* — And
to make *A* go up? — *You have to put one in B* — Isn't there another way?
— *No.* — None at all? — *No.*''

Fed (5–4). Same promisning beginning but ''*A will go up more than B
goes down because B had the weight.* — So *A* will be? — *Higher.*'' With
one in *A* and one in *B*: ''*That will make them the same size* [in
equipoise].'' With eight in *A* she succeeds in levelling the pans, but:
''What if I take one out of *B*? — *It will be lower.* — Which one? — *That
one* [*B*], *because it will have one missing.* — And if I take all eight out of
A? — It will be lower than B because it won't have its little weights then.
— And if we have five and five instead of eight and eight? — *It will be a
little bit higher.* — Which? — *Both* (indicates 4 cm higher than the level
position!).''

Jas (6–10). One in *A* and none in *B*: ''*That* [*A*] *will go down* [indicates 12
cm] *and that* [*B*] *will go up* [25 cm]. — It will go up more than it goes
down? — *Yes, because that one goes down to the bottom at the same
time, so it's heavy. That one* [*A*] *will be more heavy, so that one* [*B*] *will
be lighter still.* — Does *A* go down at the same time as *B* goes up?
—*No,*'' then hesitation and close scrutiny of the apparatus when the
weight is put on before deciding. ''And if we have one in *B* and one in *A*?
— *They'll be in the same place because they are both light.* — And if one
is added to *A* and one to *B*? — *That one* [*A*] *will go down a little bit, and
B will go down a little bit. So they will still be in the same place.* — Why
won't they move? — *They'll go down . . . wait . . . It will stay like it is.* —
Why? — *Because that one* [*A*] . . . *because that one* [*B*] . . . *because one
can't be heavier than the other.*'' Similarly with eight in both, but with
only seven in *B* ''*it will go down a little bit because it's less,*'' but after
that correct predictions.

Cri (6–3). Same correct predictions at the outset except that one falls
more than the other rises. Equilibrium correctly predicted for eight and
eight. ''And if I add five and five? — *Straight: both the same weight.* —
And if I put the five and five there and there (*A'* and *B'*)? — *Both the
same as they are.*'' But he thinks that both pans containing eight and
eight will then be slightly lower. On the other hand, with four in *A* and *B*
and four on *A'* and *B'*, he predicts that transferring two from *B* to *B'*
''*will make that* [*B*] *go down,*'' because it now has six on it.

Par (7–0). One in *B* will make it go down 4 cm and make the empty *A* rise
12 cm, but ''*one moves first,*'' because the weighted one has to move
down to begin with before it can make the other go up. Correct prediction of equipoise for eight and eight. But Par thinks that when you take

two out of *B* "*that one* [*B*] *should go up and* [*A*] *shouldn't go down.*" After the demonstration, however, he corrects his later predictions.

Generally speaking, level 1B is that of the development of constituent functions, which is to say of dependencies that are at once semilogical and semicausal because they are oriented in one direction only (that of "application"). In this particular case, each of our subjects does in fact predict that weight on one side of the scales always (or almost always: cf. Mar at the end) makes it go down, and that it "makes the other go up" (it is Mar again who uses this causal expression). So one side of the scales is already beginning to act on the other; but we are still not dealing with a reciprocity in the sense of compensation of weights oriented in opposite directions. In the first place, this rise of the light side under the influence of the heavy one is not accompanied by an equality in the variations of level, or even, frequently, by simultaneity: for Mar, *B* only goes down 7 cm when *A* rises by 25 cm because of the power *B* draws from its weight. In the second place, the action of an added weight in making a pan go down does not in any way entail—as we have already seen with B. Inhelder—comprehensions of the reciprocal action involved in removing a weight: for example, Wou thinks that if you take eight weights out of *A* "it will go down." And when faced with level pans each containing four weights, then asked to make one pan rise, all the subjects understand that one can increase the weight of the other pan, but not one thinks of diminishing the weight of the first. In the third place, and most important of all, the reasons for a state of equilibrium are still not at all well understood, and such equipoise is often wrongly predicted. For one and one, Mar thinks that one will go down but doesn't know which, and only reaches correct predictions of equipoise later by reasoning from symmetry (numerical). Wou does seem to have grasped that the level will be equal when "the two weigh the same," but her reactions to subsequent modifications of eight and eight show that she is basing her predictions solely on static symmetry (cf. Jas; the two are level because both are light) and in no way on compensations (cf. identical reactions from Fed). Cri correctly predicts the same level for equal weights, but that level changes according to the number of weights added on the beam above. Par also predicts equipoise for eight and eight, but if one removes two weights from one side then it will rise and the other will remain stationary.

So we have an interesting situation here from the point of view of contradiction. On the one hand, the subject is becoming capable of inferences and of detecting a certain regularity in the observed relations, as is apparent from the fact that after a plethora of uncertain and often contradictory affirmations at level 1A, he eventually comes to postulate that a particular action must (even in this unknown area) always lead to the same result. On the other hand, however, because of the usual persistent primacy of affirmations over negations, he still finds it difficult to conceive of contrary actions, such as removing a weight, and this leads to blanks in his understanding such as we have already noted, particularly where the notion of equilibrium is concerned. The result is, that although from this stage onward there is action of one side of the scales on the other, that action remains nonequilibrated and virtually contradictory because it lacks reversibility, or, in other words, complete compensation.

§3. Level 2A

Comprehension of the relations between the two sides of the system A and B, but initial incomprehension of their relations with the system $A'B'$:

Rot (6–6). One in A and none in B: "*It will tilt* [indicates a 12 cm fall for A and a 12 cm rise for B]. — The same amount here and there? — *Yes.* — This one won't go down just a little more? — *No, the same.* — Exactly? — *Yes.* — You're sure? — *Yes.* — Why? — *Because . . . I don't know. A goes down at the same time as B goes up.* — And if we add one in each? — *They'll stay there.* — Not go down? — *No.* — Not go up? — *No.*" Eight in A. He puts eight in B: "*so now that makes the same weight.* — And if we take two out of A? — *It will go up like that.* — And B? — *Will go down.* — The same amount as A goes up? — *No, yes, yes, the same.*" And he demonstrates 2 cm rise for A with 2 cm fall for B, a 4 cm rise for a 4 cm fall, a 6 cm rise for a 6 cm fall, and so on. With four in each pan: "What can we do to make A go up? — *Take one out of it* [A]. — Is there anything else we could do? — *Yes, if you want* [A] *to go down you can take some off* [B]. — But to make A go up? — *Nothing else.* — Can't you use the rings? — *Yes* [puts one in B]. *It goes up. Do you agree?*" Weights hung underneath A: "*It will go down.* — How far? — *Only a little. . . . No, the same as before. It's just like you were putting the ring inside.*" And hung by longer string: "*That won't make any difference.*" However, with the $A'B'$ system with one on A': "*It will make it go down not quite so much as if you put in A.* — Why is that? — *Because it's not so low down. It makes less weight.*" Then he changes his mind, but once again predicts a difference for B' and B, then corrects himself. Eight in A and eight in B: "What if we take two from A and put them on A'? — *It will stay the same. It makes the same weight.* — And eight from B to B'? — *It will still be the same weight. No, it will go down, because that will make eight here* [A] *and nothing there* [A']. — So it's B' that will go down? — *Yes, no it will go up* — Which one? — *That one* [pan B with nothing in]." But the predicted rises and falls compensate each other "*because it's as if you were putting a lot there* [A]

and nothing there [*B*]. — But is it peculiar: nothing there (*A'*) and eight there (*B'*)? — *Ah! Yes, it's the opposite . . . because A is as though you'd put more weight there* [*B*]. *Ah! No, it will make the same weight . . . because if you put them on there* [*A'* *and B'*] *it's as if you'd got them there* [*in A and B*]. *It's still the same weight."*

Iri (7–6), for one in *A* and none in *B* indicates a 12 cm fall for *A* and a 12 cm rise for *B*: *"It will be the same because A will go down a little bit and B will go up a little bit."* But then she accepts a contrary suggestion, and afterwards explains that *"both will go at the same time because that* [beam] *will move like that* [tilt toward *A*] *so that and that* [pans] *will move like that too."* For one in *A* and one in *B* she predicts that if one is added to each *"it will go to the same height. — Where? — There* [where it is with one and one]. — *They won't move? — No. — Not even a little? — They may just go down a little bit. No! They won't go down, because there and there are the same. Two rings. So that will make them the same height. They won't move."* Eight weights placed in *A*. Iri achieves equipoise by putting eight in *B*. *"And if we take two out of A? — A will go higher and B will stay still, no it will go down* (2.5 cm for a 1 cm fall in *A;* 5 cm for a 2 cm fall; 8 cm for a 3 cm fall, and so on)." With four in *A* and four in *B* how will she make *A* go up: *"I'll put in two, three, or one there* [in *B*]. — Is that the only way? — *Yes.* What if I tell you there's another answer? — *Yes, you can put one more there* [gesture as if to remove one from *A* to put it in *B*]. — Do you mean put it in *B*? — *Yes, or just taking it off.* — And if I wanted to make them both go up? — *That's impossible, because that* [beam] *can't go up.* — And if I add eight and eight, it won't go down? — *No.* — Even though it's so heavy? — *But that will only make them the same height, because that* [beam] *can't go down like that* [gesture of breaking the beam so that it slopes down on both sides]. *It can only move like this* [tilting either to *A* or *B*]." But despite these excellent explanations, Iri is unable to master the *A'B'* system right away. With one in *A'*, *A'* will move down 25 cm while the pan *A* will only go down 5 cm *"because A' will be heavier than A . . .* [and] *because when you put a ring in A' there's nothing in A."* But later, presumably influenced by her ideas about the beam linking *A* and *B*, Iri concentrates her thought entirely on equality of numbers (weights) and even resolves the problem of four in *A*, four in *A'*, two in *B*, and six in *B'* *"because four and four makes eight, and two and six makes eight too."*

Mat (7–10) thinks that with one in *A* it will go down the same distance that *B* rises, because *"A will go down and then that makes B go up the same."* In other words, the first movement governs the second.

Cat (7–5): *B* with one in goes down as much as *A* with none in rises *"because it's on just the one branch. But if it was sawed at there* [cut in

the middle] *that side [A] wouldn't go up.''* Equipoise predicted for eight
and eight "And if we add five and five? — *Well, nothing will happen.* —
What do you mean? — *It will stay where it is because it's the same
weight.''* Despite this accurate interpretation of the role played by the
beam, Cat thinks at first that a weight on *B'* "*will go down a little, but
less than if it was in the pan*" and that *A'* "*will go up a little less because
it's the same thing.''* The reason for this is that *the pan is lower down.''*
Then, when there are eight and eight in *A* and *B* she predicts that if
they're moved to *A'* and *B'* "*it won't change, I don't think, I'm not sure,
but I don't think it will.''*

Wol (8–5), to justify the equality of the rises and falls, and their simultaneity, demonstrates the movements of the pans with her hands: "*Because both will be like that, they have the same length of chains* [from
beam to pan].'' With eight in *A* and eight in *B*, she predicts a descent of
10 cm for a 1 cm fall from *B*, and "*if you take out two rings, that makes
twice as much down, like this* [20 cm]. To make *A* rise from a level four
and four "*you need to put on one here [B]*" or "*you can take one out of
A and put it in B.''* Nevertheless, even despite the initial remark about
the equality of the chains, Wou at first thinks that the weight weighs
more on *B'* than in *B*, and that the pan will move 4 cm lower "*because B
was low down and that [B'] is high up, so there's all that* [the chains] *and
there's more weight with all that.''* On the other hand, there is still
equality of rises and falls "*because it's the same plank* [= beam] *and it's
fastened in the middle* [= the arms are equal].''

Cyr (9–3), similarly answers all the *A* and B questions correctly, but
thinks that when you move a weight from *B to B'* "*it will go down because it's heavier.''* Does it do the same work, a weight in *B* and in *B'* ?
— *Yes, those in the pan push down, and those up above push a bit more
than the ones down below.''* But later he comes around to the idea of
them exerting equal forces.

Mic (9–9), for eight in *A* and eight in *B'* (after having predicted equality
with the eight in *B*), hesitates between "*I think they'll stay equal*" and
inequality: "*Because that* [pan suspended from beam] *is already pulling
down, it's heavy already anyway* [the pan by itself]. *So if you put the
weights here* [in *A*] *it pulls more underneath* [the beam] *and so it goes
even lower.''* Cf. Jac (10–3): "*it's heavier down low. It goes a little
lower.''*

Bur (9–11) thinks that a weight on *B'* weighs more "*because there's the
bar* [beam] *too, that adds some weight.''* Then later: "*On this side [B']
the wood is doing something, but . . . that doesn't matter. There's the
same weight on both sides* [A or A' and B or B'].''

Mul (9–1) starts by affirming the equality of upward and downward motions with weight on A or B: *"for it to do anything else you need to put it* [weight] *nearer the middle or nearer the end of the bar* [beam]." After which he hestitates between inequality of A and A' (*"you'd need to do sums to be sure"*) and equality because *"the bar was there when the weight is in A."* This line of argument attains the 2b level.

Kug (10–10) also begins by saying that B' will weigh more than B *"because up there it's wood* [the beam on which the B' weight rest directly] *and wood is heavier than the plate* [pan]." But later: *"No, the longer thing* [beam] *has the same weight even if you put* [the weights] *in the plate."* Again, Kug has reached 2B.

The interest of the reactions at this level lies in the fact that the subjects succeed in mastering the system of relations between pans A and B by using arguments they could perfectly well apply to the higher weights on the beam (A' and B'), yet they fail to do so, or do not do so right away, as the result of a time lag that needs to be explained.

As far as the AB system is concerned, these subjects have at last come to understand that the weights positioned in the pans on opposite sides of the scales both act in the same way, but in opposition to one another and in constant interaction. This is something we already knew from previous research, which had further related this advance to the constitution of reversible operations, which, among other things, enables a subject who is asked to make pan A rise in a four and four situation either to add a weight to B or remove one from A.

As far as contradiction is concerned, this composition of direct and inverse or reciprocal operations leads to cognitive equilibrium through compensation of affirmations and negations, while at the same time enabling the subject to understand the reason for physical equipoise when using equal weight. In this respect, it is worth noting the appearance of expressions, not met with at previous levels, that signify exclusion: "it's impossible" to make two weights go up at once, Iri says, for example, because "that [beam] can't go up or down" but only tilt on its pivot. Other reciprocal expressions, moreover, indicate an inferential necessity: the equal distances travelled by the two pans when one rises and the other falls, for example, or their simultaneity of movement, are affirmed deductively on the basis of the beam's oneness (and, implicitly, its nonflexibility). Examples of this are to be found in Iri, Mat, Car, and Wol.

This understanding of the role played by the beam therefore makes it all the more surprising that these 2A subjects display an initial resistance to incorporating the A' and B' positioning of the weights on this same beam into the set of interactions they have by now completely grasped. The arguments justifying these hesitations are of two kinds. The first kind we are familiar with from our research into the causality of weight: the latter is in practice thought to act differently according to whether it is positioned toward the top of a piece of apparatus or lower down, since its action consists in pressing or pulling downwards. The second kind consists in invoking the weight of the beam itself, or of the chains holding up the pans, as if those factors in fact add to the action of the weights. Whichever kind of argument is used, however, the subject hesitates in generalizing what he has clearly understood with regard to the positions A and B to include positions A' and B'. But as we see from Mul's and Kug's final statements, the answer to these difficulties is that the previously mentioned factors were already at work in the AB situation, since, as Mul says, the beam "was [already] there when the weight was in A."

§4. Level 2B and Conclusions

These level 2B subjects at last experience no difficulty in applying to the relations between the AB and $A'B'$ systems the same arguments, based on the symmetry and cohesion of the different parts of the scales, that level 2A subjects were already applying to the relations between sides A and B.

Lac (9–9) says firmly that moving a weight from A to A' (with one in B) will make no difference: "*No, because you have the same weight and it's the same on the same axis* [beam]." For eight in B, six in A, and two on A': that makes no difference "*because the two up above are up above, so they press just the same. It's pressing down the same on both sides.*"

Fur (9–11)). A and B: "*It pulls up the weight* [A] *exactly, because if B goes down that far, then it must make A go up because it's part of the scales.*" And B' is equivalent to B "*because it's still on the same side, it still has the same effect.*"

Bol (10–2). B' instead of B: "*It's the same as before. The important thing is that it's held . . . on the scales* [meaning that the scale's two sides are always interdependent)"

Bri (10–11): "*It comes to just the same thing, because it's the weight makes the scales go down. So whether it's up high or down low doesn't matter.*"

Mon (11–5): "*It's just as if they were in the plate . . . it doesn't make any difference because the stick stays straight.*"

The answers given at the eleven- to twelve-year level (stage 3) add nothing to those of the level 2B subjects from the point of view of contradiction, but merely provide more advanced causal explanations.

Where the coordination of the two systems AB and $A'B'$ is concerned, no further problem is encountered. It has been solved by means of an argument that is an extension of Mul's and Kug's final answers at the previous level: the scale forms a whole in which everything is connected, so that the weight of the rings is exerted on the whole of it in the same way, whether they are placed in the pans or on the beam itself.

In conclusion, if we look back over the reactions from level 1A to level 2B, as a whole, the first thing we notice is that the initial contradictions of the four- to five-year olds, or, more precisely, the incoherences between their actions and successive predictions undoubtedly derive from the three factors constantly encountered before. The first is that at this elementary level one and the same action is thought capable of leading to differing results: the weight of an object can make it rise, even though it is ordinarily a cause of descent. The second is that an action and its opposite do not produce complete compensations: by adding more weights to a pan already containing weights one makes it go down, but the same thing may happen if one takes weights out. The third is that the inferences involved do not result in the drawing of necessary consequences, but allow hesitations or partial incoherences to persist. Moreover, as we saw in section 1, the common reason for these disequilibriums is the constant primacy of the subject's continual flow of affirmations over the negations or exclusions involved, to which these younger children pay hardly any attention at all. This is, in fact, the same thing as saying that the three factors mentioned above are merely three distinct manifestations of one and the same process. The two first factors, indeed, can be viewed as a dual unit, since they both boil down in the end to a single argument: if the same action can give rise to contrary results, then, correlatively, two contrary actions can lead to the same result. As for the lack of necessity evident in the inferences drawn, chapter 2 has already shown that it can be reduced to the conjunction of these two deficiencies, and our observations in this case can serve to corroborate that point of view to a considerable extent.

To account for the processes that lead from this early stage to that of equilibration, one might limit one's explanation to saying that, since any contradiction springs from a lack of compensation between affirmations and negations, equilibration simply comes from a progress in the reversibility of operations. And since our scale constitutes precisely the kind of physical phenomenon in which the laws of equilibrium happen to be found at their simplest and their most isomorphic with regard to operatory reversibility, such an explanation would seem to be broadly sufficient, since in this case the observable facts are immediately assimilable to the deductive model they confirm. The only trouble with this, of course, is that the problem has merely been displaced, not in any way resolved: it is clear from the 1B reactions, in fact, that subjects can perfectly well predict equipoise with equal weights by reasoning from simple symmetry, and without actually grasping the compensation involved between ponderable actions in opposite directions. The real question, therefore, is to understand how the subject progresses to reversibility solely by regulating initially uncoordinated actions, taking that reversibility as a necessary point of arrival, not as a factor from which the process starts (which would explain nothing, since it is precisely the advances in reversibility we need to explain).

In the preceding results, the development to be interpreted is particularly simple: at level 1A the subject views the various actions of a single object as being quite separate, but a single action can lead to different results; at level 1B each object can act upon another, but still only in a unidirectional way; on level 2A there is interaction, the second object acting in return in accordance with the same forms as the first, but within a single system, AB or $A'B'$, only; finally, at level 2B the two systems react upon each other. This presents us with two problems: how does the subject react to the initial disequilibrium, and by what processes does the subject achieve equilibration?

The initial disequilibrium is troubling to the subject because it prevents him from predicting and comprehending successive events, and thus presents an obstacle to the subject's general assimilative tendencies. Hence a double accommodation that manifests itself at first by simple advances in awareness: in the case of action tending toward a goal (making a pan rise, and so on), attention is focussed on the perturbation, but in the case of anticipations or inferences, this is complicated by the addition (under the influence of real perturbations) of a gradually increasing feeling that there may be other possible perturbations present, in other words, noncompensated virtual tasks. Thus, although paying no attention at first to the second side of the scale when acting upon the first, the level 1A subject, when faced with the failure of his predictions, cannot help but begin to ask himself question about the possible influence exerted by the other weights, which puts him on the path toward level 1B. Similarly, the 1B subject, with his unidirectional inferences, is sooner or later obliged to feel his way toward the idea of a reciprocal action originating in the second side of the scale, which will then lead him to level 2A.

The equilibration itself is due, as usual, to the regulations these perturbations provoke. It is essential to remember, however, that the regulating mechanism does not consist, in the case of reversibility, in simply correcting the initial erroneous interpretations (in this case the irreversible links conceived of by stage 1 subjects) in order to substitute for them the idea of weights exerting reversible actions as just one concept among others. In reality, by first compensating the perturbations encountered in the action to various degrees, and then, more subtly, those imagined by the subject's thoughts during the course of his suppositions (virtual cognitive tasks), the regulations introduce, *ipso facto,* a progressive reversibility in the subject's actual actions (adding or removing weights, equalizing and achieving equipoise in the interplay of decreasing differences, and so on), and it is then this equilibration of actions that is translated conceptually by the explanatory model that enables the initial contradictions to be overcome. In short, this progressive compensation of positive and negative actions, or of affirmations and negations, constitutes an autonomous functional mechanism long before being conceptualized in an operatory form by means of a set of reflective abstractions, and this is why the essential motive force of this development is not logical contradiction (consciousness and manipulation of which presuppose this operatory completion) but rather a reaction to the successive disequilibriums of the action. It has therefore been of no small interest to verify this role played by the disequilibriums of the actions themselves (or predictions as anticipated actions), then by their equilibration, in an area where the reversibility of the process can apparently be discovered from a simple reading of the observable facts, which seem in this case to be particularly transparent. In fact, however, this adequate reading of the facts proved to be possible only after the subjects had succeeded, by means of an equilibrated coordination of their own actions, in implicitly postulating the three fundamental conditions of noncontradiction: that the same action necessarily leads to the same results; that two contrary actions compensate one another exactly; and that any valid inference must include as many exclusions as necessary consequences. It is only when this indispensable stability on the level of how the actions themselves function has been achieved that the observable phenomena provided by the scales manifest their intrinsic reversibility, whereas beforehand it remains unperceived. In a word, it is equilibration here that explains operatory reversibility, and not vice versa. And it is disequilibrium that is the starting point of the subject's progress, not contradiction expressed in a logical form (and by that very fact already overcome).

Seven

Progressive Coherence in the Interpretation of
Mirror Images and Refraction

with J. P. Bronckart (sections 1 to 5) and A. Cattin (section 6)

We saw in chapter 5 that contradiction between an anticipation and a fact that belies it does not differ in any essential way from contradictions between schemas, except that, when the fact is physical in nature, the overcoming of the contradiction cannot be deduced, but is subordinated to a sequence of further observations that complicate the model's coherence and can be the source of further contradictions. It may be of interest, therefore, to study this question in the light of essentially spatial optical phenomena, such as reversed images in a mirror, since the space involved presents a double nature according to whether it is the spatial properties of objects or the geometry of the subject's actions that are being considered. The contradictions studied in this chapter will thus be of two kinds. First, if the reversal of letters of the alphabet is viewed by the subject as a general phenomenon, what will he make of the particular case represented by symmetrical letters? Second, if it has been predicted or observed that a subject's left arm appears in a mirror to be his right arm, what will that arm point at when extended in one direction or the other?

Technique

The procedure for this experiment employs letters of the alphabet. One begins by showing the subject an asymmetrical capital letter on a card, say a capital B, and asking him to draw it. The card is then faced toward a mirror and the subject asked to draw the letter's reversed image as seen in the glass. After this simple observation of a mirror image, other asymmetrical capital letters are shown in succession, L, E, K, R, and so on, which the child copies direct from the card. Then a drawing of how each will appear in the mirror is requested. In practice, even the youngest subjects predict their reversal from the outset, and then go on to conclude that the phenomenon is a general one in obedience to a law that can be expressed as follows: in the mirror, all the letters are (or become) the wrong way round. Once this has been established, one offers in succession a number of counter-examples, A, T, M, H, asking once again for a drawing of the letter itself, then one of what it will look like in the mirror. Reaction to the contradiction is thus studied on two levels: that of action and that of verbal explanation. The most significant elements are generally observed at the action level: turning the A upside down, for example, or drawing it from right to left. Then, after the subject's predictions have been checked against the reality, the law is discussed verbally, to see how the subject modifies it, or possibly seeks to justify it despite what he has seen. This main experiment with the reversal of letters was then completed with a number of less systematic questions, two of which gave interesting results. First, asking the subject to do something ("anything you like'') with an *L,* for example, so that it will look "the right way round" in a mirror. At a certain level the subject then held up a reversed *L* (⌐) to the mirror with a correct anticipation of his reversal begin reversed. Second, an *L* on a transparent plastic card was presented to see if the subject could use it to produce the same double reversal. Two other sample tests produced no worthwhile results. First, seeing if the subject found it disturbing that a capital *A* produces no reversal whereas a lower case *a* does. In fact, none of the subjects found this at all problematical. Second, to find out if a reversed letter can become another letter to the child (as with *p* and *q*), or whether the qualitative identity of the *p* predominates even after reversal. In fact, the latter was often the case among the younger subjects, but this was merely a demonstration of their attachment to the law and the right-way-round/wrong-way-round dichotomy.

As for the second experiment, involving the reversal of the subject's left and right sides in the mirror, the technique for that will be found in section 4. The analysis of refraction will then be given in section 6.

§1. Level 1A

Apart from two five-year-olds who failed to master the law through lack of interest and active reaction, the acquisition of the underlying regularity was rapid, even among those still unable to read.

Ala (5–1) recognizes *K* as "*a letter!*" and copies it correctly. When he sees it in the mirror he first draws another *K* then reverses it: "Tell me what it's like. — *It goes to the left . . . The wrong way round.*" For *B* he anticipates "*to the left*" immediately, and repeats "*the wrong way round.*" Same prediction for *E,* the only letter he already knew. For *M* he predicts Ш without hesitation: "Tell me what it's like. — *The wrong way round. — And this one (B reversed)? — Wrong way round too. —* He predicts *T* upside down. "Look (in mirror). What's it like? — [Silence.] — Can you draw it the way you can see it in the mirror? — [*T:* correct.] — And Ǝ and ⌐, they're the wrong way round? — *Yes, both the wrong way round. —* Is it the same sort of wrong way round? — *No, because the ⌐ isn't right.*" Same reaction for *M:* "But has the letter changed? — *Yes. —* What? — *The bars aren't quite the same. —* And aren't *T* and *T* the same letters? — *No* [he points out differing details in the horizontal, then changes his mind]. — So should we say that there are some letters that change and some that don't? — *Yes. —* (He is given all the letters of the alphabet.) Now makes me two little piles: the ones that change and the ones that don't. — [Errors in the cases of *A, X, U, Q, K.*) — How would you explain it all then? — *All those* [nonchanging letters] *don't work: they're not in the alphabet.*" But at a later stage in the questioning, when asked again to predict A in the mirror, he draws it upside down, then correctly predicts reversal for a lower case a.

Mur (5–5) draws both *E* and *E* reversed in the mirror correctly, then immediately predicts correct reversals for *B* and *R*. With *A* she predicts an upside down image, then observes: *"Ah! It's like that [A]. I didn't know. I thought it would be like that* [upside down] *in the mirror."* H: *"They're not quite the same, you can't make it turn around."* She divides the alphabet up according to the two categories but makes mistakes over *I, Y, T, P, J, R, C, N,* and *Q.* "How would you explain it all? — *Those don't roll over, and those do roll over.* — *K* and *X*, if you see them in the mirror, they don't do the same (in her classification). Why not? — *Because K can be different and not that one.* — Why is that? — *Because the two bars there* [oblique strokes of *K*] *can go around to the other side, and the X can't.* — Can we say there are two groups of letters? — *Yes, those that change and those that don't change."*

Cat (5–10), after seeing *B* in the mirror, generalizes: *"When a letter's in the mirror it's the wrong way round."* Followed by correct predictions for *L, E,* and *R.* For *A,* she at first predicts *"the right way round"* then isn't so sure. *T* and *M*, however, she predicts upside down. After being shown what does happen, Cat concludes that *"they [A, T,* and *M] are all the right way round"* because *"with L there is the bar on both sides, but not with J.* — Explain what difference that makes. — *I don't know."* In classifying the letters she makes mistakes over *G, S, Q, Z, J,* and *N,* all of them in the same (reversible) class.

Pat (5–10) turns *A* upside down so as to change *"the little sticks."*

Rit (6–0). Correct anticipations for *E, L,* and *R* after having seen *B,* but predicts *T* upside down, then leaves *M* the right way round *"because the sticks can't turn."* K: *"It's turned around* [after correctly predicting that it would]."

Mar (6–6). A: *"You can't draw it because you can't turn it round* [even though she had in fact drawn Ɐ]. — So in the mirror? — *It will still be the right way round."*

The remarkable point about these initial reactions is that the law discovered by the subjects (since they all actively generalize their observation of the first letter and incorporate it into their subsequent predictions) is conceived of from the outset as referring, not to positional relationships with regard to the mirror or the presentation of the letter cards, but to the properties of those letters as objects, as if they were materially modified by the mirror. Thus Ala says that *K* "goes to the left . . . the wrong way round," and when he perceived the fact that all letters do not obey his law, he regards the letters that do not conform to it as not belonging to the alphabet, and thus as not being real letters. Mur says that the letters "roll around" or "don't roll around" and that "you can't make A turn around" as though it were a badly constructed mobile; similarly, he thinks that K's "two [oblique] bars" "can go around to the other side, and the X can't," whereas by stage 2 these segments of X will be seen as changing sides, but without one being able to perceive the fact they all look the same. Cat seems at first to have understood more fully, but in practice reasons in just the same way, since she thinks the T's two bars are preventing it from rotating. Pat turns the A upside down in order to change "the little sticks," which both Rit and Mar say "you can't turn around."

In a word, for want of the necessary distinction between an object and its image—the latter being regarded as a kind of emanation or material reflection of the former—the reversal of the letter in the mirror appears to the subject as being caused by real movements that materially modify a duplicate of the object. Conceived in this way, the law obviously ought not to permit exceptions, thus leading to the inversion of T into ⅃ and so on, without distinction between "wrong way round" meaning reversed, and "wrong way round" meaning inverted. (When Ala recognizes that it is not "the same wrong way round" he simply means that ⅃ "isn't right" in the sense that it is not confirmed by his observations.) When, faced with the facts, the subject is forced to admit these contradictions, he does not see them as the sign of a wrong interpretation, or of an incomplete and thus incorrect statement of the law, but seeks an explanation instead in resistances inherent in the object, whose elements or parts refuse "to roll" or to let themselves "be turned." In fact, then, the contradiction continues to exist in the subject's mind, not just from our point of view, but, also in his own inferences, as is made clear by the absence of all coherence when it comes to classifying the letters into those modified by the mirror and those that remain the same. For example, Cat, even though she had verbally agreed that A, G, and M all remain "the right way round," thinks later on, when classifying the alphabet, that G, S, W, Z, J. and N behave in the same way.

§2. Level 1B

This level, intermediate between the initial reactions of level 1A and the comprehension of the role played by symmetry and asymmetry that will be reached in stage 2, is characterized by two new developments: first, hesitation between the two ways of treating those letters that seem to appear in the mirror "the right way round"; second, an attempt at interpretation that is centered, not on the properties of the object as before, but on the actions of a subject, in some cases those of the experimenter (who it is thought may be turning the cards in a particular way), in others that of the child herself, who may be drawing the letter a different way round from that used in proper writing. Here are some examples:

Iré (5–10) correctly anticipates the reversal of *K*, *E*, and *L*. This leads to the law: *"The letters are the wrong way round when they're in the mirror."* For *T:* persistent hesitation between ⅃ and *T:* *"The bar doesn't change. — Is T the wrong way round? — No, the right way. — Which do you choose? — That one [⅃]."* For *A:* *"If you turn the card it will be the wrong way round. — How do you mean? — Like that [Ɐ]. — How do you know that A is still A in the mirror? — You can't change it. — And T? — No. — What about like this (a small circle attached to the left of the horizontal)? — The round changes sides. — What about the T? — The T doesn't turn . . . the T doesn't change because there's no little round."*

Luc (5–4). After predictions: *"Do you think they're all the wrong way round, the letters in the mirror? — Yes. — Always? — No, because if you put it there* [left side of mirror] *it's the right way round and there* [on right side] *then they're the wrong way round* [that is, oriented toward the left like *E*, *K*, *L*, or *R*, all correctly anticipated in mirror]." For *T* he draws nothing, then predicts *T* in the mirror. *"Is that right* [card held to mirror]? *— Yes, — Is it the right way round or the wrong way? — The right way. — And M?* [He draws it from right to left, thus conforming with his rule about the position of the cards.] *— Are the two M's* (copied then anticipated) *the same? — Yes. — And how are they? — One is the right way round, the other is . . . the right way round."* Same reaction for *A*, which he draws from right to left in anticipation of the mirror image.

Fra (5–7). Same reaction, but he says of the *A* drawn from right to left: *"It's the wrong way round,"* then: *"No, it's still the right way round, because it always has to be the right way round."* Classification of alphabet: many errors and no explanations.

Tié (5–6), after a series of correct anticipations with the asymmetrical letters, is presented with an *H*, which he tries to turn round: *"It will be the same, because there are the two bars there, and that makes it the same."* However, this is only his reading of a local result and not yet a general intuition foreshadowing stage 2, since his anticipation for *M* is drawn right to left and *"it's the same too."* Then for *A* he does the same and accepts *A "if you show it in the mirror, if you show it the wrong way round* [meaning upside down]. *— Is that the only way it can be the wrong way round? — No, like this* [on its side pointing left, or with one of its sloping sides drawn vertical, or on its side pointing right]. *— Do you know why the A doesn't change? — No."* Classification of letters:

he makes a series of trial reversals, and for letters without apparent reversal retains only *N* (wrong), *I, H, O,* and *X.* "How would you explain that there are some letters that change and some that don't? — *The ones that don't change, you put them like that, then they don't change!* — But how can you tell before you see them in the mirror? — *The R is put like that* [he turns the card upside down]."

Val (6–0) also produces an upside-down *A,* because "*you can't put it the wrong way round any other way. But a little a* [which he hasn't been shown], *that can be put the wrong way round like the others.* — And do you really think that Ɐ is what you're going to see in the mirror? — *Yes.* — Look. — *No, it's the right way round! It's a trick: you put it the right way and the others were the wrong way! All these letters* [*L, K, B*] *were the wrong way and the A has been put the right way.* Explain. — *Because the L you can put the wrong way, and the K too, and the B too, but not the A, so that's how it is* Ɐ *the wrong way, and I don't see why it hasn't been put like that in the mirror* [she turns card upside down to show what it should be]. — But is it just like the *B,* the *K,* and the *L?* — *No, you can also put the L the wrong way round another way* [she draws Γ]." Now *T:* Val predicts ⌐L. "Do you think it will really be like that? — *I don't know, but I think it will be like that: you can make* ⊣ *though, or this* [⊢]. — But do you really think it will look like that? — *No, like this* [T drawn obliquely from left to right]. *But it can be like this too* [*T:* correct]. — And *H?* — *Well I say it will be the right way round, because T and A you could put them the wrong way round but then they weren't the wrong way round.*" Classification: she is wrong over *W, N,* and *V,* and can offer no explanation.

Car (7–2) anticipates that the *K* will change and turn "*to the right*" because "*you've folded it.*" The initial general law becomes "*some of the letters become the wrong way round, and the others stay straight,*" but she can't make up her mind whether *T* changes "*because the bar* [horizontal] *will be the other side,*" or whether it doesn't change "*because it ought to go the right way.*"

Ber (7–2), like Luc, thinks that whether the letter changes its orientation or not depends upon the placing of the image in the mirror: "*If you put E on the other side of the mirror* [not at the back of it but further to one side] *it will come the same in it.*"

These children's general interpretation is thus different from that of the previous level in that it now centers on action factors (displacements dependent upon a subject) or positional factors, and no longer on the properties of the object. The general idea common to all these answers, even though it may not be explicitly formulated (though it sometimes is), is that "the wrong way round" means oriented toward the left and "the right way round" means oriented toward the right, that being the way these particular children write. Hence the curious idea, which occurs to both Luc and Ber, that the image will be the right way round on one side of the mirror (right or left) and the wrong way on the other. And hence too, later on, Val's persistent belief that the experimenter is orienting the cards to face this way or that at will, a hypothesis echoed by Tié ("the ones that change, you put them like that, then they don't change"), by Car ("because you've folded it"), and implicitly by many others (for example when Fra says of the A that "it ought always to be that way round" meaning "the right way"). It is thus this explanation by active orientation on the experimenter's part that accounts for the interesting behavior encountered in six of our subjects, which consists in drawing their A or M, for instance, from right to left, in the hope of reversing them despite such orientation, while Iré, Tié, and Val all say that you could also have turned A into Ɐ because "if you turn the card it will be the wrong way round" (Iré). One can compare Tié's "if you show it upside down," and Val's "you could put them the wrong way round but then they weren't the wrong way round," and earlier "I don't see why it hasn't been put like that in the mirror." It should be noted that these subjects are partly in the right, since it is necessary to turn the card round in order to face it into the mirror. But what they presumably imagine is that by turning the card one is reversing the letter itself (making L into Ⅎ, for example), and so believe, at certain moments anyway, that it is possible to control which way the letters appear in the mirror independently of the action of the mirror itself.

All this being so, it goes without saying that the law of mirror reversal takes on a quite different meaning from that attributed to it when it was seen as the expression of material processes inherent in the object. It now expresses simply what the mirror reflects according to the particular way in which the letters are presented to it. As a result, the exceptions to the reversal law are no longer contradictions, since they derive from different actions. At level 1A, only one action, always the same, was involved: that of sending the object into the mirror. As a consequence, all noninversions were attributed to resistances in the object, which wouldn't "turn" properly. At level 1B, on the contrary, the reversals or nonreversals of the letters are due to distinct actions directed towards distinct goals. But this, too, compromises the generality of the law (as stated, for example, by Car).

Now what the subject is beginning to sense, without yet understanding it, is that these positional relations he invokes are not confined to the relationship between letter and mirror, but also involve the connections between the various parts of the letter, and vary according to whether those parts are alike or not. The only way of generalizing the law without contradiction consists in effect in recognizing, as stage 2 subjects will, that reversal always takes place, but that if the reversal involves like elements (horizontal halves of *T*, oblique strokes of *A*, and so on), then they cannot be discerned, and the letter appears unchanged. In fact, as we have just seen, certain 1B subjects at certain moments are clearly on the verge of such an intuition: Tié senses something of the sort with *T*, and Car wonders whether the bar of the *T* "will be on the other side" or won't change, and so on. In other words, these subjects have taken a great step forward, in relation to level 1A, by discovering the role of positional relations, but because they have not yet grasped the role of symmetry and asymmetry, and therefore failed to generalize the spatial considerations within the figures presented, they do not succeed in reconciling the law with its apparent exceptions, in other words, in removing the contradictions logically.

There is one group of six subjects that merits special attention, because it represents a transitional phase between the 1B group and the stage 2 group. These six succeed in predicting the visible inversions and noninversions correctly, and sometimes almost grasp the purely apparent character of the latter, yet fail as yet to comprehend the role played by symmetry.

Tha (6–2) predicts the inversion of *E, L, K,* and so on, saying each time, in accordance with general 1B opinion: "*it will be to the left.*" For *T,* she anticipates "*to the left again,*" but after hesitation draws an ordinary *T* identical to her copy of the card itself: "How is that one then (prediction-drawing)? — *It's to the left.* — And that one (copy of letter)? — *It goes to the right and that one* [the prediction] *goes to the left!.*" The same for *A:* "*It is the wrong way round.* — The same as that one (*A* copied from card)? — *Yes.*"

And (6–6): all the letters are "the wrong way round," but he predicts right away that *A* "*will be the right way because it has two bars going up, two leaning bars*" (but still not isolating symmetry as such). As for *T:* "*You can only change it to upside down, and the others you can put the wrong way round* [laterally]."

Eri (6–11). Again his predictions are all correct. "How do you know if the letters change or not? — *I look at the bars.* — And why do these [groups of asymmetrical letters after his classification]? — *Because they don't have bars like that* [horizontal]."

Lie (6–11): same argument as And for *A.* No errors apart from *Q* in the classification, but explanation no different from Eri's: you have to "*look at the bars.*"

It is apparent from these answers that this group, all of typical 1B level age (except for one seven-year-old), are groping toward the idea of symmetry without quite being able to grasp it. Moreover, the youngest of the group does actually reach the notion (second characteristic of stage 2) that the *A* and the *T* have in fact been reversed while remaining identical in appearance to their initial state.

§3. Stage 2 and Additional Material

The two joint characteristics of stage 2 are thus the discovery of symmetry and generalization of the reversal process even when it produces no apparent change.

Yve (6–11): "*When you put the letter the right way round at* [in front of] *the mirror, you see it the wrong way round in it. —* All the letters? — *Yes, all of them. —* The *T? — It looks the right way round. But it isn't really. You see it the right way round, but . . . *" The same with *A: "It is as though it's the right way round."* Classification into categories: no errors. "*I made the letter the wrong way round in my head.*" And in order to obtain a rectified asymmetrical letter in the mirror "*you put it the wrong way round on the paper and then it's the right way in the mirror* [double reversal]."

Lau (6–10). No hesitation over predictions: "*There are letters the right way round and letters the wrong way round. —* How do you tell which are which? — *The ones that change aren't the same both sides* [symmetry]."

Asc (7–0). For *A:* "*Because if you turn it like that it stays the same. —* But it's the wrong way round all the same? — *Yes. —* And it's changed in the mirror? — *Not at all.*"

Joe (7–5): "*With the A it's always the same because the two sides are the same. The I is the same.*" No errors in classifications.

Dom (7–6): "*The ones that change aren't the same on both sides. —* And the ones that don't change, do they turn or don't they? — *they're turned the other way, but what you see is just the same.*" To obtain a non-reversed image of *L*, Dom draws it already reversed: "*If you draw them the wrong way round on the paper, then they're the right way in the mirror.*"

Ver (7–6): *M* is not reversed "*because when you turn it any side it comes to the same thing,*" like *A* and *T*. Then he corrects himself: "*If you do it like that* (lateral rotation) *it will be the same. But like that* (upside down) *it won't be.*"

Pha (8–2): "*The mirror puts them in the other direction,*" but with *A* "*you see it in the right direction all the same,*" "*because that letter has the same shape on both sides.*"

So we see that after having attributed the reversals to real movements

within the object-reflection in relation to the object of which it is the emanation (level 1A), then to positional relations or to displacements seen as
changes of position (level IB), the subject comes to generalize the notion of
reversal, so that it is now seen as the result of positional changes within the
figure itself and eventually transpositions of its parts. Thus the reversal law
becomes general, even in the case of apparent nonchanges, and the contradiction is removed, since the relation between the normal cases and those
that appear to constitute exceptions is no longer relative to anything but the
subdivision of the figures into asymmetrical and symmetrical, thus forming
two subclasses that both obey the rule.

Before investigating what these facts tell us about the theory of contradiction, however, I should like to summarize the results of two complementary
experiments which it would be tedious to recount in any great detail at this
point.

The first concerns reversal of reversal. One shows the subject a letter such
as L drawn on a card, and asks him to do anything he likes so that it will
appear "the right way round" in the mirror. Seven subjects out of about
twenty (all between seven and eight) spontaneously drew a reversed L, as
we noted earlier in the cases of Yve (6–11) and Dom (7–6), who formulate the
law. Four subjects between six years, eight months and eight began with an
ordinary L then turned it around because, as one of them remembered "the
mirror makes the letters change sides." As for the rest, they either managed
nothing or made a variety of attempts before succeeding, though it is noteworthy that some started by trying ⅃.

This synchronism between a spontaneous use of double reversal and comprehension of the apparently nonexistent effects of lateral rotation in the case
of symmetrical letters can hardly be fortuitous, since both cases involve a
composition of the reversals involved and not a generalization of previous
observations. This is, in fact, verified in the second complementary experiment, which makes use of an L drawn on a piece of transparent plastic. The
majority of stage 2 subjects predict that this L will remain unchanged when
seen in the mirror because, as one of them says, the plastic "is already like
the mirror"; the L is reversed on the side presented to the mirror, which then
rectifies it by reversing it yet again. "If you turn it," another subject of seven
years, nine months says, "then the L will be the wrong way round. If you
don't, it will be the right way because you've put it on this side and the paper
is transparent."

§4. Right and Left Arms in the Mirror

An even stronger contradiction than that of the symmetrical letters that
appear not to be reversed in a mirror may result, at least in the subject's

eyes, from the fact that when he holds up his left hand, while looking into the mirror, he appears to be holding up his right hand. This is so because he is seeing his own image reversed, as though there were some other child sitting facing him, so that the subject has to regard the raised hand as being the right hand of the mirror child, even though it is his own left hand and is still on the left hand side of the mirror from his, the observer's, point of view. This transposition of left and right, due to the fact that the subject and his mirror image are in the situation of two people facing one another, I shall term "crossover." And it should be noted that this "crossover" is not in fact directly caused by the reversing effect of the mirror: it is obvious that if one were to place three material objects A, B, and C in front of the mirror—rather than a subject confronting his own image so that both are viewed as having subjective lefts and rights, or a card that one turns round in order to project an image, as with the letters—then object C on the right would remain on the right in the mirror (whereas if B were a person then B-in-the-mirror would perceive C-in-the-mriror as being on his or her left). Since this "crossover" is thus distinct from the simple projection of a figure onto the mirror with its resultant simple reversal, it may be interesting to engineer conflicts or "contradictions" between the two.

Technique

The child is asked to indicate with his arm a road sign (visible through the window) situated to his left. He is then asked with which arm he made the gesture and which arm in the mirror will move in the reflection of his action. Once the crossover in the mirror has been observed, one asks what his arm in the mirror is indicating: is it lifted toward the same road sign (i.e., toward the window) or on the opposite side (toward the door)? If the child chooses the correct direction, then a counter-suggestion is made: the experimenter raises both arms at the same time and asks how one and the same person can point at the same thing in such a way. If the reply is "toward the door," then one suggests to the child that he move his forefinger in the mirror to see in which direction he and his image are pointing.

Needless to say, the very youngest subjects are unable to master the "crossover" phenomenon at all, since even in the simple lateralization tests (the child is asked, for example, to indicate the right hand of the experimenter sitting opposite him) no really systematic success is encountered before six and a half or seven years. Consequently level 1A subjects perceive no contradiction when asked the following questions:

Ver (–6) "Which arm are you pointing at the window? — *My left* [correct].

— And which arm is it in the mirror? — *The left.* — Sure? — *No.* — But is the little girl in the mirror pointing at the same thing as you? — *Yes.*'' Further hints and help are given, but Ver refuses to give up the idea that her left arm remains a left arm in the mirror and points to the window.

It is evident that this first reaction, consisting in simply ignoring the crossover, lasts so long because the image in the mirror is the subject's and not another person's ("It's still the left because it's my arm," another seven-year-old says). Two-thirds of the thirty-six five- to nine-year-olds reacted in this way, but the level 1A children were the only ones not to correct themselves when asked to look harder. The 1B subjects, however, become more interesting: confronted with the contradiction, they begin to hesitate and try to search for a way out of it.

Tié (5–6); see §3: "Would you mind pointing at that with your hand? (He does so.) Which hand are you using? — *My left* — And you see your reflection, which hand is it using? — *The left.* — Look hard. — *No it's the right.* — Sure? — *Yes.* — Is your reflection pointing the same way as you? — *No, it's pointing to the right.* — And you? — *To the left.* — *What is it pointing at?* — *Over there* [toward the door: opposite direction to sign]. — How is it that you are pointing to the right and to the left with the same arm at the same time? — *Even if I put myself in there* [in the mirror], *it's to the left too.* — The same way as you? — *Yes.*"

Iré (5–0); see §3: "Which of your arms is pointing at the window? — *The right, no the left.* — Which hand do you write with? — *The right.* — And in the mirror, which hand are you pointing with? — *This one* [right]. — And the little girl in the glass, is she pointing the same way as you? — *Another way.* — Which way? — *Toward the door.*"

Rin (5–10) also thinks that the mirror arm is pointing "*the other way.* — Point again and wiggle your little finger. Which way is it pointing? — *Toward the sign.* — Before, you said the other way. What do you think now? — *It is the left hand pointing in the mirror!*" So she is denying the crossover she had previously accepted.

Luc (5–4; see §3): "Which of your arms is pointing at the window? — *The left.* — And which arm is your reflection pointing with? — *The right* [no pause!]. — Why? — *Because it's in the middle.* — Explain. — *I can't.* — Is he pointing at the window too? — *No, the wall* [toward door]!"

Cia (6–0) accepts crossover after initial error, then: "*He is pointing at the door, because it's his right hand.*"

Ian (6–5). Same reactions: the arm "*is pointing at the door because the reflection is the wrong way round.*"

Pat (6–6) pointing with left arm: "And your reflection? — *The left.* — Sure? — *The right, because it's the other side.* – Is your reflection pointing the same way? — *No* [yes], *it's still pointing over there* [toward window]. How is that possible? — *No, to the wall* — What am I pointing at (simulating her reflection)? — *The window.* — Why is that? — [Silence.]"

And (6–6): immediate acceptance of crossover "*because it's the wrong way round.* — What is the reflection pointing at? — *The window.* — Why? — *Because it's its left arm.* — But you just said it's its right. — *At the door.* — Wiggle your finger. — *It's toward the window! I thought that changed too.*"

Rol (7–0): "*The left hand becomes the right hand.* — What is it pointing at? — *The door.* — Why's that? — *It's pointing two ways.* — What two ways? — *The right and the left.* — With just one hand? — *Yes.* — Is that possible? — [Silence.]"

Eti (7–6) begins similarly by saying that the reflection is pointing at the door with its right hand. "Move your finger. Now, which way's it pointing? — *To the left.* — So? — *The left hand is pointing at the sign and the right one at the door.* — Is it possible for the reflection to point two ways at once? — *Yes.*" But changes mind later.

Jea (7–10). The left hand becomes the right in the mirror. "And does it point at the same traffic sign? — *Yes, but it's not in the same place. That's what you'd expect, because if I turn around myself, then it's my right hand that's pointing.*"

Finally, here are some examples of stage 2 subjects, mostly of about seven, who succeed in distinguishing and coordinating the crossover effect and normal mirror projection.

Eri (7–9): "Raise your right hand. Which have you raised in the mirror? — *The left.* — How is that possible? — *It's as though there's someone opposite me. He will eat with his right hand, but to be like me he would have to turn around.* — Is the reflection the same as you? — *No, different.* — What is different about it? — *It's changed arms.* — Point to the sign for me. (He does so with left arm.) Now which arm will the reflection use? — *This one* [right: correct prediction]." — And will the right hand in the mirror point toward the sign or the other way? — *Toward the sign like me.*"

Nel (8–7) indicates sign with left hand. "And the reflection? — *With the right.* — What's happening? — *It does it the wrong way round.* — Is the reflection pointing at the sign or the door? — *Over there* [sign]." — But a left arm and a right arm can't point at the same thing, can they? — *Yes, because the mirror does it the opposite way round.*"

It is thus clear that, although stage 2 subjects succeed in differentiating and integrating the effects of the crossover and simple mirror projection into a whole (though we still need to investigate how), the 1B subjects are wholly unable to transcend the contradiction involved: they understand well enough that their own left arms become right arms from their reflections' points of view, but are unable to conclude from this that the sign, which is to their own left, is therefore to the right for the reflection: hence the belief expressed by Tié (who contradicts it later), Iré, Luc, Cia, and others, that the reflection's right arm is pointing in the other (door) direction and not at the sign. Rin and And both sense this contradiction and revert to the idea that the raised arm in the mirror is in fact the reflection's left one after all. Some subjects overgeneralize the crossover by amalgamating it with the reversal effect of the mirror: according to Ian (and others), everything has to be turned around the other way "because the reflection is the wrong way round." Others think that the reflection's arm is pointing at the window after all (even though it is using its right arm), but contradict themselves on the point (Pat). Rol even tries to maintain that the reflection is pointing two ways at once. The more prudent (like Jea) arrive at a compromise (to follow the terminology of Inhelder, Sinclair, and Bovet) to weaken the contradiction: the reflection is indeed pointing at the traffic sign, but the sign is no longer in the same place, because the mirror changes everything.

§5. Conclusions

The first experiment in this chapter, with letters, in which subjects were asked to give their verbal formulation of a law after a number of predictions (all of which were correct after a single observation), then presented with a number of apparent exceptions to that law to see how they would react, obliges us first and foremost to recognize the distinction stressed throughout this book: that between contradictions as disequilbriums of actions or operations (or noncontradiction as reversible equilibrium with complete compensations) and logical contradictions or noncontradictions deriving from the definition of whatever concepts are employed, and from the inferences based solely upon those definitions. It is clear, in fact, that the statement "all letters seen in the mirror are (or become) the wrong way round" is essentially ambiguous (and the researcher deliberately made no move to encourage preciser terms): if we define "the wrong way round" as implying a modification of the forms, then the law is false, since symmetrical letters are not modified. If, on the other hand, we define "the wrong way round" as referring to the reversal itself, independent of its result, then the law is general and does apply to symmetrical letters as well as to asymmetrical ones. So that the interest of the problem lies in whether or not the subject, faced with facts that contradict his law, will attempt to improve that law until he finds a logical formulation that is both general and coherent, or whether he will direct his efforts primarily toward the coordination of actions and operations, leaving the definitions of those notions used to translate such coordinations verbally more or less vague.

The answer to this problem is absolutely clear. The 1A subjects, who think of the modification of the letters in terms of objective processes, and thus regard "the wrong way round" as referring to a material result, are the only ones who take the expression of the law seriously. This is why, from the very start, they do their best to reverse the symmetrical letters, and resort to turning them upside down as a result. Then, even though experience has shown that this doesn't work, they still refuse to give up: Ala goes so far as to say he can see tiny differences in the bars according to whether the *T* or the *M* are the wrong or right way round; the others talk in terms of recalcitrance and almost of deficiency: "You can't make it turn round," "They won't roll" or even, As Ala finally claims, "they aren't in the alphabet." At the 1B level, on the other hand, by which time right and wrong way round are dependent upon actions, the law is resolutely held to be nongeneral, and thus false in its initial form. However, this does not mean that it is corrected in the direction of an operatory definition of "wrong way round": "there are some that turn and others that don't turn," one of these 1B subjects says, without suspecting that in fact they all "turn," but that from the point of view of the result, the symmetrical ones look just the same as if they were "the right way round." Only those subjects who draw the symmetrical letters from right to left, as a means of imposing some kind of reversal upon them, are really attempting to overcome the contradiction with the law, even though, because they have failed to understand the nature of the transformations, they do not actually try to modify the law itself.

As for the stage 2 subjects, they have removed the contradiction by means of a correct coordination of actions and positions. The mirror reversal having thus become operatory, it is generalized to include the symmetrical letters with a correct explanation of how it is they are not modified: "they turn, but you see the same thing" because the letters "have the same shape on both sides." In other words, the notions empolyed have become relative. But it is striking that even then the subject does not seek to perfect the law by formulating adequate definitions, and sometimes even pays very little attention to his own verbal contradictions once he is satisfied that his operations are not contradictory. For example, Yve maintains that "all" the letters are "the wrong way round in the mirror," including *A* and *T*, which are not "really the right way round," but which one "sees the right way round."

And Lau says something very similar. The child has thus understood perfectly well that "all" the letters turn, but that some of them do not change their perceptible forms in the process, yet sometimes he will use "the wrong way round" to refer to the fact of the letter having turned and sometimes to refer to the result of that reversal. In other words, the "all" and and the "some" are correctly regulated in his interpretations, which display the resulting equilibrium between affirmations and negations that such regulation entails, but, because the subject has not yet reached the level of formal operations, the definition and coherence of the formulation itself remain secondary in his mind.

That said, it is instructive to observe that transcendence of the contradiction is achieved, in the case of the spatial actions and operations studied here, without any recourse to fresh experimental information, and thus to empirical or physical abstractions, as would be the case with a problem of causality. It is at the 1A level only that the subject seeks his explanations in the material properties of the figures, whereas, once their different morphologies have been recognized, the solution arrived at consists solely in generalizing the reversal of all the letters (the operation of rotating having been acquired by reflective abstraction) by deduction, and in establishing that a symmetrical letter when reversed laterally does not change its form, thereby explaining the limitation of the changes brought about by the reversals.

As for the removal of the contradictions involved in the crossover of left and right relations in the reflection of the subject's own body in a mirror (§4), the process is closely parallel. It should be noted first of all that it is already fairly remarkable that a very young subject, one still at level 1B, should be capable of imagining that the reflection's right arm is pointing in the direction opposite to the traffic sign, when all the perceptual evidence indicates that it is in fact pointing to that sign. So the subject is in fact making a very daring inference: that a right arm extended on its own side of the body ought to be pointing at objects situated to the right, that is toward the door, even though appearances point to the contrary. The error the subject does make, in fact, lies in his failure to comprehend that if his own left arm becomes the reflection's right arm, then a sign situated to his own left must be to the right for his reflection. Here we come to the advance made at stage 2: just as the subject at this stage generalized to all the letters in the mirror (and did so deductively, not inductively or experimentally) what was in fact only evident for the asymmetrical letters, so here again the stage 2 subject generalizes deductively the reciprocity between his reflection and himself, which enables him to accept that if his own left arm becomes the reflection's right, then what the reflected arm indicates to its right must correspond to his, the subject's, left. And just as, in the case of the letters, the visible change caused by reversal is limited, and does not extend to symmetrical letters, so in the case of left and right reversals they are limited to objects presented face to face with themselves (such as letters on a card that is turned to face the mirror) and do not extend to the position of just any object interposed between reflection and subject (such as the traffic sign or the door).

Finally, as for the nature of the contradictions at work, our general hypothesis is that they result from an incomplete compensation between affirmations and negations, which is in turn due to the greater initial force of the former, which correspond to immediately observable phenomena, whereas negations (and, *a fortiori*, negations of negations leading back to affirmation) are always relative to previous assertions, and in a more or less inferential manner. In the case of our letters, the initial affirmation is in practice extremely strong from the start, excluding spontaneous searches for counter-examples or motives for doubt; but then the facts present rebuttals, which are then structured by means of a simple "all" and "some" regulation on the plane of legality: some letters are the wrong way round and others not. Yet there is one particularly deep-rooted tendency that continues to work in favor of affirmation: the 1A subjects do everything they can to confirm the law, and those on level 1B often accept that one might be able to keep it intact by regulation of positions. But it is not until stage 2 that these questions of position are generalized within the letters themselves and we find attention being paid to similar or dissimilar parts of the letters (symmetries and asymmetries): the general statement of the law is then maintained by means of a differentiation between the actions of reversal and their results, thereby leading to a subdivision into two subclasses of letters, those that change and those that don't. At this point, the interplay of affirmations and negations has finally been equilibrated.

It should be pointed out that here, as usual, the contradiction between a fact and an anticipation is subordinated sooner or later to a contradiction between schemas, so that the fact acquires meaning only when eventually interpreted by means of such schemas. In the present experiments, this situation is made particularly clear, since we have a single and unchanging fact (the nonmodification of symmetrical letters) which continues to be judged in contradiction to the reversal law for as long as the subjects fails to construct the notion of symmetry, but which ceases to be so judged the moment those spatial operations have been acquired. The only difference between the letter situation and that of the subject's own reflection, in which the contradictions exist solely between schemas, is that in the former case the contradictions arise only when the actual facts are presented, whereas in the case of the subject's own mirror image it is merely a question of coordinating two schemas which, although at first sight difficult to reconcile, have both already been adjusted at an earlier stage to facts that were troubling once (such as the fact that a tree seen during a walk is on the left leaving home and on the right coming back, and so on), but which now no longer play a role.

§6. Refraction

At first glance, it might seem that one is unlikely to find much in common between childrens' interpretations of mirror reflections and their interpretations of the refraction that occurs when a rod is dipped into liquid; but since the latter is explained, at level 2A, as being due to a sort of reflection or a directional change analogous to reflections, it would be interesting to find out whether the coordination of affirmations and negations is carried out in a similar fashion in both cases. And this does, in fact, seem to be the case.

At level IA, a pencil dipped at an angle into a glass of water is in fact regarded as being objectively "bent".

Sar (4–11): "Can we bend the pencil? — *No, no one can because it's hard.* — Let's try (pencil breaks). — *Now it's bent like the roof of a house.* — And what if we dip a pencil in this water? — *Perhaps it will break, perhaps it won't.* — [Pencil dipped in water.] — *It's bent a little bit, but not broken. Now it isn't straight any more in the water* [he feels under water with his finger]. *A little bent.* — And when you look at it? — *A little bit bent.* — And with your fingers? — *Bent* [he is distorting the observable fact]. — Why isn't it broken? — *Because if you take it out it will be straight.* — The bend will go away? — *Yes.* — Why? — *Because the water is changing it, bending it.* — Does it hurt when you hold it? — *No, it's not me bending it, it's the water.* — And in here (glass of ink-tinted water in which the refraction is not visible?) — *Perhaps it will be bent* [feels with finger]. *I can't feel a bend: the ink stops it bending.* [Feels in the plain water.] *A little bent.*" With a metal rod: "*Just a little bent, because the water's pulling very hard.* — And with your finger? — *It's bent.*"

Zul (4–9): "*It's twisted because it's dipped in the water.*" — And if we take it out? — *It won't be twisted because it isn't in the water any more.* — And like this (vertical in the water)? — *It isn't twisted because it's standing up straight.* — And in here (tinted water)? — *Twisted.* — Feel with your finger — *No, it isn't twisted in the blue water because that* [plain water] *is branch water and that isn't.* — And with your finger in the branch water? — *It's twisted.* — And if we put this rod in, what then? — [It won't be] *twisted because it's iron and it's heavy.* [Rod in.] *It has twisted* [amazement].— And if I take it out? — *It won't be twisted.*

— And like this (rod vertical in water)? — *It isn't twisted because you've put it in standing up straight. You have to put it in sloping.* — [Rod immersed totally and sloping.] — *It isn't twisted because it's all in the water.* — Why's that? — [Silence.] — If I gradually pull the rod up, will the bend be in a different place on it? — *Yes, always there* [surface of water]. — Why? — *The water has a strong push."*

Mar (5–5): It's *"bent.* — Why? — *Because it's gone all soft.* — And out of the water? — *No, because it will be dried.* — Feel with your finger (under water). — *I can feel the bend.* — Where? — *Here* [surface of water]. — (Dipped in blue water.) Is it bent now? — *It's all wet and bent.* — Is it really bent in the water, or is it just as thougt it's bent? — *Oh it's really bent."*

Fev (5–6). The pencil is not bent when upright: *"Perhaps it might become bent a little if you left it a very long time.* — How long? — *Two minutes."*

Luc (5–1) recognizes that *"it isn't bent for your fingers but it is with your eyes.* — Which is right? — *The eyes.* — And if a little ant crawled along the rod, would it feel that it was bent? — *"Yes."*

Pec (5–5): "If I take the pencil out again what will it be like? — *Not bent.* — So, was it really bent before? — *Yes.* — And straight (vertical)? — *It isn't bent because it's standing up.* — And sloping? — *Then it's bent because the water is so strong."*

There would be little point in adding to these selected examples: it seems clear that for 1A subjects the water has the power, at surface level, to "twist" or bend the pencil and iron rod, even though they remain "straight" in a vertical position, or regain their straightness when removed from the water or wholly immersed in it, and even though, as in Luc's case, touch and vision are in contradiction, in which case the latter is taken to be in the right. With the other subjects, affirmation is so resistant to the observable tactile-kinesthetic facts that they are distorted in favor (or under the influence) of the visual. As for the vertical position, for several of the children that constitutes merely an apparent exception, for, if the pencil is "straight," it is then more resistant "like the wall of a house" so that the water is unable to bend it.

At level 1B (from five and a half to six years, with a few seven-year-olds) we find an intermediate situation between the affirmations and negations inherent in the objective bending of the objects immersed.

Dor (5–6) sees the pencil bent but feels it straight: *"It's my finger that's right.* — Is it really bent? — [Silence.] — And if a little ant, crawled on it? — *It would drown, it wouldn't feel it bent* [the question evaded]. —

Why do you see it bent? — *Because of the water's strength.* — And with your finger? — *Not bent.* — Which is right? — *My finger.* — And why do your eyes tell you wrong? — *Because they can't see straight.*"

Suc (5–6): "With your finger (prediction)? — *I shall feel it straight.* — Which is right? — *My eyes, because fingers can't see, and eyes can.* — Is it bent in reality? — *No.* — What makes the iron rod bend? — *Don't know.* — So it isn't bent? — *But I can see it bent in the water.*"

Dem (5–6): "Bent in reality? — *No, it's you doing that* [but bending it objectively still]. — And standing up (vertical)? — *No, because it's hard.* — And like this (sloping)? — *It's because you're holding it that way. It's the water, you can see, there are bubbles* [connected with the bending]."

Sam (6–8): "*It's because the water forces it to be bent.* — But is it bent in reality? — *No.* — Is it your eyes or your finger? — *My finger. No, it's my eyes that are right.* —Why? — *My eyes make it go not straight.* — Have you any other ideas? — *Because the water, that forces it to be bent, but it's not true it's bent.* — So why do you see it bent? — *You see that it's bent, and you say it isn't true because the pencil isn't snapped.*"

Sum (6–6): "Is it bent in reality? — *No, it's my finger telling the truth.* — And why do your eyes tell you wrong? — *Because the water does something else: the water makes another shape happen.*"

Duc (6–10): "*The water inside only makes it look as if it makes it bend.* — But in reality? — *In reality it's bent.* — And with your finger? — *I don't know: it bends a little and I can't feel it.*"

Gae (6–6): "*The water isn't strong enough* [to bend it in reality]. — Why do we see it bent? — *It's the water that does it, with our eyes.*"

Lid (6–8): "*It seems to be bent.* — Why seems? — *Because it isn't true.* — In reality? — *No, because I can see it isn't broken.* — So? — *It's the water does that. It isn't bent, but in the water it looks like bent. It's the water's fault.*"

Vla (6–6): "*It isn't bent but that's how you see it.* — Why? — *It's the water.* — The force of the water? — *No, that's just how you see it.*"

Clearly these subjects are right: the refraction is due to the water, but the object itself is not modified, only the light reflected by it, so that "that's just how you see it," and it is quite true that "it's the water that does it, without eyes." Only, because these children are ignorant of the laws of light, and conceive of vision as going from eye to object not the reverse, they are obliged to work out a new status for the affirmation of the objects bending in the water and for its negation, provided here by the evidence of their fingers, the vertical position, or the withdrawl of the object from the water. Whereas the affirmation at level 1A concerned the material of the object itself, believed to be bent in reality, the affirmation at level 1B rejects this materialization (it isn't bent because it "isn't broken": Sam and Lid), but turns its attention to the object's form or "shape": "the water makes another shape happen" (Sum), "it looks like bent" (Lid), "that's how you see it" (Vla), and so on. This change of form is indeed due to the water: its "bubbles" (Dem) show that it is acting causally, "the water forces it to be bent" (Sam), even though nothing more is involved than a momentary modification of form, albeit one that "is the water's fault."

The only synthesis found at stage 2 consists, then, in subsuming these changes of form in certain situations (subclass A) and their absence in others (subclass A') within a general class B, but characterized in relational terms dependent on changes of direction and comparable to the reflections produced by a mirror.

Gai (6–9) already provides a rough attempt at this solution when she says that if you see the pencil bent and "*feel*" it to be straight "*it is because the water is straight and the pencil is sloping*" so "*you see it bent but it is straight in every way.*"

Kar (7–7): when the pencil is dipped obliquely "*the other end of the pencil* [= the submerged part] *slopes even steeper, because the water changes the direction.*"

Fum (7–6): the water "*makes reflections*" and "*if you hold the rod tilted, that makes it bend, if you hold it straight it's straight in the water.* — But why does it make bend? — *Because the water pushes forward a little. When you move the rod down further, the place* [where it bends] *changes too: the rod bends at the top of the water.* — And if we make the water move about? — *Yes, even if the water moves about a lot.*"

Clo (8–11): "*In the water it isn't the same as outside: there's a reflection*" and if the rod is vertical there is no reflection "*because it isn't sloping.*" Moreover, part of the rod must remain unsubmersed "*not all of it in the water.*" — Can we explain why? — *Yes, it's because of the reflection.*"

Mor (9–6): "*It's bent when you put it in sideways: it forms an angle because the water makes the pencil bend, but not really.* — What does it take to make it bend? — *Water, putting the pencil in sloping, but with some still outside.*"

Bur (10–0): "*In the water it bends. It's like a mirror because you can see yourself in water.* — How do you explain the fact that it bends? — *Because it's a mirror.*"

To the subject, this assimilation of refraction to reflection then appears sufficient to provide an account of the negatives as well as the positive cases: everything depends upon directions, and one subject of only seven was already able to remark that "it is different looking down from the top than through the glass" just as the reflection in a mirror depends upon the observer's position as much as upon the object. The general class B is then characterized by the rectilinear (without bend) form of the rod, and the subclass A by the situations in which the rod is seen as such. As for the class A', in which the objects are seen bent, Mor defines that by the three characteristics: in the water, the pencil sloping, but with part of it not immersed—only forgetting to specify, even though he knows it, the fact that the angular distortion is not sensible to feeling as to sight.

What is striking about this development, then, is how closely it parallels the results of our analysis of reflection earlier (§1–5). In both cases the affirmations of level 1A (reversals of letters in mirror or bending of rods in water) are thought of as constituting a takeover of characteristics materially given in the object, whose bars then "roll" or "turn" (the letters), or which is "bent" by the water (pencil or rod). In both cases, too, at level 1B, the modifications perceived are seen as due to actions—either on the part of a subject (experimenter turning the cards in §2 or "it's you doing that" from Dem in §6), or on that of the objects (the right or left sides of the mirror in §2 or the water changing the pencil's shape in §6—which succeed in modifying the forms of the objects, albeit without affecting their actual material. Hence a distribution of affirmations and negations in accordance with a simple regulation by "all" and "some" on the plane of legality: some letters are the wrong way round, some the right way, and in some situations there is bending of rods, in others not. Finally, in stage 3, coordination of affirmations and negations is brought about by differentiation of object from its image (or reflection), and by subordination of the latter to general laws and causal relations making it dependent upon positional and directional factors. This coordination, produced by an active construction of classes and subclasses as much as by a relativization of the notions involved, then permits the removal of contradictions that were insurmountable at level 1A (between vision and touch, vertical and inclined positions, and so on) and not wholly overcome at level 1B because the reason for the changes of form was still not truly understood.

Part Two

The Relations between Affirmations and Negations

Eight

Contradiction Produced by False Symmetries of Inclusion

with J. Montanegro

It is fairly well known that at preoperatory levels an inclusion is often conceived of as symmetrical: B. Inhelder, with a set of blue squares and red or blue circles, has already shown how strong the tendency is at four to five years and sometimes beyond to conclude from "all these squares are blue" that "all blues are squares." This phenomenon is of interest to a study in contradiction because it is probable—though this is a point that will have to be gone into later—that it derives from a disequilibrium between affirmations and negations, the former having more "weight" than the second, thus producing a lack of compensation between them. Certainly, in practice, the fact that "all the squares are blue" does result in a very deep-rooted link between "square" and "blue," so that nonsquare blues are ignored and, one might say, repressed, so as to preserve this link, which is conceived of as affirmative in both directions.

In the following experiment we shall be studying two sorts of contradiction, both latent in such a process. The first sort will be situated at the level of the child's own actions. One starts with five red cubes, which, as the subject learns from his own observation, all contain a little bell, and a number of non-red cubes which the subject does not touch, but of which some also contain a bell and others not. Despite the incompleteness of his information, one then asks the child to arrange the reds into a row, first without being able to see them and then with all the cubes visible. Since the younger subjects infer from the data that all cubes with bells are red, the row of cubes they construct without being able to see the colors contains some of the non-red cubes, and they are then surprised to see that the row of reds they have made when the cubes are visible is shorter than the previous one. Thus we have here a simple case of type 1 contradiction, in which the same action (or what is judged to be so by the subject) appears to lead to different results, but one well worth the trouble of analyzing.

However, one can also employ this situation to examine the relations between two statements of fact: that which the subject formulates at the beginning of the experiment, when he thinks there is nothing he can say about the non-red cubes (which he isn't allowed to shake), and that which summarizes what he has wrongly deduced from his attempts behind the screen that none of the extra cubes contains a bell. This will give us an opportunity to compare the role of contradictions between statements of fact with that of disequilibrium between actions. It is true that these various questions are doubly misleading: first because the subject knows only that the non-red cubes could or could not contain bells, and also because the row of reds under cover could not be constructed by anyone with certainty. But the interest of collating these incomplete data and simple possibilities is that it has in fact been entirely mastered by the majority of seven-year-olds: it is thus instructive to investigate how they achieve this success, and what prevents them from doing so earlier.

Technique

Eleven cardboard cubes are employed: five red, three yellow, and three blue. The subject is handed the five reds and asked to check whether they contain a bell or not. After his five affirmative replies, he is shown the six other cubes, which he isn't allowed to handle, and told that some of them "perhaps" have a bell in but "perhaps not." In fact, there is a bell in one of the yellows and a bell in one of the blues. All the cubes are then placed behind a screen, the data are repeated, and the subject is asked if it is possible to know what is in the yellows and blues: the reply is always in the negative. A cube without a bell is then placed in the subject's hand, and he is told: "If you're sure it's red, put it in this box (a cardboard tube that will contain exactly seven of the cubes in a row), if not, then give it back to me (still behind the screen)." Then a cube with a bell is handed to him, and after that all the others in random order. Each time a cube is put in the subject's hand the same instruction is repeated, and he is asked what the reasons are for his choice (naturally it is important for the subject to understand that he is being asked to construct a row of "reds," not one of "cubes with bells," although the very young subjects do in fact identify the two categories). When all the cubes have been processed, the child is required to summarize what he has done, then asked if he thinks he's succeeded and whether the yellow and blue cubes were empty or not.

Since the answer given by 1A and 1B subjects is that all the blues and yellows are empty, it is pointed out that his original statement "you don't know" is different from what he has just said ("they don't have bells") and he is asked if it's possible to say which is correct. After that, one asks whether there is any room left in the (still concealed) tube. When the subject has ascertained that it is indeed full (if he has inserted all seven cubes with bells in), the cubes are removed from the tube (still behind the screen). One then places all eleven cubes in front of the child, so that he can see them, and asks him to insert the red cubes into the tube a second time. When it becomes apparent that the five red cubes haven't filled the tube, one asks why.

If the subject doesn't understand that when inserting the cubes into the tube behind the screen he included non-red cubes with bells, one goes through the same classifying process again, first behind the screen then without it, asking the same questions but adding if necessary: "Is it possible that you put yellow or blue cubes with bells in them into the box as well, without seeing?"

If the subject reacts correctly from the outset (stage 2), then the questions are naturally different, and there is no need even to compare the spaces occupied by the two rows; but one does ask whether the task is possible, and why it is or isn't. One also asks what is the best way of trying to reach a solution (putting in only five cubes, or every other one with a bell, and so on).

When the questioning was over, we often confronted the subject with further problems to test his powers of quantifying inclusion: in a bunch of flowers (B), containing fifty percent daisies (A), are there more of the daisies or of the other flowers, i.e., is $A < B$? Or does the subject then compare the A solely with an A', in other words, $A' = B - A$? It might also be interesting to give tests on the intersection of classes.

§1. Level 1A

Examples:

Val (4–9). Reds handled and screen erected: "What is there behind here? — *The reds, the blues, and the yellows.* — Do you know if the yellows and blues have bells in them? — *No.*" She puts all seven bell cubes in the tube behind the screen. "What were you supposed to put in? — *The reds.* — And how did you know they were red? — *Because there was a little noise inside.* — And the yellows and blues? — *Because there wasn't anything.* — But before you said you didn't know, and now you say there's nothing in them? — *They're empty.*" The tube is observed (by touch) to be full. Repeat of classification without screen. She puts in the five reds. "Is there room inside now? — *Yes.* — And before, when it was hidden? — *Yes, there was room then too.* — Sure? — *Yes.*" Classification with screen again: "Is there room inside? — *No.* — And like this (the five reds visible)? — *Yes.* — Is that how it should be? — *It's peculiar.* — Do you think there may be blues and yellows with a bell inside? — *No.* — How can you be sure? — *Because they're not reds!*" The experimenter then had to shake a yellow cube with a bell inside in front of her before she would accept that cubes other than reds contained bells.

Pas (5–6). Behind screen: "Have they all got bells inside? — *No.* — Can you tell if the blues and yellows have? — *No.*" He tries to fill tube with reds, discards a non-bell cube, ending up with the seven bells inside. "How did you know they were red? — *Because of the bell.* — And the yellows and blues, do they have a bell inside, or can't you tell? — *They don't have bells inside.* — Just now you said you couldn't tell, and now you say they're empty. Is that right? — *Yes.* — (Question repeated.) Is that right? — *No.* — So what ought you to say? — [Silence.]*" He feels that the tube is quite full, then, after selecting reds without the screen observes unprompted that there is room left. "How has that happened? — *They weren't really taking up all the room before.*" But he only half believes this and says "*hm!*" when asked to do the whole thing over. He does both classifications again, however, then: "Why is the row longer here (blind)? — *Because they're in this box.* — Could it be possible there are yellows and blues in there too? — *No.* — Sure? — *Yes.*"

Lau (5–6) says that before the blind classification there was no way of telling what the yellows and blues have in them, but that now it's right to say they're empty "*because I shook them*" behind the screen, as if that proved something about all of them. Otherwise same reactions.

Sté (5–8) after having shaken all the reds: "And the yellows and blues, do you know what's inside them? — *No, there isn't any* [bell]. — And the reds? — *There is one.* — How do you know there isn't one in the others? — *Because I knew, because I didn't try them.* — And without trying, you know? — *Yes, I know.*" After which, he naturally accepts that the tube (filled behind screen) contains reds only "*because I shook them one by one,*" and as for the others, which he couldn't tell about before, he now knows they're empty "*because they don't make a noise* [behind screen]. *Because if I shake them and there's no noise, that's how I remember* [= know]. — But before you didn't know? — *But I did know really!*" He recognizes that the two rows occupy differing spaces but forcefully denies that he could have put any yellows or blues in the tube behind the screen.

Gro (6–11) begins by accepting that the yellows and blues "*perhaps*" have bells in, but gives up that notion after he has made his blind row: "*They're empty.*" As for the unequal spaces occupied, he attributes that to the fact that the cubes are sometimes squashed closer together than at others. "Were they the same cubes taking up more room then? — *Yes.*"

Gab (6–4) says you can't tell what's in the yellows and blues, then after blind classification: "*They didn't have any bells.*" Unequal spaces: "*Some cubes have been taken out.*" Both classifications repeated: same reactions. Failure in the inclusion test.

Fid (7–6), despite his age (he is the only one after the age of six) still gives same reactions. Faced with his contradictory statements: "*Yes, you could tell before: the reds had bells and the yellows and blues didn't.*" Unequal spaces: no solution, but he thinks it impossible for him to have placed yellows and blues in the tube blind. Failure in inclusion test.

The request made to the child with reference to the yellow and blue cubes presents him with two difficulties. The first is, naturally, that by preventing the subject from handling them, and by telling him only that "perhaps there's a bell inside but perhaps not," one is preventing him from making any affirmation about them at the outset, whereas the action of handling the reds, one by one, creates a deeply imprinted link between red and bells. Now, the facts seem to show that the need for affirmation or decision tends at this level to far outweigh the suspension of judgment implied by "perhaps." For example Sté rejects that implied uncertainty outright, and promptly translates that part of the instructions into "no, there isn't any [bell]," giving as his argument: "I knew because I didn't try them," which presumably means "because there was no point in trying them"; and when his blind tests confirm him in his idea, he adds, "But I did know really!" Another subject (not quoted above) said after being given the first instructions: "I don't know a little bit, but I do know a little bit!", which conveys much the same attitude, only in more prudent terms.

The second difficulty inherent in the instructions is that they leave the extension of the "perhaps there are some with a bell inside, perhaps not" indeterminate, without specifying whether it is "all or none" that is meant or "some yes, some no." The same tendency to prefer affirmation, or the simpler of two affirmations, will direct the subject in this case toward the "all or none." Cal, a subject we shall be quoting in section 2, and who is still almost at level 1A, translates the instructions first of all into "perhaps they all have one in, perhaps they haven't," and this all or nothing alternative is without doubt implicitly dominant in all these subjects' minds.

It therefore goes without saying that, having discovered the presence of cubes without bells behind the screen, when all the red cubes have bells, the two manifestations we have just attributed to a tendency toward affirmation will lead the child towards the immediate conclusion that only red cubes have a bell: the simple fact that there are cubes without bells thus provides simultaneous proof in their eyes that the cubes without bells are yellow or blue and that all yellows and blues have no bells inside. There is thus nothing contradictory for them in accepting that before the tests one cannot be certain, but that, once the first classification has been made, one can generalize to "all" the yellows and blues, if the question is posed in terms of "all or none." Here we have a particularly instructive example of the psychological reasons for the well known difficulty children experience at pre-operatory levels with "all" and "some" regulation.

As for the second contradiction, that of the difference in length between the two rows of cubes inserted in the tube (one behind the screen and one not), the subjects' indifference in this respect is to be accounted for by analogous reasons. What is involved is not simply a disagreement between an anticipation (same length) and a fact that contradicts it: the subject is encountering a much more profound situation from the point of view of the elementary forms of contradiction, which is that of the same action (or so the child believes) leading to different results, since the row he has made is longer when constructed blind than when he can see, even though he thinks he has inserted the same red cubes in both cases. It is therefore to be expected that the subject will begin by denying that difference (Val and Pas at first), or that he will attribute it to the removal of some of his cubes, or to their being more tightly packed in the first case. In other words, independently of the reasons previously given for his excluding the possibility of having inserted yellow or blues in the tube behind the screen, the subject is also led to assert the identity of his actions in the two situations, and to say that they were not identical would be to admit an inexplicable incoherence.

§2. Level 1B

This substage is characterized by a most instructive progression of intermediate behavioral reactions.

Cal (5–10) remembers the instructions about the yellows and blues accurately ("perhaps they have one in perhaps not") but translates it into "perhaps they all have bells in, perhaps they don't," leading eventually to: "*Some do have bells in, some don't.*" On the other hand, when making the blind row, he is certain that all the bells indicate reds and that the yellows and blues are "*without bells.*" — But didn't you say something different before? — *Because there are some that have them and some that don't.* — So is it right to say you know they're all empty? — *Yes, because there's nothing in them.*" As for the unequal spaces, the reason for that is that he hasn't enough cubes now: "*They're hidden.* — But before (behind screen) there were only reds in there? — *Yes . . . no. Yes . . .* — And it was filled right up? — *Yes.* — So why the difference? — *There aren't so many now.*"

Ver (5–9): behind screen: "The yellows and blues, do they have something inside? — *No.* — How do you know? — *Because the reds have something inside.*" As she shakes each one she says: "*It's red.*" "*It's not red,*" and so on. "But before you said (and so on). Which would be right if a boy said you can't tell and another said they're empty? Which is right? — *The one who said I can't tell if there are.* — And the other boy? — *He was right too, because they were empty.*" After observing the unequal spaces occupied by her two rows or cubes, Ver supposes at first that some reds were removed in between, or that she missed some. "How did you know they were red? — *Because they had a bell inside.* — Could there be a bell in a yellow or a blue? — *Yes, I think so.*" Second row made blind: row formed as before, and answers no when asked if the bell could be in a yellow or blue cube. But after second examination of spaces occupied: *"There are more* [behind screen], *there are yellows and blues with bells inside. —* Could you do it right if we tried again? — No, impossible, because all the ones with bells, I thought they were red."

Ber (5–9). Same initial and final reactions, but he thinks it possible to succeed blind: *"Yes, you have to have a good memory."*

Lin (6–0) says of the yellows and blues after making her blind row: *"I heard that they were* [all] *empty,"* but after examination of unequal spaces admits that there could have been non-reds inside.

Nic (6–6) concludes after blind row that the yellows and blues have no bell *"because I shook and there weren't any."* Unequal spaces: *"It's magic,"* then supposes that *"I'd put one of them* [of the blues] *inside"* and shakes one to check.

Syl (6–3). Blind: *"I put all the reds in the box. —* And the ones you didn't? — *They are yellow and blue because they haven't any bells. —* But before you said (and so on). If two little girls said (and so on) which would be right? — *The one who said they were empty."* After examination of unequal spaces: *"Because I'd put blues and yellows inside."* Second row with screen: she discards a red because the bell might be coming from a non-red: "Why don't you want that one? — *Because it isn't red.* — How do you know? — *I can't know, I can't see."*

Mor (6–10). Same initial reactions, then after examination of unequal spaces: *"There perhaps are yellows and blues with a bell."* He says no one could succeed blind.

Lon (7–0) recognizes that it's not possible to know what the non-reds contain, but, with the screen *"when they're reds I put them in the box, when they're yellows and blues I don't take them. —* But just now you said no one can tell, and now you say they're empty. Is that right? — *No, I ought to say when there's a noise they're red, and when there isn't they're yellow and blues."* Unequal spaces: *"Perhaps when I did it before I didn't put them in so tight.* [Two further rows.] *Perhaps there are yellows and blues that ring!"* He says it's not possible for anyone to select just reds blind.

One still finds a few cases of 1B reactions up to the ages of eight and nine (and even one case of ten). As for those just quoted, the following progression is evident: the most primitive case, Cal, who is almost entirely level 1A, nevertheless makes the hypothesis (after the "all or nothing" mentioned in section 1) that certain yellows or blues may have bells. Then he gives up this idea (and contradicts himself) when he is making his blind row. But after examining the unequal spaces for the second time he wavers ("yes, no, yes") when again asked if the non-reds are all empty. Ver goes further, especially after a second blind classification and a second examination of the unequal spaces: the non-reds can have bells inside. Lin accepts that hypothesis after only one examination of the spaces. Finally, Syl, despite her being only six, is the first subject not content merely to accept this supposition (the first time she is confronted with the unequal spaces, and without any hesitation): she goes further and uses it to improve her action itself, since during her second blind classification she discards a cube with a bell in because she doesn't know whether it is red or not. In other words, we have a regulation of actions added to that of ideas, and one may see this as representing a level higher than that at which interpretations alone are modified, but in fact the ages of these two categories of subjects seem to be the same: between six and seven to eight years old.

§3. Stage 2

We shall include in this stage, which corresponds to that of concrete operations, all those subjects who grasp from the start, when asked to make their classified row behind the screen, that all the belled cubes B are not reds A, for if this class A is included within B, there can be yellows or blues A' also containing bells. And it is of interest to note, before we begin, that out of the fifty children questioned, not one reached this level before the age of seven, while about three-quarters of seven-years-olds did reach it. Here are some examples, beginning with a case intermediate between stages 1 and 2:

Reg (7–10) says you can't tell what's in the yellows and blues, and with the screen up hesitates when about to place a belled cube in the tube. "Why do you think it isn't red? — *Because there aren't all reds with bells.* — Can you explain that better? — *There are perhaps other colors with bells* [In other words, this residual expression is the same as saying that A is not wholly included in B since there are some A' that are also B)." Another cube: "And this one? — [She inserts it.] *Because there are quite a lot of reds with bells in after all, as* [since] *they all have.* — Do you think it's possible to do it without seeing? — *Perhaps, but some children can't manage it.*" Unequal spaces: "*Because there are yellows and blues with bells.*"

Rau (7–1). Blind: hesitates "*because there are yellows and blues with bells in.*" When the screen is removed: "*I've gone wrong, because before I saw that there were more yellows and blues than there are now* [outside the tube]." Conclusion: "*There are some that don't have the same color and do have bells. — So is the game possible or not? — Sometimes yes, sometimes no.*" Rau succeeded in the inclusion and intersection tests.

Lin (7–3). Screen: hesitates *"because I didn't see the color. —* And to put a red in? *— I made it ring. —* When it rings you're sure? *— No, because it could be a yellow or a blue."*

Ala (7–3): "In the yellows and blues? *— There are some that have* [a bell inside] *and some that don't."* Screen: "Do you think it's red? *— I don't know. —* Could it be red? *— Perhaps. —* Or yellow or blue? *— Perhaps."* He inserts only five cubes in all: "The ones you've left out, what are they? *— Blue or yellow. —* You're sure? *— No."* Successful inclusion test.

Cat (7–3), hesitates when he gets to the fourth cube to be inserted behind screen *"because I don't know,"* discards it, then inserts another, then hesitates again for the fifth and discards it *"because I've already taken a lot . . . and when I've take a lot it's another color. —* How many reds are there? *— I didn't count. —* How can you tell if one's red or not? *— I just put them in like that, it's chance. —* And the yellows and blues? *— They're not all empty. —* Would it be a good idea just to put in the first five as they came? *— Yes. —* And can you be sure they're red? *— No."* Failed inclusion test.

Flo (7–4). Yellows and blues. *"I rather think they have them in too, some of them."* Hence hesitations during blind classification. He inserts six only: *"One I put in, the next I don't. —* And those? *— I think they're red. -* Why? *— I just do. —* Are you sure? *— Not sure, no. —* Might it be a good idea just to put in the first five? *— Yes, but that could be wrong too."*

Car (7–5): *"You can't see the color. There are yellows and blues that might have them in too."* She discards a bell-cube: *"Maybe it isn't red, so for once I'll leave it out."*

Vin (8–7). Blind: discards the fourth with bell *"because you said you can't be sure it isn't* [is] *only the reds that have bells in. —* So? *— I shook two or three times, then I said to myself: Ah, but perhaps that one isn't red. It's chance that decides, sometimes I think it's red, sometimes not . . . I must find a solution. . . . "* But he gets no further.

Oli (9–2) stops at five behind screen: *"I've already got five in. There may be more reds and I've put blues inside instead and left some reds out. —* Is it possible to win the game? *— Possible, yes, but by chance."*

The clear-cut distinction between these reactions and those of stage 1 subjects is only too evident: from the very start the stage 2 subjects interpret the instructions correctly and accept that, although the red cubes all have bells, some (and not necessarily all or none) of the yellows and blues may have bells inside, too. Hence the immediate hesitation, when a bell rings, as to whether its container is red or not red. This decisive advance goes hand in hand with the constitution of classes and subclasses, with quantification of inclusion (the test for which these subjects pass almost without exception) and more generally with regulation of "all" and "some." Only Reg, whom we regard for this reason as intermediate between levels 1B and 2, momentarily provides evidence of a residual structure, saying that the reds don't all have bells in because the others may have them in too, like the young subjects in 1B. Inhelder's earlier subjects who, presented with blue squares and red or blue circles, sometimes refused to accept that all the squares were blue "because there are blue rounds too" (their reasoning being based on a false symmetry of inclusion: "all squares are blue" = "all blues are squares," a formula contradicted by the blue circles). But Reg corrects herself immediately, and the general problems facing us are: how all these subjects achieve this correct regulation of all the "all" and "some," thus enabling them to transcend the contradictions of stage 1; what role those contradictions play in this step forward; and what the relations are between these contradictions or transcendence or them and the processes of disequilibriums or equilibration.

Before we start discussing these problems, however, let me go back once more over the various methods these stage 2 subjects have adopted in order to construct the requested row of exclusively red cubes, a task that they finally recognize as being impossible (except by chance) to perform without errors. The majority begin, as did the younger ones, by simply inserting any cube with a bell in, then hesitate and wonder if some particular cube they've handled is really red or not. More than a third of the subjects, when asked to make a second classification, insert only five cubes and discard any others after that. Some subjects (see Flo) insert every other one in the hope that they've hit upon the reds. Finally, the more cautious insert a limited number only (less than five).

§4. Conclusions

The time has now come to tackle our general problems.

1. Achievement of "all and some" regulation (all reds have bells, but all cubes with bells aren't red and among the non-reds only some have bells). The logical mechanism here is clear enough, but insufficient to explain its own formation: it is reducible to the reversibility of the operations involved and thus to a correct composition of affirmations and negations. If all the red cubes A are cubes with bells B, and there "perhaps" exist B cubes that are not A but A' (= yellow or blue with bells) we then have $A + A' = B$. If the subject masters reversibility, we have $A = B - A'$, hence $A < B$ and the exclusion of $B = A$ (false symmetry of inclusion), that is, of "all cubes with

bells are red." Furthermore, if the possible cubes A' constitute a part only of a class C (yellow or blue cubes) whose other part is without bells, in that case A' is the part shared by B and C (intersection), whereas the A (reds) are wholly included in B. That being so, B and C are not complementary or disjunct classes (such that C = non-B) and the fact of encountering cubes without bells behind the screen, that is non-red (non-A) cubes, in no way proves that non-red cubes with bells do not exist. All this becomes clear to the subject as soon as the operations of union into classes (∪, which we express by + for simplicity's sake) are conceived of as reversible, thereby making dissociations or negations possible. It is thus to be expected that when we reach the level at which these reversible operations are accessible, thus opening the way to the quantification of inclusions and the construction of intersections, these problems of cubes with or without bells cease to present any difficulty, even, remarkably enough, in the present case of a task that is in fact impossible (since the given facts are only verifiable in part).

Nevertheless, we have still not made any inroads at all upon the problem of how the subject arrives at this reversibility—which is to say at the correct composition of affirmations and negations with complete compensations between them—when at level 1A these capacities were still so very far from being acquired. As far as the initial deficiencies are concerned, the hypothesis is, then, that affirmations and negations have not achieved equilibrium because the former are naturally more deeply imprinted than the latter, so that the tendency towards affirmation outweighs that toward negation to a very notable degree. There are quite a number of reasons for this, depending upon the way in which the object is apprehended as much as upon the subject's spontaneous cognitive attitudes (two aspects that are, of course, interdependent from the observer's viewpoint but not so at first from the subject's).

As for the objects, they, needless to say, are conceptualized in the subject's comprehension before any extensions occur (this being an inheritance from earlier sensory-motor schemas). In the subject's comprehension the objects are invested with positive properties, not qualified negatively, something that happens only later, and in opposition to other objects: the yellow and blue cubes are perceived and conceived of as such, and not as non-red, which they become only as a function of an action centered on the red cubes. The fact that all red cubes have bells inside creates a strong positive link between these two properties, which weakens the search for non-red objects capable of presenting a shared attribute. Generally speaking, in an inclusion involving A and B (with $A < B$, or a significant implication between predicates $a \supset b$) the important terms are the positive terms A and B (or the qualities a and b) while elements that are B non-A (or b non-a) have no interest other than through a secondary generalization, hence the false symmetries of inclusion or implication. Even in the case of the quantitative relation $A < B$ (for example: "In this posy are there more daisies or more other flowers?") the fact that the subject then reasons as if the B elements, compared to the A elements, were reduced to A' (flowers other than daisies) seems to be evidence that he feels a need to replace the partial negation (non-daisy flowers) with a group that can be qualified positively (the rest of the flowers).

As for the subject's attitudes, here one can invoke the familiar transition from the distorting effects of centration to objectifying decentration. In the domain of affirmations and negations, the subject, by virtue of such laws, is centered at first upon the actual and thus on the positive datum which at this stage occupies the foreground, whereas the complementary classes, the limits of possible extension, and so on, figure only as peripheral virtualities, and thus carry much less weight. The "perhaps" in the preparatory instructions for the present experiment accentuates this secondary character, but nevertheless corresponds closely to all that the subject is tempted to ignore when centered on the properties that are in fact occupying him. And we have seen how that "perhaps" was activley distorted at level 1A.

In short, the disequilibrium evidenced by the initial deficiencies in "all" and "some" regulation derives, according to our hypothesis, from an initial inequality between the strength of the affirmations involved and the secondary character of the negations, hence the absence of the logically necessary compensations and the frequency of latent contradictions. In a general way, this discrepancy between the powers wielded by affirmations and negations, from the object's point of view as much as from the subject's, derives from one essential cause: that the positive characteristics of objects or actions are given directly, as observable facts, whereas their negative characteristics entail, to varying degrees, inferential mechanisms, oppositions involving other objects, or processes that will relate them to the expected results of an action or to the object's anticipated properties.

2. As for the contradictions caused by such failures of compensation, it is clear that the subject is bound to be unaware of them in the early stages, and even less able to formulate them logically, since that would presuppose the use of precisely those regulation mechanisms that he still lacks. Consequently, the two contradictions persisting through level 1A verify the general hypothesis of this book, which is that initial contradictions playing a role in development do not lie in the domain of structural and conscious relations between statements, but consist of functional disequilibriums between the subject's actions. The first of these functional contradictions consists in accepting that there is nothing one can say about the yellow and blue cubes,

then, once it has been established during the blind classification that there are cubes without bells, in affirming that all the non-reds fall into that category. From the subject's point of view there is nothing contradictory in this, since he has verified that all the reds have a bell and has later encountered cubes without bells, which are therefore yellow or blue. But there nevertheless remains a disequilibrium in this situation, since the subject has not verified that all the cubes with bells, heard but not seen, are red: there is therefore the possibility of a secondary class, which the subject does not think of, and which constitutes something like a noncompensated virtual task in a physical disequilibrium. The virtual task later becomes real, when the subject compares the lengths of the screened and nonscreened rows and observes that the former contains more elements: hence the second contradiction, which again the 1A subject fails to remove, while accepting that he has performed the same action in both cases. he then tries to get out of this difficulty either by denying the observable fact causing the perturbation, or in conceding minor differences in the actual execution (cubes more or less tightly inserted, cubes forgotten, and so on). Here again there is no logical contradiction between statements, but rather a disequilibrium, arising from the fact that a virtual task has not yet been compensated and becomes real later on with more diligent verification.

Generally, then, in all situations in which the subject forgets a complementary class A' (and concludes, among other things, that if all A are B, then symmetrically all B are A), or generalizes to "all" an indicator valid for "some," the latent contradictions contained in these affirmations are the expression of disequilibriums in the sense that the negations necessary for the system's coherence remain in the state of "virtual noncompensated tasks."

3. In order to provide an account of the transcending of such functional contradictions, and the onset of structural equilibrium, a further hypothesis then becomes necessary, but one that appears to follow with logical inevitability from that of the initial disequilibrium of affirmations and negations. This hypothesis is that, in an as yet unequilibrated cognitive system, uncompensated virtual tasks sooner or later become real and so necessarily bring about the appropriate compensation as a result of regulations modifying the initial affirmations.

This comes to the same thing as admitting, in the first place, that in any cognitive system virtual tasks already wield a certain influence on the progress of the subject's reasoning. A good example of this initially surprising mechanism is the resistance of observable facts that the subject may seek to "repress." When, in the most primitive 1A cases, the child does not wish to accept that his blind row of cubes (all supposed red) is longer than the row he made soon afterwards without the screen up, this repression of the troublesome fact is not maintained for long, for even while expressing his rejection of it, the subject has already discovered its possibility, and it is this possibility, undesirable though it may be, that goes on bothering him until he recognizes it as being a reality. Similarly, when it is a question of taking seriously the hypothesis, hitherto rejected, of a secondary class of non-red cubes with bells inside, we sometimes witness a similar process: Cal, the subject intermediate between 1A and 1B (see §3), answers "yes...no. Yes..." when asked if he has put only reds in his blind row: he is thus rejecting the supposition, but that virtual task constituted by the possible intervention of such a subclass is nevertheless already weighing upon his thought, since he is not convinced of its exclusion and will be forced, sooner or later, to change his mind when he examines the facts with more decentration or objectivity.

Generally speaking, a virtual task is a modification made possible by the given situation; for example, the fall of a body in unstable equilibrium, or the discovery of objects A' in a system $A + A' = B$, of which the subject is at present aware only of the A and B elements. In the case of a physical system, it goes without saying that the physicist alone conceives of these possibilities: if they are compensated then nothing happens, and the virtual task remains a pure possibility in the physicist's deductions. If they are not compensated, then sooner or later they are realized, and cease to be possibilities in order to emerge as realities. In a cognitive system, on the other hand, which is no longer external to the subject but internal, the subject may sense the vritual task without carrying it out, and in this case it remains a simple possibility of transformation, but one which is nevertheless a reality of thought, since it has the status of a possibility supposed by the subject (even if he at first rejects it). It is in this sense that it can already be a pressure influencing the reasoning process at that point. If it is rejected, then there is no compensation between the affirmations $+A$ or $+B$ and the possible negations $B - A' = A$, hence the error $A = B$ (unless the subject pushes coherence, which is a very late phenomenon, as far as to make A' a class alongside the others but empty, giving $A' = 0$ and $A = B - 0$). If it is accepted, then the interplay of affirmations and negations achieves coherence through their compensations, $B = A + A'$, $A = B - A'$, and $A' = B - A$.

However, might it not be said that our hypothesis comes down quite simply to supposing that the subject, having at first reasoned by means of incomplete inferences, will finally be forced willy nilly to submit to the laws of logic, since they have been at work "virtually" from the outset? That would be a little simple, since the laws of logic are formal and nontemporal, whereas the process described here is causal, and therefore both temporal and real. But if one defines the logico-mathematical universe as the world of possibles, independent of checks by the real (since formal deduction dispenses with experimental verifications), and if one conceives of virtual tasks as the margin of possibilities opened up as one goes along by real situations, then the conquest of a natural logic due to the actualizations of virtual tasks of a cognitive nature may tend asymptotically towards that knowledge of possibles constituted by the logico-mathematical sciences: in that case, a meeting between the two terms of the real and the possible becomes intelligible, without purely formal structures being evoked as causal (which would be contradictory) and preexisting factors in a historical and real development.[1]

In the results recorded earlier, one interesting indication favorable to these interpretations is the sudden and almost discontinuous transition from level 1B reactions, at which the subjects are still approaching the problem with what are clearly preoperatory attitudes and reach the solution only with difficulty, and the reasoning displayed in stage 2, where the subjects make the correct hypotheses right away, or almost. Nor, in this case, is there a clear-cut opposition between age groups, since alongside the many seven-year-olds at this stage we also find quite a large number of subjects of the same age who represent retarded cases still at previous levels. There is, however, opposition between one group of subjects and another, as if all the "virtual tasks" gradually glimpsed earlier are from now on actualized into a coherent whole. It is of no use invoking applications of operations acquired elsewhere, since it is in all the areas accessible to them that this phenomenon can be observed in varying degrees, as if long preparatory processes, on the brink of completion, were suddenly producing a sort of crystallization, or at least a suddenly accelerated structural closure. Thus we have an indication of a certain value suggesting a transition, when a certain limit is reached, from virtual to actual, though this does not mean, I must repeat, that the latter has been preformed in the first—only that it results from successive equilibrations as a result of perturbations that open up fresh possibilities at each stage.

Nine

Simple or Reciprocal Transfers
from One Collection to Another

with A. Henriques-Christophides (part one),
G. Cellerier, and D. Maurice (part 2)

Part 1. Simple Transfer of Counters between Two Corresponding Series

In light of our general hypothesis, according to which positive operations or properties are seen as carrying greater weight in early stages than negative ones, it is interesting to examine the case of actions or operations that are positive and negative simultaneously. One striking example of this will be provided by the experiment using the contacts and noncontacts between pencils when a specific requirement is made that each pencil should touch each of the others (chapter 10): in that case we shall find cases of seven- to eight-year-old subjects beginning with a juxtaposition 1, 2, 3, then, seeing that 3 does not touch 1, changing the order to 3, 1, 2 as a means of obtaining the requested contact, but without noticing right away that they have broken that between 3 and 2, thus necessitating a further permutation, and so on. Another example, this time extremely familiar, is that of the transfer of n elements from one collection or group to another when both collections at the outset are equal. In this case all the young subjects, and until quite a late age, predict a difference of n, not of $2n$, between the final states of the collections, because they retain only the positive aspect of the action performed (adding n to the second collection) and ignore its negative aspect (subtracting n from the first). Despite previous research into this problem, it seemed to us that it would be interesting to do a few tests to find out what the effect would be on the subject's mind if he was allowed to observe the entire action, rather than concealing the transfer itself so that he is allowed to see only the configurations at start and finish. Further, the two collections of shapes employed are not merely random forms, but two rows (generally of eight elements each to begin with) of objects with a one-to-one correspondance along their lengths. The child thus accepts the two rows' equality immediately, after which a transfer is first effected with one row masked by a sheet of cardboard. When the cardboard is removed, the subject then believes that the previously concealed row has increased by, for example, two elements, while his own (when he is the donor) has diminished by two. In this particular case it appears very easy to understand why the resulting difference is four not two, since the addition is represented by a lengthening and the subtraction by a shortening of one of the two rows. Nevertheless, the results obtained were in exact conformity with those familiar from past research.

§1. Level 1A

We will begin with examples of subjects to whom observation of the actual transfer was of no help at all, and who still retained their certainty that the resulting difference was one of n and not $2n$:

Mar (5–7) for a blind transfer of one refuses to believe the difference is two: "*There's one missing. —* Where? *— It's under there* [under the last counter of the donor row]. *—* So I'm cheating? *— Yes, a bit.*" When he gives three to the other row and observes a difference of six, not three, he returns the three (without screen) one by one to their initial positions and explains the six difference: "*I put three for you and three for me,*" as though they were counting positively in both places at once. This time he gives one and observes a difference of two (after predicting one): "*It's because the other moved here, it went over there* (i.e., he believes two have actually been transferred)." No screen: two transferred: "Why four? *— Because these two were there, they've been here.*" One might think this means he has grasped the principle, but for a further transfer of two in the opposite direction he still predicts a difference of two.

Mic (6–10) ends up, with screen, by sometimes predicting a $2n$ difference, but only by a simple generalization of his observations and without grasping the principle. Without screen, she gives three and counts out the difference of six: "Do you understand now? *— Yes, if I give you three you have six* [more]. *—* Why? *— Because I gave you three. —* And if you give me two? *— Five, no four! four! —* Is that what we ought to expect? *— No, it's peculiar.*"

Geo (7–10) also hits upon the law occasionally, but without understanding it. Without screen: "Give me one counter. (He does so.) How many more have I got now? *— Two, and there's the same missing here* [at the end of his row]. *—* Give me two. *— That will make you three more . . . no four. —* Why four and not three? *— Don't know.*"

Clearly, then, a complete perception of what is happening does not lead these subjects to comprehension of it, whether they limit themselves to simple observation (Mic), or whether they attempt by different means to imagine that, for a difference of $2n$, the transfer is also one of $2n$ rather than n: Mar counts the three counters in both collections, and Geo sees the gap in his own row as an indication not of an identical difference between the rows, but of the removal of two counters when he only gave one. These reactions, and many more like them not quoted above, are particularly surprising when the subject has actually perceived the transferred n counters leaving his row, where they leave a gap, and joining the other, thus making a difference of $2n$ before the child's very eyes. Yet the child still sees the transfer as an action taking place in one direction only, one that adds counters to one side but without removing them from the other, since what is subtracted serves solely to make that addition, and the counters remain the same: there is thus a total neglect of the subtraction involved as a negative element in the process, which is viewed as remaining purely one of addition.

§2. Level 1B

The subjects who have completely failed to understand the blind transfer, but who succeed in grasping it when they actually view the transaction, confirm this interpretation by becoming suddenly aware of the subtraction element, which they refer to by such terms as "taking away," "removing," and so on.

Rin (5–7), like almost all the younger subjects, begins by rejecting the facts themselves and thinking she's being tricked: "*You're cheating with that* [screen]." So then she is asked to hand the one to the other player herself: "*But that makes two again! — So it's you cheating! — No! No! —* What then? —*How do I know?* [Transfer of two.] *It's four! But how can that happen?*" [Screen removed.] *Ah, now I see. It's because you take it away from there.*"

Yve (5–9), very intelligent, understands at some moments, just from an inspection of the unequal rows, what is happening (which is exceptional for his age). At first he predicts a difference of two for two counters, but is already using the language of subtraction: "*two, because you've taken away from you and put them with me.* [Rows revealed.] *I've got four more! —* Is that peculiar? *— Oh yes, because you took away two and there are four there.*" Two transferred back. He predicts a difference of two again: "*Well! Four! And only two taken away! Oh, I see now! Someone put those two there* [= *cheated by putting two extra*]." Original transfer repeated: "*Ah, now I understand. It was me that put those two there. We had two there, first of all, so there are two missing there* [in his row] *and there are two there* [added to the other row]. *—* How many more have I got? *— Well, four.*" Screen up. Transfer of one: the difference will be two "*because I took away the one that was there, my one, and I put it there.*" On the other hand, for a transfer of three he predicts a difference of four, but seeing six gives the right explanation, linking the rows, indicating the space in the donor row with "*because it was taken away from there.*" But for a transfer of one he relapses into the initial error: "*one, or rather three, no one.* [Screen removed.] *Ah, two! Because one was taken from there.*"

Flo (6–8) begins with the usual errors and thinks she's being tricked. With the screen down she is staggered that a transfer of two gives a difference of four, but still doesn't understand and thinks there are two too many in the augmented row. She tries again with one: "*So, how many more have I got? — Two* [puzzled smile]. *—* Do you see why? —

No. — How many extra should I have? — *One.''* Further (blind) predictions all wrong. Another transfer without screen and now she's got it: *''four, because I took two away from me* [points to gap] *and I saw straight away because I saw where it began from.''* Same transfer in reverse. *''Four, because you took two away from you.''*

Lie (6–9). Usual errors, then, without screen: *''Ah! I see. It's because I took one away from there* [giving a difference of two].''

Fra (6–3), after mistakes, suspicions of cheating, and so on, sees a transfer without screen: *''That makes six because if you give me three in my row there are three missing* [in yours], *so I have six more.''*

The striking fact in these reactions is the process by which awareness is achieved. Since the transfer of counters is directed toward an addition to one of the rows, the subject at first totally ignores the fact that this addition in one direction entails a subtraction in the other, even when (Yves 5–9) the verbal description suggests otherwise: ''you took away from you and put them with me.'' It is only after completion of the action, when the gap left in the donor row is observed, in other words after seeing the material result of the act performed and not while watching the performance itself, that the subtraction is perceived as something symmetrical to the addition: hence the comprehension of the difference in terms of what is added on one side *plus* what is missing on the other, rather than, as previously, being simply equal to the addition.

§3. Stage 2

All that now remains is to give an account of how this retroactive process of grasping the role of subtraction becomes anticipatory.

Art (7–5) provides an excellent example of this transition. During the questions she systematically predicts differences of n and not $2n$ for transfers of n, and is indignant about the tricks apparently being played on her. The experiment is therefore discontinued. Some weeks later, however, without any coaching or mention of the problem in between, she begins right away with: *''When you give me one counter from you, that gives me two more, because it gives you one less. If you'd taken it out of the box* [containing extra, reserve counters sometimes used for comparisons with the row to row transfers], *then that would give me one more* [than you]. *But you took it from your row.''*

Pan (10-11) predicts a difference of two after brief hesitation: *''one.* — Why? — *No, two, because we had the same number. He took one away, that makes one less. He gave me one of his, that makes one more; that makes* [a total of] *2.''*

Without going into details of all the intermediate cases encountered between the seven- to eight- and the eleven- to twelve-year-old levels, it is already apparent how Art, by means of a striking memory reorganization, and Pan, the moment the first question is asked, both dissociate the transfer into two operations, despite the fact that they occur together within a single material action: a departure operation consisting in taking away, and an arrival operation in the form of an addition, each of these aspects being relative to one of the two simultaneously transformed collections.

However, although the two characteristics of the action in this experiment must necessarily be brought into relation, since the question bears upon the differences between the two transformed collections, it is important to remember that the situation is the same for any action or operation, except insofar as the negative aspect may not actually impinge upon the subject's attention at that particular moment, depending upon the problem being posed: to move an object from X to B is to create a lacuna in X; to join an object A to objects B is to dissociate it from another previously existing and more or less well determined whole; to attribute a quality a to the object A is to imply that other objects do not possess that quality (and thus to postulate the existence of other classes or secondary classes non-A within a single whole). The initial primacy of affirmations over negations is thus extremely natural, since action is usually directed toward a positive goal (with due exception made for corrections, or for derived actions aimed at eliminating possible perturbations). But it remains true, nonetheless, that in order to attain a state of equilibrium (albeit still relative and provisory), the subject's thought must take account of the whole formed by any possible negations, in other words, must have at its disposal a complete system of possible compensations relating to the affirmations it is employing. So the startling example provided by our transfer of counters experiments, involving addition without subtraction, is only exceptional insofar as it offers a sort of magnification of situations that are in fact quite usual, though less striking in degree, elsewhere, and which are in fact the sources of real or virtual contradictions that come to a head in the elementary stages, and whose origin in incomplete compensations we are thus able to grasp.

Part 2. An Exchange Mechanism

The difficulty subjects experience in the case of a simple transfer of n elements from one collection to another is in understanding that the difference between the new states of the two collections is then one of $2n$ and not of n. We shall now analyze a situation that is more intuitive in kind, due to the fact that there will always be an exchange of n for n, but complicated this time by the fact that the n elements exchanged are drawn in variable quantities from two different categories as well as two collections. The test was originally inspired by a well-known teaser: "if you have two glasses containing equal volumes of wine and water, and you transfer a spoonful of each liquid to the other container, then another spoonful of the resulting mixtures likewise, will there be more wine in the water or more water in the wine?" In our experiment the wine and water are replaced by two collections of twenty marbles each, collection A consisting at the outset of twenty reds, collection B of twenty whites. One then proceeds to make "fair" exchanges of, say, three for three, or five for five. In other words, the number exchanged, n must always be the same, but the marbles making up n do not have to be of the same color.

First, let us make it quite clear why there will always be as many reds A on one side as there are whites B' on the other. In the first receptacle, 1, after any n for n exchange, the reds A will correspond to their previous number less the x taken away and plus the x' added; and the whites B will have the same correspondence to their previous number, less the y taken away and plus the y' added. Reciprocally, in receptacle 2 the whites B' will be equal to their previous number minus the y' transferred to 1, and therefore taken away from 2, and plus the y that have been added to 2 and taken away from 1; similarly the reds A' will be equal to their previous number less the x' transferred to 1 and plus the x moved from 1 to 2. The total result is thus:

$$A(-x +x') + B(-y +y') = B'(-y' +y) + A'(-x' +x)$$

Now, we still have the compensations:

$$x - x' = y' - y \text{ or } x' - x = y - y'$$

since

$$x + y = x' + y' \text{ (n for n exchanges).}$$

Thus $A = B'$ (the reds A in 1 = the whites B in 2) and $A' = B$ (the reds in 2 = the whites in 1) after each exchange.

Technique

The twenty red marbles and twenty white marbles are placed in two receptacles 1 and 2. One removes the elements to be exchanged (here termed a for the reds and b for the whites), which leave red and white marks respectively in the places from which they were removed. The receptacles are then covered with a wooden frame onto which the elements removed are placed in visual correspondence, and above the respective receptacles into which they are to be transferred. A prediction is then asked for: "Will there be more red marbles in 1 than white marbles in 2, or less, or the same number? The actual result is then revealed by removing the screening frame, and a further transaction is initiated. Three types of conflict can be produced in this way.

1.) After several homogeneous exchanges (3a for 3b, and so on) with prediction then observation, one undertakes an exchange *n* for *n* in which one of the terms is uniform (say 3a) and the other mixed (2a and 1b). One then asks for a prediction, together with the reasons for it, and finally, after the actual result has been revealed, for an explanation of that.

In this particular case one has $x(a) = 3$ and $x'(a) = 1$, $y(b) = 0$ and $y'(b) = 2$, hence $x - x' = 2$ and $y' - y = 2$, but the younger subjects will naturally have a tendency to ignore the subtractions, both during the exchange itself and in the resulting states, and will concentrate on the positive terms, i.e., the elements actually transferred, and this will lead them to predict equality when the exchange is homogeneous and inequality when it is mixed.

2.) Next, one asks if it is possible "if you always give the same number of marbles, to end up with a difference of one marble between the reds in 1 and the whites in 2." After attempts have been made to produce this result, the subject is asked to explain why it cannot be done, thus providing a cross-check on the explanations of equality given for the first situation.

3. An external source of marbles is introduced. say 5a and 5b, and one adds 1a and 1b to both 2 and 1. Usually the child will predict the conservation of equality with ease. Then one adds 1b to both sides. In this case the inequality observed, after prediction of the contrary, is experienced as being extremely contradictory with the situation 1a 1b on each side. This question likewise provides a cross-check on the value of the explanations of equality given in the first situation, and enables one to ascertain whether the subject is able to differentiate and coordinate the conflicting schemas (internal transfers between 1 and 2; additions imported from outside the 1–2 system).

§4. Stage 1

From five years old to seven years old, subjects make their judgments essentially in terms of the positive and larger elements in the exchanges, without calculating the end results; and they justify their opinions either by distorting the observed facts, or by renouncing any attempt to differentiate between the colors, basing their arguments instead on the simple numerical equality ($n = n$) of the elements exchanged.

Nic (5–6) for 2a in exchange for 2b predicts and observes that *"it's the same. — And like this (1a and 1b for 2a)? — There'll be more reds with you* [so he is ignoring the fact that one red has been transferred in the other direction]. — (2*a* for 2*b*.) — *That will make two and two.* — And (2*b* and 1*a* for 3*a*)? — *The same, because three for me and three for you.* — But will there be as many reds here as whites there? — *No, you need 3b if you want it equal.*" — Make it equal then. — [He tries 3*a* for 2*b* and 1*a*.] *That makes it equal because you've got three and I've got three.* — Put them in the pots. (He does so.) How many reds in yours and whites in mine? — *Three and three.* — Why? — *Because I saw* [So he is concentrating wholly on the two totals 3 = 3]." Question 3: 1*a* and 1*b* from reserve to add to pot 1, 1*a* and 1*b* to add to pot 2: "*It will be equal* [Same number of reds in 1 as whites in 2). — And like this (one extra red in pots 1 and 2)? — *It will be equal.* — Count. — *There aren't enough.* — Can you explain? — *Because there are a lot of reds and not a lot of whites* [one less]."

Ser (5–9) for 2*a* and 1*b* exchanged for 3*b*: "*You have less whites.* — And you have more reds? — *Yes.* — Look. — [He counts.] *I've got five and you've got five. We're equal again!* — How does it happen? — *Something happened, I don't know what though.*" Fresh start with 2*a* for 1*a* and 1*b*: "*It's equal because we've given two and two.* — But it's the reds and whites we want to compare. — *It makes one white there and not here.* — And in the basket, is it the same? — [He looks.] *Yes, because before we lent equal marbles to one another. So we're equal.* — But why? — *Because ... because we're equal.*" External source: same as Nic.

Eri (5–6) for 2*b* exchanged for 1*b* and 1*a*: "*There'll be more whites and there less reds.* — Why? *Because I'm getting two whites and her one red.* — Look. How come there's the same number? — *I don't understand.* — Do the swap again so that you do understand. — (He puts 1*a* and 1*b* in the frame from each side)." Question 2: "Could you make a difference so that you have more, without cheating? — *Yes* [he gives himself 2*a* in exchange for 1*a* and 1*b* from the other]." Importation of 2*a* against 1*a* 1*b*: he predicts equality on the basis of previous observations, then discovers: "*They're not the same.* — Before it was, and now it isn't. Is that peculiar? — *No, I don't know.*" Back to exchange of 2*a* against 1*a* *and* 1*b* between pots 1 and 2: "*She'll have more reds and me less whites.* — Look — *How funny. She's got six and I've got six!* — Did you count right? — *No* [without recounting]: *she's got seven and me six* [distortion of observed fact]. — Why? — *It's not the same: she got 2a and I got 1a and 1b.*"

Myr (6–3), after several mixed exchanges using the same mixture from both sides (2*a* and 1*b* either way), predicts inequality for 2*a* against 1*a* and 1*b*: "*Now they won't be the same.* — Look — *Four and four! That's because you put a red marble back here* [into pot 1]. *You cheated.*" Exchanges without screening frame: "Can you explain? — *No.*"

Ala (6–4), similarly anticipates inequality for question 1, observes four and four, and says: "*You change it all. What is it you do?*"

The reasoning of these subjects is very simple. For question 1 they limit themselves to observing either that the same number is given by both sides, ignoring the colors, hence a prediction of equality (like Nic), or that more reds, for example, are being transferred in one direction than of the other color in the other direction, thus leadig to an anticipation of inequality. In this second case, what the subject lacks is the complex operation $x - x' = y' - y$, in other words a comprehension of the fact that if $2a$ and $1b$ are exchanged for $3a$, then three red marbles are transferred in one direction and two in the other, hence the subtraction $3 - 2 = 1$, this last red being compensated for by the white. Put another way, the subject thinks only of the positive surpluses and ignores the subtraction. With question 2, the subject assumes it is perfectly easy to produce inequality by virtue of this same principle (Eri). As for the imported marbles from the reserve (question 3), they are not distinguished from the exchanges between the receptacles 1 and 2, since the subject takes no notice of subtraction in the latter.

Since the source of the subject's prediction errors is thus his disregard of all negative operations, we can also say that it is this same systematic deficiency that prevents him from explaining the result even when he has observed it. Some subjects then contest that result by distorting the observed facts (see Eri); others repress their memory of the data; others attribute what has happened to cheating or some unobserved trick (Myr and Ala); others simply brush the bothersome question of the colors aside and return to the purely numerical totals.

In a word, this stage is characterized by a complete incomprehension due to the systematic predominance of the positive aspects of the exchange, with a consequent disregard of all subtractions. Yet the latter might be thought in one sense to be more obvious, more easily noticed, than in the case of a single transfer of n elements in which the difference becomes $2n$, since here there is exchange, and the subtractions to be grasped have their effect first of all on the comparison between the two transfers, before bringing what is taken away in each case into play. And this is what we shall find in the stage 2 reactions.

§5. Stages 2 and 3

Here are some examples from stage 2:

Cat (7–9), for $2b$ and $1a$ against $2b$ and $1a$ (under frame): "*It's the same, because we gave the same to each.* — If I give you $2b$ and $1a$ and you give me 2*a* and 1*b*, and if we compare the reds and the whites, are they equal? — *There won't be the same. I shall have one more red and you one more white* — But compare your reds and my whites, are they equal, or has one of us got more? — [Silence.] — What's bothering you? — *Because you said to look at my reds and your whites: there'll be one red with me and one white with you, and that will make it the same.* [Frame removed.] *Two reds and two whites.* — Right. Now you give me 3*b* and I'll give 1*a* and 2*b* — *There'll be 1b more with you than with me because 1a 2b and there 3b.* [Frame removed.] *It's wrong! Ah! Because you gave me 2b. It's as if some were taken away when I didn't have 2b 1a and not 3b. I gave you 3b and you gave 2b, here there are 1b and there 3a and you give me only 1a and you have 3b, so that makes four.* — And 1*b* 1*a* for 2*b*? — *That's no good. If I give you 1a 1b, you'll have 1b more than me, and I'll have . . . I need to work it out: I receive some b, that doesn't count* [for you]. *I give you 1b and you give 2b that don't count. The 2b count for you and I've given you 1b that counts. So that's 1b less for me . . . Ah! No, that will make the same amount, because, since I said there'd be one missing from yours, if we don't count the a ones, then you've given me 2b that counted and I've given you 1b that counted for me and you gave 1a that counted for you; so that means the 2b don't count for me but for you, I've given you 1b that counts and 1a that doesn't count, so it's equal.* — Could you make it unequal with equal exchanges? — *I'd have to give you one of mine.* — But then you'd have to accept one from me. — *Then we'd never manage it. If I take 1a that will make five of them, and if I give you back 1b that will make five too.* — What if we gave each other five, would that make it different? — [She counts and trys.] *You can't with five and five.* — Why not? — *Because when I give 5a and you 5b, that comes to the same thing."* Marbles from reserve: 1*b* and 1*a* each. Question: will one side have more *a* marbles or *b* marbles than the other? *"The same, because there's the same amount in the pots. Then I get a marble that doesn't count and one that does, and you the same."* However, for 1*b* or 1*a* on each side Cat hesitates between inequality and equality, then finally decides for the latter.

Alf (7–6), 1*b* and 1*a* for 2*a*: *"You'll have more a.* — Look. — *Ah! It's equal.* — Why? — *Because I thought there was one a more.* — What happened then? — *I don't know.* — Go through what we did again. — (He counts out the results but omits the subtractions.) — What about this (3*b* for 2*a* and 1*b*)? — *Now I've got . . . no, no, that's not right. It's equal.* — Why? — *Because I took away* [subtraction from his receptacle] *2a and you gave me 3a. I had one* [after subtraction], *that makes four, and I gave you 1b, that makes 4b* [in your receptacle]." — Do you think it's possible, by always exchanging the same number of marbles, to make it so that you have 1*a* more than me? — [He tries with 2*b*] *No, I'd have to take 3 back, otherwise it would be equal."* Same maneuver one by one. "Impossible? — *Yes.*" 1*b* and 1*b* added from reserve: *"Equal, because you have same,"* then he realizes: *"no, that's wrong. Why? — Because you had as many as me* [as many *b* as I had *a*)."

Tia (8–1): "3*b* for 1*b* and 2*a? — There'll be more than six with you. — (Exchange effected.) — There is an equal number. — Why? — Because the b I was given* [addition] *is the one that was there* [subtraction from other side], *that left only 2b* [with you]. *That's why it's equal."* Nevertheless, to the question "is it possible (with *n* for *n* exchanges) to have 1*b* more in mine than *a* in yours? — *Yes, if I take 2b 1a and there 3a* [thus relapsing into the same error, then unsuccessfully trying various analogous mixed exchanges] *it will always be the same number."* Marbles from reserve, 1*a* on each side: wrong prediction then generalization of observed result.

With nine- and ten-year-olds, the reactions are the same except that the references to the subtractions are often more explicit.

Fra (10–0), for example, tries to obtain unequal results with *n* for *n* mixed exchanges: *"I've understood it now, it makes exactly the same number . . . because if I make the subtraction, then I have to give as much as I lose and as much as I gain* [= I have to lose as many marbles as I gain]."

The distinguishing feature of stage 2, then, is that the subjects begin by making errors analogous to those at stage 1, but then swiftly correct them by setting losses against gains, and therefore taking subtractions into account as well as additions. Considerable deficiencies still remain, however. First, there is not always immediate generalization of what has just been discovered in a situation, but rather reequilibration from case to case, after briefer repetitions of the same uncertain advances (centration on overall total of marbles independently of color, incomplete compensations between the terms of the exchange, and so on). Later, when asked about the possibility of achieving inequality with *n* for *n* exchanges, the subject often resorts spontaneously to mixed exchanges that he has only just observed resulting every time in equalities. And above all, when his mixed exchanges once more produce the inevitable equality, this result does not lead him to grasp the logical impossibility of things ever being otherwise. He goes no further than merely accepting the factual or legal nonpossibility of the task, or even attributes it to his own subjective incapacity. Finally, when dealing with the extra marbles from outside the system, these stage 2 subjects remain unable for a greater or lesser length of time to shake off the usual errors concerning additions of 1*a* or 1*b* to each side, before grasping that the resulting inequality is due to the absence of subtraction within the collections themselves.

It is not until stage 3 that the subject moves toward a general solution:

Anc (12–5), for 3*a* exchanged for 2*a* 1*b:* "*It comes to the same: you gave me 1b and I gave 1a, so they balance out. And since there are 2a on both sides, nothing changes.*" Further, for 1*a* 1*b* exchanged for 2*b*, she explains the resulting equality by the fact that "*I took away 1b from mine, but I took back 2b, so it's as though I'd given you 2a and taken 2b* [either she meant to say 1*a* and 1*b*, or she is generalizing from the outset]."

Noc (12–0) also generalizes the subtraction in the case of 1*b* 2*a* for 3*a:* "*Because at the beginning the 3b came from you, I took 1b away from me, so that's 2b. — And the a marbles? — There's no change: two more, that makes it equal again . . . to make it not equal you'd have to take away from only one side. If you take away from both sides, then it's equal.*" For additions from outside system, prediction of inequality "*because I haven't taken anything out of the pots* [receptacles]: *there'll be more b marbles than a ones.*"

The generalizations are thus of two kinds. The first, adopted by Anc at the outset, consists in reducing the total exchanges to one-to-one exchanges in which there is necessarily either identity ("since there are 2*a* on both sides, nothing changes"), or else compensation ("you gave me 1*b* and I gave 1*a*, so they balance out"). In either case, however, this comes down to equalizing what is given by one side ($-x$ or $-y$) with what that side receives ($+x'$ or $+y'$), and thus relating subtractions to additions, both in the case of the same colors (identities) and in that of mixed colors (compensations: in this situation one has $-x = +y'$ or $+x' = -y$). The other form of generalization (used by Noc and by Anc for the later questions) consists of comparing the additions and subtractions color by color (hence $x - x' = y' - y$, and so on) as we did in our introduction. But the interest of these reactions, and what distinguishes them from those of stage 2, is that they isolate the generality of the process from the very outset: to preserve equality, Noc says, you have "to take away from both sides," and not just one. And Anc compares these differences between additions and subtractions by color to the compensations she employed earlier ("it's as though I'd given you 2*a* and taken 2*b*"). So there is no doubt, in both procedures, that it is the comparison of additions and subtractions that constitutes the common principle of the generalizations specific to stage 3.

So our results here will be found to correspond once more with the general conclusion of this book: that contradictions are due to lack of equilibrium between additions and subtractions, and that their equilibration presupposes their exact compensation, which is to say operatory reversibility. The latter, however, as we observe once again, is acquired only by successive approximations or regulations, step by step, and so represents the result and not the source of the progressive equilibration that characterizes each development.

Ten

Contacts and Separations

with R. Maier (part 1) and O. Mosimann (part 2)

Part 1. Contacts between Each Object and Each of the Others in the Construction of Spatial Configurations

When one asks subject to arrange three, then four or more pencils in such a way that each pencil touches each of the others, one encounters conflicts that involve contradiction from two points of view. In the first place, certain schemas of action are contradictory in themselves without the child being immediately aware of the fact. For example, having arranged three pencils parallel to one another and touching, in the order 1, 2, 3, and then observing, but only after being questioned on the point, that 1 is not touching 3, the subject will change the order to 3, 1, 2, and then, observing that 3 and 2 are longer touching, will proceed to the permutation 2, 3, 1, and so on, without grasping at first sight that in this situation a fresh contact must *ipso facto* eliminate a previous contiguity. In other words, we have here a very nice case of contradiction within the action itself, since the path leading to one half of the goal leads simultaneously away from the other. Second, this example shows that the subject experiences difficulty from the very outset in composing positive and negative characteristics: at the lower levels, indeed, his very projects, before any action is initiated, bear witness to a primacy of contacts over absence of contacts, according to the way in which the general relation "each touches each one" is interpreted.

§1. Stage 1

To begin with this last point, it should in fact be noted that the corre-spondance requested of one element to several others (or rather of each one to all the others) is conceived of at first as a kind of linear and transitive relation (1 touches 2 which touches 3, therefore 1 is touching 3). However, at this age transitivity itself is not very developed, so that the conception involved is, in practice, more that of an overall relationship simply requiring that the figure constructed shall be continuous and involve interdependence of its elements, thus giving an impression of general contiguity that is true in the form "each one touches at least one of the others," but without one to one contact in every case.

Eli (5–0) provides a striking example of this. She places pencils 1 and 2 parallel, but not touching, then connects them at their extremities by placing 3 at right angles to them. In her mind this means that each pencil is touching the two others, until she is questioned, then admits that 1 not touching 2. So she places 1 vertically with 2 and 3 horizontally, both touching 1 but not each other. Since 3 is now not touching 2, she returns to her first arrangement: "Is each pencil touching the other two now? — *You need another one there*," pointing to the open side of the figure. In other words, one more pencil would turn her arrangement into a square, and that would satify her. Similarly, Mar, who is six, makes a square when given four pencils, then puts 1 and 2 vertical and apart, linked at their tops by 3 and 4 horizontal and touching, so that 4 is touching neither 1 nor 2. She then makes a double T-square: 1 and 2 parallel and touching at right angles to 3 and 4 parallel and touching. But since 4 still isn't touching all the other three, she makes do with 1, 2, 3, and 4 all parallel and tight together. Phi, who is seven, begins with Mar's final arrangement, then makes an M. Mon, who is eight, still uses her four pencils to make an E, followed by a sort of F with three horizontals touching along their lengths.

It is true that these reactions might be explained by a failure to understand the instructions; but they were repeated continually, and when questioned (though not until then, and never spontaneously), the younger subjects all accepted that some particular pencil wasn't touching another. Yet this didn't stop them from continuing to search for a solution in the direction of a simply undivided whole, rather than in that of correspondence of each to each. So it is not going too far to view this tendency as an extension of the concept "touch each other" in the direction of positive relations with a concomitant disregard of the negative ones (= without contact).

§2. Level 2A

The preoperatory reactions outlined above, at level 1A, clearly continue into level 2A (seven to eight years), but with paradoxical changes of a kind already encountered.

Ros (7–0) arranges her pencils side by side: 1, 2, 3, then alters this to 2, 3, 1, and says: "*2 is touching 3 and 3 is touching 1* [ignoring 1 and 2 this time]." She likewise arranges the four pencils touching and in parallel: "*1 is touching 2, which is touching 3.* — And 1 and 4? — [Changes to 2, 3, 4, 1.] *2 touching 3, which is touching 4, which is touching 1.* — And 2 and 4? — *No, you have to put 3, 4, 1, 2.*" And so on: 4, 3, 1, 2, then 3, 1, 2, 4. When none of these is accepted, she goes back to 1, 2, 3 and places 4 crosswise, as if this made 1 and 3 touch. Similarly, Ala (7–5) puts 1, 2, 3 touching and parallel: "*Like that they all touch* [yet he had just been asked to repeat the instructions]: *1 touches 2 and 2 touches 3.* — And 1 and 3? — *Ah, no* [Changes to 2, 1, 3.] *There! 3 touches 1, and 1 touches 2.* — And 2 and 3? — *Ah! No* [1, 3, 2]. *There!*"

There are two points to be noted here. The first is that the extension of the term "touch each other" noted earlier has persevered, doubtless due to a reinforcement stemming from the subjects' budding transitivity, since three or four pencils pushed together in parallel formation are thought to be "all touching" as Ala (seven years old) puts it. But the second interesting point is that the changes of order so frequent with these seven- to eight-year-olds do not appear until this level, with the onset of operatory mobility. The fact that this advance in reversibility permits a contradiction as flagrant as this to persist in the practical construction of "touching" relations seems, on this point, to confirm the deep rootedness of positive aspects as opposed to negative ones, since noncontact is discovered in each situation only after it has been seen to occur, rather than being anticipated, as it will be by 2B subjects in the case of the parallel and touching arrangement. Indeed, what is startling in these changes of order is that at each permutation (and n times subsequently) the subject is quite satisfied if he can achieve the contact that was lacking between two pencils in the previous order, and that each time, before his attention is explicitly drawn to this point, he ignores the fact that he has thereby created a further absence of contact between two other elements.

§3. Level 2B

The interest of the level 2B results lies in the attempts to generalize to $n +$ 1 pencils the solution that has succeeded for n.

Har (9–6) no longer tries, as level 2A subjects did, to place three pencils side by side but discovers the triangle solution immediately, and says: "*1 touches 2 and 3, 2 touches 1 and 3, and 3 touches 1 and 2,*" a solution that is thus correct both as stated and in fact. But he concludes from this that with four pencils the solution is a square: "Is that right? — *Yes, 1 touches 2 and 3. —* What about 4?" He then removes 4, rearranges 1, 2, and 3 to form a triangle which he then bisects with 4, a correct solution. With five pencils he again tries to generalize: a square with 5 as a diagonal. "Is that right? — *1* [top side] *doesn't touch 4.*" So then he makes a figure with complicated angles but with two elements still not making the required contacts, then a diamond shape with a diagonal, and finally a triangle with a bisecting line and one side made up of two pencils touching along their lengths and making contact with the end of the bisector, which is a correct solution. "How do they touch? — *1 touches 2 and those three* [3, 4, 5]; *3 touches those three* [1, 4, 5] *and 2; 4 touches 1 and those three* [3, 4, 5]; *4 touches 1, 2, 3, 5; and 5 touches 4, 2, 3, 1.*" However, with six pencils he regresses momentarily to the side by side positions, then arranges 1, 2, 3, 4 in a fan with 5 and 6 laid across the fan and meeting at an acute angle.

In this case, representative of 2B reactions, we note the double tendency to generalize to n pencils, in the direction of closed and undivided figures, what is valid for three. This may doubtlessly be regarded as a final residue of the tendencies observed at the lowest levels. On the other hand, this subject can change his type of construction completely when he must (in the direction of fans or angles with contact at the points only).

§4. Descriptions and Conclusion

There is one fundamental point, however, that remains to be stressed. This is the progressive development apparent in the descriptions given by the subject of the results of his actions, particularly when they are correct. The instructions given to the child entail a one-to-several correspondance of each pencil to each of the others, and allthough level 2B subjects adopt this language with facility, as we have just seen in the case of Har, while level 2A subjects occupy an intermediate position in this respect, the children at stage 1 scarcely employ anything but one to one correspondences, even if their enumeration for a correct configuration is complete.

Osi (5–0), after succeeding in arranging the three pencils in a triangle (after attempting a side by side arrangement): "How do they touch each other? Which one is touching which one? — *2 touches 1, 2 touches 3, 3 touches 1.* — Is that all? — *Yes.*"

Dom (6 years), puts two pencils touching side by side and one across the top of them: "*3 touches 1, 3 touches 2, 2 touches 1.*"

Moreover, although the correspondence remains one to one in this way, the relation "touching" is not necessarily conceived of as symmetrical, depending on the specific parts that are in contact: "point to point" is "touching," but not "one on the other" (Dom), nor the point of one pencil touching the side of another.

So perhaps we should say that it is these characteristics, present in the subjects' descriptions of their projected or performed actions, that, by ruling out all one-to-several correspondences, provide all the explanation we need of this extension that the younger subjects give to the expression "they all touch," while disregarding the negative cases, and thus the absences of direct contact. But that would simply be to say that the child, having failed to understand the instructions, is interpreting them in his own way. So let me repeat, first of all, that the subjects do understand what is being asked of them, even though they may not do so the first time the instructions are given. That stressed, there does in fact exist a deeper and more interesting kinship between the difficulty in handling the one-to-several correspondence and the tendency to overestimate the number of positive contacts achieved. It is to be found in the fact that the younger, stage 1, subjects, lacking any overall representative plan, simply proceed in practice by relating one pencil to another as the needs of their action require, in other words, by one-to-one correspondence, so that those elements not yet involved, or those that have already ceased to be so, come to constitute a class of "others" that ought rightfully to be conceived of as a secondary A' negative class (= the non-A) in relation to the single class A actually filling their sights. So we find once again what we learned in chapter 7, which is to say a tendency to ignore the secondary class A' because it is seminegative (A' = those B that are non-A), which in this case consists precisely in dismissing or devaluing the seminegative cases (the "other" elements that do not directly touch the element being put into relation with A). In short, the tendency to translate the one-to-several correspondence into a one-to-one correspondence is the same thing as the tendency to ignore the cases of nondirect contact or to integrate them into the relation "to touch one another" taken in too broad an overall sense.

In conclusion, the present test provides us with a further example of the primacy of positive elements over negative ones, both from a physical or spatial point of view, when the subject extends the relationship "touch one another" to include cases of indirect contact or of interdependence within an undivided whole, and also from the logical point of view, when the subject reduces one-to-several (or counivocal) correspondences[1] to one-to-one correspondences by erroneously including the in fact secondary class of "others" along with those elements placed into direct relation, in other words, by disregarding those classes because they are seminegative instead of integrating them into class A as their consciously pursued aim requires.

Part 2. The Wolf, the Goat, and the Cabbage

Everyone knows the problem of the wolf, the goat, and the cabbage, which have to be ferried one by one over a river from side A to side B with the restriction that the wolf will eat the goat, and the goat the cabbage, if they are left alone together. The solution is to ferry over the goat first; then, on a second trip, the wolf or the cabbage, followed by a return journey (BA) bringing back the goat; on the next AB crossing one transports the cabbage if the wolf is on B or the wolf if it is still on A; and finally, after crossing BA with an empty boat, one brings over the goat again. There are two aspects of this little problem that can be of interest from the contradiciton point of view. The first is the role of the reverse operation BA; will the subject succeed unaided in grasping the necessity of bringing back the goat after the second AB journey, or, constantly polarized by the goal on bank B, and therefore centered on AB operations, will he regard the BA return journeys as merely necessary conditions for further AB crossings? Second, and most important, since the incompatibilities between wolf and goat (notated here W/G) or between goat and cabbage (G/C), and the compatibility between wolf and cabbage (notated $W \wedge C$), are given, and not left for the subject to construct or discover as in other experiments, how will he coordinate them? It is possible, indeed, that being so strongly centered on one incompatibility he knows he must avoid, he will provoke another, particularly on bank B if he is concentrating on A, or vice versa. Or it is possible that he will concentrate solely on the possible achievement of $W \wedge C$ and either ignore or leave in the background the incompatibilities that $W \wedge C$ implicitly entails. These are, admittedly, somewhat delicate nuances to grasp, but ones that have their interest, insofar as noncontradiction results from a general equilibration between negative and positive operations.

Technique

First, the rules of the game must be clearly established in the child's mind: a single element only to be transported at a time, but with as many trips as one wishes; the incompatibilities (if left alone, the wolf will eat the goat and the goat the cabbage, but if the boatman or keeper is present they won't hurt one another); and the compatibility (the wolf will never eat the cabbage). If the child forgets an incompatibility, one asks: "Doesn't that worry you," or something of the kind, or, if that doesn't work, one mimes devouring or being devoured. In order to facilitate the notion of a possible return journey for the goat, one places little packages on A and B which the boatman ferries to and fro occasionally, in both directions, and if it occurs to the child of his own accord to bring back G, W, or C, one asks, for example: "And what if you brought back G instead of W or C?" Naturally one demands justifications of the subject's various moves, expecially if he achieves success (which can happen by pure chance), and one tries to ascertain whether he can see any other possible solutions, as well as why he can, or cannot. Finally, in most cases one goes through the whole game again in reverse, with the wolf, the goat, and the cabbage having to be transferred from B to A.

§5. Level 1A

This first level (five to six years old) is characterized in the first place by two significant deficiencies: none of the subjects arrived spontaneously at the idea of bringing the goat G back from B to A after taking either the wolf W or the cabbage C over to B, and none of them grasped the necessity for beginning by taking over the goat. In positive terms, this is the same as saying either that the subject proceeded at random, or that, being intent on achieving the compatibility $W \wedge C$, or avoiding a particular incompatibility, he was concentrating on that element of the problem exclusively and thus forgetting the others. Moreover, it was frequent, and indeed almost universal, that as the experimenter's questions made them increasingly aware of how difficult the choices were they had to make, the subjects reacted by resorting to solutions not allowed for in the instructions: erecting a fence, deciding that the wolf or goat had changed its normal diet, or making the boat go across very quickly so that the animals wouldn't have time to eat anything.

Bar (5–5), for example, thinks at first he'd better take the goat over first *"because the wolf doesn't like that* [cabbage]," then changes his mind but remains centered on the $W \wedge C$ compatibility and takes the cabbage over first (forgetting that the wolf will eat the goat), then the wolf so as to have $W \wedge C$ on B. Later, having taken over the goat he remembers W/G and takes the wolf back to A [by hand, without, using boat], thus leaving G and C on B. He then remembers G/C and says *"the goat will eat the cabbage,"* and his illicit solution to that is: *"The goat will have to go into the yard* [outside the game altogether]." At his second attempt he takes the goat over first, but then can't think what to do next, remembering W/G then G/C when he contemplates taking over either W or C, and so *"we need two keeper men, one to take care of the cabbage* [by now on B] *and one to go and bring the wolf."* Faced with the problem in reverse (W, G, and C on B to be transported to A) he once more starts by taking over the cabbage.

Van (5–4) begins by taking the cabbage C *"so they won't eat each other* [G/C]" forgetting that there will then be W/G on A. His attention drawn to this, he then begins with the goat but doesn't know what to do next other than *"put up a little fence"* on B to keep G away from W or C. At his third attempt he begins with the wolf on B *"so the wolf won't eat the goat* [on A]." At his final attempt he once more takes W over to B first, but this time brings C over to join it *"because they are nice together* [on B]" but forgetting that the goat will already have eaten the cabbage over on A.

Thus we find that subjects at this level, when they do not proceed merely at random, concentrate either on two elements they want to keep apart (that is, on a single incompatibility) or on the two elements that can be put together ($W \wedge C$), but forgetting the two other pairings in every case. It will be remembered that in Part 1, when set the problem of n pencils to be placed in contact, many subjects choose the linear order 123, because 1 touches 2 and 2 touches 3, then seeing that 1 isn't touching 3, they permute 123 into 132 , forgetting 1 and 2 this time. Then when they see that 1 and 2 are now touching, they change to 213, and so on. The incoordination in that case is the same in nature as the one we find here, except that in this case they are being asked to effect separations (W from G and G from C) as well as the permitted juxtaposition WC.

§6. Level 1B

This level (mostly six-year-olds but with several subjects over seven) brings attempts at coordination that fail in a most instructive way: it is as though the subject is being guided through all his trials and errors by an aim, either present at the outset or discovered as he goes along, but more or less constantly pursued, which is, not to avoid the two incompatibilities W/G and G/C, but—and from the heuristic point of view this is not the same thing at all—to achieve the compatibility $W \wedge C$. And in concentrating on the latter, the subject is led to underestimate the importance of the former, for reasons that we shall have to establish.

Rac (6–1), for example, hesitates over whether to begin with the wolf, then the cabbage, and finally the goat, but seeing the disadvantage of the first two solutions, points out unprompted that if one doesn't take the goat first it would eat the cabbage, and exclaims with delight: "*Ah! I have an idea: the wolf must go first, then the cabbage, then the goat. —* Why? — *Because the wolf won't want to eat the cabbage.*" Having accepted that the goat would eat the cabbage on A, he suggest the order G, W, C, and since the wolf would then eat the goat on B, he brings G back in the boat, then takes over the cabbage and finally the goat, which is the right solution. But instead of sticking to it, when all three elements are replaced on A, and he is asked to explain his procedure in detail, he reverts to the order W, C, G. Seeing the disadvantages of this once more, he tries beginning with the goat, then says: "*I've gone wrong: it was the wolf first, and after the cabbage, and after the goat!*"

Lic (7–1) similarly, after some trial and error (the cabbage over first, then the goat, but pointing out the dangers), takes over the wolf first "*because after I can put the cabbage then the goat . . . and it's because the wolf won't eat the cabbage.*" When asked for more details she sees the obstacles, and concludes with resignation: "*What a nuisance. It's only the goat you can take first because the wolf won't eat the cabbage,*" then she takes over the wolf, spontaneously brings back the goat, then takes over the cabbage and lastly the goat, which means that she has achieved the right solution, like Rac, without outside suggestions. But in Lic's case too, when asked to repeat her success with explanations, she answers: "*You take the wolf first, the cabbage second, and the goat third.*" When the problem is reset in reverse, she keeps to the same order, and summarizing her moves she says: "*Before, I wasn't remembering the wolf doesn't like the cabbage. Then it comes* [= came] *in my head all of a sudden,"* as though she were talking about her best solution.

Dry (7–7): "*I took the cabbage first, then because the wolf doesn't eat the cabbage I took the wolf second and the goat third.*" Successive attempts make him see only the incompatibilities, and at one point, like Rac and Lic, he chances to bring the goat back from *B* to *A,* but when asked to begin afresh he is no more able to explain and exploit his success than they were. Eventually he concludes: "*Before I'd have liked to take the wolf first* [then the cabbage], *but* [then] *the goat eats the cabbage. I can't do it.*"

These reactions, of which less developed examples are already found at level 1A, are extremely curious, since each one of these subjects achieves the correct solution at some point or other, yet without being satisfied by it, so that when they start at the beginning again they once more concentrate on the compatibility $W \land C$, which is regarded not just as a necessary condition, which it is, but also as a sufficient one for success, thus producing a lack of coordination with the incompatibilities G/W and G/C. The reason for these difficulties seems to be that, since the general aim of the actions here is to bring together the three elements W, G, C, and to do so on the other side of the water, the negative aspects or moments of this procedure as a whole are regarded as possessing a lesser degree of necessity. In the first place, the return of the goat to *A* after the carrying over of the wolf to join it on *B*, although discovered spontaneously by all these subjects, does not appear to them as a necessary condition, but rather as an opportunistic expedient, rather like the illicit solutions met with earlier (building a fence, and so on), and which still occur on occasion even at this level. As for neutralizing the incompatibilities, which is to say, in practical terms, preventing the goat or cabbage from being eaten, that involves a double negation, and, other things being equal, it is rated by these subjects as inferior[2] to the positive solutions of direction union, and this leads them to devalue and ignore it. So their constantly pursued aim remains that of transferring compatible elements over to *B*, which leads them to propose W and C then G and the boatman, even if this necessitates more or less ignoring what happens on *A* during the first crossing.

§7. Level 2A

This substage (seven- to eight-year-old) is characterized by the onset of coordination between incompatibilities and compatibilities, in other words by an attribution of equal necessity to the two sorts of actions: "separating"

and "joining." However, this composition of negative and positive operations is far from being immediate, and entails an equilibration process both
laborious and, from our point of view, very instructive. It should be noted to
begin with that the attraction of the orders *W, C, G* or *C, W, G*— and thus
the primacy of compatibility or joining over the incompatibilities—remains
fairly persistent. Moreover, since the relations at work are quite numerous,
when the subject concentrates on one of them in particular he still tends to
forget the others, and this leads to a great deal of uncertain trial and error.

Sté (7–10) begins with the cabbage, then with the wolf, in order to link
the two compatible elements, but recognizes the drawback each time and
so tries to take the goat first, but without knowing how to go on from
there. "What are you thinking? — *About trying to separate: leaving the
goat there* [on *A*] *and W and C here* [on *B*]." After further attempts with
the cabbage going first, he comes back to goat first, then cabbage, but
then, on *B* "*they have to be apart. So I take* [back] *the cabbage here* [to
A]." Then he decides to take back the goat to *A* instead of the cabbage
and reaches a correct conclusion. But when asked to do the problem in
reverse (from *B* to *A*), he again begins with *W*.

Ben (8–10) likewise begins, three times running in fact, with *W* and *C*
C then *W* "*because they don't eat each other,*" then lights on goat first,
then wolf, but "*they must be kept apart.*"

Roy (8–1) uses the same expression, as well as "*what to do to stop them
eating one another?*" which is her constant preoccupation during all her
trials and errors. Moreover, she began with the goat, but despite achieving success, when asked to do the problem again in reverse, from *B* to *A*,
she follows the order *W, C, G*, as if the $W \wedge C$ compatibility could pre-
dominate somehow in the opposite direction. And the underlying idea is
certainly not that one must reverse the method because the direction of
the crossings has been reversed, because Roy does really believe she had
proceeded in this way before: "*Just now I put W, then C, then G!*"

All the subjects at this level end up by accepting the necessity of starting
with the goat, except in the case of the final, reversed test *B* to *A*, which they
view as a new problem. All of them stress, like Ben and Roy, the action of
"separating" or "keeping apart," so that respect for the incompatibilities
has become the necessary condition for the problem's solution, even though
this does not prevent the compatibility $W \wedge C$ from gaining the upper hand
quite often, during the early part of the questioning and also in the final test
reversing the direction of the journeys. In short, from now on there is an
effort to achieve coordination between bringing together and keeping apart,
even though this systematization is found difficult and still remains both
insufficient and very much a matter of trial and error.

§8. Level 2B and Stage 3

Subjects at the nine- and ten-year-old level fall into three groups. Group one continues, like most 2A subjects, to start with the sequence C then W then G (or WCG) and to aim for the compatibility W ∧ C, a persistence to be noted from the general point of view of the initial primacy of the positive operations of joining. However, they immediately perceive the incompatibilities that these orders fail to overcome and eventually, after a longer or shorter period of trial and error, decide to start with the goat, and then, after taking over the wolf, to bring the goat back to A again. In other words they are successful; but the remarkable fact is that in their final summary of how they achieved that success they still think they followed the order WCG or CWG.

> Jer (9–4), for example begins just the same as the younger subjects: "*I take the cabbage first, then the wolf, and then the goat, because the wolf doesn't eat the cabbage so they'll both be quite safe* [on B]." Then he sees that W will have eaten G on A, and begins with the goat, subsequently discovering the necessity of bringing it back from B to A after the arrival of the wolf. His success was thus still the product of trial and error, but achieved much more quickly than by the 2A subjects. The astounding thing, however, is that at the end, when giving an account of how he did it, he returns to the primacy of compatibility: "How did you do it? — *First I put the wolf* [from A to B] *then the cabbage then the goat. Since the wolf can't eat the cabbage, well, you can leave them alone* [on B]." When asked to do the problem in the reverse direction: "*I do the same thing* [W, C, G], *because there's no need to change the way I do it.*" Then he corrects himself.

The second group (equal in number to the first), on the other hand, begin by taking over the goat, then, after having brought over the wolf too, discover fairly rapidly (some right away) that they have to bring G back from B to A in order to ferry C over and then finally bring G back over a second time. But when asked to do the problem in reverse, B to A, they too resort to the order WCG or CWG, not because they are trying out a reversal of their successful A to B order, but because they are still influenced by a remnant of that extremely tenacious primacy of compatibility.

> Dal (9–0) begins with the goat, and after brief hesitation succeeds in bringing it back and resolving the problem. But when faced with the problem in reverse, he says that "*you have to do the same as before: I take over the wolf first, then the cabbage, then the goat, and like that they won't eat one another.*" Now in fact, he did nothing of the kind when solving the problem in A to B direction.

Duc (10–8) likewise follows the order *C, W, G,* for the *B* to *A* direction *"because that's how I began before,"* whereas in fact he had constantly begun with *G* in the *A* to *B* direction, except for one trial of *C,* which was not his first.

The third group is made up of cases intermediate between stages 2 and 3. They all resolve the problem more or less rapidly, but above all draw the correct conclusions from their trials and errors and then succeed in retaining them. Nevertheless, even though they no longer actually employ the order *CWG,* it does still occur to them occasionally.

Cha (11–3) finally discovers the solution unaided. But he admits to having tried another mentally: *"I did think of taking the wolf first, then the cabbage, and then the goat, because the wolf doesn't eat the cabbage. — What's wrong with that? —* [Silence]."

This temptation reappears particularly in the reverse direction test, but is likewise discarded fairly swiftly.

Finally, at stage 3 (ten to 12 years) there is simultaneous and complete coordination of joining and separation, not only in the *A* to *B* direction but in the *B* to *A* test as well.

Pil (11–4): *"It's just the same, it comes to the same whether you do it one way or the other."*

In other words, the subject understands almost from the start the necessity of beginning with the goat and that of bringing it back after the arrival of the wolf. He then uses exactly the same method in the *B* to *A* direction and remembers it when asked to summarize what he has done.

§9. Conclusion

The conclusion to be drawn from this brief analysis is naturally that once again, in the case of this particular problem, we are observing a primacy of positive actions or operations (joining the compatibles) over the negative ones (separations), as well as over the double negation involved (avoiding the incompatibilities). The particularity of this situation, however, lies in the fact that these negative aspects are extremely clear and well known from the outset: there is no difficulty in understanding or remembering that wolves eat goats and goats eat cabbages. In other words, the negative does not have to be constructed, but simply observed and remembered. The primacy of the positive therefore does not become evident at level 1A, which is that of general noncoordination, but at level 1B, as soon as the first attempts at coordination are made, and it shows itself at this point in a form that is both *sui generis* and of great interest: the positive acquires a higher degree of necessity or value. It is not until the operatory 2A level that "separating" is understood as possessing a necessity equal to that of "joining," but even then only in principle, since in practice the subject still generally begins with the order *W, C, G* or *C W, G and continually reverts to it, particularly when asked to do the problem in the B* to *A* direction. And this obsession continues to manifest itself up to level 2B, in other words up to the age of nine and even ten, often leading to the paradoxical result of successes in action, and successes perfectly grasped by the subject at that moment, yet succeeded later by the impression and mnesic illusion that he in fact followed the order *W, C, G* (or *C, W, G*), which then reappears in the *B* to *A* direction. Thus this set of facts contains a surprising case of the primacy of the positive over negative aspects clearly evident from the very outset, and a comprehension of which involves absolutely no logical difficulty.

Eleven

Contradiction and Conservations of Quantities

with C. Othenin-Girard (part 1) and S. Uzan (part 2)

Part 1. Contradiction and Conservation of Continuous Quantities

We have known for a long time that the nonconservation attitudes specific to the preoperatory stage are the sources of numerous contradictions, and the excellent studies by Inhelder, Sinclair, and Bovet on how conservations are acquired have shown that the conflicts between noncoordinated indices are even more numerous and profound than simple observation had shown. Furthermore, it seems quite clear that the conquest of conservations is dependent upon a progressive compensation of positive and negative relations (for example "higher × less wide = same quantity), so much so that there is apparently nothing more to be said about the relations between this problem and our general hypothesis of an initial disequilibrium due to the primacy of affirmations over negations: the younger subjects begin with the former ("it's higher," "it's longer," and so on) while neglecting the negative aspects that would enable them to make compensation and thus lead to conservations.

§1. Commutability

All this, however, is simply a matter of observations, and if one wishes to find the reason for these initial disequilibriums, then one needs to isolate some elementary mechanism such that the positive (or additive) character of the action entails an initially systematic ommission of its negative (or subtractive) character. It is not easy to see why this should be the case when dimensional variations alone are involved, for instance length and width, both of which are as immediately perceptible as the other. In the test described in part 1 of chapter 9, on the other hand (transferring n counters from collection A to collection B and understanding why the difference is then $2n$), it is easier to see why the action of adding n elements to B is not accompanied at the outset by an awareness of having taken them away from A, since there is only a single action involved, additive in aim, and since there is only one set of elements, which are simply displaced, and in any displacement it is the new position of the objects that is important, not the blank left where they have been.

What we need to find then, in order to explain these early nonconservations, is a mechanism of the same kind, one that endows the positive aspects of one and the same fundamental action with a primacy over its negative aspects. Such an action does exist, and plays an essential role in all questions of conservation: it is that of displacing one part of the object in relation to the others. If we define "commutability" as being commutativity in a broad sense, by simply saying that the sum (or product) of two elements is not modified when one changes the relation of their positions, it is clear that such a displacement of the parts of the object is commutable: in the transformation of a ball into a sausage, a part A of the clay that is above B in the spherical form passes to the side of B when the ball is pulled out into a sausage, yet their sum remains the same. Only, in order to reason in that way, it is necessary to remember that if one adds material in the length dimension, one is taking it away from somewhere else, and that, in consequence, the sausage is not simply "longer" by a quantity x, but is also "less something else," that is, less $-x$ in relation to the previous shape. And it is precisely this subtraction that escapes the intention of our young subject, for reasons similar to those that prevent him from understanding the $2n$ difference when one transfers n counters from one collection to another. Similarly, in the nonconservation of number, the subject thinks that the quantity increases if one lengthens a line of elements by merely increasing the spaces between them. In that case, what he fails to grasp is that an addition to the length is at the same time a subtraction, taking the form of empty spaces between the elements.

In short, the source of the disequilibrium specific to nonconservations is not only to be sought in the difficulty of keeping two modifications in mind at once while looking at the result of an action or actions: it derives at a much deeper level from the limitations involved in acquiring consciousness of the central action itself, of which the positive aspect linked to its aim (increasing the length, and so on) is alone retained, while the subtractive or negative aspect inseparable from it is disregarded, since only one action, and only one set of elements modified by it, are involved. In this interpretation it is, therefore, noncommutability that is the obstacle to conservation, whereas the latter is constituted immediately "commutability," or commutativity in the broad sense, provides an elementary form of quantification simultaneously with a now measurable form of compensation.

§2. Nonconservations

It is now easier to understand the first result of these tests, which were devised with a view to revealing the possible feelings of contradiction in preoperatory subjects by making use of the usual questions but increasing the number of transformations and significant indications of contrary meanings. At the elementary level of nonconservation it was not possible to discern the slightest indication of any consciousness of contradiction, or of any modification of subjects' reasoning under the influence of a real conflict, since the children found continual changes of quantity in materials perfectly natural, and, when faced with dead ends, reacted by merely giving up all attempt at decisions for the time being.

Cri (5–3), with the clay balls, hovers between the criteria "longer" and "fatter" as indices of superior quantity. With two sausages of unequal length (made from equal balls) he removes almost half the longer one so that there will be "the same amount to eat" and is quite satisfied with the result: "You think there will be? — [He looks carefully.] *No, you, because it's fatter.* — What can we do? — *Don't know.*" Then he suggests rolling them back into balls (as they are now): "If you roll them up, will they be the same? — *Yes.* — Look at what's on the table (the piece he cut off). Will they be the same? — *No, all that's missing, so it must be put back again.*"

Lau (5–3), herself pours two quantities of liquid into two jars so that there will be "*the same to drink in both.*" Jar *C* is wide and low, jar *A1* is less wide and taller; but Lau fills them to the same level: "Are you sure? — *Oh quite sure, because the same is in both now, just the same.*" Having poured *C* into *A2* (similar to *A1*) she observes very different levels when she'd expected equality. No amazement: "*It's not the same because here* [*A1*] *not so much was put in,*" by which she means, as became apparent later, not that she'd poured too little into *A1* in relation to *C*, but that the quantities are at present unequal. And indeed, handed *B* (taller and more slender than the two *A*) she adjusts the liquid to equal levels (with some difficulty) and announces that "*it's just the same.* — And if we pour *B* and *C* into *A1* and *A2*? — *Just like mine* [prediction of equality as formerly]. — Try. — *It's not the same, because some was spilled.* — And why does it change? — *When you pour the red* [*A2*] *it always comes smaller, and the green* [*A1*] *always bigger.*"

From the point of view of contradiction, such observed reactions, which are in agreement with injumerable others made over many years, present a meaning that we can today accept with reasonable confidence, since the experimental research of Inhelder, Sinclair, and Bovet into early learning has shown the systematic resistance of subjects on this level to modifying their attitudes under the influence of indices or conflicts employed in methodical presentations, whereas at later, intermediate levels such procedures produce a marked effect on subjects' actions. And indeed, the specific characteristic of the inferences made by these younger subjects is their lack of all necessity, both in the interpretation of actions executed and in the anticipation of their results, so that neither the disagreements between indices nor the rebuttals inflicted by subsequent observations lead to stable corrections, or indeed to an astonishment that might induce the child to seek such corrections. The reason for this is clear: the only actions the child conceives of consist in adding or taking away, and even these are regarded merely as independent or successive actions, never as indissociable poles of one and the same displacement producing changes of shape or dimensions.

Thus Cri interprets increases in length as increases in the sense of additions, and so, in order to equalize the quantities of material in the two sausages made from like balls, he removes almost half of the longer sausage and is quite satisfied with the result. When disabused, he thinks that by rolling both sausages back into balls (one of them still truncated) he will be able to achieve equality again, and he has to have the detached portion of the longer sausage pointed out to him before he thinks of reamalgamating it. In Lau's case, with the liquids, these additions and subtractions are due to the transfers: the red drink then becomes "smaller" and the green "always bigger," without the rebuttals of past predictions of equality being incorporated at all in subsequent anticipations. In short, there is no coordination between increases (in length, say) and decreases (in width) because the transformations are not conceived of as displacements that entail a simultaneously additive and subtractive effect in relation to the final and initial positions, but as due to quite separate actions. The onset of conservation generally begins, on the contrary, (and this has been checked with a kind of modelling clay called Silly Putty that makes it possible to produce very long, slender threads) with the fundamental argument that "nothing has been taken away or added" (contrary to what is believed by the younger subjects), but only the shape changed, or in other words, only parts displaced: thus Rao, at eight years old, says of both the Silly Putty's weight and substance that it is still the same "because it's spread out, that's all...and if you squash it back again it will still be the same." Compensation reasoning then follows, but only because already implied in the double, subtractive and additive, aspect of the displacement.

§3. Revertibility

One point particularly worth noting in the results obtained is the precocity of "revertibility" reactions, meaning empirical reversions to the starting point. However, this should not be taken to mean that such behavior is primitive, and the very youngest subjects never think of such possible reversions to equality, which seem to go hand in hand with the onset of constituent functions.[1] We do find Cri exhibiting such a reaction, but in a special form, since after having cut off a large section of one of the sausages made from equal balls, he supposes it possible to roll them up again in this form and thus recover the equality he now sees he has sacrificed by mutilating one of his sausages. Here, in contrast, is a straightforward example:

Her (5–6) says "*you make it bigger*" when a ball is rolled into a sausage, so "*there's more to eat because it's fatter and wider* [= *longer*]" than the other sausage. "And if we want me to have as much as you? — *Then we must be quick and make the balls* [= roll the sausages back into spheres]. — And if you make sausages? — *Yes, make them big both the same.*"

In this case we are dealing solely with direct and reversed functions (functions in fact, even revertible in both directions: reversion of sausage to ball and reversion to a second set of sausages, but this time made "big both the same"), each of which expresses a modification in one direction, but lacking conservation for want of operatory reversibility. We have always acknowledged the existence of this difference, between reversibility with conservation and revertibility insufficient to produce quantitative invariability, but it would seem that the interpretation now being offered is the only one that enables us to justify this distinction by differentiating between noncommutable changes (to add or to take away) and commutable displacements. It is the case that when there is displacement with commutability of a part *A* of the object in relation to a part *B,* if *A* is displaced in front of *B,* then there is a lengthening as a result of this new position, but there is also, and simultaneously, a subtraction at the place from which *A* was removed, hence a narrowing; the reverse operation, consisting in returning *A* to its original position, is then in its turn simultaneously additive (replacement and therefore addition of *A* to the place it came from) and subtractive (removal from its new position which it occupied as a result of the direct displacement). Thus there is complete reversibility, because the addition-subtraction in one direction becomes subtraction-addition in the other, the first of these two couples being exactly cancelled, and therefore compensated, by the second as a result of the reverse displacement. The role of the subject's external action is thus simply to produce these displacements first in one direction then in the other, but the additions and subtractions remain internal to the object, since they are joinings and dissociations of its own parts, without external additions. In the case of revertibility, on the other hand, an additive action of lengthening is conceived of as a real "making bigger," with an increase in the quantity of material, which in turn is conceived of as due either to the power of the subject, who "rolls," or stretches the clay, or the power of the receptacle that raises the height of the liquid. As for the empirical return or reversion to the starting point (revertibility), that is seen as a new action, likewise external to the object, which diminishes or takes away what was added in the first. It is thus because two separate actions are involved, and above all two actions with their sources external to the object (in the external powers of adding or taking away quantities that did not belong to the initial object, but which are produced or cancelled by those powers expressed in actions), that revertibility is irreducible to operatory reversibility and cannot lead to conservation. Indeed, from the logical point of view, if adding and taking away are actions being exerted upon the object from outside, then what we have are two distinct actions that do not compensate one another in any necessary way, whereas if those external actions are reduced to displacements in both directions of quantities already included within the object, then the additions and subtractions do compensate one another, since they are positional changes within the object, and the reverse displacement simply constitutes a permutation of them, once more characterized by a necessary commutability.

§4. Counter-proof

If revertibility is, in fact, from the subject's point of view, no more than a reversion to an initial equality as a result of quantitative increases or decreases, it should be possible to create the illusion of such equalizations arising from real inequalities which the subject has recognized as such. The experiment used here consisted first of all in presenting the child with two similar glasses, $A1$ and $A2$, containing clearly unequal quantities, such that $A1 > A2$, then letting him compare two empty glasses B (slender and tall) and C (wide and low), and asking him if they will contain the same amount, to which the usual answer is no. Next, one asks the child to predict what will happen if $A1$ is poured into C and $A2$ into B. Since the experimenter has chosen inequalities that will compensate each other, the levels in B and C turn out to be the same, and the younger subjects then have no hesitation in concluding that there is equality of quantities, despite the original inequalities, which, of course, one must make sure they still remember.

Lof (5–9) predicts that $A2$ into B will conserve its low level, and that the level in $A1$ will be reproduced in C "*because if you pour the drink from A1 there will still be the same.*" When he observes the equality of the levels in B and C, he concludes that there is the same amount to drink in both: "*The same. — How can you tell? — I can see.*" If B and C are now poured back into $A1$ and $A2$, Lof anticipates equality (though he had just said he remembered one was higher in the beginning): "Why? — *Because it's the same here* [B] *and here* [C]. — [Liquid poured.] — *That one's higher.* — Why? — *I don't know.*"

Mig (5–6). Same reactions. He laughs when he sees the drink rising higher in B that in $A2$: "*There's more red been put in!* — But you saw we didn't put any more in. So what will happen if we pour the drinks back into $A1$ and $A2$? — *We'll have the same to drink* [in both]."

Pas (5–1), on the other hand, is an intermediate case who is eventually shaken in his belief. Beforehand, however, while predicting that the $A2$ level will rise in B and that of $A1$ descend in C (a reaction found in 25%

of five- to six-year-old subjects in the form of covariations without compensations), he draws the conclusion from the equal levels in *B* and *C* that there is the same amount to drink, and anticipates that the same will be true when the liquids are returned to *A1* and *A2*. Then, having seen the original inequality reappear, he still maintains that "*there is the same to drink* [despite *A1 > A2*] *because we saw so in the others* [*B* and *C*]." At the very end, however, he begins to understand. In *B* and *C,* he says, there is "*the same height.* — And if we drink them? — *There less and here more.* — How do you know? — *Because there's more.* — But you said that they're the same height, so why does one have more? — *Because I can see it with my eyes.*"

As in the case of revertibility, then, we find that an equality can be constituted from initial inequalities (or supposed inequalities), and here, even more paradoxically, despite objective inequalities recognized at the very outset. Like the earlier reactions discussed, those quoted here thus demonstrate the connection between nonconservation reasoning (applied to differences as well as equalities) and noncomprehension of the commutability inherent in displacements, of the fact, in other words, that what is later added is equivalent to what was originally taken away. Thus in all these reactions, primacy is constantly given to the arrival points of the actions (levels of liquid) with a concomitant and systematic disregard of their starting points, even though these are not in fact forgotten.

Part 2. Iterative Correspondence and Contradiction

The interpretation of nonconservations suggested by the initial systematic primacy of positive actions over negative ones is thus that by modifying an object's form (ball of clay rolled into sausage), the subject concentrates upon what he is adding in one direction (length) but ignores the fact that this addition implies subtraction of the same quantity from some other part of the same object in its previous state. Conservation will be acquired, on the other hand, once addition and subtraction are understood as interdependent and even indissociable: in this case the modification is conceived of as a simple displacement of parts of the object, with accompanying "commutability," which is to say conservation of the sum independently of the placings (just as commutativity conserves it independently of linear order: $AB = BA$).

§5. The Problem

One indication in support of this hypothesis would consist in inducing an improvement in conservations by encouraging the subject to become conscious of the departure points of the elements displaced. This is something we once attempted earlier with a set of grooved boards, arranged in the shape of a fan, making it possible to follow the path of each counter in a widely spaced row to its arrival point in a second, more tightly spaced row, or vice versa. This experiment, however (an account of which can be found in *Mental Imagery in the Child*, chapter 8, sections 4 and 5), did not produce any very positive result, probably because the permanence or identity of the individual counters is being maintained by the grooves rather than by any specific action on the subject's part (aside from starting the counters down the slide). So the basis of our next experiment will be a situation already studied by B. Inhelder, in which it is the child's own action that encourages the acquisition of conservation. The subject is required to place a bead in one jar with one hand and a second bead in a second jar with the other hand, an action that in the majority of subjects over five leads to the affirmation that the equality resulting from this correspondence will continue indefinitely. This is because conservation is based on a recurrential type of reasoning and on a local synthesis of inclusion (each pair added to its predecessors in a class of higher rank) and order (of the repeated actions), thus producing resistent numerical iteration, among our five- to seven-year-olds, who do not have conservation of the same equivalences when they are asked to put two equal rows of counters into correspondence on a table with one row more widely spaced that the other.

The problem we have set ourselves here, then (and it is one that has already been reasearched from other angles by B. Inhelder, H. Sinclair and M. Bovet in their work on learning processes),[2] is to establish, if we begin with this iterative correspondence procedure using the beads, then pass them on from the initial receptacles (jars), still in pairs, until they form two rows of unequal length laid out flat on a table (as in the usual test), whether this will help in the acquisition of conservation. For, beginning with the initial jars, the subject does clearly see that he is taking or moving the pairs of beads away from this point of origin in order to add them to some other locations, and this may help him therefore to understand the necessary link between the negative (distancing from point of departure) and positive (arrival at and addition to the point of arrival) aspects of any displacement, which according to our hypothesis would lead to acquisition of the "commutability" responsible for conservation. It will be remembered that we are terming commutability a generalization of commutativity that, like the latter, conserves total quantity independently of position. In the commutativity $AB = BA$ there is reciprocal substitution, and thus a change in linear order. In commutability there is simply a change of position on the part of A in relation to B, but insofar as A when added to B in a new position is at the same time regarded as simply displaced from some previous position, its addition to the final position becomes interdependent upon a subtraction at the outset, thus ensuring the conservation of the whole $A + B$. In other terms, commutability is a possible commutativity, but one in which the role of substitution or change of order is played by a displacement of some sort.

Technique

We begin with three transparent cylindrical jars, A, A', and B. A and A' are identical B is narrower than A. All three jars have holes at the bottom that are stoppered to begin with, then later unstoppered. The holes provide access to two transparent tubes At and $A't$ which are about five times as long as the jars and can also be stoppered or unstoppered. There are also two small boards, a and b, each with twelve hollows into which twelve beads may be inserted. In the case of board a, these hollows are spaced out along only two-thirds of its length. In the case of b they are spaced out over the whole length. The experiment begins with the usual questions to test for conservation: the child is asked to arrange two sets of twelve beads in rows on the table, and once their equality has been accepted one row is shortened by moving the beads closer together. Only those subjects who reject the conservation of equality without hesitation are retained.

The subject is then asked to take a bead in each hand and introduced them both simultaneously into jars A and A' (then possibly into A and B as a cross-check). A further twelve pairs are then inserted in the same way, with periodic checks on the equality of the jars' contents, which is acknowledged by all subjects in every case. Once the two sets of twelve beads are in the jars, the holes at the base are unstoppered and the beads allowed to roll into the two tubes At and $A't$. Beforehand, however, prediction of the result is requested. Once again, equality is predicted by all subjects and verified by them after the beads have entered the tubes. The tubes are then unstoppered in their turn, the subject removes a bead from each in each hand, then places them in two of the hollows in the boards, one in a and one in b. When all the hollows have been filled in this way, and equality is denied, the subject is first reminded that he had accepted it in both the jars and the tubes and asked if he finds it "natural" to reject it in the case of the boards. After noting his reaction to this contradiction, the positions of the boards can be changed (into / \ or ⌐ or ⊤), and the same questions asked for each modification. Then, most important of all, one goes on to return all the beads, two by two, (one in each hand) from boards to jars A and A' (omitting the tubes in this case, of course), but only after asking for a prediction, and with requests for occasional judgments of the resulting restoration of equality and questions about the contradictions.

The interesting point about this procedure is that it eventually leads a third of the four- to five-year-old subjects to acknowledge conservation in the *a* and *b* stage (on the parallel boards with rows of unequal length) or in a rerun of the preparatory test (rows of unequal length on the table), whereas in our earlier experiment with the grooved boards arranged in a fan no such improvement was observed at this very early age.

§6. First Type of Reaction

Let us begin by describing the most primitive reactions, in which equality in A and A′ in no way leads to recognition of equivalence on the boards *a* and *b* when they are parallel, with the longer row continuing on past the end of the more tightly spaced one, even though they both contain the same number of hollows (ordinal evaluations based on the order of the terminal boundaries). On the other hand, when the boards are arranged so that they are not parallel, or at right angles to each other, or even if they are displayed too rapidly for the subject to judge the exact placings of the hollows, equality is often predicted, and, except in the latter case, maintained even after the beads have been inserted.

Jan (5–0) denies conservation of equivalence when given the preparatory test, but accepts it in the case of jars A and A′ (and even in the case of jars A and B) as well as in the case of the tubes At and A′t. When the beads are in the boards *a* and *b*, Jan accepts equality when the boards are slanted but denies it when they are parallel: "*It's not the same because there are little holes here* [= closely spaced hollows in *a*] *and big ones there* [wider spacing of hollows in *b*]. — And what if we put them back in the jars (A and A′)? — *They'll be the same.*" Beads replaced in A and A′, and Jan maintains their equality. "Now we'll but them here and there (boards displayed rapidly, then at right angles). Will there be the same? — *No.* — Let's try. — [He inserts beads and to justify prediction of inequality turns the boards parallel.] *No, because here* [*a*] *there aren't any beads* [space at end without hollows]. — Do you think it's normal for them to be the same here (A and A′) and not there (*a* and *b*)? — *Yes.* — Why? — *Because here* [*b*] *there were more.* — Then where did they come from? — [Silence.] — Is it normal? —*Yes* — Did we put the beads from A there (*a*) and the beads from A′ there (*b*)? — *Yes.* — And in the jars they were the same? — *No* [= first attempt at reconciliation] — But before you said it was the same here and here (A and A′)? — *Yes.* — And now you say not? — *Because there* [*a*] *there aren't any beads* [the third without hollows]. — Put them back in here (A and A′). — [He replaces them in pairs]. — Are they the same or not? — *There's still the same here* [A] *and here* [A′] — And there (*a* and *b*)? — *No, because here* [*a*] *there aren't any beads* [last third]. — Is that normal? — *Yes.* — Doesn't it bother you (and so on)? — *No.*"

It is clear from these initial reactions that there is ultimately no conflict between acknowledging equality between A and A' and inequality on the boards, certainly when parallel and even, later, when they are not (including at right angles). This type of reactions is found in a sixth of the four- to five-year-olds. However, just for a moment, Jan is bothered at one point by the contradiction and decides that there wasn't equality between A and A' either. Only later, after the return of the beads (in couples, one in each hand) he reverts to the equality of A and A' while continuing for all that to deny it on the boards (and without any progress when the preparatory test was repeated).

§7. Second Type

In a second type of reaction (half the four- to five-year-old subjects) the contradiction is felt, given the strength of the equalization by pairs in A and A' and also the deep-rooted impression of inequality in a and b caused by the inequality of length. The child's solution is consequently to deny the A to A' equality in retrospect.

> Pau (4–9) is convinced of the equality between A and A' "*because there's three and three*" then "*because there's five and five,*" and so on. Likewise in the tubes. But after having believed for an instant that there is also equivalence between a and b he looks at the boards harder, then energetically denies it, for the same reasons as Jan. When he replaces the beads into the jars A and A' (once again in pairs) he then disputes the equality he had affirmed earlier: "*There [A´] there are a lot and there [A] not so many. — Why? — There [A'] there are a lot because the beads have come from there [b] and there [A] there's just a few because the beads come from here [a]. — But just now you told me that A = A'. — That was wrong. There are a lot here [A] and not many there [A'] because* [same argument]."

It is clear that for subjects in this second group (when they reason like Pau) the point of origin of the beads is beginning to play a role at the point of destination, which is a first step toward commutability. Yet, interestingly enough, it works at first in favor of the conservation of nonequivalences, not that of equalities, because it is the reverse ab/AA´ journey that is being concentrated on. However, in many cases, although the child begins like Pau, he later returns to the A = A' equality as soon as he recalls the correspondence by pairs in the filling of the two jars. However, this does not stop him continuing to reject the ab equivalence, so that he then simply relapses into reactions of the first type, as evinced by Jan in the previous paragraph.

§8. Third Type

Among subjects of a third group (a third of the four- to five-year-olds), we find, on the contrary, an observable advance in the direction of conservation, albeit in steps.

Mar (4–8) represents the least advanced case. He begins with a very marked degree of nonconservation in the preparatory test. With the jars A and A', on the other hand, he accepts equivalence because "*I did like that with both my hands* [correspondence]." With A and B he hesitates "*because here* [A] *you can put in more than there* [narrower B]," but changes his mind during actual insertion. In tubes At and A't equality is conserved. As for boards a and b, there is a problem. Prediction asked for: "Will we have the same (rapid display)? — *Yes . . . no . . . yes, because we shall have the same beads* [= same number of beads?] — [Insertion] — *That one there* [a] *has not very many and that one* [b] *a lot.* — Why's that? — *Because here* [blank third of a] *there aren't any holes.* — Do you think it's normal [repetition of previous observations of A and A', At and A't)? — *Not normal.* — How do you explain it? — *Don't know* — (Back to A and A'.) Are these the same? — *Yes, the same.* — (Transfer to a and b). Are they the same? — *Yes.* — How do you know? — *I don't know. Because . . . no, I don't know* [meaning he knows they're the same but not how to explain it]." Repeat of preparatory test: success "*because it's the same size, but that one there is with this one here*," and so forth. In other words, he points out the correspondences one by one with his finger, despite differing positions of the elements and differing lengths of rows.

Fio (4–9) fails preparatory test but accepts equality in A and A' and in A and B "*because I take a bead* [in each hand] *and put them in both.*" When boards displayed rapidly he anticipates conservation of equalities, but after insertion of beads contests it to begin with, then suddenly changes his mind "*because I've looked better now.*" Repeat of preparatory test also produces success, but without further explanation.

Bea (5–0). Same reactions throughout, except that, when she discovers the equivalence between a and b she does not, any more than Fio, use A and A' as her argument, but facts that are normally used to argue nonconservations: it's the same in both "*because with a it's thinner, you can't put in your finger* [between two beads] *and on b you can.*"

Gim (4–9) in contrast justifies equality between beads on boards (rejected to begin with) "*because you take out two* [removal in pairs from tubes A and A't].*"

Hag (4–5): equality between a and b "*because there's the same there and there* [in A and A´].*"

Dus (4–11). Similar reaction: *"because in the tubes the beads are the same,"* then in *a* and *b:* *"There are the same beads in them, but they're not both as big* [indicating lengths]."

Tom (5–4) *"because there's the same there* [A and A'] *and there* [a and b]." Again success when preparatory test repeated, as with all the subjects in this group.

§9. Conclusion

These results are remarkable for four- to five-year-olds, and the facts clearly show that when centration on the displacement of elements is achieved in terms of the subject's own actions, rather than merely in terms of the apparatus (the grooved and fanned boards of our earlier experiment), then the acquisition of conservation is facilitated. It is true that in this case a particular type of action is involved, one that is in itself a source of equivalence (correspondence by pairs achieved by using both hands at the same time), but when this active correspondence by pairs is applied to the boards alone, it is in no way sufficient (any more than it is sometimes with the unequal jars A and B), and two-thirds of the subjects actually remain impervious to it (sections 6 and 7) despite its being maintained in the transfer from AA' to the tubes $At A't$ and also from the tubes to the boards. So what is new in the case of the last third of our subjects is that, in addition to the two-handed correspondences, consideration of the displacement processes themselves also plays an active part. That is, as the elements arrive at a and b they are still being thought of as emanating from sources where they were in a situation of equality. The subjects making up the first groups, in contrast, fail to link these arrival states to the departures states, or, when they do begin to do so, it is in the wrong direction, thus leading them to contest the initial equalities. To link the arrival states to the initial states in the direction of the displacement is to understand that an addition at the arrival point cannot occur without a departure having occurred at the source, and it is the grasping of this necessary interdependence that produces "commutability." The fact that such interdependence between positive elements (arrivals) and negative elements (departures) involves already corresponding couples does undoubtedly reinforce it[3] and explain its precocious nature in comparison with the results achieved by linking elements on a simple one-to-one basis (displacement of individual elements in the usual tests or that using grooved and fanned boards). But, we must repeat, this correspondence by pairs achieved by using both hands would not be sufficient in itself in the case of the boards a and b alone. It still needs the reinforcement provided by the AA' to $AtA't$ and $AtA't$ to ab displacements, even if those displacements are conducted in pairs rather than bead by bead.

In short, neither the iterative correspondence nor the materialization of the displacements succeed separately in facilitating conservation by commutability, but in conjunction they do achieve that effect, because each of these two factors concentrates the subject's attention in its own way on the departures of the beads and not simply upon their arrivals. Thus we can say that the results of this experiment constitute, not a verification of the hypothesis referred to at the beginning of this section, but nevertheless one more piece of evidence to add to all the rest in its favor.

Twelve

Contradiction and Spatial or Cinematic Conservations

with M. Labarthe (part 1), C. Gilliéron (part 2),
and A. Blanchet (part 3)

Part 1. Conflict Situations in the Evaluation of Lengths

To continue these brief remarks on conservations, it is worth pointing out that the well-known reactions relating to spatial projection of one element beyond another provide a further example of the general way in which early cognitive attitudes center on the positive aspects of actions or objective properties while disregarding their negative aspects, thus leading to disequilibriums and contradictions through a lack of compensations. The familiar test, used in so many experiments on conservation of length, in which two previously superimposed equal rods are then laid parallel but staggered, is typical in this respect, since younger subjects pay attention solely to the projection formed by the rod moved forward in relation to the other, paying no attention to the fact that its other end has also moved, thus leaving a space equal to the amount it has moved forward and creating an equal terminal disparity, or projection of the motionless rod, that compensates the first. In the case of metal rods moved by means of light taps, we shall see in chapter 14 that, up to the age of seven, the leading end is thought to move more than the impact end. It was therefore thought that it might be useful to reexamine the question of spatial differences by means of an experiment involving two "journeys" with a built-in disparity between them at the start (see section 6, chapter 8 of *Mental Imagery in the Child*). The child is shown two houses A and B, with B standing slightly further forward than A at an angle of 45° , and asked to make two people (pawns) "take two walks both the same length" by moving the pawns as they are or along paths measured by means of lined up rods (all the same unit of length or with a possible choice of two or three sets of differing unities). In addition, in certain cases one also has two little dolls, one at each end of the "walks" and a third outside, so that one can ask what these observers will think about the lengths involved, according to their different viewpoints.

§1. Level 1A

The first striking result is that, out of fourteen five- and six-year-old subjects, only one succeeded unprompted in predicting a disparity at the arrival points A' and B' corresponding to that existing at the departure points A and B. Three others did succeed eventually, but only when constrained by the measuring rods (because if the two walks include the same number of units, which the subjects find it quite normal for them to do, then the disparity at A' B' follows quite naturally). For all the other subjects, "two walks both the same length" are walks that end at the same arrival point, and when the difficulty involved is sensed, they then conclude that "that house (B) must be put side by side with the other," as Rod, among others, puts it, after having begun as follows:

Rod (5–4) walks the two pawns to the same point and claims that they have both come the same long way. "And if they go home, will they both have the same walk? — *No.* — Which will walk more? — *Him* [*A*]. — Why? — *Because his house is farther away.*" Since, on the return journey, the houses *A* and *B* constitute the arrival point, this answer is logical, if we exclude the contradiction entailed by the continuing inequality of the round trip, which does not bother the subject. "And like this (correct "walks" with terminal disparity)? — " *No, this one* [*B* ahead of *A*] *has gone more.*" But reversal on return journey. Rods: Rod places three units leading away from *B* and another three leading away from *A* but beginning a few inches in front of *A*, so that both walks still end at the same point.

Kol (5–6). Conservation test plus viewpoint of the observers at each end: "*That one is longer* [two rods staggered after congruence] *because it sticks out.* — And when this doll looks (observer at far end)? — *Then it's the other that is longer.* — Which is right? — *They don't agree, you can't make them agree.*" Houses and walks: identical arrival points despite seven units for one walk and nine for the other. Since the observing dolls still don't agree, Kol removes two units from each walk in order to attain numerical equality, giving seven and five, then five and three: "*These two walks don't have five, but all the same they're the same.*"

Nic (5–4) begins with the walks oblique, almost equal, and ending at the same point. The solution with a terminal disparity is suggested, but she rejects it because one is too long, and makes the arrival points level again. With three and three rods, walk *B* at *B'* extends beyond *A'*, so she removes the third rod, but then accepts four rods in a straight line from *A* and four with an angle in the line from *B*, thus achieving coincidence at arrival points once more. With four longer rods from *A* against four shorter ones from *B*, she accepts two parallel walks with coincident terminations: "*Yes, they both make the same walk.*"

Mic (6–11). Same absence of terminal disparity. He is asked to make the walk from *A* with three rods, then to produce the same long walk from *B*: he puts one rod from *B* to *A* (slanting) then three parallel to the first three from *A* to *A'*. "And what if we did this (correct solution with terminal disparity)? — *No, no, no! They haven't walked the same. B is longer. You've put in another stick!* [In fact, it is three and three.]" Eventually he overlaps the rods from *B* slightly so that the *B* walk won't extend beyond *A'*.

Rud (6–6). Same reactions. Shown correction solution with five rods:

"There's five and five, but the walk from B is longer [indicating terminal disparity]."

One still finds similar solutions being offered by six out of seventeen subjects in the seven- to eight-year-old group. In this same group, however, one also finds four subjects who accept the terminal disparity when constrained by the numerical equivalence of the rods used (all the same length). As for the intermediate or immediately correct solutions, we shall come to those in section 2.

At this point, however, we need to understand the reactions already quoted. Despite our familiarity with the ordinal evaluation of lengths in terms of their points of arrival (according to which longer = going further) with concomitant disregard of their points of departure, the present results raise a double problem, first because the built-in disparity between the departure points is clearly observed (to the extent that all the five- to six-year-old subjects desire to eliminate it), and second because perceptually and, moreover, numerically (measuring rods), the subjects does indeed sense, and occasionally even recognizes, that the "walks" are unequal. In addition, when the fictitious observers are invoked, these subjects (see Kol) accept the possible diversity of viewpoints, even though they cannot coordinate them. So that in this particular case we need to find an explanation that will account for such a deeply rooted centration on the order of the arrival points.

Until now we have contented ourselves with two interpretations that are not false but are, nevertheless, only partial, since both are based simply upon a kind of obliviousness on the subject's part to the order of the starting points. In the area of representational images this neglect on the subject's part can be attributed to his constant preoccupation with terminal boundaries (development of the image being influenced by the analogy with drawing), according to our early findings at least. But then our research into functions provided us with a more general view. According to this, function, like the schemas of action from which it springs, is centered upon its point of application, and is thus dependent upon the action's direction or end point. While retaining that basis, however, it now seems that, as a result of our analyses in the first work, we must also add that movement in the direction of the end point, and above all a disparity at that end point resulting from such movement, are both seen as positive quantities, since that disparity is actually being seen created, whereas the starting points are essentially points from which the movement recedes. Thus, in the case of a disparity there, it is not the projecting portion that is seen as positive but, on the contrary, the blank section corresponding to it that is seen as a negative quantity, and one not comparable in significance to the equal blank section produced by the projection at the end point.

In other words, the coordination of departure and end or arrival points presents a systematic difficulty, because it is possible solely in terms of distance (or intervals), which is to say of symmetrical relations ($XY = YX$) and of the end result of the displacement operation. Our subjects here, on the contrary, are thinking in terms of movements actually in the process of being executed, movements directed toward a goal and receding from initial placements whose relations with that goal are modified en route, since the recessions involved are progressive. This produces two striking consequences. The first is the difficulties experienced in quantification, which are reminiscent of those involved in the relations between full and empty to be studied in chapter 12: sometimes house A is said to be "further away" from the goal and house B "further forward" (Gro, 6–10) or "nearer" (Gue, 7–1, and others); sometimes, on the contrary, B is "further away" and A "nearer" (Gir, 6–10, and others), when they are thinking of the distance that has been covered by the walks. But these two meanings are not complementary, thus leading to contradictions such as that expressed by Gue, who refuses to accept the correct solution of a disparity at the end point for two reasons: because this means that "B walks further than the other" and "because his house is nearer the end of the road" (which is precisely what will no longer be the case if the idea of a common "end" at A' and B' is discarded). The second remarkable consequence is that in the majority of cases (with the exception, and then not always, of those when the measuring rods are used) the two walks leading from A and B to a common end point are said to be equal on the outward journey but not equal on the homeward journey, since A is then seen as further than B. In a word, there is no complementarity at an early stage between the two distances corresponding, for one and the same journey, to the two actions of "moving away from the starting point" and "moving toward the point of arrival," since the latter is positive and the former negative (in the sense of the logical opposite), and since they share no common measure. As a result, there can be no compensations between staggered departures and the suggested staggered arrivals, since, because the latter are positive and the former negative, there seems to the subject to be inequality between the two walks (the one projecting beyond the other at the end point being naturally the longer), thus producing a systematic tendency to equalize the two arrival points.

§2. Levels 1B and 2A

The intermediate reactions aimed at conciliation similarly require a shared arrival point in order to avoid any terminal projection of one walk beyond the other, but combine this with a detour for the pawn starting from *B*, whose walk would appear shorter if made along a straight line.

Dub (5–4) makes *B* go on "*a little tour*" in the shape of an S. When kept to straight lines, he makes the *A* pawn start level with *B*, then from *A*, when he recognizes that the walks are unequal, whereupon he bends *B*'s walk again in order to achieve level arrivals. With the rods he lays down three and three, which produces the correct disparities at either end: "Have they walked the same? — "*Yes, because if the houses were side by side it would be the same.*"

Eri (6–1) makes two straight but unequal walks with the rods so that the end points are level: "*The walks aren't the same . . . you need to push here* [terminal disparity], *but it's not the same even then.* [He introduces a bend into B.] *There, now they've walked the same* [level end points]. — And if you make *B* walk straight? — [He uses six and six rods giving a terminal disparity.] *They haven't walked the same. But there's six there's and six there.*"

Kof (7–8) begins with two straight walks ending level but with one made up of twelve rods and one of seven (all rods of equal length), then acknowledges inequality. Shown correct solution with terminal disparity, Kof rejects that, too. She then draws a new, vertical arrival line, well to the left of *A*, and makes the two pawns from *A* and *B* take slanting, parallel walks such that *B*'s is manifestly the longer: "*Now they've both walked the same and all the dolls* [observers] *are quite happy* [which was not the case before]."

Via (7–4) makes both pawns' arrival points level, but then, after consideration, decides: "*B gets there first because he's nearer.*" He then tries having their walks cross, but still ending up level at the line, and since the inequality is still there: "*I'm making B go round some bends because A has further to go.*" These bends get more and more complicated, but finally, using the rods, he announces that "*you won't have to use so many sticks to go straight as to go round bends,*" and yet "*the walks are as long as one another because of the bends.*"

And here are two examples of correct responses from the start:

Bru (7–0). The *B* pawn "*has his house further on, so his walk goes further on.*"

Cyr (7–2). Terminal disparity "*because if you put them together* [= put the two walks side by side without the projections at both ends] *they're the same.*"

Oce (8–8) measures the terminal disparity at the house end and carries it over to the arrival points: "*What you do is look at the difference between the little men* [arrival] *and between the houses.*"

The intermediate cases are interesting in that (in the case of the technique employed here) the source of the progress they make is not connected with any need to imagine a terminal projection symmetrical with that produced by the staggered departure points. On the contrary, these subjects (and there were many others like them) cling obstinately to level arrival points, and only then discover the inequality of the distances walked, either simply by perceptual means, or else by using the rods that establish the inequality by mensuration. The conflict between this need for level arrival points and subsequent awareness of the unequal distances traveled is then overcome by resorting to detours (or in Kof's case to a vertical arrival line rather than a horizontal one). In other words, for these subjects there is still no necessary complementarity between "walking away from the departure points" and "walking toward the end points," or any necessity, when the walks are straight lines, for equality between the staggered departure and a symmetrically staggered arrival, since the latter is avoided by every means possible. Dub finally acknowledges this necessity thanks to the use of the measuring rods and understands fully; Eri fails despite the equality of his measures (six and six), while the others get no further than making bends or resorting to slanting walks.

Only the subjects on the last level understand the necessity for a terminal disparity when the walks are parallel and straight, because they alone grasp from the outset the complementarity between "walking away" from A or B and "walking toward" A' or B'. Thus Bru says right away that if the house if further on then the walk goes further on, so at last there is precise compensation between the positive values X of the advance toward the goal and the negative values, non-x, of the moving away in relation to the starting point, hence $x + $ non-$x = $ constant, which makes possible the equalization of the outward and homeward trips over the same distance, as well as the construction of two equal journeys despite staggered points of departure.

Part 2. Conservation of Lengths and Perceptual Illusions

In what follows, we began by asking ourselves what would happen to certain perceptual illusions that are normally strong in young subjects (Müller-Lyer and also vertical-horizontal) if the straight lines to be compared were to consist of rods that the subject himself selects for their equality before they are placed in the illusion-producing apparatus. However, the subjects used for this experiment were also tested for conservation of length in straight lines, first congruent then staggered, and it turned out that among the four- to five-year-olds the number of conservations or quasiconservations was greater (about 50% of the group) than had ever been observed before, thus providing a second problem for discussion: that of the status of these quasiconservations occurring before operatory quantification.

Technique

For the two illusions, the procedure consists in asking the subject to select from six rods any two that are equal in length (there are only two in fact). The two selected are then arranged either for the usual vertical-horizontal illusion test (an inverted *T*) or on a card covered with convergent and divergent featherings so as to create the Müller-Lyer illusion. The subject is then asked to look carefully at the rods and say whether they are the same length or whether one is longer than the other. In other words, he is being prompted to describe "how they look." Then, and only then, the question is put: "What are they like really?" This second question can entail a reference back to the choice of two equal rods made earlier by the subject himself; but naturally the wording of it must not suggest such a reference.

§3. Stage 1

The first remarkable result was that at this stage (four- to six-year-olds) 57% of the subjects in the vertical-horizontal illusion test and 72% in the Müller-Lyer test declared the two straight lines to be equal. (Only 21% in the first case, and 10% at the most in the second, "saw" them distorted in the usual way, while 20% and 18% wavered between the two.) It should be made clear, however, that the subjects affirming equality between the lines were not differentiating between what they knew and what they perceived, but simply claimed to "see" the lines as equal. Here are two representative examples:

Kol (5–8). Müller-Lyer: "Are the two sticks both as long as each other or not? — *Yes.* — There isn't one longer than the other? — *No.* — How do you know? — *Because I can see it.* — Doesn't one go a little bit further than the other? – *No* [because he can see it doesn't]."

Ver (6–6). Vertical-horizontal: "*Both the sticks are as big as one another.* — But when you look at them are they the same? — *Yes.*" Müller-Lyer: same answer. "Are you seeing them the same, or do you just know they are? When you look isn't there one big and one little? — *When I look they're both the same.* — So what have you done? — *I've seen that they were the same size, the sticks.* — When? Was it when you chose them, or now, looking at them? — *Before and now.*"

Even though these illusions are both very tenacious ones, and often studied before with subjects of these ages, we nevertheless conducted a control experiment to check that the subjects would in fact still perceive them if they had not previously chosen the rods themselves for their equality. And this was indeed the case. The only possible interpretation that remains, therefore, is that these subjects are refusing to accept a possible distinction between perception, a possible source of subjective errors, and their conceptual or representative knowledge, in this case based upon previous observations and above all on their earlier active selections. The result is a sort of "repression" of the observed facts analagous to that in so many cases already encountered where there is a conflict between present perceptual data and preconceived ideas.

As to why this notional knowledge, which is able to win out over perception at stage 1 in this way, should not itself be distorted in the ⊥ position, or when the lines occur in simple succession, when it is to so much greater an extent when the lines are staggered ($-\!\!=\!$), the explanation for this must be that in the latter situation there is projection of one line beyond another, and that factor is fundamental in the ordinal evaluation of lengths (in contrast with metrical evaluations based on the interval between the two ends), whereas it does not come into play at all in the configurations ⊥ or — —. It is thus quite normal in these latter cases that the subject should refer back without conflict to his previous choices and observations, whereas in the case of the configuration with terminal projection he finds himself confronted by a new problem, and one equally notional in nature.

To conclude this examination of stage 1 we will look at two examples of the rare cases in which the subject, despite having selected two equal rods earlier, does not "repress" the distortions, and does agree that the lines are unequal, both in the vertical-horizontal test and in the Müller-Lyer test. In this case, however, he of course believes that they have been modified in reality, and makes no distinction between objective size and apparent or perceptual size.

Win (4–5) chooses the red and brown rods as being equal, which is correct. The red is placed vertically, the brown horizontally: "*The red is too big* [for the conservation of equality]. — Why? — *It's longer.* — What if an ant walked along them both? — *The red is* [= goes] *further, the brown is shorter.* — And the ants? — [On] *the red the ant would walk more, it is bigger.* — And like this (brown and red interchanged)? *Well, it would be that one* [vertical brown] *that would walk more.* — But before we began? — *I chose two the same.* — And now? — *That one is bigger.*"
— But he can find no explanation, other than that he may have made a mistake in his choice of rods.

Pat (5–11). Same reactions for vertical-horizontal. "Why did you choose these two sticks? — *Because they were the same length.* — And now? — *That* [vertical] *is longer.* — How can that be? — [Silence.] — Is it all right? — [Silence.] — [Vertical and horizontal interchanged.] — *That one* [red vertical] *is longer.* — Before it was the brown and now it's the red? — *Yes.* — How can that be? — [Silence.]" Müller-Lyer: "*One is bigger.* — Why? — *Because there is a bigger space*" entailing a lengthening of the stick.

Thus is no conservation of length under the effect of perceptual distortion. But the latter, as we saw in chapter 7 with reflections in a mirror and refraction, is regarded as a real modification of the object's properties, in this case the lengths of the rods. This objective length (evaluated among other methods by how far an ant would have to crawl) is thus judged either to be constant, in which case the perceptually observable facts are rejected and "repressed," as with Kol, Ver, and the great majority of subjects, or else to be variable, as in the cases of Win and Pat, though without any explanation (in contrast to the results of our reflection or refraction experiments).

§4. Stage 2

As for the later stages, it is at level 2A, between seven and eight years old (often after a brief intermediate phase), that distinction is made between perceptual appearances (though these are not yet understood as subjective) and "knowledge" derived from measurement.

Cri (7–9) Vertical-horizontal test (*V-H*): "*You might say that one* [*H*] *is smaller than that* [*V*]. — What do you think? — *I think they're the same because of measuring before.* — And like this (rods interchanged so that *H* becomes *V* and vice versa)? — *Well, now it's the opposite. It's that one* [previous *H* now *V*] *that looks smaller than the other.* — But is it really? — *No.*" Müller-Lyer: same reaction, when one looks "*this one is smaller than that one . . . It's funny, because they're both* [in reality] *the same size.*"

Pil (7–6): "*It's as though there's one longer than the other, but they're the same.* — How do you explain that? — *I don't know.*"

Sos (8–6): "*That one* [*V*] *is longer than the other, but if you put them like this* [parallel] *then they're the same! They're magic tricks; it's as though that one is longer than that one.*" Müller-Lyer: he imagines at first he must have chosen sticks that weren't really equal, then, after checking their equality: "*They're the same length.* — And when you look? — *Ah! No.*"

Buc (8–7). *H-V: "They're not the same* [he checks the objective equality he had established]," then: *"They're not the same: V is bigger. But if you put H where V is, then it becomes bigger. So they're the same."* So $(V > H) + (H > V) = (V = H)$.

Flu (8–7): *"It's as though V is longer. — Is it really or just as though? — They're the same, only with them put differently ... No, it isn't* [longer]. — And if two ants walked along them, would one have to walk further? — *Yes, that one ... But that's not right, because the two sticks we put in were the same length* [and therefore, objectively, still are]."

Finally, toward nine to ten years old (level 2B), it seems that the distortion is being regarded as perceptual in the sense of subjective:

Lav (9–6): *"It's as though V is longer, but it isn't. It's because this one you're looking at from on top and that one you see straight* [= horizontal]." Müller-Lyer: *"One seems bigger ... because these arrows go the same way here* [convergent feathering] *and there they go further away* [divergent]."

San (10–6). H-V: *"It's only as though. It's because V is straight* [vertical] *and when it lies down flat it makes it look as if it's littler, but if it's like that* [V], *then it gets bigger."*

Gun (10–2): *"That one seems bigger, because one is looking with one's eyes,"* but measuring tells us the truth. *"And without measurement? — You could try feeling with your fingers."*

A parallel experiment using the Hering illusion (the effects of angles) gave the same results.

§5. Discussion

These conflicts between perceptually observable facts and notional and inferential knowledge possess a certain theoretical interest because they are in no way reducible to the ordinary antithesis between errors or illusions specific to perception as a subjective process and the certainty characteristics of objective comparisons by congruence or measurement, but derive, on the contrary, from the fundamental transformations of the very acts of affirming and denying as they develop, and from equilibrations tending to eliminate the contradictions linked to their elementary forms (see part 1 of chapter 15). Indeed, the reactions of the stage 1 subjects (see section 1) confronted with their perceptual illusions (when there have been preparatory observations linked to the choice of equal pairs made by the subject) are clearly comparable to what we find in the case of objective distortions in no way reducible to perceptual subjectivity: refraction, mirror reflections or unexpected mechanical curves dependent on conditions inherent in the apparatus.

In all these cases, as in the present situation, what we in fact find is a preoperatory stage 1 in which affirmation consists in a direct taking over of the object's intrinsic and absolute characteristics without the internalization or relativization that will later enable the subject to bring that affirmation into relations with positional factors, differing viewpoints, and so forth, or with his own activity regarded as susceptible to approximations or errors (except in an all or nothing situation). Thus in this preoperatory stage the bars of a letter reversed in a mirror have "rolled" one way or the other (chapter 7), the rod seen refracted has been "bent" by the force of the water, the pencil fixed to the wheel (mechanical curves) has gone wrong and not followed the path "it ought to go on," the imperceptible difference between elements (chapter 1) cannot exist if you can't see it, and so on. In the case of the present perceptual illusion it is therefore natural for the subject to find himself forced to choose between "seeing" the two rods as equal, because he "knows" they are (hence a simple repression of the troublesome observable fact), and believing them to have become objectively unequal (as happens with a minority of subjects), albeit without being able to find any cause for this modification (hence the rarity of this kind of reaction). So what is there that is similar in all these various forms of behavior, since in the case of the reflections, refraction, or the aberrant mechanical curves, the distortion is not denied by attributed to external perturbations, whereas in the case of perceptual illusions, presented as they have been here, the distortion is generally denied, and the perturbation eliminated by repression of the observed fact? Now there does exist, nonetheless, a characteristic that is common to all these early reactions: it is the refusal to accept that the two states A (permanence of form or size) and A' (optical or mechanical or perceptual distortion) *are both true at the same time* and relative to two distinct but compatible referentials.[1] Thus there is affirmation of A or of A' and nonaffirmations and negations combined to produce $A + A' = B$. In short, these affirmations of the first type are not accompanied by negations presenting the form of the secondary classes: making A elements with characteristics a and b (and therefore included among the B) correspond to A' elements with b but non-a characteristics. The only form of negation made use of at the moment thus remains the sort of practical but not yet stated sort of negation that consists in rejecting or even denying all perturbations threatening the predictions that are regarded as correct.

Level 2A presents an intermediate situation. Here we find recognition that both the states do exist: the real size A (equal rods) and the apparent size A'

(one "seems" bigger, "it is as though" and so on). However, because there is no comprehension ("I don't know," "why," "it's funny," and so forth, or "perhaps I measured wrong at the beginning,") there is still no subsumption of A and A' into a class B with its shared characteristics and its subdivisions, both of them stable. Hence a disequilibrium and resultant fluctations, as in the case of Flu, made manifest in an instability of expressed negation, so that "not the same" may be dependent upon either the object or the subject, with no firm ground for decision.

With level 2B, internalization and relativization acting interdependently with affirmations and negations make the solution possible: the general class B becomes stable (the rods really are equal) as do the two subclasses A and A', now that they are seen as relative to the positions and the subjective "impressions" dependent upon "looking": when superimposed, the rods remain equal (A), but in the positions V and H, or with convergent or divergent feathering behind them, they appear different (A').

§6. Qualitative Identity

This development of affirmations and negations in the two interdependent directions of an internalization (endogenous developments) and a relativization is naturally very closely linked with the advances made in quantification, first intensive (construction and regulation of "all" and "some" for secondary classes), then extensive ("commutability," then measurements) characteristic of the operatory levels. One of the interesting features of the present results is their confirmation that in situations where two rods are first placed in congruence, then staggered (one projecting at each end) one may find, before quantitative and operatory conservations, kinds of preoperatory quasiconservations whose status we are now concerned to establish.

Technique

Two distinct procedures were employed, both of which tend to provide the subject with assurance that the two rods involved are indeed equal at the outset, even though one projects beyond the other later.

The first procedure, which we shall term B, is a familiar one. The subject is offered several small rods and asked to select two that are exactly equal. These two rods are then placed parallel and in congruence on the table so that they are horizontal from the subject's viewpoint. Then one is slid along so that it projects by about half its length beyond the other, and the child is asked if they are still the same length. Some subjects say thay are, others contest it because of the projection.

The second procedure, which we shall term D, employs drawings in addition. The subject selects a rod, then is asked to draw a line the same length beside it, very carefully and making sure their equality is exact. Then the rod is slid along so as to project by about half its length beyond the drawn line, and the child is asked if it is longer, shorter, or the same length as the line. Next, the experimenter draws another line of the same length alongside the rod in its new position, but of a different color than the child's line. Now the new line and the rod are compared, after which the rod is removed and the same questions are repeated in relation to the two different colored lines, which are, of course, staggered by half their lengths.

These two procedures taken together, interpreting success very broadly, produced 66% quasi-conservatory reactions at four years old and 48% at five years old, conservations rising to 60% at six years old and to more than 75% at seven years old. It would seem, therefore, that we have a bimodal curve, but since there were hardly more than fifty replies in the four- to six-year-old group we would be reluctant to assert this unreservedly. On the other hand, if we take the considerable number of favorable cases at four years old, plus the fact that at this age quantification is still rudimentary and that the predominant form of affirmations (referred to in the preceding paragraph) tends to reinforce the qualitative identities of the objects involved, one is naturally led to think that these precocious quasiconservations are different in kind from operatory conservations. However, before attempting to analyze them, it should be recorded that a further test was carried out with the same four- to five-year-old subjects in order to compare the two procedures employed in light of the two possible orders in which they can be used. The results came very close: 50% favorable cases using the drawing technique first, and 44% percent using the more familiar one first, which appears to indicate quite simply that the first (D) reinforces centration on the initial equalities very slightly. That said, here are some examples:

Bol (4–10). *D:* "Look at your red line and my blue line. What can we say about them? — *That one is the same line as the one here.* — Are they the same size, or is one big and the other little? — *Both* [he indicates the rod and the two lines]." *B:* "*That's not right. It isn't the same because that goes further.* — And their sizes, are they the same, or is there a big or a little? — *That one is big and that one too.*"

Cec (4–6). B: "*They're not the same the two of them, not in longness.*— Which is longer? — *That, because it's at the top.* — [Rods returned to congruence.] — *The two are the same lenth.* — And like this (staggered), are they the same length? — *No, because there's one at the top and one at the bottom.*" D: Rod and Cec's line not staggered: "*The line and the stick, well it's the same length.* — [Staggered.] — *They're not the same lenth* [same reasons given]. — (Two staggered lines without rod): "Are they both the same length? — *Yes, because one is at the bottom and the other at the top* [D counted as a success, but not B]."

Syl (4–6). B: "*One that's little and one that's long, because it's like that* [staggered]. — Which is longer? — *They're both the same* [pushing them back into congruence]. — And like this (staggered again)? — *One longer. One put at the bottom and the other at the top.* — Both the same lengths? — *Yes, because one has been put like that and one like that* [indicates compensating projections at two ends], *so that makes them short and then long.* — Both the same long? — *Yes, because that one ought to be at the top and* [= or] *that one at the bottom: both the same.*" D: "*Not the same now, because that one's at the bottom and that one at the top. They're the same.*"

Ger (5–3). B, staggered: "What do you think? — *It's not right, they'ght ought to be the same size.* — But one is bigger? — *They're both the same size.*" D: "*They're the same, there's just one that's a little bit longer.* — But their size? — *They're both big, it's the same.* — But one's longer? — *That one.*"

Mic (5–6). B: "*That one's smaller.* — How do you know? — *Because it's lower down.* — Are the two the same size? — *Both the same.* — How do you know? — *Because I saw they were before.*" D: same reactions.

Fin (5–1). D: "*It's longer, it's been put further along.*" B: "*There are the two both big.* — The same size or not? — *Yes.*"

Dar (5–6). D, after havering: "Are they both the same bigness? — *No; (yes) the same; (no) bigger there, that sticks out over the line a bit.*"

Von (6–6). D: "Same length? — *No, this one is lower.* [As will be apparent from earlier reactions, it is the upper of the two horizontal elements that is staggered to the right, so its projection is always in the direction of the movement and thus positive.] — And if they were paths? — *Both the same, if I do like this, that one is bigger and this one more high. If you put this and this like this* [superimposed] *it's the same size.*"

These then are samples of the quasiconservation reactions representing about 50% of the four- to six-year-olds, in contrast to those who, despite continual prompting and repeats of the questions, accept and maintain inequality with the staggered formation. We need therefore to establish the status of these partial reactions, which are linked, as the hesitations or waverings at all the transition points show fairly clearly, to the cases of nonconservation (see Dar). To do this, we must naturally first establish the significance of the notions employed ("same size" "the same," and so on) by subjects still possessing no means of quantification other than ordinal or perceptual ones (though we have seen what liberties they take with regard to perception).

The case of Ger is especially enlightening in this respect: the rods "are the same, there's just one that's a little bit longer.... They're both big, it's the same." This reply is very reminiscent of those given by Xan and Nic (chapter 2 part 2) who, faced with a large oblong of four by eight centimeters, and asked if they can make one with all its sides equal, think they have resolved the problem by drawing an oblong of similar dimensions to the first but very small, because in this way the sides are the same size because "*they are all little. — Exactly the same little? — Yes.*" In other words, "the same size" here is not a quantitative equivalence but a qualitative identity. To say "both big, it's the same" or "the same size but just one a little bit longer" is no more contradictory to the subject than to say, as many children do at a certain level in the development of their ideas of weight, that two objects can have the same weight even though one weighs a little more (because it's situated slightly higher, for instance). When Bol says "that one is big and that one too" or Fin "there are the two both big" and so on, there is nothing to indicate that they are referring to anything but such a qualitative identity.

On the other hand, we must remember that the same four- to six-year-old subjects (see section 3), when confronted with two extremely strong and tenacious optic-geometric illusions, announce that the straight lines they are asked to compare are in fact equal, both because they have affirmed them to be so before the perceptual distortion, and because the kind of affirmation characteristic of this level consists in a taking over of qualitative characteristics that are judged to be both permanent and constituent as far as the object is concerned. Such an attitude leads much more readily to qualitative identies than to quantifications, and thus to the use of absolute predicates (big or little, and so on) much more than to relations capable of seriation. It is therefore just such absolute predicates that are employed at this level by 50% of the subjects—in place of the quantifications they have still to construct—and employed, moreover, in the face of projections that are already partly leading them (and successfully in the case of the other 50% of subjects) toward an ordinal quantification. More precisely still, the qualitative identity at work in the reactions just noted presents us with two interdependent meanings: choice of what is taken to be a stable predicate in order to constitute an equivalent class despite the possible variations (the two rods are both "big") and permanence of that predicate in one particular object (this rod stays "big"). The fundamental difference between these qualitative identities and quantitative conservations—as also, as we have seen, between revertibilities and reversibility—is that the first are essentially expressing the characteristics of the overall actions performed by the subject on the object, as well as those of their schemas of assimilation (selecting two equal rods, assimilating them into a single class of equivalence, placing them in different positions without wondering whether the projections at either end are equal, returning them to congruence, and so on), whereas the second (conservation and reversibility), while of course also entailing actions by the subject, bear upon the object's parts (parts displaced during a modification of its shape, size of terminal projections when the rods are staggered, and so on), which *ipso facto* implies quantifications, even anterior to any measurement. Thus ordinal quantifications are situated halfway along the path that leads from qualitative identities to operatory quantifications, and this explains why they prove insufficient to ensure conservations in the case of 50% of the present group of four- to six-year-olds.

This being so, it becomes easier to understand the analogies, as well as the profound differences, between the quasi-conservation arguments employed at this four- to five-year-old level and the much more familiar ones found among eight- to nine-year-olds who are beginning to acquire quantitative conservation. The analogy is, of course, the reversion to the starting points at which the rods (or the drawings of them) were selected because they were shown to be equal either by congruence or lateral juxtaposition: "Both the same . . . because I saw they were before" (Mic). But this reversion can have two very different meanings. At the operatory level, as we have stressed in so many of the chapters in this book, every action of transference (transfer of one part of the object in the case of a change of shape, or displacement of the whole object as here) is understood as necessarily and interdependently including an additive or positive aspect at its arrival point (addition of something, or the approach to a goal, and so on) and a subtractive or negative aspect at its departure point (removal of a part of the object or recession from the starting point). So that it is this necessary compensation of affirmations and negations, or of positive and negative elements that ensures "commutability"—or conservation of the whole formed by the parts exchanged—and that accounts for the fact that conservations and compensations can be constituted before measurement, this balancing out of additions and subtractions doubtlessly representing the most general and most elementary form of nonordinal quantification. In the case of our youngest subjects, it is affirmation that holds unrivalled sway in every domain, and negation still remains in its rudimentary form of practical negation or suppression of perturbations. As a consequence, the three arguments employed by the four- to five-year-olds have a very different meaning from the corresponding arguments used at the operatory levels, and can all three be reduced to a return to the point of departure nearer to revertibility than to operatory reversibility.

Let us begin with the apparent compensation between terminal projections of staggered lines (Syl, Von, or Cec at the end). It is clear that these do not involve any metrical equality between the projections, since such equality is mutually dependent upon quantitative conservation,[2] but that they are essentially an indication provided by the subject as to what should be pushed forward or back in order to cancel out the terminal disparity and restore the initial congruence. In other words, what we are witnessing is not a quantitative compensation, but a practical compensation or feedback mechanism, as it were, amounting to an elimination of the two causes of perturbation in relation to the original equality.

As for this return to the starting point as such, we cannot assimilate that to operatory reversibility either, since both the direct and reverse operators in the latter are quantified or quantifiable. The difference consists in the fact that in the case of true reversibility there is compensation or cancellation $(T.T^1 = 0)$ performed intrinsically by composition of additive and subtractive elements internal to the action displacing the parts of the object, whereas in the revertibility from which these reversions stem there are two distinct actions modifying the objects from outside, and not yet an "addition $\times$ subtraction" reversed into a "subtraction $\times$ addition" (See chapter 11, part 1).

Finally, there is the question of identity (these rods are the same because "I saw them before," and so on). Again it goes without saying that we are not dealing here with "identical operations" ($\pm$ 0) within an operatory grouping, which are additive ("nothing added nothing taken away"), but with the qualitative identity of which this whole set of experiments has thrown up so many examples, beginning with those truly remarkable reactions to the perceptual illusion tests.

In conclusion, these quasi-conservation reactions allied with the refusal to accept the perceptually observable facts constitute a particularly rich and complex example of insufficient compensations between the positive and negative elements of the action concerned. Hence the permanent situation, if not of manifest contradiction, at any rate of unstable equilibrium, and thus of latent disequilibrium, in which these subjects' reactions show them to be, in particular the way in which they use the same arguments either for or against the thesis they are defending: "It's not the same now," Syl concludes for example, "because that one's at the bottom and that one at the top. They're the same"; or Dar: "No [they're not the same size]. . . . It's the same . . . It's bigger there, that sticks out over the line a bit." And yet we refuse to believe that it is possible to make these subjects say just what one wants them to say. The truth is that already, even before logical or operatory structuration, the pursuit of equilibrium is no empty phrase, because the reasons for disequilibrium have proved to be very much deeper at these levels than one might at first glance imagine.

Part 3. Conservation of Flow and Delivery Rate

Although so many of our research projects have been concerned with conservations, there is one we had forgotten until F. Halbwachs brought it to our attention. It is the one that examines reactions to rates of flow when water passes from a large diameter tube into one of smaller diameter, or vice versa. In such a case, in order for the same quantity of water to be delivered in a set time, it is necessary and sufficient for the decrease in diameter to be compensated for by an increase in the rate of flow, since otherwise contradictions will be encountered, such as, for example, having to accept that a normal rate of flow in large tubes will not be disturbed by the passage of the water into narrower tubes.

Technique

This consists in fixing a rubber tube AB in length to a faucet A, then extending AB with two large glass tubes in series, which we shall call $T\,BC$ and $T\,CD$, point C being the joint between BC and CD. First, one makes sure the subject understands that the water flows without interruption from A to D. Then one suggests replacing one of the glass tubes T with another glass tube t which is the same length as T but of perceptibly smaller diameter, so that the order will be $T\,BC \rightarrow t\,CD$ or sometimes $t\,BC \rightarrow T\,CD$. Then one asks for a prediction of what will happen, in particular where the rate of flow in t is concerned. To make this more easily perceptible, one can inject small bubbles of air at C with a syringe; but the younger subjects often think that the speed of the bubbles is independent of that of the water. One then goes on to observations and asks for explanations of the water speed in t, especially if the subject acknowledges that it is higher than that in T. One also asks questions about the quantities of water involved and, in order to measure the rate of delivery, one asks the child to indicate at which point one could fill a glass more quickly, at C (outlet of T) or at D (outlet of t). In addition, one can tilt the first of the two glass tubes (T or t) and ask for a prediction as to whether the speed of the water in the tube will be higher with it sloping or with it flat.

A second part of the experiment consists in reminding the child of the *bisses* to be found in Valais, which are irrigation channels bringing water down to the fields. The model *bisse* displayed is made up of a sloping section of open conduit (1–2) followed by a horizontal section (2–3) of the same width but visibly deeper, which compensates the very apparent slowing down of the water as it passes through this section 2–3. The same questions are put as in the first section of the experiment, then, at the very end, one reverts to the tubes *T* and *t*.

§7. Stage 1

The reactions of level 1A (four- to five-year-olds) are characterized by correct or false intuitions, all of which are local and noncoordinated.

Sol (5–2) accepts that the bubbles *"go as strong the same everywhere"* but that the water goes quickest emerging from *D*. No conservation of delivery rate: *"There is more water there [T BC] than here [t CD]."* *"If you prick here* [syringe at *C*] *it will go quicker there [T BC:* i.e., upstream of *C] and there* [T CD, downstream].*"* For the conduit, the water goes quicker along 2–3 *"because it bends* [becomes horizontal].*"*

Vad (5–4): the water goes at the same speed everywhere, but it doesn't all go from *T BC* into *t CD*: *"Where does it go then? — Into the tap* [as if it could flow back up again].*"*

Cec (5–6) thinks that the water in *t CD* *"goes slower because it's littler"* but the bubbles in it go quicker. In 1–2 *"it's sloping, so it goes very quick,"* but paying no attention to what happens in 2–3. Likewise: *"Is there as much water in t CD as in T BC? — No, here [C] and there [t CD] it becomes smaller and smaller."*

Clearly, then, there is no conservation of the quantity of water passing from one tube into the other, and the subjects show the usual initial imperviousness to the contradictions arising from this. For example, there is less water in the little tube than in the big one, but the speed is the same (Sol and Vad), or it is less and slows down because it's smaller (Cec), without any problem being experienced as to what happens to the excess that isn't coming through. The observable facts may be distorted or denied as well as correctly stated, and the speed of the bubbles remains independent of that of the water (Cec) unless (as with Sol) they possess the power to make the water go faster.

The level 1B subjects anticipate a conservation of the quantity of water, and in general a deceleration of the speed of flow in the thinner tube, without seeing that the combination presents a problem. Then, having observed the facts, they either accept them or distort them in the direction of various compromise solutions that then endanger their original conservation itself.

Mur (6–8): "What if we put *T BC* onto *AB*? — *There's the same amount of water going through.* — And if we put on *T CD*? — *Still as much and still a little longer.* — And with *t CD* instead of *T CD*? — *Yes, but that will go through for longer* [more slowly] *because it is narrower.* — [*t* is affixed.] — *It goes quicker!* — Why? — *Don't know. The water from the fat one pushes harder, so then it goes quicker in the little one.* — And is there the same amount of water? — *Yes, t CD is longer and thinner, but there's still the same water going through.* — Is it longer (measurement)? — *No, it isn't longer, it's narrower.* — So? — *It's here* [*T BC*] *that there is more water!* — [Bubbles injected.] — *In the fat one the water takes a long time. When it's thin it goes quicker.*" Nevertheless she puts the glass to be filled at *C* and not *D:* "*Here* [*C*] *it's going quicker.*" Conduit: "*There's more water going through in 2–3. In 1–2 there's not so much water, so it's longer to fill up* [she puts her glass at 3].''

Dom (6–10) likewise predicts the same quantity of water in *t* and *T,* and the same speed: "How will it manage to get through? — *It gets more rounded* [smaller diameter] *because it's thinner.* — It's thinner because it's more rounded? — *There* [*T BC*] *there is a lot of water and there* [*t CD*] *not much water.* — So? — *I don't know.*" Conduit: "Will there be the same amount of water all along? — *No. There* [*1–2*] *it will go quicker and there* [*2–3*] *more slow.* — And to fill your glass? — *There* [*3*], *because it has more water.* — But you said that it goes quicker there [1–2], so wouldn't it come out quicker [at 2]? — *I don't know.*"

Cat (6–8) puts her glass at *D:* "*There's a lot more water because it goes slower, No, there's more when it goes quick.*" Observation: "*There's a lot more water* [in *BC*] *when it's fat, and that goes slower.*" Conduit: "*There's not so much in 1–2. There's less water but going quicker.*" Back to tubes: "*It goes faster with the little one and more slowly with big, because there's more water in the big and less in the little.*"

Nic (6–6). *T BC* and *CD:* "*The same amount of water both sides* — (*T* and *t?*) — *The water is smaller. It's the little tube that makes the water littler*" but "*going the same speed.*" Observation: "*In the big it goes slower and in the little faster*" hence his prediction for the conduit that in 2–3 "*there'll be more water so it will go quicker.*"

Pac (6–5), after observation: "*In t there's not so much water going through and it will go quicker.*" Later, however, he claims the opposite: "*faster because there's more water.*"

Pie (6–2) predicts that the thin tube will make water go slower. Then: "*I see that as it's littler it goes quicker.* — Only this time, or always? — *Only this time.*" Conduit: "*In 1–2 it will slide down quick. There* [*2*] *it will stop a bit, and if there's a lot it will go on running along the top.* — Where will it go quickest? — *There* [*1–2*]. — Where is there more water?

— Here [2–3]. — And to fill your glass quickly? — There [3]. — Why? — There's more water coming at the same time at 3. There's not much water there [1–2] but it's quick, so it must keep running to keep up, so it's quicker than at 3."

So all of these subjects predict a conservation of the water as it passes from *TBC* into *TCD*, which is easy; and often they do the same for the contents of *T* into *t*, but suppose a slowing up in *t*, without seeing that in that case they need to explain where the water flowing faster in *T* is being stored. When a greater speed is observed in *t CD*, the subject no longer knows how to get out of this difficulty because of his lack of coordination between quantity and units of time, in other words, because he is unable to construct the synthetic notion of "delivery rate." Mur tries to find a way around by supposing *t* to be longer, then seeing that this is not the case, abandons conservation: "There is more water in *T BC*." Then further contradictions present themselves: more water "takes a long time going through," as though it were solid bodies to be transported one by one. Cat reasons in the same way, but wavers between "more water = more slowly" and "more water = quicker" (see also Pac). Pie is led to believe that sometimes one and sometimes the other is the case and, with the conduit, gets out of this difficulty by thinking that the surplus water in 1–2 goes "along the top" of the water in 2–3.

§8. Stages 2 and 3

At level 2A (seven- to eight-years-old) we find an early form of coordination occurring. This cannot as yet provide conservation of the relative quantity of water deliverd, but it does begin to provide an explanation of why the water speed increases in the narrow tube. This new attitude is manifested in two ways: first, the connection between narrowness and increased speed takes on a causal value ("because") and is thus no longer a matter of simply stating a law; second, the subject starts looking for an explanatory model in the direction of a compression of the water or a decrease in its volume.

Ber (7–3) of *T* and *t*: *"The water goes quicker because it's the little tube, it will go quicker [in t CD] because it's smaller."* The reason for this is that *"the water is squeezed here [t CD]"* and elsewhere isn't squeezed. But in that case *"there's less water [in BC] and more in CD,"* so the glass will fill quicker at *D*.

Car (7–5) says likewise that *"there [BC] the water gets fat, and there [t CD] it has to get thin, and because it's thin it has to go faster. — Why? — If we put in bubbles it would go very quick there [t CD] and not so fast there. The water has to make itself thin.''* As to the quantity of water, Car sometimes thinks that *"there's more of it in the big one''* and sometimes more in *t CD,* so the glass must be placed at *D.*

Ryk (7–8). Same reactions. *"The water will get small''* in *t* and *"it will go very quick.''*

Yor (8–5): *"The water will be thin and can get through more easily''*; *"it goes quicker or slower when you change the volume.''*

Lyo (8–7): *"It will go quicker* [in *t*], *there's less water at the same time,''* which is almost a definition of delivery rate, *"because the hole* [diameter] *is smaller than with the big one.''* But the glass must be put at *C "because there will be more water coming out all at once.''*

Luc (8–10) predicts that in *T BC "it will go a little faster and here* [*t CD*] *not so fast.' The first is fatter, the second smaller, that flattens the water and so the water from the first tube pushes the water in the second.''* But the glass should be put at *C "because the first* [*T BC*] *is bigger and it won't take so long to flill. That one* [*t CD*] *is smaller and it will need longer to fill.''*

From now on, then, there is a causal connection between the thinness of *t* and the speed of the water, the thinner tube being seen as "squeezing" the water, making it thinner too, or even "flattening" it, so that it can "get through more easily" and therefore flows faster. However, although the water's speed has been brought into relation in this way with its "volume" (Yor) or with the tube diameter (Lyo's "hole"), there is still neither compensation nor, consequently, conservation of delivery rate, so that these subjects still expect the glass to be filled at different rates at *C* and *D.* At level 2B the coordination beginning to appear at level 2A emerges more strongly, but still doesn't produce conservation.

Ral (9–2) is quite clear at first that *"it's the same number of water going through.''* Then, for *T* and *t*, *"It's thinner and the water goes quicker,''* so that he first puts the glass to fill at *D,* then changes his mind and puts it at *C* after all *"because it's fatter.''*

Ari (10–11) finally feels her way to the solution. She begins by thinking that in *t "not so much water can get through . . . it gets blocked at C''* but not understanding in that case where the surplus water is being stored, so that she concludes that *"there is the same quantity of water but there* [*T*] *it goes slower and there* [*t*] *quicker. — So where should we put the glass? — It's the same. Here* [end of *t*] *there's more speed and less water, and there* [end of *t*] *there's less speed and more water* [at any one moment, not more being delivered].''*

At stage 3 the speeds are at last predicted from the outset, and coordination achieved.

Lea (10–9): "*In t CD it will go quicker then in T BC because there's less room and the same number of water, so it will hurry to get out. —* Should the glass go here (*C*) or there (*D*)? — *If you don't change the volume of water it comes to the same.* — But here (*C* at the end of *T*) it's fatter? — *No, because there's no more water there* [than at *D*]."

Cla (11–3). *T* and *t:* "*It comes to the same thing. Here* [*t*] *there is a small volume. In T it has to take up more room and that makes it slower. —* And the glass? — *The same at both: there there's a lot of water but it's going slower, and there there's not so much water but it's going quicker.*"

Den (12–3): "*In t it will go rather faster, because it's smaller. You have to have the same amount of water coming through a smaller diameter.* — And the glass? — *It's the same* [at *C* and at *D*]: *If there is the same rate of flow it doesn't matter which.*" Choice between *t* and *T:* "*If you put them side by side there's the same amount of water going through. —* And with one sloping? — *That might help; no, I think it's still the same: in the end it's the same.*"

From level 2B onward, one senses that the subjects are clearly feeling around for an invariable, hence the apparent regression in certain cases that makes them believe, despite the observable facts, in a uniform speed, albeit only as a substitute for the uniform delivery rate they are looking for. In other cases, as with Ral and Ari, it is the quantity of water that must then be brought into relation with its speed as an inverse function of the diameter. This leads to the correct anticipations and explanations at stage 3, the index of understanding of the compensations involved being provided by the choice of place to fill the glass, with Den finally saying quite explicitly that "if there is the same rate of flow it doesn't matter" whether you put it at *C* or at *D*. It is also noteworthy that these older subjects finally (though not always immediately) manage to avoid the trap represented by sloping the tubes, rejecting the temptation to regard the water in the tubes as being like spheres rolling down a slope because they see that the speed in *T* is dependent on the delivery rate in *t*.

§9. Conclusion

The five phases of which we have just given a brief description present us with a conservation that is cinematic in nature as opposed to one relating simply to static quantities. The question we now face, therefore, is to establish whether this cinematic conservation entails a compensatory mechanism balancing out additions and subtractions, or other positive and negative elements, analogous to the one we have posited as intervening in other, previous situations. This is indeed the case, but with this one difference, that the unequal tubes are usually presented in the order $T \rightarrow t$ and not $t \rightarrow T$, so that the younger subjects expect there to be less water in t and an equal or decreased speed relative to T. As a result, there is a centration on subtraction and the negative elements at the end of the path, whereas in the case of modifications to a clay ball by making it into a sausage, or in that of transferring liquids from container to container, it is the apparent increase in quantity that becomes the focus of attention, at the expense of the preliminary subtraction. But this makes it all the more remarkable that this (as it were) imposed diminution in quantity of water and speed of flow is not brought into relation with the positive elements anterior to it, in other words causes no problem, even though the problem seems so evident to us (and to the 2B subjects later): where is it going to, this water that is somehow being "left over" at point C, between the fat tube T and the thin tube t? At the 1A level, the subject resorts to imagining a kind of flowback, as if the bubbles were able to move against the current (Sol), or as if the water could go back up into the faucet (Vad), but only if the question is specifically put. At level 1B this question is still never raised by the subject. The level 2A reaction is different: the subject acknowledges that the water is going faster in t, but being unable to grasp as yet that this acceleration is what ensures the conservation of quantity, he supposes that the liquid is compressed in some way (is "squeezed," "flattened," or whatever), a hypothesis from which he easily frees himself in the case of the tests involving interchanges of liquid between containers. It is not until level 2B that this problem is faced up to seriously, so that we find Ari saying that "it (the water) gets blocked at C (end of tube t)" because of the narrowness of t, then adding "I don't understand," and finally overcoming her puzzlement by discovering the principle of the constant delivery rate.

In short, a subject who expects a conservation of both the quantity of water and its speed as it passes from T into t—which happens at stage 1—but then decides that both will decrease when he observes the smaller diameter of t, is failing to relate this subtraction to the previous quantities (in T). As a result, he does not ask himself how it is possible or what it means. Thus it is this lack of coordination or compensation between the subtraction and the previous positive values that brings about nonconservation and the multiple contradictions found at stage 1. Whereas conservation is immediatly on the way to being constituted as soon as the subject brings this decrease in diameter introduced by *t* into relation with an increase in speed viewed as its necessary result, since the water must go through without being "blocked" (as Ari puts it) at the entrance to *t*. But this constitution is delayed at first by the rather too *ad hoc* hypothesis of a compression of the water (level 2A), so that conservatoin is not in fact acquired until there is an exact compensation between the diminution in diameter and the augmentation in speed, that is, when the apparent excess of water in *T* is seen as flowing through *t* in the same amount of time. This equality between the amounts of time the water takes to pass through both tubes, a necessary condition of the conservation of delivery rate, is verified in practice by the equal times taken for the glass to fill at *C* and *D*, or by placing the two tubes *T* and *t* side by side, as Den suggests. In sum, we do in fact find once again that it is exact compensation of additions and subtractions that gives rise to conservation, insofar as the passing of all the liquid (and not just some of it as before) from *T* into *t* is conceived of as a general displacement, without blockage, and thus necessarily accompanied by "commutability." For one cannot say, in fact, that the compensation between the thinness of tube *t* and the speed of the water passing through it is simply a quantitative composition of two variables that neutralize each other, since there is mensuration of neither (any more than of the height and width in the case of modifications made to the shape of a ball of clay, for example): compensation does not take place until the moment when the subject grasps that all the water in *T* must go into *t*, since the water in *CD* came from *BC*, and indeed from *AB*, and it is this cinematic connection of the starting and end points of the flow with the equality of the quantities leaving *A* and those arriving at *D*, that simultaneously ensures local compensation of the diameters and speeds and also conservation of delivery rate. It is in this sense that a cinematic conservation of this kind is comparable to the results of so many of our investigations into the conservation of lengths.

Thirteen

Full and Empty

with A. Henriques-Christophides

We are all probably only too familiar with at least one joke based on the old tautology that a glass half empty is the same as a glass half full. But is that equality self-evident at any age, one may wonder, and why—or why not? And then one might also wonder whether one ought not to find out whether such statements as "almost full" and "almost empty," for instance, when applied to the same glass, appear contradictory at any age. But might not such an investigation turn out to be merely of semantic interest? We think not, and for the following reason: one of the central hypotheses of this book is that the functional disequilibriums of early levels of cognitive development derive from a predominance of positive values over negative ones, and consequently of af!rmations over negations, thereby leading to a lack of compensations that constitutes the functional equivalent of contradictions, even if they are not experienced as such by the subjects. However, as we have seen, the primacy of affirmations is due to a number of causes, and the principal one, perhaps, is that the positive properties of objects correspond to directly perceptible facts, whereas negations are relative to previous affirmations, and are in general not established except by more or less inferential means.

It is precisely such positive and negative characters, in a very familiar form, that fullness and emptiness represent in the case of such everyday objects as glasses or bottles, and although emptiness is indeed relative to the water or wine one might have been expecting, as it is in the nature of negative characteristics to be, it nevertheless corresponds to what is undoubtedly the most frequent state of a glass, and has been endowed with a specific name that evokes its representation (unlike such negations as non-red, non-square, and so on), so that noting its presence might seem as easy as in the case of fullness. The problem we are setting ourselves, then (an instructive one from the point of view of contradiction conceived of as an incomplete compensation), is to establish whether or not we find a lack of symmetry even between fullness and emptiness, suggesting that the former constitutes a stronger or more immediately penetrating notion than the latter.

Technique

The first part of the questioning consists in establishing not only the subjects' vocabulary in this area, which is indispensable, but also to a large extent the concepts they start off with. The subjects are shown three identical, completely cylindrical bottles, all 15 cm high and 3 cm in diameter, containing different levels of water: I up to three-quarters of its height, II up to a half, and III up to a quarter. A description of these bottles is requested, and if the child talks merely about a lot of water, or a little water, then one asks him to be more precise and to use terms such as "full" or "more" or "less full," and "empty." One then talks about (or draws) another bottle, IV, which has water right up to the stopper, and a further bottle, V, which has no water in at all.

Next, one asks the subjects to point out which of these bottles is "almost full," "almost empty," "half full," "a little bit empty," and so on. There are some children who reject such expressions as "almost empty" or "a little empty," and this is taken into account in the later stages.

The bottles are then hidden from view and one asks three series of questions, to each of which the child is required to reply both verbally, with any explanations that may occur, and also by making drawings. Here are the questions:

Series A: This concerns the impossibility of an object presenting *a* and non-*a* characteristics at the same time.
  A1: "Can a bottle be at the same time full up and not quite full up?"
  A2: "Half full and not half full?"
  A3: "A little full and not a little full?"

Series B. The contradiction here involves the quantifiers (once more only the varieties of ± full, since the emptiness variants are covered adequately by the child's responses to the *C* series).
  B1: "Can a bottle be at the same time almost full and a little bit full?"
  B2: "Almost full and half full?"
  B3: "Half full and a little bit full?"

Series C. Finally, we come to the relations between fullness and emptiness. When the quantifiers applied to both are the same (as in *C1, C3,* and *C4*) the relation is clearly contradictory, except in the case of half/half (*C2*). In the latter case, and in the case of *C5* and *C6* with their differing quantifiers, the relation is one of complementarity.
  C1: "Can a bottle be at the same time full and empty?"
  C2: "Half full and half empty?"
  C3: "Almost full and almost empty?"
  C4: "A little full and a little empty?"
  C5: "Almost full and a little bit empty?"
  C6: "A little bit full and almost empty?"

In practice, it is the *C* questions with which we shall be most concerned here, since the *A* and *B* questions are satisfactorily resolved by almost all age groups, except when *A2* is assimilated to *C2*, and except also for certain 1a subjects who simply eliminate the negations in series *A* and translate the terms used in series *B* into others of their own. It should be noted, in this respect, that a repetition of the exact wording of the question by the child himself is often indispensable (after the subject's first answer) if one wants a proper answer. The terms employed are in practice frequently modified in a way that is, in fact, helpful in judging how the relations involved are being understood.

§1. Stage 1

The most general criterion is failure in the case of question *C2* (half/half)..
the youngest subjects it is possible to question (four-year-olds) still have difficulty with the quantification of fullness, but their difficulty with emptiness is markedly greater. For example, Pat (4–4) begins by showing bottles II, I and IV (half full, three-quarters full, and full) for "full up", and I (three-quarters full) for "a little bit full," whereas to him "almost empty" means V (empty) and "a little bit empty" produces the answer "there isn't one." By the time the subject is five years old, however, one can begin to talk of a level 1A at which the evaluations of fullness are more or less correct, but at which the same quantifications are not successfully applied to emptiness.

Vir (5–5) shows the correct bottles for "full up," "almost full," "a little bit full," and "half full," but when it comes to complementarity she shows two bottles at the same time: "Do I have a bottle here that is at the same time a little bit empty and a little bit full? — [Shows 0 and 1/4.] — Almost full and almost empty? — [Shows 3/4 and 1/2]"

Edw (5–6) calls I (3/4) "*a little full,,*" II (1/2) "*middle full,*" III (1/4) "*a little less full,*" IV (full) "*still more full,*" and V (empty) "*empty.*" But she refuses to describe the first four at all in degrees of emptiness. Nevertheless she points to III (1/4) when asked for "almost empty," but does the same (after three repetitions of question) for "a little bit empty," and refuses that description for I, which in fact fits it. Questions *A-C:* she succeeds only with *B3* (half and a little bit full) and *C1* (full up and empty), that is with one total opposition and one distinction between "half" and "a little bit." With the three contradictory questions *A1-3* she takes note of the affirmative parts only and ignores the negations. With *B2* "almost full" and "half" are translated into "*they are almost a lot full.*" *C2:* "half full" is correctly drawn and "half empty" shown as quarter full. *C3* is accepted "*because they have almost the same bigness of water*": half drawn for "almost full" and quarter for "almost empty." *C4:* "a little bit empty" again drawn as quarter full, as is "a little bit full." Above all, the equality in *C5* is rejected because although "almost full" is correctly understood "a little bit empty" is reduced to a little bit of water, and so "*it isn't the same amount of water.*"

Nic (5–9) describes bottles I to IV well in terms of "full" but is less successful in terms of "empty." III, from "*even less full* [than II], *it has very little,*" becomes "*it is all empty, it has a lot of emptiness in,*" and when a bottle is asked for that is "a little bit empty," he points twice to III. He refuses vehemently to regard I as "a little bit empty": "*no, you can't.*" The *C2* equality is rejected because "half full" is drawn as two-thirds full and "half empty" as a quarter full. Similarly with *C5* ("almost full and a little bit empty"): "*No, because otherwise you'd need two bottles.*"

Ren (6–4) shows all the degrees of fullness correctly but gives III (1/4) for "half full." "And almost empty? — *There isn't one.* — Not one? — *No.* — And a little bit empty? — *There isn't one.* — What does it mean, "a little bit empty"? — *There's a little paint in* [colored water]. — But a bottle that's a little bit empty? — *There isn't one.* — And half empty? — [¼.] — And almost empty? — *Isn't one* — And almost full? — [¾.]"

Ser (6–1) quantifies degrees of full well but identifies "almost empty" with "a little bit empty." "Do I have a bottle that is at the same time half full and half empty? — *No.* — Why not? — *Because there* [¾ and 1] *it's full up, and there* [½] *it's half full, but there* [¼] *it's half empty.*"

Fra (6–2) also points to III (1/4) for "half empty" then for "a little bit empty" points to III again on two nonsuccessive occasions: "Is it I or III that is a little bit empty? — *It's III.*" So to him, a little bit empty meant "containing only a little bit of water." For "half full" he correctly gives II: "And the other half, what's that? — *Full up* [he has topped it up in imagination and is describing the result]. — You couldn't say it is half empty? — *Yes* [without conviction]." But a moment later his reply to *C2* is: "*No, because if it's half full it can't be half empty.*" His *C2* drawings are the same as Nic's: 2/3 and 1/4. Likewise with *C5*: "*No, because if it is almost full it can't be a little bit empty.*" *C6* equality also rejected although the terms were understood: "a little bit full" is drawn about 1/4 full and "almost empty" about 1/8 full: "So it's the same thing? — *No.*"

Next one finds an intermediate 1B level at which question *C2* (half full/half empty) is not always answered correctly, which it will be at stage 2, but at which *C5* is, at least in the straightforward cases.

Flo (6–6) makes the transition from level 1A to level 1B because, although she at first gives III for "a little bit empty" she later corrects herself and points to I. She sees no contradiction in *A2* and translates it into a form that seems to herald a correct answer to *C2*: "*yes, because there's a little in like that,*" meaning both when half full and not half full. But when *C2* is asked she rejects it vehemently "*because first of all it's half full and then it's half empty,*" which to her seems contradictory. *C4* is accepted because "*a little bit full* [correct 1/4 drawing] *and a little bit empty* [identical drawing] *that's almost the same thing.*'' The *C5* equality is then rejected for the same reason. So there is a regression on this point in relation to 1A type reactions.

Lud (6–4) points out II for "a little bit empty" after having already correctly indicated it for "half full." III (1/4) is given on various occasions as *"half empty,"* *"almost empty,"* and *"a little bit empty."* Then, having acknowledged that III may be *"a little bit full,"* he describes I, unprompted, as *"a little bit empty."* So Lud's vocabulary seems to be getting more accurate. But then he rejects the *C2* equality *"because it can't be . . . it can be half full but not half empty."* His drawings give 1/2 for half full but 1/4 for half empty. When it comes to the *C5* equality however (almost full and a little bit empty), after first rejecting it *"because the water can't be right up at the top and a little bit at the bottom,"* He draws "almost full" and "a little bit empty" at the same level (about eight- or nine-tenths full) and accepts identity. To *C6* he then answers (after previous failure) *"A little bit full is the same thing as almost empty. — How did you work that out? — Well, I listen. Sometimes I go a bit wrong, so then I work in my head. — And what do you do in there? — I do things with my thoughts. It works all right in there, so then I draw it all right on the paper."*

Cat (7–9) finally indicates I for "a little bit empty" (after having given III twice), and II for "half empty." She nevertheless rejects the *C2* equivalence *"because either it's half empty or it's half full"* accompanied by usual drawings of 1/4 for the first and 2/3 for second. On the other hand, having first rejected *C5* she then draws two identical levels of about 4/5: *" 'almost full' needs a little bit more to be full and 'a little bit empty' there's that much water (4/5) and that left over* [the empty 1/5]." Her reactions to *C3* (almost full and almost empty) and *C4* (a little of both) are also worth noting. She was successful with *C3* but when it came to *C4:* *"If it is a little bit empty, that's because it's almost empty. Yes, if it is a little bit full it's that* [1/8], *that's the same thing as almost empty. It's possible* [for the bottle to be a little empty and a little full as in *C4*]." — What is? — *A little bit empty, that's almost all empty, and a little bit full that's almost all empty as well."*

It thus seems quite clear that there is a very strong asymmetry present during stage 1 between full and empty. A first indication of this, and one not without value, is the difficulty (which at 1A is actually an impossibility) experienced in describing the bottles presented in terms of greater or lesser emptiness, as if the language of fullness were the only natural one (whereas oppositions such as "little" and "big" occur very early in a child's vocabulary). One of the very few 1B subjects (not quoted) who does use emptiness spontaneously in his descriptions (albeit at 7–0), still does so in terms relative to fullness: for II and III "they still need that much water," indicating the empty portions, and for I "it still needs that."

A second remarkable indication is the general failure with question *C2* (half full/half empty), and for a very significant reason: there is no compensation between the positive or full half and the empty half, as is made plain by the fact that in general the first is shown as 3/4 full and the second as about 1/4 full. It may be said that in this case the emptiness is sometimes overestimated, since it is shown as taking up 3/4 of the bottle, but it is quite clear that this is not so, since it will become evident later how tenacious the conception is (defined by Noh in section 3 and persisting throughout stage 2) that "a little bit empty, that means it has almost no water left in" (cf. Flo, Lud, and Car among the cases already quoted). In other words, drawing a quarter bottle of water for "half full' is a devalorization of that half. It may also be suggested that there is nothing more involved than the conventions of quantification, and that, if the child wants to call unequal parts "halves," then it is up to us to follow him in his reasoning. But the fact remains the children of five or six are already perfectly capable of dividing "full" quantities into (equal) halves, and also that when this inequality between halves occurs it is invariably at the expense of emptiness, which is what interests us here.

And indeed, another noteworthy reaction common to levels 1A and 1B (one that we shall also find again later) is that, although the terms "almost" and "a little"—which are familiar enough quantifiers, even though they do include a seminegation, since they refer to what is missing—are employed correctly when it is full parts that are involved, they give rise to systematic difficulties when applied to emptiness. We shall return later to these reactions, since they persist in scarcely attenuated forms beyond level 1B.

There is one exception to what we have just noted, however: the general success in answering question *C5* from level 1B onward (with rare exceptions) after constant failure at level 1A. Moreover, this failure at level 1A is, once again, because "a little bit empty" is regarded even in this case as the equivalent of "containing only a little bit of water." At substage 1B, on the other hand, this same expression, when it occurs in question *C5,* is correctly understood, apparently under the influence of "almost full," which suggests a small empty space to be filled. It therefore seems that the phrase "a little bit empty" can change meaning according to the quantity of "fullness" with which it is associated from one question to another. This is made clear, for example, in the case of Cat, who when asked *C4* defines "a little" as "almost all empty" and synonymous with "a little bit full," whereas when she is answering *C5* "what is left over" (meaning the empty 1/5) is also called "a little bit empty."

Taken as a whole, then, we can say that stage 1 reactions generally seem to display a fundamental asymmetry between positive terms relating to fullness and negative terms relating to emptiness. This asymmetry produces a systematic difficulty in achieving compensations, which in turn leads to contradictions, such as that exemplified in particular by the reactions to our key *C2* question, which leads to "halves" being conceived of as unequal. And yet these reactions still leave one with a certain uneasiness about the hesitations and incoherences displayed by these subjects. Their answers are not, in other words, the kind of wrong but stable answers one often receives at this level to questions involving some causal explanation, but rather simple expressions of noncomprehension, disturbingly vague and changeable in nature. However, this uneasiness will be dissipated at levels 2A and 2B, when we shall find seven- to ten-year-olds, whose thought is manifestly coherent and who resolve the half/half *C2* question without difficulty, still stumbling over the terms "almost" and "a little bit" when applied to emptiness as opposed to fullness.

§3. Level 2A

Since stage 2 is the one at which operatory reversitility normally begins to occur, it is to be expected that the necessary compensation between fullness and emptiness should be grasped from the outset in simple cases such as that exemplified by question *C2* (half full/half empty), success with which is the distinguishing feature of levels 2A and 2B. However, interestingly enough, one difficulty does persist. It is that presented by "almost empty" or "a little bit empty," both of which entail the composition of a negation (empty) with a seminegation (almost or a little), whereas the "almost full" of question *C5* is mastered as early as level 1B, since that entails only the attenuation of an affirmation. Because certain seven- to eight-year-olds (four out of eleven) do eventually grasp "almost empty" or "a little bit empty," for a while we thought it might be best to classify the others as simple cases of transition between 1B and 2A. However, since those "others" represent seven out of eleven and one was over nine, we shall refer to them all under the heading 2A. Here are some examples:

Bri (7–11) correctly describes III as "*almost empty,*" then, after hesitating over the meaning of *C2*, finally exclaims: "*Of course, yes you can have that. There's a bottle that's half full, and then the other side is empty. You can.*" But with *C3* (almost full and almost empty): "*It's the same principle as before: you have a bottle almost full and at the top it's almost empty.*" *C4* (a little bit empty and a little bit full) the difficulties emerge more clearly: "*Naturally you can. If it's a little bit full then there's water in the bottom of the bottle, and if it's a little bit empty there as well there's water in the bottom of the bottle.*" Despite this, however, his drawings are correct and very close to the models (the by now concealed I and III): "Well, are they the same? — *No, they're not!* — And both are a little empty? — *Yes.* — But they don't contain the same amount of liquid? — *No, but they're both of them almost empty!*" C5, however he resolves easily: "*When it's almost full there is a little bit empty left at the top.*"

Emi (7–9), albeit without providing such fascinating developments as the previous case, reasons similarly for *C3:* "*Almost full and almost empty* [at the same time], *you can say that, yes.*" The drawings this time are indeed identical, both like I, but described thus: one "*is almost empty* [1/4] *and a little full* [3/4 full in fact]" the other "*is almost full* [again 3/4 in fact] *and a little empty* [1/4]." *C2, C5,* and all the other questions, however, answered successfully.

Noh (8–5) resolves *C2* correctly with correct drawing of bottle half full and half empty. *C3* is judged contradictory: "*If it is almost full it won't be right up to the stopper, and if it's almost empty that means a little bit of water left in the bottom.*" The difficulty thus seems overcome, but is raised again with *C4:* "*A little bit empty, that means it has almost no water left in, it is* [only] *a little bit full.*" Drawings identical (both III, i.e., 1/4): "So a little bit empty and a little bit full? — *They're the same thing.*" Question *C5* understood perfectly however.

Sté (8–6) describes bottle III: "*It is almost empty, half empty, a little bit empty* [repeated], *or rather almost empty,*" and indeed, when asked later to draw "a little bit empty," he shows the one he did correctly (albeit after hesitations) for "almost empty." Moreover he stumbles at *C6* and draws 1/10 of water for "almost empty" then about 2/10 "a little bit full": "*It can never ever be the same thing.*"

Joe (8–6) describes III (1/4) as "*a little bit full*" (as opposed to half full and the rest). "Can we say 'almost empty?'—*It's not very accurate.*" He describes I and III well in terms of more or less full, but can't handle "empty" in the same way at all. So then he is asked to show which bottles fit which descriptions "A little bit empty? — [Shows III.] — A little bit empty, is that a lot of water or little? — *Only a little water.*" Questions *C2* and *C5* answered easily (with correct gestures), but *C3* produces the same confusions as before until he is asked to produce a drawing, the "*I made a mistake. That* [drawing of III] *is almost empty.*" Nevertheless, at the end of the session, when asked again to show "almost empty" he shows I, then: "*Oh! No, that's almost full,*" despite which he again relapses a moment later.

Cha (9–1) succeeds right away with questions *C2*, *C5*, and *C6*, but with *C3* and *C4:* *"Yes, it can be almost full and almost empty"* and *"Yes, it will be the same thing, it can be a little bit full and a little bit empty."*

These subjects are more interesting than the earlier ones because, having reached the level of operatory reversibility, and thus being capable of the quantifications that implies (conservations, and so on), they are attempting to give a precise meaning to the terms they employ. This means that for a "half full" bottle they will no longer draw a bottle, as stage 1 subjects did, two-thirds or three-quarters full, because emptiness has less value in their eyes than fullness. So question *C2* is resolved without difficulty, and on this point there is exact compensation between positive and negative.

Although the quantification of fullness no longer raises any problems, however, it is noteworthy that the same is still not true of emptiness, other than in this one particular case of the relation "half empty." There are thus two questions that remain: that of "almost empty" and, above all, that of "a little bit empty." In the case of "almost," this has a precise meaning in the domain of positive quantities, which is "all, less a small part," which thus presupposes a division into parts, comparison of the extents of those parts, and a negative operation of subtraction. But emptiness is a very strange kind of class, because it isn't there; so that dividing it into parts is a different matter altogether from dividing up fullness, and subtracting from it even more complex still. The implicit solution our subjects arrive at is thus to go on treating it as a whole, so that "almost empty" means simply "partially empty." The fascinating case of Bri seems quite clear in this respect: for "a little bit full," he draws his bottle a quarter full, and for "a little bit empty" he draws it three-quarters full; but then, when astonishment is expressed at this difference, which his words seem to contradict, he maintains that they "are both almost empty," which can have only one possible meaning (at 7–11!), which is that they are both "partly empty." Sté likewise identifies "almost empty" (in fact the upper quarter) with "a little empty" and, although very vague about his quantifications of emptiness, later refuses (when trying to pin down his thoughts more exactly) to homologize it with its corresponding "full" term, because he draws "a little bit full" as two-tenths of water and "almost empty" as one-tenth, and "they can never, ever be the same thing." Likewise, for Joe, a quarter of water is "a little bit full" but "almost empty isn't very accurate." Cha, at nine years old, is still sturdily maintaining that "almost full and almost empty will be the same thing" while "almost empty" can be "a little bit empty."

Thus the division needed for "almost" receives merely a general solution in the sense of "partially," but there is also another problem, and one that becomes acute in the case of "a little bit empty." "A little bit" is in itself simply a seminegation signifying "not much" in the sense of "nothing except for a small part" or "all except for a large part." The trouble is, however, that emptiness is itself a negative quantity (or zero class), so that the expression "a little bit empty" is in fact a partial double negation, whose first term partly cancels out its second, which comes to the same thing as lending it the meaning "fairly or almost full." It is true that 2A subjects do have a general understanding of the double negation (the opposite of the opposite of beautiful), and can even master the rule of signs in concrete forms. Thus the interesting point here is that the partial double negation, when applied to emptiness, is totally rejected, as if in the case of nothing the two negations added up instead of restricting one another, and so produce "very little of something." Since emptiness is only being thought of with reference to the water, we end up with Noh's definition, which is in fact general at this substage: "a little bit empty, that means it has almost no water left in, it is [only] a little bit full." Or, more succinctly (from Joe), a little bit empty is "a little water."

So, even in the early stage of concrete operations, when operatory reversibility is coming into force with the quantification of the positive properties specific to manipulable objects, we find that there is still not complete compensation between direct operations and those that should be bearing symmetrically upon negative realities like emptiness. The quantification of the latter, and its complementarity with relation to fullness, are certainly mastered in the very straightforward cases, such as the half full and half empty of question C2, but as soon as a more refined regulation of all and some is involved, with the interdependent affirmations and negations it entails, the problems remain unsolved.

§4. Level 2B

The difficulty of "almost empty" and above all that of "a little bit empty," on occasions, is finally overcome, albeit after varying periods of hesitation and uncertainty.

Oli (7–5) describes bottles I to III as three-quarters empty and a quarter full; half full and half empty; and a quarter full and three-quarters empty. He shows III for "almost empty" and I for "a little bit empty." Question C2: "Yes, if it's half full it's also half empty." C3: "No, because if it's almost full it can't be almost empty." C4: "Yes, because if it's a little bit full it's a little bit empty." But after repetition of question: "Ah! No, because if it's a little bit full it's a lot empty and not a little." C5: "Yes, because if it's almost full it stays a little empty." C6: "Yes, because if it's a little bit empty the rest is full." Question repeated: "No, no, because if it's a little full, then it's a lot empty and not a little." Thus on two occasions Oli can still momentarily confuse "almost empty" with "a little bit empty."

Kar (7–11). *C1* to *C4:* no problems. With *C5* she at first denies that the bottle can be almost full and little empty, then immediately giggles: *"Of course it's possible. Yes,"* *C6* she begins by translating into *"a little empty and a little full"* and accepts it as possible in that form (a little empty = almost empty), then she repeats the question correctly and confirms it is possible, in which she is correct.

Rin (8–1) describes III as *"almost empty, just a bit full. — And I? — That's almost full* — Can you say the same thing without using the word full or filled? — [Hesitation.] *A little bit empty.* — Does that seem odd to you? — *We don't say it at home. I like almost full better."* *C2: "Yes, there's still the same amount: if it's half full there's a half there in it, and if it's half empty there's also a half in it."* *C3: "No, because if it's almost full it has a little water missing, and if it's almost empty there's a little bit of water still in* [with correct gestures]." *C4: Yes, it can be a little bit empty and a little bit full, that doesn't change."* The drawing, her only one, shows a very small amount of water: *"That way it's a little bit empty and a little bit full, it's the same."* But no problem with *C5:* *"Almost full it has a little bit of water missing and a little empty it also has a little bit of water missing."* *C6* produces another right answer. She is then asked to compare her answers to *C3* and *C4,* and with hindsight she comes up with the correct answers: *"There's just one thing different: a little bit empty and almost. — Are they the same? — No, because a little empty is a lot of water and almost empty is a very little bit of water."*

Ver (9–4) gets *C3* right: *"No. Almost empty is right at the bottom and almost full up at the top."* However, for *C4: "Little bit empty, just a bit at the bottom, little bit full, that's the same."* But the drawing is correct and she understands her mistake. After she has answered *C3* a counter-suggestion is made: "Why not?" Whereupon, like Char (§3) she draws a half and a half bottle: *"In the middle it's almost full and almost empty."*

Jac (9–3). *C3:* for a moment Jac still confuses "almost empty" and "a little empty" since he draws "a little empty" with less than a quarter of water and then attempts to put things right with a truly admirable compromise: *"It is a little empty with water."* Then he gets it right: *"When it's a little empty there's a lot of water in it."*

Ler (9–11). Same reaction as Ver to *C4: "It's the same thing,"* followed by a correction.

Pie (10–9) exemplifies the difference between verbal concept and graphic concept in his reply to *C4: "Yes, a little full and a little empty. — Can it be both those? — *Yes, a little full there's a little* [water] *and a little empty there's a lot.* — And it's the same thing to you, a little full and a little empty? — *Yes, the same thing.*'' But he changes his mind when it comes to drawing them, doubtless because ''same thing'' had meant to him the identity of the relation between ''a little'' and ''all,'' but forgetting that it is reversed in one case, something the drawing forced him to remember.

There is nothing that need be added regarding these 2B subjects, unless it is that the quantification of emptiness, still not reached at the previous level, has at last become accessible, albeit after trial and error. It will be noted that the procedure finally used consists in no longer thinking first about emptiness on its own, then about fullness on its own, before eventually linking them together in some way or other (including by equivalence, since Rin still says ''a little bit empty and a little bit full are the same thing'' before understanding the contrary), but in reasoning explicitly in terms of complementarity, as exemplified by Oli when he says ''if it is a little bit full it's a lot empty and not a little.'' In other words, complete compensation between positive and negative, the source of noncontradiction, is finally being respected in this particular case of empty and full.

§5. Stage 3 and Conclusions

At about the age of eleven, all the questions are at last being answered correctly without hesitations, except occasionally over one point (*A2*), but that for grammatical reasons, not logical ones.

Gid (10–7). *C3:* ''*No, because if it's almost full, then* [it has a little missing] *and if it's almost empty it has a lot missing.*'' He draws I for a little empty and III for a little full, then demonstrates their complementarity: ''*If you take that and put it there* [I on III, or III on I] *it makes a bottle that's full up.*''

Nic (11–7). *C2:* ''*Yes, if it's half full there's water in one of the halves and it's empty in the upper half.*'' *C3:* ''*No, because if it's almost full there's a lot of water in it and if it's almost empty there's only a little.*'' *C4:* ''*No, because if it's a little bit empty there's a lot of water in, and if it's a little bit full there's less water.*'' On the other hand, when asked *A2*, a question correctly solved by almost all age groups (half full and not half full), Nic takes it to mean ''half full and half not full'', which is of course the same as *C2* (half full and half empty). However, this error was purely linguistic and thus irrelevant.

Lau (11–7). *C2:* ''*Yes, because if it's half full it can't help being half empty.*'' *C3:* ''*No, if it's almost full it's almost up to the top, and if it's*

*almost empty there's only very little in it.'' C4: "No, if it's a little bit full
there's only a little water in the bottom, and if it's a little bit empty it
goes almost to the top.''*

Thus complementarity eventually comes to be recognized as the criterion
governing the possibility or compatibility of the combinations of full and
empty (see Gid's demonstration), while the situations without complementary are judged to be contradictory (see Nic's *C3* answer: "a lot of water"
and "only a little"), this reasoning also being applied in the case of emptiness (see Gid's *C3* answer: "a little missing" and "a lot missing").

To conclude, the results of this experiment seem to us to lend particularly
strong support to the hypotheses being defended in this book: that contradiction being the result of incomplete compensations between affirmations and negations ($x.\bar{x} \neq 0$), the cognitive disequilibriums characterizing
elementary levels of development are due to a systematic predominance of
the first over the second, or of the positive elements of action, representation, and thought over the negative elements. That notions as familiar as
fullness and emptiness, in subjects who are filling and emptying their cups
and glasses many times each day, should involve such an evident and such a
persistent asymmetry between positive and negative seems to show fairly
clearly that there is a general problem present, and not one specific to complementary classes alone (chapter 8).

However, we still have to examine our results to see what they can tell us
from the point of view of contradiction. Once again they provide us with a
particularly fine example in that we have at our disposal not only the subjects' concrete and active representation of their reasoning in the form of
drawings, but their verbal thought as well (and even a set of preliminary
definitions, as it were, provided by the first phase of the questioning, when
the child has to make the five bottles I to V correspond to discriptions, in the
description → designation direction as well as the other way around). As
usual, what we find is a difference between logical contradiction on the verbal
statement plane, and what one might call functional contradiction, or disequilibrium on the plane of the actions and preoperations actually carried
out: these two planes do finally come together when, by then furnished with
an adequate operatory apparatus due to reequilibrations, the subject becomes capable of making the contradictions conscious and formulating
them, which immediately enables him to avoid them or transcend them. In
the early stages, however, they are very distinct, and this state of affairs can
even continue until quite a late stage, as with the problems studied in this
chapter (naturally we are ignoring in these remarks the easy contradictions
that are sensed and avoided at even the very earliest levels, such as that in
A1: "full up and not full up at the same time").

On the verbal statement and definition plane, one might perhaps maintain that our younger subjects never contradict themselves at any particular point: to define ''a little bit empty'' as containing a little bit of water and ''a little bit full'' in the same way does indeed make it possible to maintian their identity (question *C4*). But even if that is the case in the immediate present as each question is put, one must not forget that these definitions vary from one situation to another, and that this same ''a little bit empty'' takes on a diametrically opposite meaning with question *C5*, which is correctly answered as early as level 1B. This must be taken, then, as the sign of a fairly remarkable instability, and it is this fact that obliges us to make our distinction between the two planes: that of verbal statements or their ''logical'' or prelogical form, on which the subject always manages to justify his tendencies at any given moment, even though their source naturally remains unconscious, and that of these deep tendencies themselves, manifesting the mode of coordination of his actions or preoperations and changing as he gets older. It is on this fundamental plane that we observe, at stage 1, a constant disequilibrium stemming from the lack of compensation between positive and negative, which is to say, in this case, from the lack of complementarity between the full and empty parts of the bottle: to say that ''a little bit empty'' denotes a little bit of water *A*, and that ''a little bit full'' does the same, is to ignore that part of the bottle *A'* which is then not being included in either empty or full. It may be said that, in question *C2*, to say that ''half-full'' and ''half-empty'' are equivalent two-thirds and a quarter respectively, if one defines ''halves'' as unequal parts, is ''logical''; but 2/3 and 1/4 do not take up the whole.[1] In short, however ''logical'' the subject may strive to be in each particular case, by making verbal adjustments, such thought remains profoundly contradictory.

If these functional contradictions, and therefore this disequilibrium, stem from a lack of compensation between affirmations and negations, how will equilibration be achieved?

The answer is given by the stage 2 results. On the one hand the subject has become capable of quantification (and of conservation) in the domain of positive quantities, and has acquired, in particular, correct regulation of all and some. On the other hand, however, he is still at sea when it comes to quantifying emptiness, notably in the cases of ''almost'' and ''a little bit.'' Such a double situation naturally provokes efforts to establish stabler relations. At first (cf. cognitive ''virtual tasks''), these efforts take the form of what one might call presentiments, and of tentative gropings. Then, increasingly guided by the idea of a necessary complementarity between full and empty (full part + empty part = whole bottle), the necessary condition for noncontradiction is established: hence the universal solution of question *C2* (half full and half empty). In a sense, then, one might say that the initial disequilibrium creates an unease, which becomes conscious as soon as the subject ceases to forget his previous answers to the questions when tackling a fresh one, and attempts to link all his reactions to the complementarity of full and empty. And if we take what is common to all these factors, then we do in fact find that it is the growing compensation between affirmations and negations that produces equilibration.

Fourteen

Contradictions Relating to "Almost Not"

with T. Vergopoulo (part 1) and C. Dami (part 2)

R. Carreras has had the excellent idea of investigating how children deal with the elementary forms of the infinitesimal, and will eventually be publishing his remarkable results in book form. Meanwhile, we are most grateful to him for his kind suggestion that we might like to analyze some of the problems he has devised from the point of view of contradiction. We have selected three to describe here. The first two will be dealt with in part 1, and these failed to meet with any solution until a rather late stage (stage 3 levels of eleven- and twelve-year-olds, and some at 2B). The third, on the other hand, to which we shall devote part 2, was mastered early on in stage 2 (seven- and eight-year-olds) and partly at least as early at level 1B. the instructive nature of the results obtained, insofar as the analysis of situations of contradiction is concerned, stems just as much, as we shall find, from the contrast between these two sorts of reactions as from our analyses of the individual problems.

Part 1. Displacement of Rulers and the Weight of a Grain of Salt

The first of the questions to be investigated consists in understanding the fact that a very light blow does not apparently cause an object to move, but that after n blows a displacement is observed. This question involves the problem of contradiction in two ways. First because there is a contradiction in the terms to be accepted, in other words that $(n \times 1) > 0$, something the younger subjects certainly balk at. But second because of the difficulty we have already observed of achieving compositions between the positive and negative (for example, between complementary classes in chapter 8 and full and empty in chapter 13) on account of the general tendency, at early levels, to confer primacy on affirmation and neglect negation. In the present case, the process imposed by the subject's successive observations seems to set out from negation and then replace a succession of negations with a final affirmation. So how will the relation between these terms be structured?

The questions relating to visible and invisible displacements (first part of *Techniques*) will be supplemented by some further short questions (second part of *Techniques*) on an analogous, but purely static problem: supposing that a grain of salt weighs "nothing," how much will a pinch or a little pile of salt weigh? The resulting incomplete compensation $(0 + 0 + \ldots) > 0$ is thus all the more paradoxical and instructive in that the subject can no longer take refuge in the force of the blows and other dynamic factors.

Techniques

1. A ruler, A, large, flat, 50 centimeters long and thus quite heavy, is laid

on the table. It is then struck repeatedly but lightly on one end with a thin rod. No one blow appears to make *A* move, but after several blows it is observed that it has in fact moved slightly after all. Predictions are asked for at the outset, then the subject is asked after each blow if the ruler, *A*, has moved or not, and if not, then which blow will make it begin to move. One also asks if the displacement is the same at both ends of *A*, and if not why not. Next one moves on to more analytical questions. Another ruler, identical to *A*, has been cut into three segments: *B* and *B′* are each 15 centimeters long, *C* is 20 centimeters long. Questions are put to the subject about each segment individually, or after inserting *C* between the two others widthwise. The ruler is then put back together and the initial questions repeated (the point of these variations being to find out whether a long ruler moves more or less than a short one, and what the reasons are for the possible differences). It is also sometimes advantageous to push the ruler by hand.

2. For the questions about the weight of salt, one has two identical eggcups, one empty and the other three-quarters full. On a sheet of black material one places a single grain of salt from an external source, asking whether it weighs anything or not. It is then placed in the empty eggcup to see if that modifies its weight or not. Same questions for 1 + 1, then 1 + 1 + 1 grains, and so on. Then comes the question how many grains of salt are needed to obtain any effect: the answers can be anything from 10 to 30, 100, or "a pinch" and so on. Next the questions are put in the reverse order: if we take one grain out of the three-quarters full eggcup, does that make a difference to its weight, and so on. Finally, if a single grain is thought to have no weight at all (in the additive direction) one asks whether the same grain weighs something for an ant, a mouse, and so on, and if yes, does it weigh something to us and whether, in reality, it does have weight or not.

§1. Stage 1

First, here are some results:

Bor (5–0). 1. One tap on *A:* "Did it move? — *No because it's too heavy.* — How many taps must we give it? — *Two.* [Another tap.] *No, it's too heavy.* — Will ten move it? — *No.* [Taps given.] *It moved.* — At the first tap? — *No, the eighth.* — And at the seventh it didn't move at all? —*No.* — Between the first and the seventh, it's as though we didn't do them? — *Yes.* — So why did it start at the eighth? —*Because you tapped a little bit harder.* — When we tap here (start of *A*) does it move along as much as there does (end of *A*)? —*No because it's much more at the end.*" The idea is put to her that the other (impact) end takes the blow, but she remains unshaken. Bar *B*. One tap. "Did it move? — *Yes.* — Will ten taps make it move? — *Yes* [Taps given.] *Yes.* — Which tap made it start moving? — *The first . . . no, a little later, a little before the last, the third.* — It didn't feel anything at the second? — *A little bit.* — And at the first? — *No.* — (Same movement at both ends?) — *Yes, the same as the start.*"

2: "With a grain in the eggcup is it heavier than before? — *No, because it's very tiny so it doesn't weigh.* — And one more (= 2)? — *No.* — And one more (= 3)? — *No, It's very tiny, so it can't make weight. You have to put it all in.* — (A pinch put in.) Is that enough? — *Yes.* — It's heavier than before? — *It needs another* [pinch]. — (Pinch put in.) Is it heavier than before? — *Yes.* — And if I take out one grain is it lighter than before? — *Yes.* — And if I take another one out? — *Yes.*" And so on. "I'm taking out one more, leaving just one. Is it lighter than before? — *Yes.* — Now if I take one out there'll be none left in. Is it lighter than before? — *Yes.* — Now there's nothing in. If I put in one grain, won't it be heavier than before? — *No.* — But when I took one grain out you said it would be lighter than before, didn't you? — [Silence.] — And now I have none and I add one and it's not heavier than before? — [No] *you need to put in like before* [a pinch]. — If an ant had to push the grain of salt, would it think it was heavy? — *A little bit.* — And a mouse? — *Not so heavy. A mouse is bigger.* — But it's still the same grain, so how can it change weight? — *It's still the same. If it had changed it would be more heavy.* — Who is it heavy to? — *No one.* — But you say that a pinch of salt weighs something, and a pinch is a lot of grains. And you say a grain weighs nothing. So can a nothing plus a nothing plus a nothing make something? — *Yes.*"

Lia (5–7). 1: He thinks that *A* moves after the second tap, then after the third "*sometimes at the second, the third, the fourth, or the fifth.* — What does it depend on? — *How hard it's hit.*" The lightness of the blows is heavily stressed. "Doesn't it feel the first? — *Yes, sometimes, but it moves more often with the second.* — But with one tap, does it move a very little or not at all? — *Sometimes with the first it moves, but most times with the second and the others.*" He begins by thinking there is greater forward motion at the impact end than the other, then leans toward equality.

2: The grains of salt weigh nothing, but after several pinches: "*Now it's almsot a bit heavy. Before it didn't weigh, now it does weigh.*" Removing one grain at a time makes no more difference to the weight than adding them. But by pinches: "*Now it's not so heavy as before but it doesn't weigh.* — I'll take out some more. — *It's less, less heavy. Zero heavy.* — I'm leaving in a very tiny bit. — *It's zero heavy.*"

Sej (5–6) 1: *A* doesn't move until the third tap, but moves less at its leading end "*because it's pushed*" at impact end. This doesn't apply to *B* because "*it's short.*" With *B* then *B'*; "*It's at the end* [of *B'*] *it goes along more. At the start* [of *B*] *it goes along less, at the end* [of *B'*] *more.*" But for *A* he returns to his original idea: "*at the end less, because it's pushed at the start.*"

Pad (5–7) 1: Pad, on the contrary, thinks that *A* moves forward "*only there* [end] *because you're tapping here* [start]." This isn't so with *B*, which is heavier, but is so again with *B'* (extension of *B*) "*because the iron* [*B'*] *gets bigger.*"
    2: One grain weighs nothing "*because there's just one. — And one more (= 2)? Is that heavier than before? — No, not yet. — And one more (= 3)? — No, not yet. — How many do we need to put on to make it weigh? — A lot.*" A pinch put in. On the other hand: "If we take out one grain is it lighter? — *Yes.* [and so on]. — And if I leave just one in? — *It's lighter still.* — And lighter still again if I take out the last one? — *Yes.* — And if I put one back in, is it heavier than before? — *No* [and so on, up to three]."

Bro (6–1). 1: One tap: "*No, that wasn't hard enough. —* But with several taps? — *No* [Taps given.] *It did move a little bit because there were several little taps, that makes a big tap. —* Which of the little taps made it begin to move? Did the first make it move? — *No, the second or third I think. You can't move with the first of all. —* Is it as though it didn't exist? — *Yes.*" As for the displacement: "*It's the end end that moves most. —* Why? — *Because . . . it's more there. —* If it moved along a square (on squared paper) at the beginning end, how much there? — *Oh, two squares at the end end. —* And with a harder tap? — *If it goes along a square at the end, then it's a half a square at the beginning, because the beginning goes along less than the end.*" With *B* + *B'* + *C* (in line) the whole will move "*at the third tap. —* Not at all at the second? — *A tiny little bit. —* And at the first? — *No it wasn't hard enough, it can't start right away* [so "hard" = repetition]." — And does it move along the same here (start of *B*) and there (end of *C*)? — *No, it's still the front* [end of *C*] *that moves along most. —* Why? — *Because the beginning* [impact end of *B*] *is lighter than the end. —* Why? — *It's not so heavy. —* How do you know? — *Before I had the answer. Now I can't remember.*"
    2: One grain more or less makes no change, nor do two or three, only piles: "*A pile is heavier than the grain. —* And a half pile? — *That is too. —* And a quarter of a pile? — *A little bit more heavy. —* And an eighth of a pile (the quantity demonstrated), is that heavier than the grain? — *No, they're the same.*"

Can (6–5). 1: "*There* [impact end of *A*] *it moves less than at the end.*" But this is not the case with *B*: "Why not? — *Because it goes slowly,*" whereas *A* "*goes quick because it's big.*"

Bru (6–10). 1: *A"didn't move till the fourth tap* [of fifteen given]. —
Didn't it feel the others? — *No.* — What happens to make it feel the fourth?
— *Don't know.* — At the fourth, does it move a little or a lot? — *A
very, very little.* — And at the fifth? — *A middle amount.* — And the
sixth? — *More still.* — And the seventh? — *More still.* — And the
eighth? — *More still.* — And at the third? — *Nothing at all.*" But for
Bru the leading end of *A* moves less than the impact end. However, this
is not so with *B* "*because A is longer.*" *B* + *B*′ doesn't move till third
tap: "*the first two didn't feel* [weren't felt].*"
    2. One grain of salt more or less makes no difference, but "*perhaps
fifteen will.*"

Gio (7–7). 1: After one tap then ten taps *A* moves forward "*at the second
and then at all the others. — It didn't move with the first? — No.*" Both
A and *B* move more at their leading ends "*because it's at the end it
starts to move, the end at the end is bigger because it's the one that
moves along. — And the end we tap doesn't move along? — Yes, but not
so much.*" But *B* + *B*′ in line doesn't move at the first tap: "*No, at the
eighth because when there is an end bit* [*B*′] *it doesn't let the first bit* [*B*]
move." But after having accepted a small displacement at the seventh
tap, at the sixth "*a tiny little bit less,*" and at the fifth "*no it didn't
move,*" he changes his mind about the relative terminal displacements:
"*No, at the hitting end* [of *B*] *it moves forward more, because when you
give it a tap it starts off at that end, because B pushes B*′" and furthermore the displacements at both ends have finally become equal "*because
B goes along a way then B and B*′ *move together.*"

It is apparent, then, that these subjects are perfectly happy to accept that
the first light taps (one to six, say) administered to a ruler don't make it
move, whereas succeeding ones do produce movement by means of a simple
cumulative effect; or that a grain of salt weighs nothing, but that a little heap
of grains does have weight. Hence the formula accepted by Bor without the
slightest difficulty: a nothing plus a nothing plus a nothing makes something.
The problem posed by the reactions of this stage is thus that of noncoordination between positive (displacements or weights) and negative (apparent lack
of both). However, we cannot simply say here, as we so clearly seem to be
able to do in other situations, that the former must necessarily be given
primacy over the second, since in this particular case the negative corresponds to the nonperceptible, which makes the difficulty in structuration
natural. But since it has seemed in earlier cases that this primacy of the
positive stems from its immediately observable nature, while the negative is
in varying degrees inferred from an expectation, the present situation constitutes a kind of borderline case well worth investigating: that in which the
decision lies between "nothing" (no displacement, no weight) and "almost

nothing" (minimal displacement, minimal weight) and must be made exclusively on grounds provided by the postive observable facts (repetition of blows with final visible effect, augmentation of number of grains finally producing a perceptible result).

Now, since such a coordination presupposes an adequate quantification of the positive as a precondition, it is natural that we should find total failure at this stage, and even total unawareness of the continual contradictions, since such quantification is still lacking. Thus where the displacement of the ruler is concerned, most of these subjects think that the leading extremity of the member moves forward more than the end receiving the impact (the remainder of the subjects think the contrary): this makes it clear that this lack of differentiation between displacement and elongation favors the notion that the former is able to arise *ex nihilo* from the repetition of the blows without the first few of those blows having had any effect. The implicit idea in all the subjects' minds, as far as this repetition is concerned, is actually made explicit by Bro: "Several little taps, that makes a big tap." In other words, the subject is ignoring the fact that the taps are discontinuous, each one acting separately, with addition of their successive effects not of the force of the blows. So that the child is joining them all together illegitimately to make one big bang. The idea that the blows become stronger by repetition is evidence of the same erroneous additivity (the subjects all know that the taps are very light). As for the answers to the part 2 questions, they reveal the nonrelational conception of weight so familiar at this level: light is not just the negative of heavy (except purely verbally on occasions) but another quality altogether, so that we find certain subjects expressing the idea that the addition of a single grain of salt adds no weight, because it doesn't weigh anything, whereas its removal makes the whole lighter, since one is taking something away.

§2. Level 2A

The criteria for this level (seven- and eight-year-olds with two cases of six-and-a-half- and some nine-year-olds) are affirmation, usually correctly justified, of equality between the displacements at the two ends of the ruler, and perplexity over the additivity of the successive displacements after the first, nonperceptible ones.

Mic (6–6). 1: After ten taps on *A:* "*It began to move with number eight* [He does the tapping himself.] *I'd already given it some* [before]. *After, it began to move.* — And the ones before didn't count? — *With those, they didn't make it move.* — When did it begin then? — *With number six.* — And before that what was happening? — *With the first and second it didn't move.* — Not at all? — *No.* — And the third? — *It did begin.* — Why didn't it begin right away? — *Because the first tap is lighter.* — But you're doing them all the same. — *Ah, perhaps I didn't look hard enough."* Prediction for *B:* "*No, not with just one light tap, but with a lot it will move."* Displacement at leading and impact ends are equal, likewise in case of *B + B'*, because "*They will both push one another.* — Watch both ends. — [He tries.] *It's hard to see them both at once.* — Well, what do you think anyway? — *It moved the same all the way along* [same response for *BB' + C + A*]." Next, B + B' + D: "*It doesn't move.* — Fifteen taps. — *At number eight it began to move.* — Don't you find that peculiar? — *Perhaps it began to move with the first one, because all the taps are the same.* [Tries one tap.] *I didn't see anything, but I think it moves at number three or four.* — When you can't see anyting, can it be moving all the same? — *No, that's not possible."*

2: One grain (+ 1, and so on) weighs nothing: "*You need to put in at least nine.* — And if I take one out? — *Then it will weigh even less . . . There would have to be only three left in for it not to weigh anything at all again."* But to an ant "*it weighs a little."* Then he can't decide whether the ant is right or whether it really doesn't weigh anything.

Par (7–7) I: "If I give one little tap will it (*A*) move? — *Yes.* — Where? — *At the beginning* [impact end] *and the end, it's all the same thing.* [one tap.] *No, it's too heavy.* — And with fifteen light taps? — *It will move a little.* [Taps given.] *Yes, just a very little.* — So with one it didn't move and with fifteen it did? — *Yes.* — Why? Do you think that's what should happen? — *Because fifteen light taps make one big tap."* With *B* and *B'* he supposes, after observation, that the movement begins with the third tap and he perceives that after fifteen taps "*it has moved along a lot more . . . because fifteen is more than three.* — So, is three more than two? — *Yes.* — And two than one? — *Yes.* — And one than zero? — *Yes.* — But before you said that it began with tap three, and that the two first taps didn't count. Is that right? — *Don't know.* — Here it moved at tap three? — *Yes. one millimeter.* — And how much at the second tap? — *Nothing at all.* — And is two bigger than one tap? — *No.* — It moves a bit more with each tap? — *Yes.* — And the first two taps don't do anything? — *Yes* [they don't]. — And three is more than two? — *Yes.* — And two than 1? — *Yes.* — And it doesn't move, is that right? — [*Silence.*]"

2: One grain (and so on) weighs nothing, whether added or removed; only a pile weighs something. "If I start taking them off, when will it start getting less heavy? — *When half has gone.* — What if I take away just a little less than half, does that count as zero? — *Yes.* — You don't think that's peculiar? — *No."*

Ser (7–6). 1: After ten taps: "*You made the taps harder every time.* — (We start again.) What were the taps like then? — *Light.* — And it moved? — *Yes.* — When did it begin moving? — *At tap five.* — And at number four, did it move then? — *No.* — Is it as if the first four didn't exist? — *The fourth pushed a little, but the fifth more than the fourth.* — And the third? — *It didn't move then. If you push there* [impact end] *the other end moves away the same amount.*" With $B + B' + C$ the movement begins at the sixth tap: "So the sixth is as if it's the first? — *Yes.* — (One tap given.) Did it move? — *Before you made the sixth one harder.* — No I didn't. Now, why hasn't it moved? — *Don't know.* — Is it because there simply has to be a fifth before it? — *Yes because with the fifth that begins to give the feeling it wants to move and then* [with the sixth] *it moves.*"

2. One and two grains weigh nothing, but "*three, that's heavier than two and one.* — But two isn't heavier than one? — *Yes.* — But you said just then that two equal zero? — *If you take out one grain it weighs less than with one in.* — And you told me earlier that one equals zero. Which is right? — *That* [1 = 0 and 2 = 1 = 0]. — And would it be heavy to a little ant? — *Yes, because the ant's littler than us, so he feels the weight.* — So does a weight only exist when you can feel it? — *Yes . . . yes, it exists but you can't feel it.*"

Ket (7–8). 1: "*With the fourth, if you give a lot of taps then it moves along . . . One tap* [any one tap] *doesn't do much, but a lot of taps make it move along.* — And do three make it move? — *No.* — Didn't it feel the first taps? — *No.* — And why then, suddenly like that? — *Because it's been given taps before.* — Is that normal or peculiar? — *Peculiar.* — What would you expect normally? — *For it to move with the first. Perhaps we didn't see it.*" But then, with $B + B'$ and the rest, he reverts to denying the effects of the early blows: "*It didn't feel anything till the fifth.* — Why not at the fourth? — *Because you hadn't given enough taps* [before the fourth]." On the other hand, the ruler moves along in a homogeneous fashion "*because it's not cut in two, it's the same thing* [at both ends] *when you give it a tap.*"

2: Usual reactions: plus or minus one makes no difference. "And (0 + 0 + 0 . . .), do they make half a gram (the weight Ket has assigned to a "pile")? — *No.* — Can things that don't exist make up something that does? — *Yes.*"

Rab (7–6). 1: "*Of course both sides* [both ends of A] *have moved along. If you push at the start end it makes the same amount.*" But the first few taps don't do anything "*because they're just touching it, they don't push.*" Later, a change of mind: "Does it move at the first tap? — *You can't tell.*" But later again: "*not at all.*"

2: Plus or minus one makes no difference. But the single grain has weight for an ant. But a small child *"can't feel anything at all, it hasn't any weight."*

Cav (8–7). 1: *"If it moves along at the beginning* [of *A*] *then it must move along at the end because the whole little plank moves,"* but *"because it's heavy it doesn't move till the fifth tap . . . you have to tap it several times to have a harder tap."*

2: Adding a grain makes no difference, but taking one away makes it less heavy.

Ham (8–3). Same reactions for 1:*"When you hit several taps quicker* [= at a faster rate], *it moved."*

2: Adding grains or taking one away makes no difference.

Fla (8–7). 1: One tap, no result *"because it was too gently. —* And ten gently? *— A little because there are several."* In 2, on the other hand, one grain is *"a tiny little bit"* more heavy and one taken away the reverse, but only *"when there are several is there any weight."*

Fis (8–10). 1: *A* moves forward at fifth tap and *"perhaps before. —* At the third? *— No, nothing at all then. —* Could we say the fourth is the first? *— No, it's still as if they existed all the same* [from one to three], *it made a noise. —* So why didn't it move till the fourth? *— Because there is a power."*

Sel (9–7). 1: *"A lot of taps give more force than one and it moves. —* What if I began at the third? *— You have to begin at one or it doesn't move."*

All these subjects belong to the level when concrete operations begin to appear, together with all the advances that entails from the quantification and conservation point of view. They all affirm, in particular, the quality of the displacements at the two ends of the ruler when it is pushed, because as Caf puts it, "the whole little plank moves." Conservation of lengths in cases of displacement is not so easily achieved as it might seem, for, when one of two equal and previously superimposed lengths is moved so that its leading edge projects beyond the end of the other, one generally has to wait until a later level for a solution affirming the quantitative equality of the two projecting portions.

Given these advances in quantification, every one of these subjects is sooner or later visibly bothered by the observed fact that, although ten or fifteen taps make the ruler move, a single tap, or the first two or three, apparently have no effect. They then offer two solutions. The first seems obvious enough: "perhaps I didn't look hard enough," Mic says, and so "perhaps it began to move with the first one." But this being the level of concrete operations, at which budding operatory logic is applied solely to the manipulable and the perceptible, this solution of a nonperceived displacement is resolutely dismissed almost at once, so that when asked later on whether something can be moving even if you can't see it moving, Mic answers: "no, that's not possible." Similarly, however readily they accept that the little ant can feel the weight of a single grain of salt, these subjects still maintain that it doesn't exist for us if we can't feel it. (See Rab, and others. Despite Ser's verbal claims to the contrary, he still goes on thinking that $2 = 1 = 0$). This identification of the existing with the perceptible, which persists almost throughout stage 2, is something to be kept in mind when it comes to analyzing the relations between positive and negative, which together govern any question relating to contradiction, since such an identification excludes the notions of "almost nothing" or "almost not" that are indispensable for any quantification of the negative (cf. chapter 13, where the reactions to "almost empty" and "a little bit empty" are strikingly parallel to the results here, even though in that case we were dealing with extremely perceptible bottles!).

Hence the second solution, which is that although those first taps do not produce any actual movement of the ruler A, they are nevertheless necessary in some kind of preparatory role: "you have to begin at one," Sel says, "or it doesn't move." And Ket, when asked why it moves suddenly at the fourth tap, says "because it's been given taps before." Nor is this idea of preparation still the same simple overall additivity of stage 1 (to which Per still resorts, with his "fifteen light taps make one big tap," before observing the additivity in practice of the small displacements between three and fifteen, albeit without being able to generalize it to one, two, and three). It is being conceived of here more as a qualitative and dynamic, but cumulative action, which consists in giving "it the feeling it wants to move" (Ser, hence his "taps harder every time" even though he knows and admits that they are "light") or as "a power" (Fis). And similarly, when Cav says "you have to tap it several times to have a harder tap," or when Ham talks of hitting "several taps quicker," they are thinking of a transmission of successive cumulative effects. So we are now on the way toward quantification, and between "nothing" (zero displacement) and the visible effects, an intermediate term is on the verge of appearing: "It's as if they existed all the same," Fis says of taps one to three.

The same tendencies are found in the case of the salt grains. Ket thinks that the addition or removal of one grain has no effect, yet he rejects the equation

$$0 + 0 + 0 + \ldots = 1/2 \text{ gram}$$

(the weight he ascribes to a "pile"). Fla thinks that it is only "when there are several'' that there is ''any weight,'' but a single grain is already ''a tiny little bit heavy,'' even though he then makes it clear that this isn't quite the same thing as ''weight.''

§3. Level 2B and Stage 3

At the first of these levels the necessity for the initial taps becomes clearer:

Fab (9–7). 1: bar B doesn't move until tap three: *''It's the third tap that counts. But the first and second count too, otherwise the third would be the first and wouldn't move it. The first and second move it a tiny bit. —* (B' added to B.) Does B' feel anything if you tap B? *— Yes, it will vibrate, and that goes from B into B'.''* She later maintains that with one tap B doesn't move but just vibrates.

2: $+ n = -n = 0$ up to 200.

Ari (9–5). 1: ''Did A move at the first tap? *— No, at the fourth, a little tiny bit. —* Not at all at the third? *— I'm not sure it was the fourth. But if it was the fourth, then the third would have started it shaking a tiny bit, it was preparing itself, but you didn't see it. —* And at the second? *— Well, less than at the third. —* And at the first? *— Not at all, but it gives a little shock, and that makes the second shake it, and the third, and with the fourth it begins to move.''*

2: One grain *''doesn't make any weight.''* But: ''If I add one grain where there weren't any? *— It makes it a very tiny bit''* more heavy.

Bon (10–9). 1: A doesn't move until the fifth tap. ''So if I began at the fifth, would it move? *— No, it must begin from the start, the first ones do make it move a little tiny bit. —* But it doesn't really move until the fifth? *— Yes.''*

2: opposite reactions from Ari: Bon maintains that *''a grain of salt has only very, very little weight,''* but that if you add it to something it won't make that something any heavier: ''You need a lot.''*

Dom (10–3). 1: ''*It [A] moves along on number 5, but very little. —* So the first four didn't count? *— It moves, but you can't see it. —* And with two? *— Even if you can't see it, it doesn't move. —* So it's as though one and two didn't exist? *— No, you have to hit three times all the same. —* But the first two don't count? *— They count beginning with the second, but you can't see. —* And the first? *— It does move it really, but you can't see anything.''*

2: One grain: *''It weighs something, but we've got a lot of strength, it's as though there's nothing there so we can't imagine it.* — And if I take off a grain, does it weigh less? — *Yes, but almost nothing less.* — And do two grains weigh more than one? — *Yes, twice as much as one."*

Ros (10–9). 1: Movement first at sixth tap *"because the first hasn't the strength of the sixth,"* but then he wonders whether, even at the first *"it will move a tiny bit."*

2: "One grain in the eggcup, is it heavier than before? — *Yes, a very tiny amount."*

Duv (11–0). 1: *A* doesn't move until *"the ninth tap. — And at the eighth? — It begins a little. — And at the seventh? — No. — As if nothing at all happened? — Yes. — As if it was motionless? — It was just a little tiny start. — But at the sixth completely motionless? — Yes. — And from the first to the sixth? — It was beginning to come. — How? — It moves a little this way* [quivering gesture]." *B* and *B'*: *"It moved at the third tap. — And at the second? — It began to shiver but it didn't move. — At the first? — It shivered, but less than at the second."*

2: One grain: *"It weighs more than before; you're adding the weight of the grain to the eggcup."*

And here, finally are some stage 3 subjects with their immediate correct answers:

Evy (11–3). 1: One tap: *"I didn't see."* After ten taps: *"It moved because you gave them all one after the other. — From the very first one? — No, at first you can't see anything. Yes, it must have done, otherwise it wouldn't move* [at the tenth]. *Perhaps it moves a little, just a little, without your seeing it, otherwise it would never move. — Does it move the same distance at the end that's tapped and the other? — Of course it does. It can't shrink."*

2: One grain: *"It has a slight amount of weight that we can't feel."*

Ngu (11–5). 1: *"You have to begin with the first because the first and the second are as if you were giving not very strong taps and it increases . . . as if you were tapping harder and harder."*

2: One grain: *"*[He laughs.] *A thousandth of a milligram heavy!"*

Isa (11–10). 1: *"If it doesn't move the first time it's not going to move the fifteenth!"*

Gat (11–11). 1: "First tap? — *Perhaps it moves very very little, and if you give it several taps you notice."*

2: One grain: *"Very little, almost not, it weighs almost nothing."*

Liv (11–4). 1: After ten: "And the first? — *It's as though it moved. In fact it moves, but you don't see it. — Why do you say in fact? — Because you give it a tap. It's bound to move a slight amount."*

So at level 2B we find perceptible progress has been made in coordinating the perceptible positive and the invisible negative: something is happening as a result of those first taps, even if that something isn't yet displacement proper. Ari is the most explicit: the first tap produces "a little shock," which at the second tap "shakes" the ruler, shakes it even more at the third, and finally, "at the fourth it begins to move." Duv's solution is much the same: at the second tap "it began to shiver but it didn't move." This idea is then extended to the first tap, so that it becomes possible to say that during taps one to six "it was beginning to come," or, as Ari puts it, "It was preparing itself." So there is an idea there, among these subjects, that somewhere between negation of visible displacements and their affirmation there must be a middle term, since their appearance does not occur until after the first few taps: hence the necessity for a quantification of these intermediate degrees and for a continuous additivity. But since they are still convinced, in accordance with the usual stage 2 laws, that the nonperceptible doesn't exist, they refuse as yet to talk about very small displacements and resort instead to explanations in terms of dynamic transitions: shocks, shaking, vibrations, and so on. Finally, others make the leap and accept, with Dom, that the first tap "does move it really, but you can't see," which is the stage 3 solution, but reached with greater difficulty and hesitation.

As for the weight of the grain of salt, the solution offered to that problem is closely parallel (and this parallelism between two such different situations is remarkable) Ari and Bon both make a distinction between possessing weight and making heavier, even though Ari endows the grain of salt with the first of these properties and not the second while Bon reverses the attibution. Dom, on the other hand, accepts both, even though it is not possible "to imagine" such minuscule quantities, so that if you remove one grain it is "almost nothing less!"

Finally, the stage 3 answers mark the decisive developmental characteristic of this period of formal operations: primacy of necessary deduction over submission to observable phenomena. "Yes it must have," Evy says, when asked if the ruler moved at the first tap, "otherwise it would never move." And Liv: "It moves in fact, but you can't see it." And Isa: "If it doesn't move the first time it's not going to move the fifteenth!" Thus we finally have additivity of the small displacements themselves, each of which is imperceptible but whose sum can be seen, rather than the earlier cumulative dynamic effect (for although Ngu talks about tapping harder and harder, he is careful to preface this with "it's as if"). As for the grains of salt, they no longer present any problem. A single grain of salt, Evy says "has a slight amount of weight that we can't feel."

§4. Conclusions

In the majority of situations involving coordination of affirmations and negations, it is the former that are overestimated (excessive generalizations, and so on) and the second that are deficient. In the present experiments, on the contrary, there are more negations involved than is ultimately seen as legitimate, and this not from an initial tendency to overvalue them, but because the lack of perceptible results produces an imperative need to draw false inferences (nondisplacements). Thus the problem then becomes, as usual, that of coordinating these affirmations and these negations by finding degrees of quantification that will be complementary to one another in both domains, positive and negative. The solution appears to be a simple one: taking as one's starting point a visible displacement whose existence can be asserted after ten to fifteen taps, it will be sufficient to construct a negative operation (division or subtraction going back along the series of taps one by one) capable of revealing the minimal elements present, in other words, the small displacements the multiplication or addition of which gives the final total displacement. But since this elementary change of position is "almost not" a displacement, since it remains invisible, while already being a "very small" part of the finally observable whole, this coordination of affirmations and negations, which would present no difficulty whatever if each element were visible, becomes a matter of pure inferences, an analysis of which thus becomes most instructive with regard to the coordination of affirmations and negations.

At the very outset noncoordination is total, since we have $(0 + 0 + \ldots) > 0$, as a result of the fact that a positive displacement is emerging from a number of zero displacements which are nevertheless necessary, just as n grains of salt have a weight while none of the individual grains does. The first solution the subject thinks of is interesting in that it immediately transposes the problem from the displacements themselves to their causality, or, in other words, to the factor of positive production that provides an account of them, that is, the force of the blows. The negative effect is then explained by an inadequacy on the part of this positive action, so that the first few taps are claimed to be too light, even though, as Bro is already claiming at stage 1, "several little taps, that makes one big tap." The question then arises, however, of what the nature of this additivity is, and above all of where or in what it resides. Where can those light, successive taps be making their mark, where are they being stored in such a way that their sum produces one hard tap? The first answer must of course be "inside the person administering the taps," hence the argument that he is tapping harder and harder. But this interpretation, which would effectively explain the sudden and discontinuous appearance of a displacement, is rebutted by the fact, acknowledged by the subject, that all the taps in the series are light. Hence the next solution, found at level 2A: the taps are stored within the object, and before actually causing it to move they produce within it "a feeling it wants to move" or "a power," because, as Fis says of the first three taps, "it's as if they existed all the same," which is a very pretty compromise between negative and positive (but also a fine example of incomplete compensation). With level 2B we find a further form of transition leading to the displacement: the "shaking" or "vibration" imparted to the object by the taps that "makes it ready" to move. But it is not until stage 3 that the contrary operations of division and collection are coordinated from the start, thus ensuring solution of the problem.

The strange fact in this development is that the child, rather than accept the existence of very small displacements that can't be seen (which the subject declares for a long time to be "impossible"), but that would produce a simple additivity with evident reversals, resorts first of all to various sorts of cumulative dynamic effects that are no more perceptible than the tiny displacements (for one cannot see the feeling it wants to move, the power, or even the vibrations), and that cannot be quantified other than in an ordinal and qualitative way. In practice, then, until stage 3 the subject continually fails to coordinate the negative (reverse) and positive operations, and what he puts in the place of partial negations (small, invisible displacements) are no more than weakened affirmations, merely stressing what is still lacking for the taps to produce an actual displacement. In other words, what the subject is actually looking for, in order to remove the contradictions, is an "almost displacement" instead of an "almost zero" displacement, the whole point of which is that it is not absolutely zero. It is in this sense that these results, while reminiscent of those given in chapter 1 concerning imperceptible differences, are also parallel to those in chapter 13 concerning difficulties in coordinating empty and full, which persist until the constitution of a quantification enables the subject to achieve composition of affirmations and negations.

As for the grains of salt problem, where at the outset no single grain was conceived of as possessing weight, whereas adding them to form a pile suddenly did produce weight (from 9 to 100 or 200, and so on), the noncoordination of negations and affirmations there is even more flagrant. However, this problem proved less rich in solutions, since in this case there are no causal actions involved, such as administering a blow, but merely unions or dissociations, and because such unions, viewed as acts, do not present a greater or lesser degree of force. This, indeed, makes it all the more striking that for such a long time the subject sees no contradiction in the composition $(0 + 0 + \ldots) > 0$, when it is the properties of objects alone that are involved.[1] However, we must remember the existence of one surprising and quite commonly expressed opinion, which is that removing one grain from the pile makes it lighter, whereas the addition of an identical unit doesn't modify the total weight at all. The results just studied suggest a possible explanation for this: a pile less one grain is "almost the same pile" but is no longer the entire pile, whereas a pile plus a grain is still the same pile, as long as one is prepared to thumb one's nose at all forms of cardinal quantification.

In sum, we find in these two groups of results a further example of disequilibrium produced by noncoordination of affirmations and negations, or of direct and reverse operations. Furthermore, although we do not find the primacy of affirmation demonstrated in quite such spectacular fashion as in chapter 13 in relation to empty and full, we are nevertheless able to discern its essential cause, which is the primacy of observable fact, in the sense of the directly perceptible, over that which cannot be seen. Indeed, the younger subjects, despite being so unanimous in acknowledging that the grain of salt is heavy to an ant, still go so far as to refuse it any weight whatever on the grounds that it has no weight perceptible to us.

Part 2. Piling Up Paper

Another problem suggested by R. Carreras consists in having the child construct two piles of equal height from thin sheets of paper, showing him how to check the equality of those heights by linking their tops with a ruler, which the child can then judge to be either horizontal or not, and then asking him if the piles will remain equal, and the ruler horizontal, if a single sheet of paper is removed or added to one of the piles.

Technique

The techniques employed have varied slightly, but the general principle behind them all is very simple. The child is first asked, by way of introduction, to make two equal piles from six to eight sheets of some thickish material, such as hardboard, arranging them in biunivocal correspondence and checking the equality of his piles with a ruler. Then one makes, or has the child make, two piles made up of eighty to one hundred sheets of thin paper, invoking the same procedure by correspondence. One then asks if a difference of one sheet will modify the heights, which are verifiable by means of the ruler, or how many one needs to add or remove in order to achieve a real modification.

§5. Introduction and Examples

The questions asked thus seem totally equivalent to those in part 1 of this chapter, but there is one difference that could be of importance. In the case of the displacements as a result of taps, or in that of the grains of salt, the quantitative evaluations had as their basis elementary additive operations bearing upon a single variable: displacements or tiny movements whose combined lengths gave a larger displacement, individual grains of salt or small quantities resulting from their addition (weight of a "pinch" of grains of salt, and so on). In the present case, on the contrary, the evaluations can remain ordinal or qualitative (height of one pile projecting up above the other or not, and the ruler remaining horizontal or not), but do not need to, since they can also be based on the biunivocal correspondence used in the construction of the two piles to be compared. Either case, however, requires two variables to be brought into relation.

These differences may play a role. In particular, except for one or two cases, we found no oppositions between the effects of removing a sheet or adding one, as was the case with the grain of salt questions in part 1. In fact, it could hardly be otherwise, for, although one can conceive that removing a grain from a small pile modifies that pile's integrity, whereas adding one leaves it "still the same pile," the question involving the elimination or addition of a single sheet of paper to one of two piles is not posed in terms of identity (identity, that is, of the "before" and "after" heights of a single pile) and absolute height, but only in terms of whether one is higher than the other. And given such a viewpoint, there are no longer any differences between adding and subtracting. Here are some level 1A reactions:

Isa (6–6) predicts that after a sheet is removed from one side the piles *"aren't the same height any more"* and that the ruler will *"be sloping.* — Sure? — *Yes.* — Look. — *It's still straight.* — And two off? — *No, another as well* [three sheets removed]. *No the ruler's still flat. The sheets aren't very thick, so if I take off one it will be the same height still.* — And if you take off two? — *You can't tell.* — with this pile (four)? — *With that pile you can tell. They're thick, those pieces?"*

Fav (6–6). Same initial reactions, then after trials: *"It's not sloping.* — No differences in height? — *No.* — How many would you have to take? — *Ten."*

Nad (6–7): *"They're so fine, it's as if you hadn't taken anything off at all. — And two? — Still not. — And three? — Still not. And four? — Still not. — And five? — Now it's changing. —* It's number five that changes the pile? *— Yes. —* But it's just the same as the others? *— Of course, but it's because we took away some little by little: that makes a difference in the end."* Later, Nad moves up to stage 2.

One can also establish a 1B level characterized by hesitation on the subject's part:

Vic (5–10) answers all the preliminary questions with the two piles of hardboard sheets easily. "And if I take away a sheet of paper from here, will the two piles of paper stay the same? *— No.* — And the ruler? *— It will be sloping.* — Like with the boards? *— Yes.* — [Sheet removed.] *— It isn't sloping.* — Why not? *— It's still the same layers.* — But I did take a layer away from this side? *— Yes.* — Like with the boards? — [No] *they were fat.* — And the paper? *— That's very fine.* — And if I take one off, does it make a difference? *— Yes, a little bit lower.* — And the ruler? *— You can't see a difference because it's the same height.* — And if I put another sheet on, is it the same height? *— No* [he places his hands on the piles]. *When I put my hand there it's lower* [than the other side]. — And the ruler? *— It will be slopinga little.* — Watch. *— Yes.* — Is it sloping? *— Yes, I can see it.* — And if I take away a sheet? — [Hesitates.] — And if I add? *— Both as flat.* — How many for it to be higher? *— Put three there."*

Fra (6–7) predicts that the ruler will slope after one sheet removed. After it's been done: *"No, it's stayed straight . . . Perhaps it's the same height, too. If you take all* [= more] *off, it will slope.* — But if we take one? *— It doesn't slope at all . . . If you take two at once it slopes* [will slope]. — And if I add one *— The same height still, because the sheet of paper gets flat."*

Before we analyze these reactions, here are some stage 2 reactions:

Ral (7–0), without the preliminary demonstration with the boards: "If I take away one sheet? *— That makes it a very tiny bit smaller.* — Can you see it? *— You can scarcely see it . . . you almost can't see it at all, but it isn't the same.* — And the ruler? *— You can't see anything, but it's not flat any more."*

Cha (7–3), after one sheet: *"The ruler is flat because the sheets are thin.* — And the two heights? *— To tell the truth* [= in reality] *they're not the same because a sheet has been taken off."*

Mos (7–5): *"You can't see that the ruler is sloping, because it's* [the paper is] *too fine."*

Gri (7–5): *It looks as though they're the same, but in effect* [= in fact] *they aren't the same height."*

Cal (7–3): *"The two piles aren't the same height but you might think so. But there's one sheet gone all the same."*

§6. Level 2B

If we consider merely the succesive stages of this development, then it can be seen as broadly identical with that seen in the reactions to the part 1 problems: the nonperceptible inequalities are at first regarded as nonexistent (as with the two most typical 1A subjects Isa and Fav) then finally as certainly existing but not visible, because of the thinness of the paper (stage 2). Yet in comparing these two sets of results, one is also struck by a series of noteworthy differences.

1. First, there is a considerable disparity in the ages at which a satisfactory explanation is achieved. For the invisible displacements this does not occur until stage 3, at about eleven or twelve years old, and for the grains of salt not until level 2B at about ten years old, whereas in the present case, involving the differences in height between two piles, almost all the seven-year olds answer correctly as soon as they reach stage 2, and some even manage to do so at level 1B.

2. The second noteworthy difference is that, while even the stage 2 subjects, when asked about the displacement of a ruler, reply that it is "not possible" for a movement to be caused without one seeing it (even though they resort to the hypothesis that they haven't "watched properly"), in this part the subjects find it quite natural as early as seven years old (despite the "concrete" character of operations at this 2A level), and are at least entertaining the idea at level 1B when no more than five and a half or six years old, that one pile of paper can be lower than another, and a ruler slightly inclined as a result, without one's being able to observe the effect visually because one sheet of paper is "too fine" or too "thin" for one to observe its thickness. So we can say that there is a fairly startling contrast between the judgments made on the displacements or the weight of grains of salt (which is not zero for an ant but is for us, because it is imperceptible) and the interpretations of differing heights.

3. A third difference, already mentioned, is that we find scarcely any oppositions between "adding" and "taking away" a sheet of paper, whereas they are frequently found in the case of the grain of salt, and always in the same direction (adding produces no modification but taking away changes the pile). Among the present subjects, Vic thinks for a moment that taking away a sheet of paper doesn't change the height of the pile but that adding

one, on the other hand, makes the ruler slope sufficiently (he claims) for him to see it, whereas for Fra, taking away modifies that slope and adding has no effect, because the ruler makes the sheet of paper "get flat" (a clever compromise, but still contradictory because even when made thinner a sheet of paper still retains a thickness).

Our problem, then, is to explain these three sorts of difference between the reactions to the displacements and the reactions to the different heights when both are imperceptible. From the point of view of additions and subtractions, that is, of positive or affirmative elements and negative ones, it is clear that there is an opposition of structure between these two processes: a projection of one length or height beyond another necessarily supposes two terms, A that projects beyond B and B being projected beyond, whereas a displacement or simple movement does not become relative until a certain level of comprehension (cf. Galileo's relativity compared to the absolute movements of the Aristotelians). As a result, a projection constitutes from the very outset an asymmetrical relation whose values are seriable, whereas a displacement can continue to be conceived for a long time in terms of absolute qualities. Furthermore, if A projects beyond B, then every further advance of A beyond B is translated into an inferiority of B expressed in terms of "less far" or "less high," a fact that coordinates the modifications into simultaneous positive and negative forms. On the other hand, a displacement of A alone being judged little or big in no way implies as yet (before the relativization of these predicates) that "littler = less big" or "bigger = less small" or, therefore, that "almost nothing = a very small something." In sum, any projection implies a series of possible and relative values extending from zero projection (equality of levels and horizontality of ruler) to very large disparities, whereas displacements are conceptualized in the form of nonrelative affirmations that are affirmed or negated as a single unit. From all this it follows that a diminishing series, such as clearly visible projections, slightly visible projections, scarcely visible projections, and invisible projections, slightly is much less shocking to early stage 2 subjects than displacements that are supposed to exist yet remain imperceptible.

To these logical considerations we must also add the conditions of metrical evaluation involved, since they may well play a role in the early stages and by stage 2 have become an essential factor. For in practice, the degree to which the subject recalls the way in which his two piles of paper were constructed (that is, by a more or less diligently observed one-to-one correspondence), the addition or removal of a sheet will entail the disruption of that correspondence, and thus once more reinforce positive and negative relations by means of a necessary coordination (more on one side = less one the other). The displacements of the ruler or the changes in the number of grains in part 1, on the other hand, are simply a matter of increases or additions, without subtractions (though with the possibility of reversal in the case of the grains), and above all without any correspondance implying the coordination of positive and negative relations. It will be remembered, in this context, that as late as level 2B (part 1, §3) - and ten-year-old subjects who are still continuing to exclude the possibility of real yet invisible movements prefer to imagine "almost displacements" (shaking, vibration, "feeling like moving," and so on) rather than "almost zero" displacements, which is to say positive but imperceptible ones. But, and especially if the subject has a biunivocal correspondence as his reference, it is not feasible to speak of an "almost projection," because the addition or removal of a sheet of paper, however thin, has already introduced an inequality, for the simple reason that such a change must always be to the advantage of one pile and to the disadvantage of the other.

In short, the notable differences between the results described in parts 1 and 2 are as instructive as the contradictions themselves in part 1, the persistence of which, in comparison with those observed in part 2, and their final removal, demonstrate to us the fundamental role of compensations between positive and negative in the equilibration of a thought seeking to eliminate its conflicts. Such a coordination, and indeed nothing but such a coordination, makes it possible to master the paradoxical notion of the "almost not," which succeeds in reconciling the minimum of positive with the maximum of negative that is compatible with some positive, and even in conferring on this concept the dynamic and relative meaning of a seriable magnitude as opposed to static and absolute predicates.

Fifteen

Contradictions in Cases of Multiple External Factors

with T. Vergopoulo (part 1), M. Gainotti-Amann (part 2),
and J. de Lannoy (part 3)

Part 1. Relative Movements

Every action, however doubly positive in the (logical) characterization of its objective and in the (cinematic or vectorial) movement that brings it nearer to that goal, entails two kinds of negations or negative property. The first are external and consist in excluding that which is not the action itself, and in particular those neighboring but distinct actions with which it might be contradictory to confuse it. The others are internal and bring about a recession from the action's point of origin to correspond with its positive advance toward its goal. We have already seen (chapter 9, part 2) to what contradictions the disregard of these second negative conditions can lead, but it is in the domain of relative movements that both kinds are particularly important. When a movement A is brought into relation with another movement B, it is essential, first, to distinguish that movement A from the displacement A' in the opposite direction, and, second, to take into account its point of departure and not solely its point of arrival. These problems of relative movements have been familiar to us all for a long time, but we thought it might be interesting to investigate an especially simple case here: that in which a traveler moves along inside a train while the train is going through a tunnel, the question being whether the traveler will stay a longer or shorter time in the tunnel according to whether he stays in his seat, walks in the same direction as the train is moving, or walks against the movement of the train. In this particular case we intend to examine, among other things, whether success will be as delayed (eleven to twelve years) as in the case of our earlier relative movement problems, and whether the difficulties and contradictions do in fact stem from a disregard of the two kinds of negative conditions just referred to.

Technique

The equipment consists of a long cardboard tunnel with a top that opens like a book so that one can see inside, and a long train that runs through it. Two people, one black (B) and one white (W) can remain where they are (situation 0) each at one end of the train, the question then being whether one of them will stay longer in the tunnel than the other or not (they are both inside for the same time in fact). In situation 1, B moves from his place at the front of the train toward W at the back, against the movement of the train. Situation 2: B is at the back, W at the front, then B walks toward the front, moving in the same direction as the train. Situation 3: B at the front of the train moves toward W at the back, but when he is about halfway he goes back forward to fetch his newspaper before setting off again to join W at the back. Situation 0 can be supplemented with B and W still not moving but both at the front of the train, and situation 2 can be supplemented with situation 2a in which W and B both start at the back but B moves to the front.

§1. Stage

At the level up to four years the subjects don't understand the problem. At level 1A, at about five, however, they answer the questions and concentrate either on the entry to the tunnel or, more usually on the exit.

Luq (5–10). Sit. 0 (no movement): "Did they both stay the same time in the tunnel? — *No, when (W) was behind the other [B] was in front.* — But B went in first? — [He does the journey again.] *Yes, because B goes into the tunnel, then B comes out and the other one too.* — So they were both in there for the same time? — *No, W stays longer because he stays in afterwards.* — But B went in first? — *Yes.* — So it was the same? — *No, W stays longer, because W is in the tunnel when B is outside.*" Sit. 2: "Were they in there for the same time? — [He makes B do his walk to the front again.] *Yes, because B went to see his friend* [so they emerged together]. 2a: "The same time? — *No, W longer* [correct] *because he was right at the back* [wrong reason]." Sit. 1: "*The same time inside, because B went to see his friend* [so they emerged together]." Sit. 0 again: "*B more because he was the first inside.* — Who came out first? — *B.* — Who went in last? — *W.* — Who came out last? — *W.* — So were they in the same time? — *No, W more because he was behind.*"

Bon (5–11). Sit. 0: "*It's W who stays in longer, because B goes in first and W last.*" Sit. 1: "*Both the same time in the tunnel.* — Why? — *Because B wanted to go to see W and they came out of the tunnel together.*" Sit. 2a: "*It's W more because he came out last* [correct answer, wrong reason]."

Bac (5–5). Sit. 0: "*W stays in longer than the other.* — Why? — *Because he's behind, he stays longer in the dark.*" Sit. 2a: same reaction as Bon.

Kas (5–9). Sit. 0: "*B goes in first and stays in longer.* — But he comes out first too? — [Silence.] — Don't they both stay in for the same time? — *Yes . . . No, W stays in longer when it comes out and B when it goes in. They stay in the same.* — Not one more than the other? — *W longer because he comes out last.*" Sit. 1: "*Both the same because they come out together,*" but then "*W stays longer because B goes in first and W after.*"

Can (6–1). Sit. 3: "*They stayed in the dark at the same time, and after, B stayed* [went back to] *in his seat a little while to get his newspaper* [which was clearly of no importance]. — So did B stay inside more, or

less, or the same time? — *The same time: when B was there* [at back
after joining *W*] *they stayed a little while in the dark."*

The characteristic of these reactions is thus to ignore the internal movements and their directions, even though they were correctly perceived and
reproduced, and to base all judgments as to the length of time spent in the
tunnel essentially on the order of emergence, although the order of entry was
also referred to. Kas does perceive momentarily that in situation 0 (motionless at both ends) the two orders compensate one another, but then, after
having at first given greater weight to *B*'s earlier entry, reverts to the general
idea that the last out remains in the longest time.[1] Even situation 3, with the
return for the newspaper, makes no dent in this idea with Can.

With level 1B, the internal moves begin to play a role, first negative then
positive, but still independently of their direction in relation to that of the
train.

Ala (6–5). Sit. 1: *"The W stayed longer. Why? – Because he didn't move.
The B stays not as long* [incorrect] *because he moved."* Sit. 2: *"W stays
longer. He didn't move."* Sit. 0: *"They both stayed in longer. The W and
the B stayed in the same long time.* — Not one longer than the other? —
No, it's the B and the W that stay in longer. — Why? *Because they
didn't move, so they stayed in their seats.* — So people who move about
stay in? *– Not such a long time.* — Why? — *Because the other, he . . ."*
Later, Ala changes her mind momentarily, presumably under the influence of this unanswered question, but then reverts to the idea that
movement diminishes duration.

Gia (6–9) also thinks with sit. 1 that *B* stays less time inside because he
walked, whereas *W* stays in longer *"because he was at the tail end and
stayed in his seat.* Same reply in sit. 2a, but for sit. 0 Gia reverts to 1A
reactions: *W* longer *"because he went through after the other."*

Cat (6–4), on the other hand thinks that in sit. 2 the *B* stays in longer: *"It
must be the black because he has to walk to get to his friend."* Similarly
with sit. 1: *"He has to walk to meet his friend."* Sit. 0: *"The same time
inside because they both stayed in their seats."*

Cor (7–7). Sit. 1 and 2: *"B stays in longer because he walked."* Sit. 0:
"They stay in the same time because they didn't move."

Cat's and Cor's reaction seems the more normal: walking takes time, so
that increases the time spent inside the tunnel. The opposite reactions are
doubtless to be explained by a compromise between vestiges of type 1A (the
one at the back of the train stays in longest) and an attempt to take the
movements into account. But taking the movements into account, if they are
still viewed as independent of the train's direction, can clearly lead just as

well to the idea that each movement brings the mover closer to one end, and thus diminishes the time spent in the dark, as to the contrary idea, expressed by Cat and Cor, which is sometimes found among certain 1A subjects. Moreover, it should be noted that all the answers up until now were given after observation, since predictions were beyond these younger stage 1 subjects. It is possible under these conditions, by increasing the number of observations, moving the train in slow motion, or asking leading questions to help the subjects, to obtain a correct account of the in-tunnel durations, but never with explanations, and only on condition that no more than two people, B and W, are involved. If one adds a third party in situations 1 and 2 (B's wife F, who remains throughout in B's initial place), the relations between W, B, and F become too complex for the subjects to read the situation at all.

§2. Stages 2 and 3

Level 2A marks certain perceptible advances in comprehension after observation, and in the subsequent explanations, but we still do not find correct anticipations.

Rau (7–1) predicts for sit. 1 that W will stay in longer *"because he is behind,"* which is thus a stage 1 reaction. On the other hand, after observing the actual process twice: *"B will stay in longer because W stays where he is and B goes toward W."* For Sit. 2a (observed): *"W stays in longer because he's behind all the time and B was in front . . . and came out before."* Sit. 0: *"Both stay in the same. – —* Why? — *Because W rode along and B too: they rode the same."* (So Rau doesn't simply invoke their immobility as opposed to the displacements of the other situations, but also one and the same movement of the train for both!) But one boy told me B stays in longer because he goes in first. — [He laughs.] *Yes, B went in first and W after, but W came out after."*

Did (8–3) predicts for sit. 1 that B *"stays in longer because it's B who moves along,"* which is a 1B reaction. Likewise with sit. 2. But once the two situations have been demonstrated, he cottons on at once, and is amazed that B stays in longer *"because if he'd stayed where he was he'd have come out first."* On the other hand, for sit. 2a: *"it's W who stays in longer because he's at the back of the train. —* But B was too, wasn't he? — *Yes, but because he moved along he stayed not so long in the dark."* Sit. 3: *"The B longer because he went into the tunnel first and came out* [at the back] *with his friends. —* And if one wanted him to stay in the same time as his friend? — *Then we could have put him with his friend and he'd have stayed there. —* What about like this (one at each end)? — *Yes, because B went in first and W last and B comes out first and W last."* However, with the three characters (*W, B,* and *F*), Did curiously relapses into stage 1 reactions, even when observing: For sit. 1: *"B* [walking back against the direction of the train] *and W* [not moving at the back] *stayed in longer, and F* [not moving at the front] *stayed in not so long";* and for sit. 2a *"all three the same,"* then *B* longer than *F* [at front] *"because he was at the back of the train and walked to the front."*

Taken as a whole, the explanations given at level 2A were not up to the level of correctness exemplified in those quoted, and even Rau and Did floundered for a while at first. Moreover, 2A reactions were characterized by two universal deficiencies. First, there was the total failure of all subjects in their predictions, which in practice remained at the level of the stage 1 explanations (after the event). Second, they all failed again totally when faced with the situations involving three characters, so that their answers once more regressed to the levels of stage 1 reactions to *B* and *W* alone.

On the other hand, their reactions after observing the demonstrations with two characters only showed noticeable progress. With situation 0, these subjects no longer simply say, as 1B subjects did, that *B* and *W* stay for the same length of time in the tunnel because they stay in one place rather than one of them moving: Rau says that they both "ride along," thereby invoking the fact that they share the single duration of the train's passage through the tunnel, and Did is most explicit about the fact that if one of them goes into the tunnel first he also comes out first. With situations 1 and 2 they both grasp that if *B* walks in the opposite direction to the movement of the train, then he will emerge later in time than if he had stayed at the front, and that if he walks in the same direction as the train then the opposite is true. In short, they are relating the order of entry and emergence while simultaneously comparing *B* and *W* and taking into account the direction of the characters' displacements.

2B subjects are successful in predicting the answers to questions involving two characters, as well as in explaining the trio situations, after correct observation, but not predicting the solutions to these latter problems.

Ari (9–3). Sit. 1 (anticipation): *B will stay longer because he goes in first into the tunnel and they come out together* [*W* and *B*], *so he stays in longer."* Sit. 2a (prediction): *"It's the opposite, because B went along* [inside the train] *and came out first."* Sit. 3 (prediction): *"It's the same thing as the first question, it seems to me."* Sit. 1 with *W* and *B* at front, *W* at back, *B* walking to *W*: *"W stays in less long and F and B stay in the same,"* which is twice wrong, once for *F* and *B,* and once for *W* in relation to *F.* Demonstration: *"Oh, yes, of course: B stays in longer than W and F: if you put them in order of how long, then B is longest, and F and W will be equal because F goes in first and comes out first, and W goes in last and comes out last.''* On the other hand, even at the prediction stage Ari generalizes her reasoning and reverses it for sit. 3 with three characters.

Stage 3 subjects resolve these three character problems even at the prediction stage, sometimes with spontaneous reference to the composition of relative speeds.

Pel (10–4). Sit. 2: *"B stays in less time than W because if you take the speed of the train, then B is going faster, so he finishes quicker. It's as if you added up the two speeds, the train's and B's. That makes a bigger speed for B and less speed for W* [who is motionless in relation to the train speed].'' Sit. 1: *"If he goes backwards he stays in the darkness longer, because by moving to the back he is going slower than the train until he reaches his friends.''*

Isa (11–3). Sit. 2 with three characters: *B* stays less time in the tunnel because *"the train is always going the same speed, but B runs, he walks* [in the same direction as the train] *so it's as if the train is running twice for him.* — And in the opposite direction? — *He stays longer in the tunnel because he comes to the back, and it's as if he's going twice as slowly* [as the train].''

So, despite the fact that these problems are easier than our previous tests for relative movements,[2] we still find that composition of relative speeds does not appear until the eleven- to twelve-year-old level. Yet it is already implicit in the level 2A answers, but in terms of comparisons between the entrances and exits, and not, as here, in the form of direct compositions of speeds.

§3. Conclusion

If we examine this development as a whole, then we find, as predicted, that the primary source of the contradictions observed is connected with the fact that the starting point of the actions or movements is not brought into relation with their end. In the present situations, even though they involve neither the displacement of an object nor, in every case, the displacement of people, the arrival point of the changes under consideration, which is to say the emergence from the tunnel, is nevertheless accorded clear predominance as usual over the departure points (entries into the tunnel), since the unshakeable argument used at level 1A is that the one who comes out last is going through the tunnel for a longer time, and that when the emergences are simultaneous then the durations are equal, independently of any possible previous movements made by *B* or *W*. At level 1B things appear to change, since the characters' movements are beginning to be taken into account. However, they are still not viewed as imposing a relation of entrances to emergences, and thus of the beginnings and ends of the action, but rather as actions that appear to bring B nearer to the goal (emergence) or that simply take time. Thus it is not, as is customary, until the level of concrete operations (2A) that the attempt to relate the starting and end points of the actions begins, and even then only after they have observed the event, since their anticipations remain just as centered as ever upon the arrival points, right up until level 2A for the two character situations and even up to stage 3 for the three character problems.

This first source of contradictions, so durable and systematic in itself, is accompanied here, however, by a second: that which we attributed earlier, in the introduction to this section, to those external negations, as opposed to earlier internal ones, indissociable from the positive aspects of the action (these being relative to the characteristics of the goal or to the movement directed toward it). This then involves a failure to distinguish and appreciate the opposition between a particular action and those that are different from it but with which the subject confuses it. In the present case, the varieties of action to be distinguished, in terms of their direction, are the various displacements of B. In practice, throughout stage 1 these directions, whether with or against that of the train, still play no role. At level 1A the only question raised is whether or not B "goes to be with his friend," or, in other words, whether they emerge together or not. At level 1B the only concern is to distinguish between movement and nonmovement, so that the very different actions of walking toward the end of the tunnel or walking away from it remain undifferentiated. Thus, once again, it is not until the operatory stage 2 that this second source of contradictions is eliminated, at first partially (2A after observation but not in predictions), then almost entirely (level 2B), and eventually completely by means of deduction endowed with intrinsic necessity (composition of relative speeds at stage 3).

In short, this experiment has shown, like so many others, that the sources of the initial contradictions is to be sought in a neglect of the negative aspects (internal as well as external in the senses given in the introduction to this section) specific to any action: recession from its starting point and opposition in relation to neighboring but distinct actions.

Part 2. The Role of Negation in the Conjunction of Two Factors: The "Not Only"

In our accounts of previous experiments, we have confined ourselves to considering only actions that necessarily entail a positive component and a negative component (adding after having taken away, moving toward an end

point while receding from a starting point, and so on). In this section, however, which once more deals with the equipoise of weights on a scales (thus
completing our research in chapter 6), we are dealing with actions that
involve two positive factors acting simultaneously: the weight and its position (that is, its distance from the central axis), and initial reactions naturally
consist in retaining the more immediately striking of the two, in other words
the weight, and in ignoring the other. There may nevertheless be some
interest in examining this situation from the negation point of view, since,
although it does not involve an incomplete negation ("almost not" as in
chapter 14) or a relative or restricted negation (secondary classes $A' =
B$.non-$A$ as in chapter 8), it does entail, when two conditions are necessary, a
particular and important type of negative connection characterizing both
incomplete and relative negations: that of the insufficient yet necessary condition, which one may denote in ordinary language by the words "not only."
What the subjects at later levels discover is that equipoise depends "not
only" on the absolute weights but also on their position (technically, this is
the same as saying that these two notions combine to form "moment," but
we shall go no further than the point of view of our most advanced subjects,
who still perceive them as two distinct factors).

The development of this notion of "not only" is interesting because we
find that before eventually acquiring it, the subjects will first try all sorts of
modifications of the single factor at first envisaged, including observable
phenomena connected with it, rather than abandon the idea that its role is an
exclusive one.

§4. Stage 1

At level 1A one can almost say that the subject does not yet know of, and
does not even look for, any necessary and sufficient conditions that will
ensure equipoise of the scales (the only task set, but with five different sorts
of weights: $A > B > \ldots > E$). They do accept, it is true, that a heavy weight
on one arm will make it go down, but even that, as we saw in chapter 6, is not
absolutely universal. That aside, they invoke all sorts of other factors, including (and this noteworthy) the positioning of the weight, though naturally
without any comprehension of the actual role played by the weight's distance from the fulcrum.

> Sid (5–5) places an A (the heaviest kind of weight) on each side: "*If you
> put those, it stays.* [It doesn't. He tries different positions.] Why isn't it
> working? — *Because it's heavy.* — But before you said it needed to be
> heavy? — *No . . . yes* [he places an E on each side: success]. — Why? —
> *Because they're light. You have to have little ones.*"

Pat (5–0): "*You need very little ones that don't make it go down.* —
Where should we put them? — *I'd put them in the middle, not at the
side, then it wouldn't go down.*" He then puts an *A* on one side only,
then another on the other side but positioned differently. "And if you put
them both at the same time, would that work? — *I don't think so,
because I can't make it go up again.*" Success: "*There, it's staying.* —
Why? — *Because they're near enough the edge.*"

Syl (5–1) when the scales remains tilted rectifies it with his hands for a
moment to make it stay still in equipoise. After a success: "*It's because
they were put right.* — So are there right places and wrong places? —
No, it's right everywhere."

Got (5–3): "*It stays more still with the big ones. Ah! It's going down.
You need to put a lot on.*"

Car (5–11): "*You have to put them on together* [identical piles on both
sides]."

Mer (5–10): "*I know why it isn't working: it's the big ones that are the
nuisance, they're too heavy.*"

So in certain cases it is helpful if the weights are "put right" (Syl), but it
isn't necessary, since Syl also says that "it's right everywhere," an apparent
contradiction that becomes more understandable when one remembers that
Syl also thinks it's possible to achieve the same result with one's hands, as
though holding the scales in equipoise for a short time will stabilize it in that
position. Sometimes the heavy weights work best, albeit on condition that
they are not "too heavy"; sometimes the light ones seem preferable because
they will cause less disturbance. Sometimes "you need to put a lot on,"
sometimes it's best to put them on "together," in other words forming two
identical volumes. But putting weights on both sides at once brings a danger
of the scales "going up." In sum, one seeks in vain, in this phenomenism,
for any trace of necessary conditions, each one being conceived of in turn as
sufficient, but never, so far, as necessary and sufficient.

The necessary condition relation begins to appear in rudimentary form at
level 1B (six- to seven-years-old), but in a purely legal form without causal
comprehension: equipoise is achieved when there is symmetry in the equality of the weights. From the point of view of the relations between affirmations and negations, it is interesting to find that as this condition becomes
necessary, the subject begins to view it as sufficient, and it does not occur to
him, even when the results contradict this belief, that the placing of the
weights may also play a role, even though that role can also be viewed as
included within the term symmetry.

Heb (6–5): Success with *B* and *B:* "Why? — *It's both of them being the same size.* — And with *A* and *A?* — *Don't know* [places them at different distances]. *They're too heavy.*" No reference to positions.

Ber (6–10): same reactions. After failure with equal weights but incorrect positioning: "*It's heavier here than there.*" He adds a little weight. By regulating the distances in the action he succeeds: "*I put them on better than before. I got them settled better.*"

Mor (6–10) finally moves weights in toward center: "And at the ends? — *No, that won't work.*"

Cer (6–10): "*It's as if the scales is heavier on one side than the other.*"

Nat (6–6): "*You need to put one on each side.* — How? — *Well, two the same size.*" Then with *A* and *A:* "*They are the same weight, the same size, the same shape,*" but she puts them at unequal distances from center: failure "*because they were too big.*" Then she puts on *ABD* on both sides, but without concerning herself about positioning: "*I can't seem to do it . . . Perhaps that one* [*A*] *is smaller than that one* [the other *A*]." Failure again, then regulation (in action) of positions leading to success: "Why? — *Perhaps because before I let go the scales too suddenly.*" Later Nat nevertheless seems to have become conscious of the positioning factor: "*I put on the same bolts and the same way away,*" but pays no further attention to it. So that after an *A* and *A* failure: "Why? — *It's heavier here than there.* — Why? — *Don't know.* — Think — *I put them almost in the same place, but not quite.* — Try again. — *The two mustn't touch, that makes too much weight.*"

For these subjects, then, there is necessity for symmetry of the selected weights, in number and so on, but not in their positions, and failures are attributed to mysterious inequalities that make it plain the role of the distances has not been grasped. There is sometimes regulation of the distances in the actions, but without conscious appraisal: Ber attributes his success to the fact that he got the weights "settled better," and Nat, who gets nearest to the solution, eventually thinks that her symmetrical positioning works because she has moved the weights apart.

§5. Stage 2

At level 2A (seven- to eight-years-old), which is that on which the reciprocal and compensating action of equal weights is understood (as we say in chapter 6), the subject begins to grasp that symmetry of the weights themselves is not sufficient. However, the discovery of the role played by their positions is still not due to a conceptual negation, that is, the equality of the weights is still not judged as being a necessary and yet "nonsufficient" condition. So that it is trials and errors, regulations of the action alone, that lead to an adjustment of the positions, and it is only after they have led to success that the subject becomes conscious of why. For it should be noted that the motor trials and errors brought to bear on the positionings do not presuppose an anterior hypothesis as to their role. When placing a weight on the scales, the subject may set it down twice on successive occasions in almost the same place, without conscious intention, or move others to make room for it, and then, upon observing the movements of the scale, regulate the positions one by one according to what happens. Thus it is not until after the event that he will perceive the fact that equal weights must also be placed in symmetrical positions.

Gon (7–2) begins with equal weights independent of positions: *"No, that doesn't work* [active regulation]. *There it was heavy, but not there. So I pushed the four over a bit so the weight came nearer the end."* After further attempts: *"The same bolts must be in the same place. — Why? — Because every time it's a bit heavier here* [one end] *if you push the others toward the middle."*

Kar (7–1). Same beginning. Then: *"I really can't see."* Numerous trials and errors with four elements, then: *"If there's one that's more over there* [toward center] *it goes down. They must be in the same place."*

Dep (8–0). Same reactions, then: *"The distance away can help you somehow. — How? — That's what I'm wondering."*

Isa (8–6): *"I noticed that if one is more forward, it goes down that side. When you put them in the same place it works. If you don't it doesn't."*

Here, finally is a level 2B example showing comprehension from the outset:

Mag (9–0): *"These two big ones are the same weight, so they'll make it balance with one at each end. — How exactly? — First of all, you must make sure you measure the weights to be in the same place. If you put one here and the other there, then it sinks down at the end."*

Taken as a whole, this development shows how far from natural it is for young subjects, once a necessary condition has been found for ensuring the equipoise requested, to entertain the notion that it is not also sufficient, despite the contradictions between observed facts and anticipations based on that single condition. We have to wait until level 2A before regulations of their action lead to conscious awareness of the role played by a second condition. Although it is a matter, in this case, of a negation relative to the meaning of the condition already discovered, and one that in no way entails exclusion or reversal of that condition itself, this difficulty in establishing its "nonsufficient" status constitutes a particular case of the general resistance to all forms of negation, no matter how multifarious their varieties. As to these special negations intervening in "necessary but not sufficient" relations, one can compare them to those characterizing an intersection of classes: if classes A_1 and A_2 have a common part A_1A_2, we then have two secondary subclasses A_1non-A_2 and A_2non-A_1, each of which thus includes a restricted negation. Similarly, if the weights a_1 and the positions a_2 both play a necessary role, only their conjunction a_1a_2 is sufficient to regulate the equilibrium, hence the restricted negations $a_1$non-a and $a_2$non-a_1 characterizing the "nonsufficient" relations. Only unlike the properties of the classes A_1 and A_2, which are given and observable in all situations, once the classes here have been constructed the properties "necessary and sufficient" or "necessary but not sufficient" are always relative to causal or logico-mathematical deductions: hence the derived, but not less essential, character of this type of negations, neglect of which is the source of contradictions.

Part 3. Combinations of Three Factors

The previous section introduced us to that particular form of negation that intervenes when a condition, while being necessary to the production of a phenomenon, is nevertheless not sufficient, something neither easily nor quickly comprehensible for the subject. Here we shall be dealing with a situation in which three factors intervene, and which is for that reason even more complex, even though it takes the form of a game with which all our subjects were familiar, and whose various aspects would seem to be easily explicable. The game, *balle-pelote*, a sort of "wall tennis" much played in Belgium, consists simply in throwing a ball against a wall, which it must strike above a horizontal line, in such a way as to make it return close to the thrower or striker and thus prevent his opponent or opponents striking it in turn (the "racquet" being in this case the open hand). There are three distinct factors involved in achieving this aim: the distance of the thrower from the wall, the height of the ball's point of impact on the wall, and the force of the throw or shot, and their conjunction is of course necessary, since no single one is sufficeint to determine the result. In consequence, one must take into consideration a complex set of negations, all of which are just as indispensable as the positive elements, in order to comprehend the processes at work.

To be more precise, there are two implications involved here (far ⊃ hard and high ⊃ hard) and two exclusions or negations of the implication (soft and far or soft and high), so that we are left with four acceptable combinations and four excluded ones:[3]

Acceptable	Excluded
1. Far, hard, and high	5. Far, soft, and high
2. Far, hard, and low	6. Far, soft, and low
3. Near, hard, and high	7. Near, soft, and high
4. Near, soft, and low	8. Near, hard, and low

Clearly, then, the two implications specific to the four acceptable combinations entail a dissymetry: corresponding to "hard" we have three possibilities (1, 2, 3), and to "soft" only one (4). Reciprocally, if the thrower is "near" he can throw the ball "hard" and "high" (a "sky lob" which will return almost vertically) or he can throw it "low" and "softly," whereas if he is "far" he is bound to throw "hard," irrespective of the height of impact on the wall. It is this lack of symmetry that may create in the subject a feeling of unease, expressed by such words as peculiar, funny, not quite right, and so on, because he finds it too difficult to take all three factors into account at once. However, this is in fact no more than a "pseudocontradiction" since it is removed as soon as a sufficient combination of variables intervenes.

Technique

The procedure is very simple. One begins by asking the subjects (the experiment was conducted near Brussels) how one plays *balle-pelote* and how, if one is near the wall, one should throw the ball to make it fall back to the ground beside one. One also asks what one should do to make if fall a long way behind one (say ten meters: normally excluded combinations because they favor the opponent). Then everyone goes outside and actually plays, investigating the various possibilities. At times the experimenter herself may join in, adopting combinations not predicted by the subject. Next, one questions the subject as to how far his anticipations agreed or disagreed with the actions observed, and asks him to explain those actions. Finally, one returns to the subject of the dissymmetries between "far" and "near" to find out what the child thinks about them now.

§6. Level 2B

Before this level children are either too young to play the game or, if they can, employ only a few combinations and accept any new ones they see used quite simply, without showing the slightest surprise about anything, except as unexpected effects they can't explain.

Dep (10–11) refuses to make any prediction about the "near" position: "*If you throw hard, then it will come back, but you can't say where. —* Never? — *Perhaps very far or very near.*" He has a few tries: "*Well, I thought that if you didn't throw it hard it was still going to go a long way.*"

Pau (10–10) is amazed that one can lob the ball from close in and make it fall back so close to one; "*It's as if the wall was turned around, as if you were throwing the ball from farther away and it was coming back to you.*"

Boc (10–1) thinks that, despite not being exactly close in, "*if it goes right up high, then the ball won't be strong enough to go as far as there* [far]. *It will go like that* [less far] *and it means hitting very hard to get that.*" If one aims lower "*then there's more chance it will make a longer trajectory.*" Asked about the dissymmetries between far and near: "*well I can't see anything odd about that: if there are three or four ways of hitting, that's it and all about it.*"

Bar (10–4) doesn't think one can predict whether a ball thrown high from far will return near or far: "But what makes it hit the ground near or far from the wall? — *Because it must have a strong impulse to go high and hit the wall, and it doesn't have enough power left to hit the wall very hard then come back ten meters away.*" Hit from close in "*you must give it a powerful impulse for it to go high, and for it not to have* [enough] *force to go* [on return] *ten meters.*" Or again: "*when it goes up high it hits the wall, and it can go in one direction or the other.*"

Ver (11–5) thinks that by throwing high from close in the ball "*will come down further out*" and not near the wall.

Although each of these subjects possesses a natural knowledge that a ball thrown obliquely against the wall will rebound in the opposite direction from which it is thrown, it is clear that, despite their age, when the points of impact vary in height they predict the directions and distances of the rebound very inaccurately. Thus they are still incapable of combining the three factors, and often even just two of them, not just in their anticipations but even in their explanations after the event. It therefore goes without saying that they will not experience any feelings of contradiction, or even unease, when confronted with the dissymmetries that are pointed out.

§7. Stage 3

At the next level (3A), on the other hand, the subjects who are beginning to coordinate the variables, but in terms of particular or local situations, do find this asymmetry odd when it is brought to their attention.

Jak (11–6) describes the principal possible shots fairly correctly, except in the case of the distance factor from the close in position: "*When you're far away the ball lessens its speed* [so you have to throw harder] and *when you're near, then it's directly against the wall, so there's bigger speed and it can go a long way.*" So he fails to predict soft shots from near in, but accepts that the ball when thrown high will fall back beside the thrower near the wall: "*When you swing it up high it doesn't quite hit, it goes against the wall, but not with a thump like when you throw straight at it,*" hence the "sky lob" descent. When the two possibilities for the near in situation are pointed out: "*It's funny . . .* [but] *I can't explain what's happening. I know what I do, but I couldn't teach anyone else.*"

Dem (12–3) hadn't predicted the two close in possibilities either: "*I'd never have thought of it . . . but if you have two possibilities for the one you ought to have two for the other.*"

Ren (12–10) accepts quite naturally that "*if I were close to the wall, well! the ball would fall down near me,*" but he thinks that by throwing high he will necessarily make the ball return away from the wall: "*The ball goes quite high, and since it's quite high it can come back quite a way away*" He is then troubled to see the "sky lob": "*Normally, there's one of the two solutions that shouldn't happen* — Why not? — *Because if I throw low and if I throw hard up high it isn't the same thing,*" in other words, two distinct actions ought not to give the same result. But he is forgetting what he said earlier: that near the wall the ball would come back near him, albeit ommitting to add that he would have thrown it gently.

Del (12–4) agrees that one must always throw hard from a distance because "*if one wants to get it a long way naturally one must put some force into it. It's normal that there's only one possibility if you want to reach the spot you want to reach.* — But what about when you're near (he has already demonstrated the two possibilities himself)? — *Yes, but perhaps there are more possibilities that I don't know about in both cases. There are more possibilities perhaps in the first case.* — What others? — *It's possible there are but I don't know, do I? So I can't say.*"

Xav (13–2), close in, "*first I threw a very short ball, just tossing it, so that it came back to my feet. After that I tried a different sort of shot that would come back to my feet in a different way, but it didn't work.*

Then a second time it came back almost just beside me. — So how's it done? — *This possibility happens just by accident, because the ball turns, then it brakes a bit. Or, instead of that, naturally you mustn't throw too hard, and especially not high up.* — So from far out there's only one possibility: throwing hard. And close in there are two. Isn't that odd? — *A bit, yes, that there are two possibilities for one and only the one for the other. It ought to be the opposite* — The opposite? — *Yes, if you throw quite hard, but upward, then the ball ought to go behind too* [as when thrown from far out]. *You throw them both hard* [from close and far] *and you don't get the same result?* — Is that normal? — *Well yes, because it happens all the time* — Normal but peculiar? — Yes! [great conviction]''

The perplexity of these subjects is plain. For some, like Xav, a single action is achieving differing results, which is contradictory. For others, like Ren, it is two distinct actions leading to the same results, which seems to them equally inadmissible. So too, in a general way, does the lack of symmetry between the two possibilities in the close in position, producing similar effects, and the single possibility (throwing hard) in the far out position. In fact, these feelings of unease relate solely to an inadequate analysis, at the anticipation stage, of the various possible combinations, acceptable or excluded, between the three factors present, the subjects either forgetting one factor out of the three or sticking to their habitual associations. Those subjects who produce the best analyses beforehand, like Del and Xac, either hypothesize other, unknown possibilities (Del), or attribute real results to simple accident, as with Xav and his "sky lob." The trouble is, however, that such an analysis is made difficult by the double interplay of negatives it implies, and this explains why it is not mastered until so late, and certainly not by these level 3A subjects, as we have seen. For on the one hand we have three variables A, B, and C, and for these variables eight possible combinations involving negations and affirmations symmetrically: ABC, $\overline{A}$BC, A$\overline{B}$C, AB$\overline{C}$, A$\overline{BC}$, and so on. On the other hand, if these eight combinations are in themselves symmetrical, then four of them are excluded by the fact of the asymmetry of the implications involved, hence the dissymmetry of the variables "hard" and "soft."

At level 3B, on the other hand, the subjects no longer find anything abnormal in the lack of symmetry, despite the suggestions of the experimenter, because their analyses of the combinations of the three variables is more thorough.

Hoa (11–10): "*It's normal: since you're quite close to the wall, well that means you have to throw not so hard, and you have several possibilities. If you feel like throwing higher then you do it harder to get it back to you,*" whereas from a distance "*you only have one possibility because you must throw much harder.*"

Gui (12–1): "*Yes, it's odd that there's only one possibility to throw the ball behind* [= away from the wall] *and two for throwing it near. — Is it* normal, would you say? *— No, but yes, because when you throw a long way you're forced to do it hard to get the distance, but when you're close in, then you can do what you want.*"

Wil (13–7), after statement of the possibilities: "*I forgot to say that* [close in] *if you throw high that comes back, too.*" he thus refuses to find the lack of symmetry pointed out to him at all "odd": "*All that depends on the position you're in after all.*" But he ultimately transposes the asymmetry within the concepts themselves: at a distance it's the force that matters, whereas close in it's "*the same power whichever way you look at it. Force is what you use to get quite a long way, whereas power, you use that to get any place at all.*"

The removal of the contradictions (or pseudocontradictoins) of the previous level is thus due to two factors: a better preliminary analysis of the possible simultaneous combinations of the three variables, and the fact that they take into account the two implications "far ⊃ hard" and "high ⊃ hard" together with the exclusions entailed by their lack of symmetry. To these implications, pointed out by Hoa and Gui, Wil adds an additional one embracing the whole: "force" implies what he calls "power," but without reciprocity. It is thus clear how far the solution of a problem not yet understood at level 2B, understood but not resolved at level 3A, and finally mastered at level 3B, is in fact conditioned by gradual, explicit or implicit comprehension of the interplay of negations, with its symmetries in relation to the affirmations in the table of possible combinations and its asymmetries in that of the implications which decide which combinations are acceptable and which are excluded.

General Conclusions

Let us first recapitulate the problems we set ourselves when projecting this work. What we were essentially concerned to do was to establish the operatory status of what is commonly termed contradiction in natural thought, even though the distinguishing characteristics of this contradiction are fairly far removed from those of logical or formal contradictions, while at the same time being closer to those of what is called "dialectic contradiction."

Introductory Remarks

Logical contradiction consists, in fact, in sumultaneously asserting the truth of p and of non-p, or, if $q \supset p$, in simultaneously asserting $q.p$ and $q.$non-p, and to do so despite a set of definitions, axioms, and theorems hitherto accepted, as well as in the face of rules laying down the use of negation and implication. In other words, logical contradiction consists in an error of formal calculations in relation to a procedure that would have enabled it to be avoided, and that will suffice to correct it as soon as the error has been perceived, whereas on the plane of natural thought contradictions are presumably inevitable, because they arise with regard to questions that the subject ought to have asked himself without being able to resolve them in advance (for lack of the formal mechanism that possesses a sort of built-in precorrection of error): these questions consist, in practice in asking oneself whether an action a is compatible with an action b, or even favorable to its execution, or whether they are incompatible or simply an impediment to each other. The only method at the disposal of natural or nonformalized thought is to try those actions out and to judge from the results whether they accord or not. A more developed stage of thought will consist in anticipating these trials and results, or in conceptualizing them to various degrees. But even if the stage of making definitions is reached, those definitions will still consist solely in conscious acquisition of previous actions, as long as formalization remains incomplete. Our first problem, therefore, was to establish what the "contradictions" in this natural thought are, from the point of view of the subject's actions and operations (later formalizations of which can certainly be considered ultimately as a particular case, but a borderline case, implying a profound reorganization of methods once that borderline has been passed).

Our second problem was to determine what the nature of "transcendences" will be in relations to these "natural" contradictions. Here again the contrast with formalized thought is fairly clear-cut, for one does not "transcend" a logical or formal contradiction[1], one either eliminates it or discards it by means of local correction or a change of theory. In practice, no logic of transcendence exists, as Henriques has shown at our Center, and if one can, and must, speak of "dialectical transcendence" in many domains, that merely serves to indicate that dialectical contradiction is nearer to that of natural thought than to that of formal logic.

The third central problem examined in this work has been that of in what relation these "natural" contradictions and transcendences stand to the processes of equilibration, which have always seemed to us to be constitutive of cognitive development. These relations are naturally ones of quasi identity, for if this "natural" kind of contradiction is not formal in nature, and if no logic of transcendence exists, then it must certainly follow that the first consists solely in oppositions and conflicts, and thus in disequilibriums, and that transcendence of it is a reequilibration. But in what do these disequilibriums and this reequilibration consist?

Thus we are led on to our fourth problem, the one that ultimately, because of the unforeseen results of the researches we have just described, turned out to be the one with which we have been principally concerned in this book: how are we to explain the plethora of contradictions we find during the early stages of development as compared to the later ones, when one might equally well have expected to find unforeseen contradictions cropping up at any stage, and with more or less constant frequency (since each new problem or each new construction, whether operatory or preoperatory, may involve contradictions at its frontiers)? Indeed, why do their absolute numbers not increase, thus providing a constant frequency of occurrence in proportional relation to the continual extension of the cognitive domains (and despite their overall progressive character)? Yet in fact, it does seem that contradictions, sometimes experienced as such, but most often remaining unnoticed and unconscious, abound above all at the preoperatory levels, and are characteristic of a sort of chronic state at level 1A (restricting ourselves, naturally, to those virtual contradictions which will be acknowledged as real by the subjects themselves at later stages, without reference to the cognitive stage of the adult researcher). So that there is indeed a problem here: upon what factors do such initial disequilibriums depend? This was a new problem for us, since hitherto we had regarded these initial disequilibriums, quite wrongly, as going without saying, or as something to be attributed to various difficulties of synthesis, both of which explanations are ultimately, in fact, tautological, whereas the present results, most of which were unexpected, provide the basis on which to construct a solution.

The Nature of Contradictions

Examination of the first of the four problems stated has led to the following observations. At a first approximation, we find ourselves faced with three main classes of contradictions.

1. The simplest result from the fact that the same action can seem to produce results that are regarded as contrary, which gives the impression of an identification deficiency, whereas what are really involved are either distinct actions or results representing two particualr cases of a more general relation yet to be discovered. As an example of the first of these two possibilities, we might cite the wheels on the sloping board in chapter 5, which sometimes roll downhill and sometimes roll slightly uphill. Here the two movements do not result from the same action, because the wheel's center of gravity (a weight on its rim) is sometimes facing the downhill side and sometimes the uphill side. As an example of results apparently distinct to the subject but in fact identical, we have the case, in chapter 7, of the letters seen in the mirror, which sometimes appear to be reversed and sometimes not, whereas in fact they are all reversed, but some of them appear not to be so because their forms are symmetrical.

2. A second main category of contradictions is characterized by an incomplete opposition between classes of objects which should be disjunct, because one entails negation of certain properties of the other, and which are erroneously regarded as containing a part in common, this overlap being contradictory in its very composition. As an example of this we might cite the classes of equivalence constructed by our younger subjects when dealing, in chapter 1, with the imperceptible differences between neighboring elements $(A = B = C = \ldots = G)$ that become very visible when the end elements are compared $(A < G)$. In this particular case the younger subjects construct two distinct classes, as for example:

$$(A = B = C = D) < (D = E = F = G)$$

without seeing (or seeing at first) that the element D cannot without contradiction belong to both at once.

3. A third set of contradictions results from erroneous inferences, and in particular from false implications. This is the case, for instance, with the red cubes a all containing a bell g in chapter 8. From the resulting $a \supset g$ the subject continues for quite a long while to conclude that, reciprocally $g \supset a$, which in this case is false, although he regards it as actually necessary.

The common characteristic of these three classes, and thus the most general definition of contradiction, is to consist in incomplete compensations between affirmations (attributing the quality a to the class A) and negations (attribution of non-a to the complementary class A' under $B = A + A'$, whether B is the whole of the discourse or any class including a property b common to A and to $A' =$ and exhausting $A + A'$). This definition applies directly to our category 2, which thus constitutes a prototype. But it is also applicable more indirectly in the case of category 1, since the subject's error then consists in failing to see, either that the action under consideration in fact corresponds to two classes of subactions A and A' whose effects are distinct, or that the apparently different results A and A' are in fact equivalent within B (reversal in mirror) and simply have distinct manifestations (letters either asymmetrical [A], or symmetrical [A']). As for category 3, that of erroneous inferences or false implications, these consist either in forgetting that if $a \supset b$ then one has $a.b \vee \bar{a}b \vee \overline{ab}$, and that the conjunction $a.b$ excludes $b \supset a$ since it is its negation, or, more generally, in supposing an implication $x \supset y$ when one in fact sometimes has $x.\bar{y}$, which excludes it. Thus in all three categories contradiction results from an incomplete compensation between negations and affirmations, something that goes without saying from the logical point of view, but which, from the point of view of the relations between logic and natural thought, has a double interest for us here.

To begin with, it should be remembered that from the logical point of view the strict definition of the contradiction $p.\bar{p}$ or $p.q$ if $q \supset \bar{p}$ is to constitute the reverse operation of the tautology $p * q = p.q \vee p.\bar{q} \vee \bar{p}.q \vee \bar{p}.\bar{q}$. As a result, it is equally contradictory to affirm simultaneously in an identical situation both the truth of an operation, say $p \vee q$, and of its reverse $p.q$. But from the point of view of natural thought the broader and vague notion of incomplete compensations possesses two kinds of advantages. First, it enables one to distinguish degrees in the contradiction according to whether the overlapping section $(A.\bar{A})$, erroneously supposed to exist between two complementary classes, is larger or smaller, or includes a greater or smaller number of contradictory characteristics $a.\bar{a}$. Second, it raises the psychogenetic problem, which we shall return to later, of the respective power possessed by affirmations and negations to take root in the child's mind, and of their nature, according to whether the negations are more or less internalized (from the existence or properties of an object to the construction by the subject of classes with more or less negative characteristics) and the affirmations more or less relativized (from absolute predicates to relative qualities. See under *Contradictions between Actions*, p. 299.)

Further Classfications

This leads us on to further possible classifications of contradictions, all of which will remain subordinate to the categories considered above. First, there is a fundamental distinction which would hardly have occurred to one before it was rendered unavoidable by the results already recorded: that between pseudocontradictions and real contradictions, the first being constituted by links that appear contradictory to subjects at an early level and cease to be so at later levels, while the second are contradictory to subjects at later levels, even though they may not be noticed or contested as contradictory at earlier levels. As examples of the first we might cite the case in chapter 13 of the bottles that are simultaneously half full and half empty, something the younger subjects refuse to accept as possible (since they lack relativization of the notions of full and empty). An example of the second are the bottles, in the same chapter, that are simultaneously "almost full and almost empty," a combination that only begins to trouble subjects when they have constructed a sufficient quantification of the quality "empty" (since before that "almost empty" = "partially empty", whereas "almost full" is correctly assimilated or restructured).

This distinction between pseudocontradictions and real contradictions, the bearing of which may possibly go far beyond the frontiers of psychogenesis (for does not the dialectical "contradiction" of being and nonbeing, the transcendence of which leads to the notion of becoming, participate to some extent in the nature of pseudocontradictions?), is in no way opposed to the definition of the contradictory by incomplete compensations, except that, in the case of the former, it is the error itself bearing upon the delimitations of what is or is not contradictory that results from such an insufficient regulation of compensations between affirmations and negations.

Another subdivision might also be introduced: that of the contradictions or conflicts intervening between a schema of actions or operations of the subject and another schema of similar nature, and that of the contradictions between a prediction on the subject's part, and thus an anticipatory schema, and an external fact undermining that prediction. But, as we have observed repeatedly, the difference between these two forms of contradictions is much less great than one might suppose, for, although the prediction is naturally a function of a schema, observation or recording of the fact that then contradicts it are also indissociable from an interpretation, and thus from one or more schemas of assimilation, just as was the case with the facts either wrongly or rightly predicted and previously accepted. The result is, in one sense, that further contradictions or agreements arise between the subject's schemas, the only remaining difference being that, given conflicts between two schemas alone, correction or transcendence is effected by accommodation of one with the other and by reciprocal assimilation with endogenous construction of negations as well as affirmations, whereas, in cases where unexpected facts intervene, these same processes are also accompanied by a necessary submission to new and external data, together with negations imposed from outside. However, there is a further general difference of another nature: in the case of contradiction between a new fact and a prediction, this conflict is immediately, or rapidly, made conscious, whereas a contradiction between schemas alone can remain unconscious for a greater or lesser length of time. We shall return to this point in the section *Transcendences* (see below).

Hence a third variety of possible subdivisions stemming from the progressive and more or less slow process of bringing the contradictions involved into consciousness. And here we must begin by distinguishing between two cases: that of contradictions between successive affirmations or observations, in which the subject simply forgets this past, however recent, and that of conflicts between actual and simultaneous statements, which, being more or less durable, are the only kind of interest. So in their case, in turn, we must now distinguish between those contradictions that become conscious rapidly and those that do not force their way into consciousness until much later, and even not until the moment when the subject becomes capable of removing them by a more or less successful transcendence. We may then speak of virtual contradictions, in the case of those that remain unconscious, and actualized contradictions in the case of those that have begun to present a problem to the subject's reflection. However, and this we would like to stress' yet again, we have the right to speak of virtual contradictions only insofar as the subject will actualize them at later levels. In other words, we do not have the right to use that term when referring, at all levels up to twelve to fifteen years old, to contradictions perceptible solely to an adult observing them from outside.

A further point: contradictions that arise between a prediction and a fact, as well as contradictions that remain for some time merely virtual, fall, like pseudocontradictions, into the broader category of incomplete compensations between affirmations and negations. As for the degrees of consciousness involved, they naturally make no difference. In the case of the intervention of a new fact F', it never contradicts an anticipation other than partially, in the sense that the prediction was based upon other facts, F, and that the error consisted solely in believing those F to be more general than they were, since in fact there exist F' that are non-F, and the task that now presents itself is to reconcile these two groups by subsuming them within a law L which will apply to the whole F + non-F. So we see once again that the contradiction stems from the disregard of partial negations (non-F) and that its transcendence comes to the same thing as compensating affirmations and negations in a new system whose simplest general form is $B = A + A'$ in which $A' = B.\text{non-}A$ and $A = B.\text{non-}A'$.

Transcendences

This brings us back to the second of the problems recapitulated in the *Introductory Remarks*, which is that of the structure of transcendences. As all the experiments have shown, and as we have stressed several times, these transcendences appear to be effected in every case in accordance with two interdependent processes, one extensional, the other in comprehension: a widening of the referential and a relativization of notions. These two processes, both of them constructive, always go hand in hand to varying degrees, since the first, by widening the field, introduces new elements and consequently new relations, thus rendering the notions present at the outset more flexible. When the subject discovers, as in chapter 15, part 2, that weight alone leads to contradictory results when placed on a scales, and is obliged to supplement it with distance from the center (that is, in fact, the "moment"), there is simultaneous extension of the referential and relativization of the action of the weights in terms of their positions.

What needs to be pointed out now, however, is that both these aspects of any transcendence require fresh compensations between affirmations and negations. To say that weight alone does not suffice to raise the contradictions encountered, and that it is therefore necessary to supplement it with a positional (or distance) factor, is certainly to alter the classification of the factors involved, and to complete an original primary class A (or several) with secondary classes A' that will be non-A in the closest interlocking relation, thus requiring more negations or seminegations, as well as more affirmations, in order to equilibrate the new referential. But the same is necessarily true where relativization is concerned as well. As long as the subject has already mastered conversion (heavier = less light, and so on), he will now succeed in acquiring more complex inversions that will reinforce the compensations (heavier × less far from center) = (less heavy × further from the center).

Although all this has already been observed and stated with regard to the individual experiments, this is a suitable point at which to add two further remarks concerning facts that, up until now, have been stated but not explained, both of them relating to this hitherto somewhat mysterious process that leads to consciousness of many contradictions being acquired so late and with such difficulty. For it is indeed a puzzling thing to understand the fact that so many contradictions, despite being so glaringly obvious to our eyes (and also to those of children who have reached a sufficient operatory level), remain unnoticed for so long by younger subjects. Why is it, for example, that a five- or six-year-old subject is able to assert the inequality of two rows of elements, even if he is centering on the two rows' different lengths, when he has only just constructed the two collections involved himself, employing simultaneous correspondence, and certified their durable equivalence? More generally, why is it that the contradiction between two schemas (here the correspondence then the ordinal evaluation of the staggered rows) can remain unconscious for so long?

There are two facts that require more detailed analysis with regard to this question, and in light of what we have just been saying, namely, that transcendence consists in compensations achieved by resorting to negations constructed to that end. The first of these facts is that, as we pointed out a moment ago, achieving consciousness of contradiction is much easier when it appears between a prediction and some new external datum that rebuts that prediction. This makes the answer quite simple: it is that in such a case the negation has not been constructed. It has been imposed from outside by the new event that has appeared, and that now only needs to be situated within a wider referential, a task that presents a more or less easy or difficult problem of transcendence, and no longer one of achieving consciousness of the contradiction.

The second fairly general fact is that consciousness of a contradiction between schemas is not produced until the level at which the subject becomes capable of transcending it, whereas in the previous case the subject can often search for a long time before successfully integrating the new fact (together with the negation it entails) into an adequate system of positive and negative elements (secondary classes, and so on). In the case of a contradiction between schemas, only this system to be constructed is capable of making the necessity for the negations evident, and without those negations the subject's thought simply proceeds by a series of local and isolated affirmations, each factor continuing to reign undisputed in its own domain (equality for the correspondances, inequality for the rows of different length, and so on), thus explaining the subject's unawareness of the contradiction.

Put more simply, since a contradiction is the acceptance of an overlap between two complementary classes $(A \times \text{non-}A) > 0$ or of a conjunction between two exclusive qualities $(a.\bar{a} > 0)$, in order to sense it one must be in possession of the negation, $\overline{A}$ or $\bar{a}$, so that although such a contradiction may seem obvious to us the subject does not see it, for the simple reason that he does not yet possess it because he needs to construct it. This being so, he reasons solely with the positive characteristics of these classes or properties, when in fact the only way to bring them into new relations (which is precisely what happens at the point of transcendence, but only then) is to perceive their negative aspects as well. So that we have a situation here very different from those in which the negations are imposed from outside, and thus in relation to an anticipation they rebut.

Contradiction and Equilibration

We must now address our central problem: that of the relations between contradiction and equilibration, since it is clear even at first sight that if, for whatever reasons, affirmations are going to overwhelm negations in a systematic way during the early stages, then the considerations set out in our previous sections will take on much more than a merely descriptive significance.

Before we reach that point, however, let us first recall why it is that the contradictions characteristic of our elementary levels consist of disequilibriums and not of logical contradictions. Our previous section has already provided us with a clue: it is clear that a contradiction of which the subject fails for a long time to become conscious can result solely from "noncompensated virtual tasks" and not from any formal incompatibility between premises. But our results show that there is a much more general reason, since they have presented us with a whole spectrum of intermediate stages between what we must term contradictions in action and contradictions in thought, for contradictions in action can indeed exist. An example would be, for instance, wishing to attain a goal but setting off for no reason in the opposite direction (hence the difficulties of detour behavior). In that case there is naturally nothing more involved than sensorimotor procedures that either reinforce or work in opposition to one another, which is a characteristic of equilibration processes and not of formalization. In chapter 3, when the subject is asked to make judgments about the results of turning an object around once, then twice, or when, in part 2 of chapter 10, it is a matter of arranging things so that a wolf does not eat a goat, or the goat a cabbage, we are still close to such practical situations, hence all the possible transitions between such situations and the operations of thought. Until we reach these latter, then, what we term contradiction on the plane of natural thought consists solely in conflicts or virtual or actualized oppositions, or in other words in disequilibriums whose logical contradictions constitute only an end point reached quite late in the child's development.

What we now need to do, therefore, is to isolate and establish why these disequilibriums occur, why they occur with such frequency in the early stages, and, above all, why they are overcome so slowly. These are real problems, because the simpler the actions are the less they ought to produce conflicts; and indeed, on the plane of pure, or sensory-motor action the oppositions we find scarcely ever stem from any cause other than obstacles or perturbations from external sources. Here again, however, their difficulty remains relative to the aims pursued, and as long as the aims remain modest so do the obstacles. Moreover, the conflicts and disequilibriums we have been studying occur essentially in the domain of the conceptualization of actions, and thus of the comprehension of situations. In that case, however, why does this intellection remain in conflict instead of progressing in a straight line by means of a succession of small but cumulative successes? It is of course true that we have to consider the difficulty of the necessary decentrations relative to the subjective illusions arising from centrations of which the subject is unaware. But why should the distortions due to these illegitimate centrations produce contradictions as their end result rather than simply easily corrected errors of fact?

If what we said earlier is correct, if, that is, contradictions do in fact consist of incomplete compensations between affirmations and negations, then we ought to find a general reason for the initial disequilibriums that does not stem simply from external obstacles, or from just subjective centrations generally, but from such centrations polarized in a systematic way around one of these two terms at the expense of the other. Now this is indeed what proved to be the case when our experiments dealt with simple positive and negative elements requiring to be brought into relation. Thus chapter 8 demonstrated the difficulty experienced in constructing the secondary class with partial negation ($A' = B.\text{non-}A$) in the case of the non-red cubes containing bells, as if it followed from "all red cubes have bells" that all cubes with bells are red. Chapter 13 described the asymmetry present in elementary quantifications of full and empty; chapter 14 revealed the resistances encountered by the notion of "almost not." In all these situations, whose number we could well have extended considerably, we did indeed observe a systematic disequilibrium favoring affirmations, constituting the more natural and spontaneous behavioral reactions, over negations, which, being much more difficult to construct and handle, invariably lag behind affirmations until one reaches operatory levels.[1] In particular, for a long time the subject completely fails to perceive that every action must necessarily and intrinsically entail a negative aspect (moving away from the starting point and destroying the initial state) as well as a positive one (moving toward the goal and producing a final state) accompanied by a transfer which entails a sort of initial subtraction (taking something away at the start) as well as the final addition (adding at the arrival point). However, we shall return to these negations within the actions themselves in the section *Contradiction between Actions* (p. 299).

Affirmations and Negations

What we must do to begin with, then, is to establish the general reasons for this initial primacy of affirmation over negation. These are multiple, and we find them at all levels of the behavioral hierarchy. At the perceptual level, only positive characteristics are perceived, and negation is not a process occurring in perception. It is true, in a sense, that one can perceive the fact that an object is no longer where one saw it before, or is not in its usual place, but in that case these are not pure perceptions: they are observations in response to an expectation, and that expectation, like the observations, depends on the entire action and thus goes beyond the realm of perception proper. One might also invoke the relatively negative characteristics of "background" in relation to "figures" (devalorization of magnitudes belonging to the background, perception of a space in depth if a background remains without boundaries or figures, and so on), but in fact we happen to know, owing to the work of *Gestaltpsychologie,* that perception of the background is not that of an absence or negative element but, on the contrary, that of a necessary support to any figure.

At the level of sensory-motor action we encounter no endogenous negative behavior, but only movements directed at removing an obstacle, and thus subordinate to a positive goal, since any complete action pursues such goals. In the case of retroactions or feedbacks the same is true, and these reversions in the course of trial and error processes are not yet reverse operations, but rather simple repetitions, or fresh attempts merely continuing the pursuit of the positive goal involved.[2] Furthermore, the activity of any scheme of actions comes to the same thing as assimilating objects in the double sense of utilizing them in the pursuit of satisfaction (positive) of a need and of conferring on them, or recognizing in them, similarly positive properties. It is true that when interindividual behavior occurs, even before language, rejection reactions appear, but once again this is a matter of removing an obstacle or source of distress, not yet of endogenous negations.

With the beginnings of conceptualization, on the other hand, we observe the formation of elementary negative judgments, but always in relation to previous positive affirmations or elements: for instance, the child will say of an object "it is little, not big," or "grandpa gone," indicating the direction in which the departure took place. In such cases the primary procedure always remains that of statement, which is of necessity positive, or of justification, whereas negations presuppose relating processes or inferences that are secondary formations and much more limited because linked to disappointed expectations, rebutted predictions, or changes modifying an object's position or quality.

At the level of verbal expression, there is the striking fact that language, even adult language, never expresses more and less relations except in positive terms: "more or less heavy" can thus be applied to very small values as well as others, whereas "more or less light," which is logically equivalent, denotes only a certain order of light weights.[3]

In fact, the use of negation makes progress only with the gradual construction of whole structures, and does not become systematic until the latter attain operatory status. To take an example from the early stages of the development of classifications, for instance, a child at level 1B, when dividing a set of round counters B into whites A and reds A', will certainly say of the latter that they are "not white," but this does not mean that he has constructed a secondary class of "non-white rounds" or $A' = B.\bar{A}$, because if you then ask him if there are more rounds than there are whites or reds, that is, $B > A$ or $B > A'$, he is unable to quantify this inclusion, and no longer compares A or A' to anything but that group complementary to it, as if the rounds B had been reduced to that group. Thus we have to wait until the operatory level before we find negation being correctly manipulated in such a case; and this remains true of all the other "groupings" of concrete operations. And indeed, this is something that in fact goes without saying, since the operatory reversibility not attained until level 2A consists of bringing a reverse operation, and thus a negation, into correspondence with *each* direct operation or affirmation.

Levels of Affirmations and Negations

Now that we have established some of the reasons for the intial primacy of affirmations and for the corresponding lack of negations at early stages, we need to go on from there and characterize the successive statuses of both in the course of the development leading to ultimate compensation between them.

I. As far as affirmations are concerned, we can distinguish three successive forms of these, each corresponding to one of the three principal levels of cognitive functions.

1. Since elementary action means to modify the object and assimilate it at the same time, the first form of affirmation consists in a taking over of the object's characteristics (anterior or modified, observed or predicted) without adding anything to them, because schemas of assimilation are centered first of all on "comprehension" without consciousness as yet of their "extension."

2. At the level of preoperatory conceptualization, the common characteristics of objects or their links are isolated and organized in the form of more or less coherent systems of classes and relations, the structures of which are added to the properties of those individual objects while providing them with frameworks. A second type of affirmation will thus bear upon the positive characteristics of these frameworks and on the relationships enabling them to subsume the various categories of external data.

3. At the operatory levels, these frameworks having been structured and subdivided in a stable and consistent fashion, affirmations will be regulated by the interplay of the operations performed and will in this way acquire new

forms, notably through the organization of primary or secondary classes, or by the relational form taken by hitherto undifferentiated and absolute predicates.

In short, the succession of these three forms of affirmations is ascribable to a double process of internalization by endogenous construction and of relativization due to successive adjunctions enriching the assimilation of exogenous data.

II. Corresponding to these three phases of affirmation there are three principal forms of negations, less easy to delineate because of their rarity in the early stages and the numerous avatars marking their development.

1. Corresponding to the properties of objects that affirmations of the first kind tend to take over, we find in the negative realm external perturbations in opposition to the modifications and observations either desired or predicted. The first form of negation emanating from the subject is then a kind of motor or practical negation, if one may so put it, which tends to suppress the perturbation, or compensate it, in an attempt to restore the positive anterior state. In the case of failure, there is accommodation, thus leading to fresh affirmations. In both cases the negation is thus no more than transitory, and subordinate to a primary need for affirmation.

It should also be noted that this first situation corresponds to what, in the domain of equilibration, I have elsewhere termed α type behavior,[4] in which the perturbations must merely be suppressed or neutralized and are not yet required to be integrated as variations within the systems involved.

2. With the progress of conceptualization and the construction of classes and relations which enclose objects inside a framework that is still fairly open in overall structure but susceptible of local organization, a second type of negations is constituted. This consists in refusing an object inclusion within a class or participation in a relation. This new kind of negation is thus no longer simply practical but constative in nature, and its role becomes less negligible as the conceptual framing of objects permits the integration into these interpretative systems of an increasing number of external perturbations, which then take the form of functional variations which must be considered in their own right and no longer simply eliminated (β behavior in the domain of equilibration): these constative negations then serve to exclude some particular variation from some particular relational framework, as they are able to do in respect to any funciton or relation, or to oppose to that framework whatever is not ascribable to it.

However, since at this level the conceptual framework remains local, and does not attain the consistency of general operatory structures, it goes without saying that the number and qualitative precision of the negations still remain much inferior to those of affirmations: even in this constative form negation does not as yet play more than an occasional and fleeting role, never attaining the durable character of the reverse operations that typify an operatory structure. It is thus not surprising that its developments, both in extension (for example when quantification of emptiness as opposed to fullness is required, as in chapter 13) and in comprehension (characteristics of secondary classes, as in chapter 8) remains markedly inferior to that of affirmation, thus leading to a still extremely resistant primacy of positive elements over negative ones.

3. Finally, at the stage of operatory structures, we find that each affirmation has its corresponding negation (for example, every class A has its complementary non-A class, every domain of relations a complementary domain to which it does not apply, and so on) and, in the form of reverse operations, negations become as permanent as affirmations, especially since these reverse operations henceforth take in and make over, in the form of internal variations within the system, that which until now had remained partly in the form of external perturbations (γ behavior in the domain of equilibration).

If we look closely at this development of negations, we find that it contains the two processes of internalization or increase of endogenous constructions and of relativizations, that characterized the development of affirmations, but with a systematic timelag in phases 1 and 2, in which the positive elements retain a far more deeply rooted and powerful influence, insofar as the conceptual or operatory frameworks arising from the subject's activities remain too sparse to dominate the whole formed by the objects' characteristics. Furthermore, this picture of the formation of negations applies essentially to those situations in which the subject accepts the rebuttals of experience. When that is not the case, as we found in part 2 of chapter 5, in the case of the mechanical curves (where the subject's prediction errors are first attributed to errors made by the pencil, then to resistance on the part of the equipment, then to material defects in his own action, and only finally to errors in his own generalizing reasoning), the timelag that ensues in the succession of forms 1, 2, and 3 of negation confirms *a fortiori* the difficulties of internalization and endogenous construction, as well as of the relativization of negations.

Contradictions between Actions

Corresponding to these three successive forms of affirmations and negations (with a systematic timelag of the latter at levels 1 and 2) we find, finally, the three forms of contradictions continually encountered in this book, and which we are now able to analyze from the point of view of the negations internal to the actions themselves.

Corresponding to those affirmations that aim at a direct taking over of the properties, whether anterior or modified, of individual objects, and to those negations that are merely an elimination of perturbations, we find a first form of contradiction consisting of oppositions between actions. Although in theory immediately conscious and also relatively easy to remove in the case of uncomplicated actions, these contradictions proliferate and become more resistant as soon as the actions themselves become more complicated, and above all as soon as the need to organize them arises, thus bringing into play a measure of prediction which reveals the reasons for such contradictions. We need only recall, for example, what we found in parts 1 and 2 of chapter 10, where, when asked to arrange three pencils so that they all touch one another, subjects simply placed them in 2 and 2 associations, forgetting the need for contract between 1 and 3; or how, in order to take over the wolf, the goat, and the cabbage, they concentrated on ensuring the compatibilities on one bank while forgetting the incompatibilities existing on the other; or, again, how subjects transferring n elements from one collection to another do not see that the difference between the collections is then going to be one of $2n$, and so on.

In all these cases, the reason for the contradiction stems from the fact that the subject, being centered on the goal or arrival point of the actions because they are positive values, ignores the concomitant negations, subtractions or negative factors. It will be as well, therefore, in these concluding remarks, to recall the logical conditions governing the execution of any action, since it is these conditions that, in the last analysis, dominate the entire problem of contradictions. I shall state two of them.

The first of these conditions stems from the fact that every action, however simple it may be, and even when considered as an individual and isolatable action (independent of the class or schema to which it belongs), is distinct from all others. For example, to place an object at one point is a different thing from placing it elsewhere, or from leaving it where it is; to leave a cabbage in the presence of a wolf if different from leaving it beside a goat. In other words, the affirmative or positive character of an action is indissociable from a negative aspect or exclusion, which sets that action a in opposition to that which is not itself, which is to say the totality of non-a actions, whether one takes this totality to embrace the whole of all other possible actions, or whether one restricts it to the extension of the most nearly interlocking class or schema. This first condition of coherence has its importance, in that it does not always go without saying for the subject, even at levels beyond the most elementary. We have seen, for example, in the section *The Nature of Contradictions,* for example, that one of the three common classes of contradiction stems from the fact that the subject sometimes believes an identical action capable of giving rise to opposite results, and this apparent identity error is caused by the fact that the subject is confusing two actions that are in reality distinct and is thinking of them as one.

The second very general logical condition governing any action is that its positive result is always and necessarily interdependent on a transfer originating in a negative starting situation: to introduce a modification into an object is, in effect, simultaneously and indissociably, to enrich it with a new and (in that sense) positive state and also to abolish the previous or initial state, which consists in a negation or subtraction. This second condition, although universal, is much less apparent to the subject simply because, during the course of an action, he is always centered on the goal to be reached, and consequently upon the positive and final state. Moreover, when the source of what is taken away at the outset remains external to the domain of the objects being modified or the action being executed, this negative factor may play no role: to drive in a nail at some given point may constitute a successful action if the nail is taken from an external source of some kind, whereas its origin presents a problem if it has had to be removed from some other point where it was serving a useful purpose. In the situations in which we have seen the subject entangling himself in contradictions, it is precisely because the transfer linking the initial state to the final state, by remaining internal to the system in question, could not be ignored without compromising comprehension, and even the success, of the actions being carried out.

In sum, any action, however positive its goal, is interdependent upon two systems of negations, one external, which sets it in opposition to that which is not itself when viewed as affirmatively characterized by that goal, and the other internal, rendering the positive character of the transfer, in the direction of the goal, interdependent upon a subtraction and moving away from the point of origin. Thus it is neglect of such negative aspects that engenders contradictions.

Contradictions between Subsystems

The second form of contradiction, that between schemas or subsystems, which corresponds to our type 2 affirmations and negations, relating to the conceptualization of actions and to the conceptual framing of objects, raises analogous problems, even though they appear at first sight far removed from those in the previous section.

In a general way, these contradictions stem from a lack of coordination, and for that reason remain unconscious for a fairly long time, since transcendence of them cannot be achieved other than by the intervention of overall operatory structures, whose common characteristic is their intrinsic necessity (serial transitivity in chapter 1, additive composition of parts into a whole equal to their sum in chapter 2, and so on). The problem that faces us first, therefore, is that of the logical conditions governing all necessary coordination. And, as we shall see, this is once again a matter of compensations between the positive or affirmative factors of arrival and the negative factors of departure.

The first of these conditions (corresponding to the second of those the set out in the *Contradiction between Actions*) consists, in effect, of a set of transfers between the initial state and the final state providing compensation between what is deducted or removed at the outset and what is added at the end: to collect a set of parts into a whole that is equal to their sum is to remove each of those parts from its initial local situation in order to add it to others in a final situation, and, at the level of concrete operations, this transfer consists in a displacement that ensures the conservation of the parts in their new position. To construct a relation $A < C$ in a transitive sequence from $A < B$ and $B < C$, is to extract the difference between A and B (ignoring their absolute value) in order to add it to that separating B from C and so derive a new totality AC. In particular, we should remember the importance of these transfers from initial states to final states in all actions which consist in modifying the form of objects, and which involve questions of conservation (of material, weight, and so on). The universal nonconservations that characterize the preoperatory levels of development result, in this case, precisely from the fact that the subjects ignore or disregard such transfers, and then imagine that the augmentations observed in one or other of the object's dimensions (increase in length, say) are due to additions at the end point of the action but without subtraction at its starting point, thus producing nonconservation. Once the necessity of the transfer has been perceived, however, what is added at the arrival is seen to correspond to what is taken away at the start, so that the change of position of the transferred elements is accompanied *ipso facto* by what we may term a "commutability" (if one part A of the object changes position in relation B, then their sum $A + B$ remains constant), which is a more general form of commutativity ($A + B = B + A$) and a source of conservation.

But these transfers linking the initial states and arrival points of composition are accompanied by another fundamental characteristic, the second condition of all necessary coordination, which consists of a series of exclusions whose negative character is indissociable from the construction's positive or affirmative character. In a general sense, in effect, to impose a conclusion with necessity is to exclude all other possibilities: to assert the necessity $A < C$ is to exclude $A \geq C$, to assert that the whole W is equal to the sum of the parts P is (as our preoperatory subjects in chapter 2 signally failed to see) to exclude $T \leq \Sigma P$, and so on. And, at the outset of one's construction, to transfer an element such as a class A, extracted from its initial, isolated situation, in order to include it in an interlocking class B, is to exclude from A the secondary complementary class A', as well as any common part between A and $A' = B.\text{non-}A$.

In short, every necessary coordination, like every simple action, is likewise interdependent upon two sorts of negation, one sort external, setting it in opposition to what it is not (with whatever positive element is entailed in its result), and the other internal, insofar as the transfers required by its realization, and oriented positively in the direction of that realization, imply subtraction at their point of origin.

Thus we may now perceive the profound analogy between the logical conditions governing the carrying out of any action and the construction of any inferential coordination, since in both we find a transfer ensuring compensation between what is taken away on one side and what is added to the other, together with a set of complementary exclusions of the positive characteristics. These two factors thus ensure the identities or conservations necessary to actions and coordinations alike, without underestimating the characteristics of the construction, since there are changes and a production of new factors. So that it is neglect of the negative aspects proper to these initial situations, or to these exclusions, that, by compromising the compensations indispensable to the coherence of the whole, accounts for both our type 1 and type 2 contradictions, and particularly for the noticeably more resistant type 2 contradictions involving relations between subsystems or between schemas.

Contradiction and Operations

Finally, when affirmations and negations reach their third form, so that each affirmation has its corresponding negation, as is the case with operatory structures, the contradictions that can then arise within these structures, or in their immediate applications, no longer consist of anything more than momentary errors or defects in reasoning, leading to the brief omission at some particular point of this necessary compensation between positive and negative elements, or, in other words, of this necessary correspondence between direct and reverse operations. For such operatory systems do in fact constitute what one may term, with Ashby, "perfect regulations," whose principal property is to provide a precorrection of errors, as opposed to corrections after the event, and thus to transcendences modifying the system. Thus we are now coming very close to what characterizes logical or formal contradictions, the one difference being that logical systems add different degrees of formalization, whereas natural thought, even at its higher levels, goes no further than making use of the operations proper to the various structures, without providing itself with reflexive or theoretical models of them. And there can be no doubt that this results in a fairly durable opposition: the contradictions proper to natural thought do bear essentially upon the content of actions or judgments, whereas the logical principle of noncontradiction is limited to the prohibition of simultaneously asserting a and non-a, or of applying an operation and its reverse at the same time, and lacks the power to make any decision, on its own, as to the truth or falsity of the contents this structures. Only, since natural thought in its spontaneous development ends up by giving those contents an operatory form, and since logical formalization consists of enriching that operatory form with a precise and correct procedure that completes it, there is ultimately convergence between the two, so that logical contradictions and noncontradictions may be regarded as ultimate cases of the contradicitons and noncontradictions proper to natural thought. All of this can undoubtedly be taken to justify the interpretation of contradictions, adopted throughout this book, as incomplete compensation between affirmations and negations. As for dialetical contradictions, let me simply repeat that since natural thought is essentially dialetical in its development, being a succession of disequilibriums and reequilibrations, dialectical contradictions are bound to fall within the province of such mechanisms, even though we must always remember that these contradictions, "dialectical" and natural alike, are merely the expression and not the causal source of those disequilibriums.

However, although from the level at which formalization begins onward a distinction is unavoidable, despite their relations, between formal contradictions and those that involve contents, it must not be thought that the latter kind no longer appear in rational thought in general or even in scientific thought. To take only the latter, it is in fact clear that in the stage before that of (provisorily) completed and already formalized theories, there is an earlier stage of scientific thought to be considered, a whole set of problems still under study, and still giving rise to various hypotheses or explanatory models either proposed for testing or adopted on a more or less temporary basis. Moreover, it often happens that a new fact ultimately destined to exclude a previously accepted theory will at first not be understood in that light, and so gives rise in the meantime to a series of retouches of anterior theories before it becomes apparent that it is in fact their coherence itself that is under threat. In such areas it is thus easy enough (albeit after the event) to demonstrate the existence of contradictions. When analyzing them, one naturally finds that they result from the use of excessively general and ill-defined notions, from which later progress will eliminate the ambiguities, or of notions that, without being false, were conceived of as being more universal than was the case, so that retouches or fresh differentiations were required in the new areas to which they were being extended. In all these cases it is then possible to see that the contradiction did not in fact stem from the positive cahracteristics of the concepts or principles later recognized as insufficient or nongeneral, but essentially from the fact that it was difficult or impossible to discern where exactly the boundary lay beyond which it remained necessary to introduce restrictions, partial negations, or incompatibilities. In other words, for any characteristic a (continuity, for example) of which the negation non-a has an equally common meaning (discontinuous character of granular or crystalline structures, and so on) the problem is, in a new and as yet undeveloped area, to determine in what and on what point any unforeseen data fall into the realm of non-a when the positive property a appears to be imposing itself. In a moving and highly instructive passage in his memoirs, Max Planck tells how difficult and distressing he found it to acknowledge that his early work on the radiation of black bodies, together with the mathematical formulations he was already succeeding in deriving from it, in fact implied the negation of the continuum and the hypothesis of quanta, which he rejected, almost as it were on moral grounds, so evident did the necessity of continuity seem to him at the time. In such cases, and they are in fact innumerable, although this example is particularly well known and, indeed, so weighty as almost to overstate the case, it is clear how the equilibration of affirmations and negations remains a general problem for all developing thought from its first tentative steps through to the level of early childhood, and right on up to the transformations and hesitations that may characterize the phases of transition and invention proper to the highest scientific advances in periods of crisis or renewal. The fact is, that the more numerous the variables, the more difficulties one encounters in establishing whether a new datum b is compatible with a more or less general characteristic a, or whether, either in the short or long term, it entails the negation non-a. In this respect, just as in elementary cases, negation presupposes a whole secondary development with a necessity for mediating implications working in opposition to the much more direct apprehension of positive properties, even though the latter may also be inferred and not, as in earlier stages, directly observed. It was therefore very much worth our while to retrace, from a psychogenetic point of view, the beginnings of this complex phenomenon presented by contradiction on the plane of natural thought, and the obstacles that delay the correct manipulation of negations in the very difficult process of equilibrating them with affirmations.

As for that equilibration process itself, in the course of this book we have frequently stressed the fact that transcendences of contradiction, in their double aspect of an extensional widening of the referentials and a qualitative transformation of notions in the direction of relativization, are both active and constructive in character. And here again the analogies with the development of scientific thought are innumerable. However, the two characteristics that these transcendences present, of compensation in relation to perturbations as the sources of contradictions on the one hand, and of construction resting sooner or later on reflective abstractions on the other, are both to be made the object of separate studies in future publications.

Notes

Introduction

1. In the body of this book we shall simplify our vocabulary and use the general term "contradictions" to denote the elementary functional forms of contradiction (disequilibriums) as well as the more developed, logical forms, except, of course, on those occasions when it is useful to differentiate between the two varieties.

Chapter Two

1. See §6, also Piaget and Inhelder, *Mental Imagery in the Child* (New York: Basic Books, 1971), chapter 6.

2. Together with the general considerations of ordinal projection and differences of perimeter noted earlier.

Chapter Eight

1. We have already written elsewhere (in Inhelder and Piaget, *The Growth of Logical Thinking: From Childhood to Adolescence* [New York: Basic Books, 1975]) about the "causality of the possible," but in the following two senses: (1) the "materially possible," when the subject hesitates between two actions or hypotheses and chooses one while being conscious of the possibility of the other; (2) the "structurally possible," when the subject is grasping an overall structure that includes a variety of operations but can as yet perform only some of them (for example, a simple reversal but not yet a double reversal). In such a case he has nevertheless acquired the skill to perform the others, and this "aptitude" or "competence" can be said to act causally, as it were, in the sense that it renders the actualization of a hitherto virtual operation probable when the situation demands it. Here, however, we are thinking of a third and broader category, one in which the new operations are not inscribed within a structure, certain of whose compositions the subject has already realized, but in which recently acquired structures are opening up fresh possibilities, for example in the form of interactions with other structures, or hitherto unfamiliar operations being constructed on the basis of previous operations (as in the case of proportions).

Chapter Ten

1. It should perhaps be pointed out that our previous analysis of function showed a clearcut anteriority of "several-to-one" correspondences over those that are "one-to-several."

2. Just as, in mathematics, reductions to the absurd, rejected by Brouwer for infinite wholes, can seem less convincing than direct demonstrations.

Chapter Eleven

1. Emilia Ferreiro has shown the significance, one more general than might be expected, of such revertibility behavior and its correlation with certain psycholinguistic levels involving the expression of temporal relations see *Les relations temporelles dans le langage de l'enfant*, Droz, 1971).

2. The present experiment was in fact directly inspired by one of those devised by Inhelder, Sinclair, and Bovet (*Learning and the Development of Cognition* [Cambridge: Harvard University Press, 1974], chapter 2). In their work, the above authors employed iterative correspondence in several consecutive tests, with first balls then granules being interchanged between two small, identical glasses, thus providing a means of transition between the discrete and the continuous and establishing improved conservation as a result. In the present experiment we are not concerned with that particular problem, but are making a futher study of the effects of initial iterative correspondences when facilitated by centration on the path of the beads by means of long transparent tubes. In both cases, however, the reason for the progress observed is a return to the sources of the equalities as a mode of the operatory construction of those equalities.

3. And particularly since this reiterative paired correspondence, by stressing it with repetition, leads to centration on the departures at the same time as upon the source of the initial equalities.

Chapter Twelve

1. In this respect, the present results are directly comparable with those in chapter 1, in which the subliminal objective is rejected in favor of the macroscopic subjective, whereas here the macroscopic objective is repressed in favor of earlier choices and observations that are taken as presenting the exclusive truth.

2. See tables 141–43 in *Mental Imagery in the Child*.

Chapter Thirteen

1. It might be said also that it is in fact the wording of *C2* itself they find contradictory; yet when they divide a length, a group of beads, or any positive quantity into two halves, those halves are regularly conceived of as being complementary.

Chapter Fourteen

1. It will be remembered that we have already encountered an analogous additive composition in chapter 2, where the whole is not equal to the sum of its parts. In the rather simpler situation here with the grains of salt, it seemed to us that the action involved did not yet constitute an operatory addition (comparable to a displacement in the sense that what is added to one side is necessarily removed from another) but remained analogous to those additive actions without complementary subtraction to be observed at the level of nonconservations, the action then producing a new material adjunction (increase in the quantity of material, and so on). In this particular case, however, the irrational nature of the production is even more paradoxical, since the action of collecting into a pile actually engenders something (>0) from nothing.

Chapter Fifteen

1. It is true that one might suspect there being a systematic semantic misunderstanding involved here, since the phrase "stay longer in the tunnel" can mean either

"come out later" despite equal durations inside, or "remain inside for a longer duration." However, during the course of long periods of questioning, much of it not included in the quoted extracts, we naturally took every precaution that the terms employed should be understood as referring to duration and not to the order of emergence. The trouble is, however, as we have clearly seen elsewhere, that these two kinds of notion, metric and ordinal (cf. spatially, "longer" = "going furthest at arrival point"), remain indifferentiated at stage 1, not from any simple verbal misunderstanding, but for reasons of actual conceptualization.

2. Jean Piaget, *The Child's Conception of Movement and Speed* (New York: Basic Books, 1969), Chapters 5 and 8.

3. The term "low" meaning "low down near the line on the wall but remaining above it," and only those cases being accepted as possible in which the ball returns to the position from which it was thrown. In 8, the ball rebounds past this point, but a skilled player could naturally intercept it in flight.

General Conclusions

1. In the work I did with B. Inhelder (J. Piaget and B. Inhelder, *The Early Growth of Logic in the Child: Classification and Seriation* (Atlantic Highlands: Humanities Press, 1969) one of the things we studied was the development of negations. We displayed eighteen objects differing in shape, size, and color, asked subjects to indicate "which of these things are not" A and B or A, B and C. The development of the answers from four- to seven-years-old showed a fairly clear-cut tendency: reference to the distant classes diminishes with age, whereas negation in relation to neighboring classes (that is complementarity in relation to the closest interlockings) increases from fourteen to sixty-seven percent. In another test, in which subjects were asked to comment on negations such as a dog or a daisy, and so on, "not being a tulip" we obtained answers such as "the dog ... is more not a tulip" than the daisy, and of the negation involving another flower that it "is a little more right because it is in the category of flower as well," thus making the negative relations more useful.

2. With, it is true, certain corrections in the form of negative feedback; but these can be conceived of as improvement processes.

3. Similarly, "more or less big" or "more or less little," and so on. In one Ivory Coast dialect, *Baoulé*, there is a word for "bigger" but no word to express the relation "smaller."

4. See my work on *L'equilibration des structures cognitives* (to be published by Presses Universitaires de France).